Travel Dis

D1491203

This coupon entitl[...]s
when you book your trip through the

TRAVEL NETWORK®
RESERVATION SERVICE

Hotels ♦ Airlines ♦ Car Rentals ♦ Cruises
All Your Travel Needs

Here's what you get: *

♦ A discount of $50 USD on a booking of $1,000** or more for two or more people!

♦ A discount of $25 USD on a booking of $500** or more for one person!

♦ Free membership for three years, and 1,000 free miles on enrollment in the unique Travel Network Miles-to-Go® frequent-traveler program. Earn one mile for every dollar spent through the program. Redeem miles for free hotel stays starting at 5,000 miles. Earn free roundtrip airline tickets starting at 25,000 miles.

♦ Personal help in planning your own, customized trip.

♦ Fast, confirmed reservations at any property recommended in this guide, subject to availability.***

♦ Special discounts on bookings in the U.S. and around the world.

♦ Low-cost visa and passport service.

♦ Reduced-rate cruise packages and special car rental programs worldwide.

Visit our Web site at http://www.travelnetwork.com/Frommer or call us globally at 201-567-8500, ext. 55. In the U.S., call toll-free at 1-888-940-5000, or fax 201-567-1838. In Canada, call at 1-905-707-7222, or fax 905-707-8108. In Asia, call 60-3-7191044, or fax 60-3-7185415.

---

* To qualify for these travel discounts, at least a portion of your trip must include destinations covered in this guide. No more than one coupon discount may be used in any 12-month period, for destinations covered in this guide. Cannot be combined with any other discount or promotion.

**These are U.S. dollars spent on commissionable bookings.

***A $10 USD fee, plus fax and/or phone charges, will be added to the cost of bookings at each hotel not linked to the reservation service. Customers must approve these fees in advance. If only hotels of this kind are booked, the traveler(s) must also purchase roundtrip air tickets from Travel Network for the trip.

Valid until December 31, 1998. Terms and conditions of the Miles-to-Go® program are available on request by calling 201-567-8500, ext 55.

WDC234

Frommer's® 98

Washington, D.C.

by Elise Hartman Ford

Macmillan • USA

About the Author

Elise Hartman Ford has been a freelance writer in the Washington, D.C., area since 1985. She contributes regularly to such newspapers as the *Washington Post,* and to *Washingtonian* and other magazines. In addition to this guide, she is the author of two books about places to rent for special events and meetings: *Unique Meeting, Wedding and Party Places in Greater Washington,* now in its fourth edition, and *Unique Meeting Places in Greater Baltimore.*

MACMILLAN TRAVEL

A Simon & Schuster Macmillan Company
1633 Broadway
New York, NY 10019

Find us online at **www.frommers.com**.

ISBN 0-02861892-0
ISSN 0899-3246

Editors: Kelly Regan, Dan Glover, Bob O'Sullivan
Production Editor: Stephanie Mohler
Design by Michele Laseau
Digital Cartography by Raffaele Degennaro and Ortelius Design

Special Sales

Bulk purchases (10+ copies) of Frommer's and selected Macmillan travel guides are available to corporations, organizations, mail-order catalogs, institutions, and charities at special discounts, and can be customized to suit individual needs. For more information, write to Special Sales, Macmillan General Reference, 1633 Broadway, New York, NY 10019.

Manufactured in the United States of America

Contents

6   Where to Dine in Washington, D.C.   95

7   What to See & Do in Washington, D.C.   142

List of Maps

AN INVITATION TO THE READER

In researching this book, I discovered many wonderful places—hotels, restaurants, shops, and more. I'm sure you'll find others. Please tell me about them, so I can share the information with your fellow travelers in upcoming editions. If you were disappointed with a recommendation, I'd love to know that, too. Please write to:

Frommer's Washington, D.C. '98
Macmillan Travel
1633 Broadway
New York, NY 10019

AN ADDITIONAL NOTE

Please be advised that travel information is subject to change at any time, and this is especially true of prices. We therefore suggest that you write or call ahead for confirmation when making your travel plans. The authors, editors, and publisher cannot be held responsible for the experiences of readers while traveling. Your safety is important to us, however, so we encourage you to stay alert and be aware of your surroundings. Keep a close eye on cameras, purses, and wallets, all favorite targets of thieves and pickpockets.

WHAT THE SYMBOLS MEAN

✪ Frommer's Favorites

Our favorite places and experiences—outstanding for quality, value, or both.

The following abbreviations are used for credit cards:

AE American Express	EU Eurocard
CB Carte Blanche	JCB
DC Diners Club	MC MasterCard
DISC Discover	V Visa
ER	

FIND FROMMER'S ONLINE

Arthur Frommer's Outspoken Encyclopedia of Travel (www.frommers.com) offers more than 6,000 pages of up-to-the-minute travel information—including the latest bargains and candid, personal articles updated daily by Arthur Frommer himself. No other Web site offers such comprehensive and timely coverage of the world of travel.

Introducing
Washington, D.C.

The most dramatic way to arrive in Washington, D.C., is by air travel, touching down at Washington National Airport. The flight path follows the flow of the Potomac River and teases you with a rushing view of the city's most famous monuments and memorials. And thanks to an 1899 act of Congress limiting the height of downtown buildings, it's easy for even a first-time visitor to pick them out. You can spy the White House, the Washington Monument with its pencilpoint tip thrust into the sky, the rounded roof of the Jefferson Memorial, the wedding-cake tiered dome atop the sprawling Capitol, and the gleaming white columns of the Lincoln Memorial.

But regardless of how you arrive in the nation's capital, your impression of the city will surely center on these images. Washington, D.C., is one of the world hubs of power and diplomacy; its buildings carry the country's history, past, present, and future. Nearly 20 million visitors come to D.C. each year to see the shrines to great Americans, the home of our president, the chambers where Congress debates policies and principles, and the hall where the Supreme Court settles America's legal questions once and for all. You could spend your entire visit touring the Capitol Hill/White House circuit, but you'd miss a whole lot of what this city has to offer.

Washington, D.C., is a uniquely cosmopolitan city. Just walk around and take in the feel of it, with its wide, Parisianlike avenues and charming architecture. Consider the diversity of its neighborhoods, from the stately Embassy Row/Dupont Circle area with its restored town houses, grand mansions, and embassies, to the ethnic feel of Adams Morgan, whose streets are lined with quirky boutiques, hip nightclubs, and intimate eateries. Sample the many languages being spoken—by tourists like you; by diplomats and their staff; and by the Hispanic, Asian, Eastern European, African, French, and Italian peoples who call D.C. home. Feast on the cross-cultural mix of cuisines available; cravings for Vietnamese, Japanese, French, Thai, Russian, American, barbecue, Chinese, Ethiopian—you name it—can be well satisfied here.

D.C. is also a city teeming with culture. Within the city limits (67 square miles), there are more than 50 museums, including the National Gallery of Art, the Smithsonian Institution's 14 museums, and the country's oldest modern art museum, the Phillips Collection. In addition, D.C. is home to about 70 art galleries. Its performing arts venues range from the renowned John F. Kennedy Center for the Performing Arts, which stages world-class opera, orchestra, ballet, and theater performances, to stand-out community productions. Check out the thriving club scene for a night of jazz, rock, blues, swing, or country music by local and headliner acts alike.

Finally, for all the delights contained within Washington buildings, a tremendous bounty of pleasures also awaits outdoors. D.C. is quite an attractive city—the Potomac River runs alongside it and verdant, beautifully landscaped, people-friendly Rock Creek Park runs through it. Great green spaces, like the Mall, and smaller gardens and parks pepper the landscape. Everyone knows about the cherry blossom trees which sprout each spring along the Potomac River Tidal Basin, but some lesser-known outdoor sites include the C&O Canal and its towpath and the 88-acre Theodore Roosevelt Island wilderness preserve.

So while you're in Washington, be adventurous. Take in the monuments, of course, but don't stop there. If your hotel is in one part of town, hop on the Metro (clean, well-lighted, and safe) to another neighborhood for dinner. Visit a museum off the Mall. The compact size of the city and its excellent public transportation system make exploring easy. Use this guide to help you decide which D.C. areas or attractions intrigue you most, then go and explore.

1 Frommer's Favorite Washington Experiences

- **Visit the Lincoln Memorial After Dark.** During the day, hordes of rambunctious schoolchildren may distract you; at night, the experience is infinitely more moving.
- **Take a Monument and Memorials Walking Tour.** You'll need a good map for this one. Take the Metro to Foggy Bottom, and start out with a hearty breakfast at Aquarelle, in the Watergate Hotel. (For a quicker, cheaper, but still delicious fix, stop at the Watergate Pastry shop on the lower level of the complex.) Explore the Kennedy Center across the street (save in-depth touring for another time, but do go to the upper-level promenade that girds the building and enjoy the magnificent city and river views). Then double back to the Vietnam and Lincoln Memorials; follow the cherry tree–lined Tidal Basin path to the Jefferson Memorial; and finish your tour at the Washington Monument. This is a long but beautiful hike; afterward, head to the charming Old Ebbitt Grill (make reservations in advance) for a strength-restoring lunch, or eat at the food court in the nearby Shops at National Place.
- **Ramble through Rock Creek Park.** A good place to ride a bike, run, or even work out. A paved bike/walking path extends 11 miles from the Lincoln Memorial to the Maryland border. You can hop on the trail at many spots throughout the city—it runs past the National Zoo, behind the Omni Shoreham Hotel in Woodley Park (where you can use the $1^1/2$ mile Perrier parcourse, jogging to each of the 18 calisthenics stations), near Dupont Circle, and across from the Watergate/Kennedy Center complex. You can rent a bike from Big Wheel Bikes at 1034 33rd St. NW (☎ 202/337-0254), in Georgetown, and from the Thompson Boat Center (☎ 202/333-4861), located on the path across from the Kennedy Center. For a really long bike ride, trek to the Lincoln Memorial, get yourself across the busy stretch that connects the parkway to the Arlington Memorial Bridge, and cross the bridge to the trail on the other side; this path winds 19 miles to Mount Vernon.
- **Spend a Day in Alexandria.** Just a short distance (by Metro, car, or bike) from the District is George Washington's Virginia hometown. Roam the quaint cobblestone streets, browse charming boutiques and antique stores, visit the boyhood home of Robert E. Lee and other historic attractions, and dine in one of Alexandria's fine restaurants.

- **Sip Afternoon Tea at the Top of Washington National Cathedral.** On Tuesday and Wednesday afternoons at 1:30pm, you can tour the world's sixth largest cathedral, then succumb to tea, scones, and lemon tarts served on the seventh floor of the West tower, whose arched windows overlook the city and beyond to the Sugarloaf Mountains in Maryland. $15 a person, reserve as far in advance as possible (☎ 202/537-8993).
- **You Be the Judge.** If you're in town when the Supreme Court is in session (October through late April; call ☎ 202/479-3000 for details), you can observe a case being argued; it's thrilling to see this august institution at work.
- **Admire the Library of Congress.** The magnificent Italian-Renaissance–style Thomas Jefferson Building of the Library of Congress—filled with murals, mosaics, sculptures, and allegorical paintings—is one of America's most notable architectural achievements. Be sure to take the tour detailed in chapter 7.
- **See the Earth Revolve.** The Foucault Pendulum at the National Museum of American History provides empirical evidence that the earth is revolving; don't miss it.
- **Spend a Morning on the Mall.** Arrive at about 8:30am (take the Metro to the Smithsonian), when the Mall is magical and tourist-free. Stroll behind the Smithsonian Information Center (the Castle) through the magnolia-lined parterres of the beautiful Enid A. Haupt Garden. Exit on Jefferson Drive, walk east to the Hirshhorn, and cross the street to its sunken Sculpture Garden, an enchanting outdoor facility. Then cross back on Jefferson Drive, walk past the Hirshhorn, and turn left on the brick path that leads into the lovely Ripley Garden—yet another gorgeous green space on the Mall. (If it's Sunday, you can have brunch in the Castle, served from 11am to 3pm in the dining room, styled in 12th-century Norman design. For details call ☎ 202/357-2957 before 10am and after 3pm.)
- **Debark at Union Station.** Noted architect Daniel H. Burnham's turn-of-the-century beaux arts railway station is worth a visit even if you're not trying to catch a train. Dawdle and admire its coffered 96-foot-high ceilings, grand arches, and great halls, modeled after the Baths of Diocletian and the Arch of Constantine in Rome. Then shop and eat: the station's 1988 restoration filled the tri-level hall with shops and eateries, everything from Ann Taylor and Crabtree & Evelyn to a high-quality food court and the refined B. Smith's restaurant.
- **Cut a Deal at the Georgetown Flea Market.** Pick up a latte at the Starbucks across the street and spend a pleasant Sunday browsing through castoffs of wealthy Washingtonians, handpainted furniture of local artists, and a hodgepodge of antiques and collectibles. Everybody shops here at one time or another, so you never know who you'll see or what you'll find. Wisconsin Ave. NW at S St. NW in Georgetown; open March to December, Sunday from 9am to 5pm.
- **Enjoy an Artful Evening at the Phillips Collection.** Thursday evenings from 5 to 8pm, you pay $5 to tour the mansion-museum rooms filled with Impressionist, post-Impressionist, and modern art, ending up in the paneled Music Room, where you'll enjoy the jazz, blues, or other musical combinations performed by fine local musicians. It's a popular mingling spot for singles (there's a cash bar and sandwich fare). Call ☎ 202/387-2151 for information.
- **Stroll Along Embassy Row.** Head northwest on Massachusetts Avenue from Dupont Circle. It's a gorgeous walk along tree-shaded streets lined with beaux arts mansions. Built by fabulously wealthy magnates during the Gilded Age, most of these palatial precincts today are occupied by foreign embassies.
- **People-Watch at Dupont Circle.** One of the few "living" circles, Dupont's is the all-weather hangout for mondo-bizarre biker-couriers, Washingtonians of all sorts who like to play chess (stone pedestals ring an inside section of the circle), street musicians, and lovers. Sit on a bench and be astounded by the passing scene.

- **Order Drinks on the Sky Terrace of the Hotel Washington.** Posher bars exist, but none with this view. The experience is almost a cliche in Washington: When spring arrives, make a date to sit on this outdoor, rooftop terrace, sip a gin and tonic, and gaze at the panoramic view of the White House, Treasury Building, and the monuments. Open from the end of April through October, for drinks and light fare (☎ **202/347-4499**).
- **Attend the Kennedy Center Open House.** In late September/early October, and again in spring, the weather almost always cooperates for this fun, free, mostly outdoor celebration of the arts. Diplomats and office drones alike can't resist shimmying to the beat of music played by top Washington musicians on the terraces. Call ☎ **202/467-4600** or 800/444-1324.
- **Shop Saturday Morning at Eastern Market.** Capitol Hill is home to more than government buildings; it's a community of old town houses, antique shops, and the veritable institution, Eastern Market. Here, the locals barter and shop on Saturday mornings for fresh produce and baked goods, and on Sunday for flea market bargains. At 7th St. SE, between North Carolina Ave. and C St. SE.

2 Washington Today

Washington, D.C., is the capital of our country and a city unto itself, and therein lies a host of complications—control of the city being the main issue. Because it's the seat of our country's government, Washington is under Congress's thumb (by order of the U.S. Constitution), which means, in particular, that Congress controls the city budget. But an elected mayor and council govern the city, thanks to Congress's granting of home rule to D.C. in 1973. This awkward relationship is compounded by other factors. For instance, Washington's economy relies heavily upon the presence of the federal government, the city's single largest employer: about 16.7% of area residents are federal employees. The flow of tourists who come here to visit federal buildings and sightseeing attractions nourishes D.C.'s hotels, restaurants, and other hospitality businesses, and makes tourism the city's second largest industry. And, strangely, Washingtonians may vote for president but not for Congressional representatives. (Residents do elect a delegate, a kind of lobbyist for the District without power to vote within Congress.)

As President Clinton put it in a December 1996 press conference, Washington suffers from a "not quite" factor: The capital is not quite a city and not quite a state, but something else altogether. In this statement, the president was addressing the District's situation in response to the city's request for federal aid.

Current home rule by the notorious, mismanaging Mayor Marion S. Barry has brought the city to the brink of financial ruin. Congress has taken bold steps to limit Barry's power and clean up his mess, with the appointment of a financial control board and the assignment of a chief financial officer to improve fiscal management. President Clinton, meanwhile, did respond to the request for federal funds. In early 1997, the president submitted to Congress a federal budget that included a D.C. aid package, the details of which, even at this writing, Congress and the administration wrangle over as Washingtonians wait.

Or maybe not. The district's woes may have little, if any, tangible effect on you as a tourist, but many residents are tired of dealing directly with the city's turmoil. As many of them head for the suburbs, they point to the problems of crime (the District's homicide rate increased 10% in 1996 while homicides decreased in many other large cities), inadequate schools, high taxes, and an obstructive city bureaucracy. *The Washington Post* reports that Washington has lost more than 50,000 residents in the 1990s.

How, then, could Washington have placed fourth in the *1997 Places Rated Almanac* ranking of "best places" in the country to live and work, and eighth in *Fortune* magazine's 1996 listing of top cities?

Based on criteria that measured the abundance and quality of such items as the arts, jobs, climate, crime, recreation, and transportation system, the two surveys found a lot to praise in the capital. And, during your visit, so will you. The capital is still the capital, and federal funds will always see to the upkeep and appeal of much of Washington. Most of the city's attractions are in relatively safe parts of town, and they're operating normally. And if the city has suffered at the hands of Mayor Barry, it nevertheless continues to thrive from the resources and attention showered upon it from other quarters.

Today, even as some homeowners and renters flee, developers and entrepreneurs are flocking in. The neighborhoods of Georgetown, Foggy Bottom, Dupont Circle, Adams Morgan, and Capitol Hill are as charming as ever. But the really remarkable news concerns the downtown area, especially the district bounded by Pennsylvania and Massachusetts avenues, between 7th and 15th streets NW. This part of town is truly blooming after a 50-year downslide. Within a few short blocks are at least five theaters, including the National, the Warner, and the Shakespeare Theater. (The term "revitalization" is apropos, since this area was the city's center of theatrical activity during the 19th and first half of the 20th centuries.) The defunct department store Woodward & Lothrop's, at 11th and G streets NW, is due to reopen as the home of the Washington Opera House in about 5 years.

In the meantime, the debut of the immense MCI Center is making a big splash. This is the arena for Washington's basketball (the Wizards) and hockey (the Capitals) teams, but the 5-acre complex also stages concerts and conferences, and includes a three-level Discovery Channel retail store, an interactive National Sports Gallery, and several large restaurants.

Restaurants like Hard Rock Cafe, Planet Hollywood, Cafe Atlantico, and Bice are already entrenched in the community, and more restaurants are opening all the time. Local artists persist in taking over the empty spaces of old office buildings along the 7th Street corridor, in particular, sometimes forming cooperative arrangements, intent on creating a flourishing new arts scene. Nightclubs, always loyal to the heart of the city, are prospering here and along the U Street strip, further north. The clincher, though, is the fact that people are now venturing downtown, prompting a push for the development of more apartment buildings and condos along these streets.

The upshot of all this activity is . . . well, activity. Streets once dark are bustling into the wee hours. And while Congress takes Mayor Barry to task and talks of a federal takeover, artists, entrepreneurs, and diehard Washingtonians are bringing new life to the capital.

3   History 101

Today, whatever criticisms people make about Washington, they're bound to admit that the city itself is one of the most beautiful in the nation. But it hasn't always been a showplace of gleaming marble monuments and beautiful tree-lined thoroughfares. From the late 18th to the late 19th century, the world wondered why America had chosen for its capital "a howling, malarious wilderness."

Dateline

- 1608 Capt. John Smith sails up Potomac River from Jamestown; for the next 100 years, Irish-Scotch settlers colonize the area.
- 1783 Continental Congress proposes new "Federal Town"; both North and South vie for it.

continues

- 1790 A compromise is reached: If the South pays off the North's Revolutionary War debts, the new capital will be situated in its region.
- 1791 French engineer Pierre Charles L'Enfant designs capital city but is fired within a year.
- 1792 Cornerstone is laid for Executive Mansion.
- 1793 Construction begins on the Capitol.
- 1800 First wing of the Capitol completed; Congress moves from Philadelphia; Pres. John Adams moves into Executive Mansion.
- 1801 Library of Congress established.
- 1812 War with England.
- 1814 British burn Washington.
- 1817 Executive Mansion rebuilt, its charred walls painted white; becomes known as White House.
- 1822 Population reaches 15,000.
- 1829 Smithsonian Institution founded for "increase and diffusion of knowledge."
- 1847 Cornerstone laid for first Smithsonian museum building.
- 1861 Civil War; Washington becomes North's major supply depot.
- 1865 Capitol dome completed; Lee surrenders to Grant April 8; Lincoln assassinated at Ford's Theatre April 14.
- 1871 Alexander "Boss" Shepherd turns Washington into a showplace, using many of L'Enfant's plans.
- 1885 Washington Monument dedicated.
- 1889 National Zoo established.
- 1900 Population reaches about 300,000.
- 1901 McMillan Commission plans development of Mall from Capitol to Lincoln Memorial.
- 1907 Union Station opens, largest train station in country.
- 1908 Federal Bureau of Investigation (FBI) created.
- 1912 Cherry trees, a gift from Japan, planted in Tidal Basin.

continues

A WANDERING CONGRESS   To say that Washington got off to a shaky start is putting it mildly. For openers, our capital came about as the result of a mutiny. In 1783, 250 Revolutionary War soldiers, understandably angered because Congress was ignoring their petitions for back pay, stormed the temporary capitol, the State House in Philadelphia, demanding justice. The city of Philadelphia, sympathizing with the soldiers, ignored congressional pleas for protection, and as the soldiers rioted outside, the lawmakers locked the doors and huddled within. When the soldiers finally returned to their barracks, Congress deemed it politic to move on to Princeton. They also decided that they needed a capital city whose business was government and the protection thereof.

This was not an altogether new idea. Congress had been so nomadic during its first decade that when a statue of George Washington was authorized in 1783, satirist Francis Hopkinson suggested putting it on wheels so it could follow the government around. Before settling into Washington, Congress met in New York, Baltimore, Philadelphia, Lancaster, Princeton, Annapolis, York, and Trenton.

A DEAL MADE OVER DINNER   When Congress proposed that a city be designed and built for the sole purpose of housing the government of the new nation, fresh difficulties arose. There was a general feeling that wherever the capital might be built, a great commercial center would arise; thus, many cities vied for the honor. Then, too, northerners were strongly opposed to a southern capital—and vice versa. Finally, after 7 years of bickering, New Yorker Alexander Hamilton and Virginian Thomas Jefferson worked out a compromise over dinner one night in New York. The North would support a southern site for the capital in return for the South's assumption of debts incurred by the states during the Revolution. As a further sop to the North, it was agreed that the seat of government would remain in Philadelphia through 1800 to allow suitable time for surveying, purchasing land, and constructing government buildings.

ENTER L'ENFANT TERRIBLE   An act passed in 1790 specified a site "not exceeding 10 miles square" (that's 100 square miles) to be located on the Potomac. President and experienced surveyor George Washington was charged with selecting the exact site and appointing building commissioners. He chose a part of the Potomac Valley where the river becomes tidal and is joined by the Anacostia. Maryland gladly provided 69¼ square miles and Virginia 30¾ for the new Federal District. Virginia, whose portion included Arlington and Alexandria, later complained that the District was developing too slowly. Virginia's 30¾ square miles were deemed unnecessary, and so they were returned to the state in 1846. The District today covers about 67 square miles.

President Washington hired French military engineer Pierre Charles L'Enfant to lay out the new federal city. It has since been said that "it would have been hard to find a man better qualified artistically and less fitted by temperament" for the job. L'Enfant arrived in 1791 and immediately declared Jenkins Hill (today Capitol Hill) "a pedestal waiting for a monument." He surveyed every inch of the new Federal District and began his plan by selecting dominant sites for major buildings. He designed broad, 160-foot-wide avenues radiating from squares and circles centered on monumental sculptures and fountains. The Capitol, the "presidential palace," and an equestrian statue (the last to be erected where the Washington Monument stands today) were to be the focal points. Pennsylvania Avenue would be the major thoroughfare, and the Mall was conceived as a bustling ceremonial avenue of embassies and other distinguished buildings.

L'Enfant was a genius, his plan a masterpiece, but he was also a temperamental artist with no patience for the workings of a bureaucracy or the exigencies of politics. He refused to cooperate with Washington's appointed surveyor, Andrew Ellicott, or the building commissioners in charge of the federal city. Worse yet, he went out of his way to offend one of the latter. Without so much as a by-your-leave (in fact, in spite of an injunction to the contrary), he tore down the manor house Commissioner Daniel Carroll was building because it blocked one of his cherished vistas.

George Washington diplomatically assuaged Carroll and arranged compensation, but L'Enfant continued to create difficulties. His plan itself dismayed landowners who had been promised $66.66 per acre for land donated for buildings, while land for avenues was to be donated free. L'Enfant's

- 1914 World War I begins.
- 1922 Lincoln Memorial completed.
- 1941 National Gallery of Art opens; United States declares war on Japan.
- 1943 Pantheon-inspired Jefferson Memorial and Pentagon completed.
- 1949 Interior of White House rebuilt.
- 1957 Helicopters first seen on White House lawn.
- 1960 Population reaches almost 800,000.
- 1971 John F. Kennedy Center for Performing Arts opens.
- 1976 Metro, city's first subway system, opens in time for Bicentennial.
- 1982 Vietnam Veterans Memorial erected in Constitution Gardens.
- 1987 Arthur M. Sackler Gallery, a new Smithsonian facility focusing on Asian art, opens on Mall; expanded Museum of African Art, also part of Smithsonian, moves to Mall.
- 1991 Population exceeds 3 million.
- 1993 U.S. Holocaust Memorial Museum, documenting the horror and tragedy of Nazi era, opens near Mall.
- 1994 Marion Barry is elected to a fourth term as mayor, after serving time in prison.
- 1995 Korean War Veterans Memorial is dedicated. Pennsylvania Avenue closed to vehicular traffic in front of the White House.
- 1996 The city goes through tough times, plagued by municipal and federal budget woes.
- 1997 Federal government offers aid package to save D.C. from bankruptcy. Franklin Delano Roosevelt Memorial is dedicated.

160-foot-wide avenues and 2-mile-long Mall were therefore not appreciated. Of the 6,661 acres to be included in the boundaries of the federal city, about half would be avenues and the Mall.

A more likable man might have won over the landowners and commissioners, inspiring them with his dreams and his passion, but L'Enfant exhibited only a peevish and condescending secretiveness that alienated one and all. The price of genius became too high when L'Enfant ignored Washington's repeated urgings to produce at least a preliminary blueprint so that fundraising could begin. A year after he had been hired, L'Enfant was fired. For the next few decades, he was a familiar figure "haunting the lobbies of the Capitol . . . pacing the newly marked avenues"— keeping a bitter and lonely vigil (with a mangy dog for company) over the developing city. Capitol architect Benjamin Latrobe wrote in his diary: "Daily through the city stalks the picture of famine, L'Enfant and his dog." A grateful Congress offered him $2,500 compensation for his year of work, and James Monroe urged him to accept a professorship at West Point. Insulted, he spurned all offers, suing the government for $95,500 instead. He lost and died a pauper in 1825. In 1909, in belated recognition of his services, his remains were brought to Arlington National Cemetery. Some 118 years after he had conceived it, his vision of the federal city became a reality.

HOME NOT-SO-SWEET HOME   In 1800 the government (106 representatives and 32 senators) and its effects arrived, according to schedule. What they found bore little resemblance to a city. "One might take a ride of several hours within the precincts without meeting with a single individual to disturb one's meditation," commented one early resident. Pennsylvania Avenue was a mosquito-infested swamp, and there were fewer than 400 habitable houses. Disgruntled Secretary of the Treasury Oliver Wolcott wrote his wife, "I do not perceive how the members of Congress can possibly secure lodgings, unless they will consent to live like Scholars in a college or Monks in a monastery. . . ." The solution was a boom in boarding houses.

Abigail Adams was dismayed at the condition of her new home in the presidential mansion. The damp caused her rheumatism to act up, the main stairs had not yet been constructed, not a single room was finished, and there were not even enough logs for all the fireplaces. And since there was "not the least fence, yard, or other convenience," she hung the presidential laundry in the unfinished East Room. To attend presidential affairs or visit one another, Washington's early citizens had to drive through mud and slush, their vehicles often becoming embedded in bogs and gullies—not a pleasant state of affairs, but one that would continue for many decades. There were many hitches in building the capital. Money, as always, was in short supply, as were materials and labor. The home of the world's most enlightened democracy was built largely by slaves. And always, in the background, there was talk of abandoning the city and starting over somewhere else.

REDCOATS REDUX   Then came the War of 1812. At first the fighting centered on Canada and the West—both too far away to affect daily life in the capital. (In the early 1800s, it was a 33-hour ride from Washington, D. C., to Philadelphia—if you made good time.) In May 1813, the flamboyant British Rear Admiral Cockburn sent word to the Executive Mansion that "he would make his bow" in the Madisons' drawing room shortly. On August 23, 1814, alarming news reached the capital: The British had landed troops in Maryland. On August 24, James Madison was at the front, most of the populace had fled, and Dolley Madison created a legend by refusing to leave the White House without Gilbert Stuart's famous portrait of George Washington. As the British neared her gates, she was calmly writing a blow-by-blow description to her sister:

> *Our kind friend, Mr. Carroll, has come to hasten my departure,*
> *and is in a very bad humour with me because I insist on waiting until the*
> *large picture of General Washington is secured, and it requires to be unscrewed*
> *from the wall. This process was found too tedious for these perilous moments;*
> *I have ordered the frame to be broken, and the canvas taken out; it is done. . . .*
> *And now, dear sister, I must leave this house, or the retreating army will make*
> *me a prisoner in it, by filling up the road I am directed to take.*

When the British arrived early that evening, they found dinner set up on the table (Dolley had hoped for the best until the end), and according to some accounts, ate it before torching the mansion. They also burned the Capitol, the Library of Congress, and newly built ships and naval stores. A thunderstorm later that night saved the city from total destruction, while a tornado the next day added to the damage but daunted the British troops.

It seemed that the new capital was doomed. Margaret Bayard Smith, wife of the owner of the influential *National Intelligencer,* lamented, "I do not suppose the Government will ever return to Washington. All those whose property was invested in that place, will be reduced to general poverty. . . . The consternation about us is general. The despondency still greater." But the *Intelligencer* was among the voices speaking out against an even temporary move. Editorials warned that it would be a "treacherous breach of faith" with those who had "laid out fortunes in the purchase of property in and about the city." To move the capital would be "kissing the rod an enemy has wielded." Washingtonian pride rallied, and the city was saved once again. Still, it was a close call; Congress came within nine votes of abandoning the place!

In 1815 leading citizens erected a brick building in which Congress could meet in relative comfort until the Capitol was restored. The Treaty of Ghent, establishing peace with Great Britain, was ratified at Octagon House, where the Madisons were temporarily ensconced. And Thomas Jefferson supplied his own books to replace the destroyed contents of the Library of Congress. Confidence was restored, and the city began to prosper. When the Madisons moved into the rebuilt mansion, its exterior had been painted gleaming white to cover the charred walls. From then on, it would be known as the White House.

THE CITY OF MAGNIFICENT INTENTIONS   Between the War of 1812 and the Civil War, few people evinced any great enthusiasm for Washington. European visitors especially looked at the capital and found it wanting. It was still a provincial backwater, Pennsylvania Avenue and the Mall remaining muddy messes inhabited by pigs, goats, cows, and geese. Many were repelled by the slave auctions openly taking place in the backyard of the White House. The best that could be said—though nobody said it—was that the young capital was picturesque. Meriwether Lewis kept the bears he had brought back from his 4,000-mile expedition up the Missouri in cages on the president's lawn. Native American chiefs in full regalia were often seen negotiating with the white man's government. And matching them in splendor were magnificently attired European court visitors. The only foreigner who praised Washington was Lafayette, who visited in 1825 and was feted with lavish balls and dinners throughout his stay.

Charles Dickens gave us the raspberry in 1842:

> *It is sometimes called the City of Magnificent Distances, but it might*
> *with greater propriety be termed the City of Magnificent Intentions. . . . Spacious*
> *avenues, that begin in nothing and lead nowhere; streets, miles long, that only*
> *want houses, roads, and inhabitants; public buildings that need but a public*
> *to be complete; and ornaments of great thoroughfares, which only lack great*
> *thoroughfares to ornament—are its leading features.*

Tobacco chewing and sloppy senatorial spitting particularly appalled him:

> *Both houses are handsomely carpeted, but the state to which these carpets*
> *are reduced by the universal disregard of the spittoon with which every honorable*
> *member is accommodated, and the extraordinary improvements on the pattern*
> *which are squirted and dabbled upon it in every direction, do not admit of being*
> *described. I will merely observe, that I strongly recommend all strangers not to look*
> *at the floor; and if they happen to drop anything . . . not to pick it up with an*
> *ungloved hand on any account.*

But Dickens's critique was mild when compared with Anthony Trollope's, who declared Washington in 1860 "as melancholy and miserable a town as the mind of man can conceive."

A NATION DIVIDED   During the Civil War, the capital became an armed camp, with thousands of camp followers. It was the principal supply depot for the Union Army and an important medical center. Parks became campgrounds, churches became hospitals, and forts ringed the town. The population doubled from 60,000 to 120,000, including about 40,000 former slaves who streamed into the city seeking federal protection. More than 3,000 soldiers slept in the Capitol, and a bakery was set up in the basement. The streets were filled with the wounded, and Walt Whitman was a familiar figure, making daily rounds to succor the ailing soldiers. In spite of everything, Lincoln insisted that work on the Capitol be continued. "If people see the Capitol going on, it is a sign we intend the Union shall go on," he said. When the giant dome was completed in 1863 and a 35-star flag was flown overhead, Capitol Hill's field battery fired a 35-gun salute, honoring the Union's then 35 states.

There was joy in Washington and an 800-gun salute in April 1865 when news of the fall of the Confederacy reached the capital. The joy was short-lived, however. Five days after Appomattox, President Lincoln was shot at Ford's Theatre while attending a performance of *Our American Cousin.* Black replaced the festive tricolored draperies, and the city went into mourning.

The war had enlarged the city's population while doing nothing to improve its facilities. Agrarian, uneducated ex-slaves stayed on, and poverty, unemployment, and disease were rampant. A red-light district remained, the parks were trodden bare, and tenement slums mushroomed within a stone's throw of the Capitol. Horace Greeley suggested that the capital go west.

LED BY A SHEPHERD   Whereas L'Enfant had been aloof and introverted, his glorious vision was destined to be implemented 70 years later by Alexander "Boss" Shepherd, a swashbuckling and friendly man. A real estate speculator who had made his money in a plumbing firm, Shepherd shouldered a musket in the Union Army and became one of General Ulysses S. Grant's closest intimates. When Grant became president, he wanted to appoint Shepherd governor, but blue-blooded opposition ran too high. Washington high society considered him a parvenu and feared his

Impressions

I know of no other capital in the world which stands on so wide and splendid a river. But the people and the mode of life are enough to take your hair off!

—Henry Adams

My God! What have I done to be condemned to reside in such a city!

—A French diplomat in the early days

ambitions for civic leadership. Instead, Grant named the more popular Henry D. Cooke (a secret Shepherd ally) governor and named Shepherd vice-president of the Board of Public Works. No one was fooled. Shepherd made all the governor's decisions, and a joke went around the capital: "Why is the new governor like a sheep? Because he is led by A. Shepherd." He became the actual governor in 1873.

Shepherd vowed that his "comprehensive plan of improvement" would make the city a showplace. But an engineer he wasn't. Occasionally, newly paved streets had to be torn up because he had forgotten to install the sewers first. But he was a first-rate orator and politician. He began by hiring an army of laborers and starting them on projects all over town. Congress would have had to halt work on half-finished sidewalks, streets, and sewers throughout the District in order to stop him. It would have been a mess. The press liked and supported the colorful Shepherd; people forced out of their homes because they couldn't pay the high assessments for improvements hated him. Between 1871 and 1874, he established parks, paved and lighted the streets, installed sewers, filled in sewage-laden Tiber Creek, and planted more than 50,000 trees. He left the city bankrupt—more than $20 million in debt! But he got the job done.

L'ENFANT REBORN Through the end of the 19th century, Washington continued to make great aesthetic strides. The Washington Monument, long a truncated obelisk and major eyesore, was finally completed in 1884. Pennsylvania Avenue was becoming the ceremonial thoroughfare L'Enfant had envisioned, and important buildings were completed one after another. Shepherd had done a great deal, but much was still left undone. In 1887, L'Enfant's "Plan for the City of Washington" was resurrected. In 1900, Michigan Senator James McMillan—a retired railroad mogul with architectural and engineering knowledge—determined to complete the job L'Enfant had started a century earlier. A tireless lobbyist for government-sponsored municipal improvements, he persuaded his colleagues to appoint an advisory committee to create "the city beautiful."

At his personal expense, McMillan sent this illustrious committee—landscapist Frederick Law Olmsted (designer of New York's Central Park), sculptor Augustus Saint-Gaudens, and noted architects Daniel Burnham and Charles McKim—to Europe for 7 weeks to study the landscaping and architecture of that continent's great capitals. Assembled at last was a group that combined L'Enfant's artistic genius and Shepherd's political savvy.

"Make no little plans," counseled Burnham. "They have no magic to stir men's blood, and probably themselves will not be realized. Make big plans, aim high in hope and work, remembering that a noble and logical diagram once recorded will never die, but long after we are gone will be a living thing, asserting itself with ever growing insistency."

The committee's big plans—almost all of which were accomplished—included the development of a complete park system, selection of sites for government buildings, and the designing of the Lincoln Memorial, the Arlington Memorial Bridge, and the Reflecting Pool (the last inspired by Versailles). They also got to work on improving the Mall; their first step was to remove the tracks, train sheds, and stone depot constructed there by the Baltimore and Potomac Railroad. In return, Congress authorized money to build the monumental Union Station, whose design was inspired by Rome's Baths of Diocletian.

Throughout the McMillan Commission years, the House was under the hostile leadership of Speaker "Uncle Joe" Cannon of Illinois who, among other things, swore he would "never let a memorial to Abraham Lincoln be erected in that goddamned swamp" (West Potomac Park). Cannon caused some problems and delays, but on the whole the committee's prestigious membership added weight to their usually accepted recommendations. McMillan, however, did not live to see most of his dreams accomplished. He died in 1902.

By the 20th century, Washington was no longer an object of ridicule. And it has continued to develop apace. The Library of Congress, Union Station, and the Corcoran Gallery were all built around the turn of the century. The Museum of Natural History was erected in 1911 (already extant Smithsonian buildings included Arts and Industries, the Old Patent Office Building, and the Castle), the Lincoln Memorial was completed in 1922, and the Freer Gallery in 1923. A Commission of Fine Arts was appointed in 1910 by President Taft to create monuments and fountains, once again with Olmsted as a member. Thanks to Mrs. Taft, the famous cherry trees presented to the United States by the Japanese in 1912 were planted in the Tidal Basin. And thanks to Taft's commission, neoclassic architecture and uniform building height became the order of the day. During the Great Depression in the 1930s, FDR's Works Progress Administration—WPA, *We Do Our Part*—put the unemployed to work erecting public buildings and artists to work beautifying them. More recently (1971), the John F. Kennedy Center for the Performing Arts, on the Potomac's east bank, filled a longtime need for a cultural haven.

In 1974, the opening of the new Hirshhorn Museum and Sculpture Garden on the Mall met the need for a major museum of modern art. Another storehouse of art treasures is the modernistic I. M. Pei–designed East Building of the National Gallery of Art, which opened in 1978. It was designed to handle the overflow of the gallery's burgeoning collection and to accommodate traveling exhibits of major importance. In time for the Bicentennial, the National Air and Space Museum opened in splendid new quarters, and the first leg of the capital's much-needed subway system, Metro, was completed. The 45 acres between the Washington Monument and the Lincoln Memorial were transformed into Constitution Gardens, and in 1982 the park became the site of the Vietnam Veterans Memorial.

In 1987, Washington got a new $75 million Smithsonian complex on the Mall; it houses the Arthur M. Sackler Gallery of Art, the relocated National Museum of

Impressions

The whole aspect of Washington is light, cheerful, and airy; it reminds me of our fashionable watering places.

—Mrs. Frances Trollope

Washington . . . enormous spaces, hundreds of miles of asphalt, a charming climate, and the most entertaining society in America.

—Henry James

African Art, the International Center, and the Enid A. Haupt Garden. In 1989, renovation of the city's magnificent Union Station was completed. Its brilliant architect, Daniel Burnham, also designed the palatial City Post Office Building which, in 1993, became part of the Smithsonian complex as the National Postal Museum. The same year saw the opening of the United States Holocaust Memorial Museum, adjoining the Mall, a grim reminder of civilization gone awry. In 1995, the Korean War Veterans Memorial was dedicated. Washington's fourth presidential monument—and the first in more than half a century—was dedicated in May 1997 to honor Franklin Delano Roosevelt; it is the first memorial in Washington purposely designed to be totally wheelchair accessible. In late 1997, a Civil War memorial opened, recognizing the efforts of African-American soldiers who fought for the Union.

4 Hollywood on the Potomac

On a cold February morning in 1997, a cab pulls up in front of the Willard Intercontinental Hotel on Pennsylvania Avenue NW and discharges two well-dressed passengers: a woman, somewhat distracted, chattering to an intense-looking man moving hurriedly. As the couple ascends the steps to the hotel's entrance, the man glances over to see former Housing Secretary (and Bob Dole running mate) Jack Kemp descending. "Hey, Tommy, how ya doin," yells Kemp to the man. "Tommy" smiles a greeting and executes a smooth wave, hardly pausing on the steps, as Kemp calls, "We'll talk later."

This scene was shot last year in Washington as part of an episode for the popular television series *Chicago Hope*. The woman, Dr. Kate Austin (played by actress Christine Lahti), is anxious about having to testify before a Senate subcommittee on health care reform. Austin's ex-husband, Tommy Wilmette (played by Ron Silver), will also testify, but he remains calm and focused. The episode uses recognizable Washington locations—the Capitol Building, a part of Union Station's exterior, the Lincoln Memorial—and Washington personalities like Kemp and Senator Ted Kennedy to convey a sense of the authority and particular glamour of the place. In fact, by story's end, the viewer senses that this is Wilmette's swan song. His self-possession and acceptance among Washington insiders signifies his imminent departure from Chicago and from *Chicago Hope*.

Chicago Hope is just one of scores of Hollywood productions that have used Washington as a location for a movie, TV, commercial, music video, documentary, you name it. The Washington, D.C., Office of Motion Picture and TV reports that, on the average, 6 films and anywhere from 10 to 20 TV productions are shot here each year, although the number for Washington-based films tends to go up in election years: 14 movies were made here in 1996, including *Mars Attacks, The People vs. Larry Flynt, Absolute Power*, and *Independence Day*. When you are in Washington visiting, you may well stumble upon a filming or taping in progress, especially since the capital's most famous tourist attractions are also producers' favorite backdrops. Nothing packs a Washington punch like a flash of the White House on the screen.

But if movie- and TV series-making are on the rise in Washington, the practice of using Washington—and politicians—as a subject for films has long been fashionable. Starting in 1915 with *Birth of a Nation,* the lineup includes *Mr. Smith Goes to Washington* (1939), *All the King's Men* (1949), *Advise and Consent* (1962), *All the President's Men* (1976), *Broadcast News* (1987), *Bob Roberts* (1992), and the newly released *Wag the Dog* (to name just a few).

Given Washington's popularity among TV and film producers, its sometime nickname, "Hollywood on the Potomac," seems apt. The funny thing is, though, that the appellation derives not from the capital's frequent use as a film location or subject, but from its magnetic appeal for Hollywood celebrities. Although we have had an actor become president, it isn't Ronald Reagan with whom the concept is associated, but with our current president, Bill Clinton. His affinity for movie stars is matched by his aptitude for employing star power in fundraising and electioneering efforts.

Barbra Streisand, musicmeister/billionaire David Geffen, and studio chairman Lew Wasserman are among those who have raised major bucks for Clinton's campaigns. The most honored friends of Bill's ("FOBs") get to spend the night in the Lincoln Bedroom (guests have included such stars as Candice Bergen and Richard Dreyfuss). Clinton's inaugural balls in 1993 and 1997 brought so many Hollywood types to Washington that for days it was difficult to wander anywhere in the city without spotting a star: Kim Basinger coming out of H.H. Leonards' B&B on O Street, Gregory Hines puffing on a cigar in the Fairfax Bar of the Ritz-Carlton, Kevin Costner walking down a hallway of the Willard.

The phrase "Hollywood on the Potomac" refers to another growing phenomenon, the use of "star" testimony on Capitol Hill. Depending on the type of hearings being held, you might see anyone as you tour the Capitol, from actor Ted Danson testifying on behalf of environmental causes to Alec Baldwin lobbying for federal funding for the arts.

Politicians, on the whole, rarely mind doing a star turn for the cameras. Next time you watch a movie or TV show with a Washington twist, be on the lookout. You may spy George Stephanopolous popping up on the sitcom *Spin City*, Bob Dole putting in a good-sport appearance on "Saturday Night Live" (after losing the 1996 election), or senators Christopher Dodd, Alan Simpson, Paul Simon, and Howard Metzenbaum playing themselves in the film *Dave*.

5 Famous Washingtonians

Benjamin Banneker (1731–1806)   When Pierre L'Enfant left Washington in 1792, Banneker, a black mathematician, astronomer, and surveyor, re-created his maps and city plans from memory.

Art Buchwald (b. 1925)   Pulitzer Prize–winning syndicated columnist and political satirist.

Frederick Douglass (1818–95)   Born in slavery, he escaped and fled north to become a driving force in the abolitionist movement and its most impassioned voice.

Edward (Duke) Ellington (1899–1974)   Native Washingtonian, bandleader, pianist, and songwriter, he composed "Mood Indigo" and "Sophisticated Lady."

Katharine Graham (b. 1917)   When *Washington Post* publisher Donald Graham killed himself in 1963, his wife Katharine (Kay) Graham took charge of the newspaper and developed the *Post* into the must-read national publication it is today. Her memoir, *Personal History*, published in 1997, provides fascinating insights into her life, the life of the newspaper, and how Washington works.

Helen Hayes (1900–93)   The First Lady of the American Theater was well known for her roles in *Long Day's Journey into Night* and *The Glass Menagerie*.

Pierre Charles L'Enfant (1754–1825)   Brilliant French military engineer who, invited by George Washington, laid out plans for the national capital in 1791.

Dolley Madison (1769–1849)   President Madison's wife and capital society's first queen, she rescued Gilbert Stuart's famous portrait of George Washington from the British in the War of 1812.

Perle Mesta (1891–1975)   Official Washington's "hostess with the mostest," especially during the Truman years. She was the inspiration for the musical *Call Me Madam.*

James Smithson (1765–1829)   Although he never set foot in the United States, he should be considered an honorary Washingtonian because he left his fortune to this country for the museum complex that, bearing his name, has become the largest in the world.

John Philip Sousa (1854–1932)   America's bandmaster, known as "The March King," composer of "Semper Fidelis," "Stars and Stripes Forever," and "The Washington Post."

Walt Whitman (1819–92)   American poet, author of *Leaves of Grass* and *O Captain, My Captain,* the latter a tribute to Lincoln, whom he greatly admired. He thought of himself as the great poet of democracy.

2

Planning a Trip to Washington, D.C.

As you might imagine, Washington is one of the most visited cities in the country. Tourists come year-round, although April is the busiest month. Take this into account as you plan your trip and make reservations in advance if you want to book a particular hotel (at a particular rate). Remember, too, to check theater and concert schedules ahead of time, in case you want to purchase tickets for a show; performances often sell out quickly. As I mention below, it is possible to arrange months ahead for special tours of certain sightseeing attractions, thereby avoiding long lines or even the disappointment of missing a tour altogether.

Having said all that, I have to add that the impromptu experience in Washington sometimes becomes the most memorable—going for an early run on the pathway paralleling the Potomac as the sun comes up over the monuments, or sitting at Martin's bar in Georgetown and listening to fourth-generation owner Billy Martin tell tales about Washington legends (the Kennedy clan, Lyndon Johnson, Sam Rayburn, Art Buchwald) who have made Martin's their regular hangout since the place opened in 1933.

1 Visitor Information & Money

Before you leave, contact the **Washington, D.C., Convention and Visitors Association,** 1212 New York Ave. NW, Washington, DC 20005 (☎ **202/789-7000**), and ask them to send you a free copy of the *Washington, D.C., Visitors Guide,* which details hotels, restaurants, sights, shops, and more. They'll also be happy to answer specific questions.

Also call the **D.C. Committee to Promote Washington** (☎ **800/422-8644**), and request free copies of brochures listing additional information about Washington.

ADVANCE RESERVATION CONGRESSIONAL TOURS

Based on ticket availability, senators and/or representatives can provide their constituents with advance tickets for tours of the Capitol, the White House, the FBI, the Bureau of Engraving and Printing, the Supreme Court, and the Kennedy Center. This is no secret. Thousands of people know about it and do write, so make your request as far in advance as possible—even 6 months ahead is not too early—specifying the dates you plan to visit and the number of

What Things Cost in Washington, D.C.	U.S. $
Taxi from National Airport to downtown	10.00–12.00
Bus from National Airport to downtown	8.00 (14.00 round-trip)
Metro from National Airport to Farragut West (non-rush hour)	1.10 (downtown)
Local telephone call	.25
Double at the Jefferson Hotel (very expensive)	175.00–305.00
Double at the Canterbury Hotel (expensive)	109.00–215.00
Double at the Radisson Barceló Hotel (moderate)	89.00–169.00
Double at the Embassy Inn (inexpensive)	59.00–125.00
Dinner for one, without wine, at the Willard Room (very expensive)	55.00
Dinner for one, without wine, at Jaleo (moderate)	23.00–25.00
Dinner for one, without wine, at Il Radicchio (inexpensive)	6.00–15.00
Bottle of beer in a restaurant	3.50–4.00
Coca-Cola in a restaurant	1.50
Cup of coffee in a restaurant	1.25
Roll of ASA 100 film, 36 exposures	6.50
Admission to all Smithsonian museums	Free
Theater ticket at the National	20.00–70.00

tickets you need. Their allotment of tickets for each site is limited, so there's no guarantee you'll secure them, but it's worth a try. (Advance tickets are not necessary to tour an attraction; they just preclude a long wait.)

Address requests to representatives as follows: name of your congressperson, U.S. House of Representatives, Washington, DC 20515; or name of your senator, U.S. Senate, Washington, DC 20510. Don't forget to include the exact dates of your Washington trip. When you write, also request tourist information and literature.

Note: Before writing, you might try calling a senator or congressperson's local office; in some states you can obtain passes by phone.

One other tip: If you have acquaintances who work at any of the sites, or within a related organization, by all means, contact them. For example, an employee of the Justice Department may be able to obtain FBI tour tickets for you, hassle-free.

THE CAPITOL   Congressional passes are not for tours but allow you to sit and observe Congress in session. (Regular guided tours, for which you need no ticket, take place Monday through Saturday, from 9am to 3:45pm, and last 45 minutes.) Check the Senate and House calendars first to see what days Congress is in session and in recess. Call ☎ **202/225-3121** to check the House schedule and ☎ **202/224-3121** to check the Senate schedule. The *Washington Post* also publishes a daily calendar that notes the times Congress will be in session and the issues to be debated.

THE WHITE HOUSE   Tuesday through Saturday between 8 and 8:45am, the doors of the White House are open for special VIP tours to those with tickets. Once again, write far, far in advance, because each senator and congressperson receives no more than 10 tickets a week to distribute. These early tours ensure your entrance during the busy tourist season when thousands line up during the 2 hours daily that the White House is open to the public. The VIP tours are also more extensive than those held later; guides provide explanatory commentary as you go. On the later tours, attendants are simply on hand to answer questions but don't give formal talks in each room.

THE FBI   The line for this very popular tour can be extremely long; March through September you can expect to wait for 1 or 2 hours. Guided congressional tours take place on the quarter hour, from 9:45 to 11:45am and from 1:45 to 2:45pm. Contact your senator or representative, at least 3 months ahead, to schedule an appointment for constituent groups of six or fewer.

BUREAU OF ENGRAVING & PRINTING   Guided VIP tours are offered weekdays at 8am, except on holidays.

THE KENNEDY CENTER   Congressional tours depart Monday through Saturday at 9:30am year-round and at 9:45am April through September. These tours are free, but you must have a letter from your senator or congressperson. Call ☎ **202/ 416-8303** at the Kennedy Center for more information on these tours.

THE SUPREME COURT   Contact your senator or congressperson at least 2 months in advance to arrange for guided tours of the building led by a Supreme Court staff member.

2 When to Go

CLIMATE

Probably you'll visit when you have vacation time, a business meeting here, or when the kids are out of school, but if you have a choice, I'd recommend the fall. The weather is lovely, Washington's scenery is awash in fall foliage colors, and the tourists have thinned out.

If you hate crowds and want to get the most out of Washington sights, winter is your season: There are no long lines or early morning dashes to avoid them, and hotel prices are lower. People like to say that Washington winters are mild—and yes, if you're from Minnesota, you will find Washington warmer, no doubt. But our winters are unpredictable, bitter cold one day, an ice storm the next, followed by a couple of days of sun and higher temperatures. Pack for all possibilities.

Spring weather is delightful, and, of course, there are those cherry blossoms. Along with autumn, it's the nicest time to enjoy D.C.'s outdoor attractions, to get around to museums in comfort, and to laze away an afternoon or evening at the ubiquitous Washington street cafes. But the city is also crowded with visitors and school groups.

The throngs remain in summer, and anyone who's ever spent a summer in D.C. will tell you how hot and steamy it can be. The advantage: This is the season (especially June and July) to enjoy numerous outdoor events—free concerts, festivals, parades, and more. There's something doing almost every night and day. And, of course, Independence Day (July 4th) in the capital is a spectacular celebration.

Average Temperatures (°F) in Washington, D.C.

	Jan	Feb	Mar	Apr	May	June	July	Aug	Sept	Oct	Nov	Dec
Avg. High	44	46	54	66	76	83	87	85	79	68	57	46
Avg. Low	30	29	36	46	56	65	69	68	61	50	39	32

WASHINGTON CALENDAR OF EVENTS

The District is the scene of numerous daily special events, fairs, and celebrations. Listed below are the major annual events. When in town, check the *Washington Post,* especially the Friday "Weekend" section. The Smithsonian Information Center, 1000 Jefferson Dr. SW (☎ **202/357-2700**), is another good source. For annual events in Alexandria, see chapter 11.

January

- **Presidential Inauguration,** on the Capitol steps. After the swearing-in, the crowd lines the curbs as the new or re-elected president proceeds down Pennsylvania Avenue to the White House. The event is heralded by parades, concerts, parties, plays, and other festivities. For details, call ☎ **202/619-7222.** January 20 in years following a national election.
- **Martin Luther King, Jr.'s Birthday.** Events include speeches by prominent civil rights leaders and politicians; readings; dance, theater, and choral performances; prayer vigils; a wreath-laying ceremony at the Lincoln Memorial; and concerts. Many events take place at the **Martin Luther King Memorial Library,** 901 G St. NW (☎ **202/727-1186**). Call ☎ **202/789-7000** for further details. Third Monday in January.

February

- **Chinese New Year Celebration.** A friendship archway, topped by 300 painted dragons and lighted at night, marks Chinatown's entrance at 7th and H streets NW. The celebration begins the day of the Chinese New Year and continues for 10 or more days, with traditional firecrackers, dragon dancers, and colorful street parades. Some area restaurants offer special menus. For details, call ☎ **202/ 638-1041.** Late January or early to mid-February.
- **Black History Month.** Features numerous events, museum exhibits, and cultural programs celebrating the contributions of African Americans to American life. For details check the *Washington Post* or call ☎ **202/357-2700.** For additional activities at the **Martin Luther King Library,** call ☎ **202/727-1186.**
- **Abraham Lincoln's Birthday,** Lincoln Memorial. Marked by the laying of a wreath and a reading of the Gettysburg Address at noon. Call ☎ **202/619-7222.** February 12.
- **George Washington's Birthday,** Washington Monument. Similar celebratory events. Call ☎ **202/619-7222** for details. Both president's birthdays also bring annual citywide sales. February 22.

March

- **St. Patrick's Day Parade,** on Constitution Avenue NW from 7th to 17th streets. A big parade with all you'd expect—floats, bagpipes, marching bands, and the wearin' o' the green. Past grand marshals have run the gamut from Tip O'Neill to the Redskins' "player of the decade" John Riggins. For parade information, call ☎ **202/637-2474.** The Sunday before March 17.

Cherry Blossom Events. Washington's best-known annual event: the blossoming of the famous Japanese cherry trees by the Tidal Basin in Potomac Park. Festivities include a major parade (marking the end of the festival) with princesses, floats, concerts, celebrity guests, and more. There are also special ranger-guided tours departing from the Jefferson Memorial. For parade information—or tickets for grandstand seating ($12 per person)—call the **D.C. Downtown Jaycees** (☎ **202/728-1137**). For other cherry-blossom events, check the *Washington Post* or call ☎ **202/789-7038** or 202/547-1500. Late March or early April (national news programs monitor the budding).

April

Smithsonian Kite Festival. A delightful event if the weather cooperates—an occasion for a trip in itself. Throngs of kite enthusiasts fly their unique creations on the Washington Monument grounds and compete for ribbons and prizes. To compete, just show up with your kite and register between 10am and noon. Call ☎ **202/357-2700** or 202/357-3030 for details. A Saturday in early April.

• **Easter Sunrise Services,** Memorial Amphitheater at Arlington National Cemetery on Easter Sunday. Free shuttle buses travel to the site from the cemetery's visitor center parking lot. Call ☎ **202/685-2851** or 202/789-7000 for details.

White House Easter Egg Roll. The biggie for little kids. In past years, entertainment on the White House South Lawn and the Ellipse has included clog dancers, clowns, Ukrainian egg-decorating exhibitions, puppet and magic shows, military drill teams, an egg-rolling contest, and a hunt for 1,000 or so wooden eggs, many of them signed by celebrities, astronauts, or the president. *Note:* Attendance is limited to children ages 3 to 6. Hourly timed tickets are issued at the National Parks Service Ellipse Visitors Pavilion just behind the White House at 15th and E streets NW beginning at 7am. Call ☎ **202/456-2200** for details. Easter Monday between 10am and 2pm; enter at the southeast gate on East Executive Avenue, and arrive early.

• **Thomas Jefferson's Birthday,** Jefferson Memorial. Celebrated with a wreath-laying, speeches, and a military ceremony. Call ☎ **202/619-7222** for time and details. April 13.

• **White House Spring Garden Tours.** These beautifully landscaped creations are open to the public for free afternoon tours. Call ☎ **202/456-2200** for details. Two days only, in mid-April.

Taste of the Nation. An organization called Share Our Strength sponsors this fundraiser, which takes place in more than 100 cities throughout the nation every April. In Washington, about 90 major restaurants and wineries set up tasting booths at Union Station and offer some of their finest fare. For the price of admission, you can do the circuit, sampling everything from barbecue to bouillabaisse; wine flows freely, and there are dozens of great desserts. The evening also includes a silent auction. Tickets are $65 if purchased in advance, $75 at the door, and 100% of the profits go to feed the hungry. To obtain tickets call ☎ **800/955-8278.** Late April.

• **The Smithsonian Craft Show** features one-of-a-kind limited-edition crafts by more than 100 noted artists (it's a juried show) from all over the country. It takes place at the National Building Museum, 401 F St. NW, during 4 days in late April. There's an entrance fee of about $8 per day. For details, call ☎ **202/357-2700** (TTY 202/357-1729) or 202/357-4000.

May

• **Georgetown Garden Tour.** View the remarkable private gardens of one of the city's loveliest neighborhoods. Admission (about $18) includes light refreshments. Some years there are related events such as a flower show at a historic home. Call ☎ **202/333-4953** for details. Early to mid-May.

• **Washington National Cathedral Annual Flower Mart,** on the cathedral grounds. Includes displays of flowering plants and herbs, decorating demonstrations, ethnic food booths, children's rides and activities (including an antique carousel), costumed characters, puppet shows, and other entertainment. Admission is free. Call ☎ **202/537-6200** for details. First Friday and Saturday in May.

- **Memorial Day.** At 11am, a wreath-laying ceremony takes place at the Tomb of the Unknowns in Arlington National Cemetery, followed by military band music, a service, and an address by a high-ranking government official (sometimes the president); call ☎ **202/685-2851** for details. There's also a ceremony at 1pm at the Vietnam Veterans Memorial—wreath-laying, speakers, and the playing of taps; call ☎ **202/619-7222** for details. On the Sunday before Memorial Day, the National Symphony Orchestra performs a free concert at 8pm on the West Lawn of the Capitol; call ☎ **202/416-8100** for details.

June

Smithsonian Festival of American Folklife. A major event with traditional American music, crafts, foods, games, concerts, and exhibits. Past performances have ranged from Appalachian fiddling to Native American dancing, and demonstrations from quilting to coal mining. All events are free; most events take place outdoors on the Mall. Call ☎ **202/357-2700,** or check the listings in the *Washington Post* for details. For 5 to 10 days, always including July 4.

July

Independence Day. There's no better place to be on the Fourth of July than in Washington, D.C. The festivities include a massive National Independence Day Parade down Constitution Avenue, complete with lavish floats, princesses, marching groups, and military bands. There are also celebrity entertainers and concerts. (Most events take place on the Washington Monument grounds.) A morning program in front of the National Archives includes military demonstrations, period music, and a reading of the Declaration of Independence. In the evening the National Symphony Orchestra plays on the west steps of the Capitol with guest artists (for example, Leontyne Price). And big-name entertainment also precedes the fabulous fireworks display behind the Washington Monument. *Note:* You can also attend an 11am free organ recital at Washington's National Cathedral. Consult the *Washington Post* or call ☎ **202/789-7000** for details. July 4, all day.

August/September

- **National Frisbee Festival,** on the Washington Monument grounds. See world-class Frisbee champions and their disk-catching dogs at this noncompetitive event. For details, call ☎ **301/645-5043.** Labor Day Weekend.
- **International Children's Festival,** Wolf Trap Farm Park in Vienna, Virginia. At this 2-day arts celebration, the entertainment—all of it outdoors—includes clowns, musicians, mimes, puppet shows, and creative workshops from 10am to 4:30pm each day. Admission is charged. For details, call ☎ **703/642-0862.** Late September.
- **Washington National Cathedral's Open House.** Celebrates the anniversary of the laying of the foundation stone in 1907. Events include demonstrations of stone carving and other crafts utilized in building the cathedral; carillon and organ demonstrations; and performances by dancers, choirs, strolling musicians, jugglers, and puppeteers. This is the only time visitors are allowed to ascend to the top of the central tower to see the bells; it's a tremendous climb, but you'll be rewarded with a spectacular view. For details, call ☎ **202/537-6200.** A Saturday in late September or early October.

Annual Kennedy Center Open House Arts Festival. A day-long festival of the performing arts in early to mid-September, and again in spring (that one is called "Spring Celebration"), featuring local and national artists on the front plaza and river terrace (which overlooks the Potomac), and throughout the stage halls of the Kennedy Center. Past festivals have featured the likes of Los Lobos, Mary Chapin

Carpenter, and Washington Opera soloists. Kids' activities usually include a National Symphony Orchestra "petting zoo," where children get to bow, blow, drum, or strum a favorite instrument. Admission is free, although you may have to stand in a long line to gain admittance to the inside performances. Check the *Washington Post* or call ☎ **800/444-1324** or **202/467-4600** for details. A Sunday, one usually in early September, the other in April, noon to 6pm.

October

- **Taste of D.C. Festival,** Pennsylvania Avenue between 9th and 14th streets NW. Dozens of Washington's restaurants offer international food-tasting opportunities, along with live entertainment, dancing, storytellers, and games. Admission is free; purchase tickets for tastings. Call ☎ **202/724-4091** for details. Three days, including Columbus Day weekend.

- **White House Fall Garden Tours.** For 2 days, visitors have an opportunity to see the famed Rose Garden and South Lawn. Admission is free. A military band provides music. For details, call ☎ **202/456-2200.** Mid-October.

- **Washington International Horse Show,** US Airways Arena, 1 Harry S Truman Dr., Landover, MD. This is one of the nation's most important equestrian events, featuring a hunt night, Jack Russell terrier races, international team show jumping, and dressage. Admission (about $18) is charged. Call ☎ **301/840-0281** for details and ☎ **202/432-SEAT** for tickets. Eight days in late October.

- **Halloween.** There is no official celebration, but costumed revels are on the increase every year. Giant block parties take place in the Dupont Circle area and Georgetown. Check the *Washington Post* for special parties and activities. October 31.

- **Marine Corps Marathon.** More than 16,000 runners compete in this 26.2-mile race (the fourth-largest marathon in the United States). It begins at the Marine Corps Memorial (the Iwo Jima statue) and passes major monuments. Call ☎ **800/RUN-USMC** or ☎ **703/784-2225** for details. Anyone can enter; register up to a week ahead. Fourth Sunday in October.

November

- **Veterans Day.** The nation's war dead are honored with a wreath-laying ceremony at 11am at the Tomb of the Unknowns in Arlington National Cemetery followed by a memorial service. The president of the United States or a very high-ranking government personage officiates. Military music is provided by a military band. Call ☎ **202/685-2851** for information. At the Vietnam Veterans Memorial (☎ **202/619-7222**), observances include speakers, a wreath-laying, a color guard, and the playing of taps. November 11.

December

- **St. Nicholas Festival,** at the Washington National Cathedral. An evening for families that includes a visit from St. Nicholas, dancers, choral groups, crafts, caroling, bell ringing, and much more. Call ☎ **202/537-6200** for more information or to inquire about other Christmas concerts, pageants, services, and children's activities. Early December.

- **Christmas Pageant of Peace/National Tree Lighting,** at the northern end of the Ellipse. The president lights the national Christmas tree to the accompaniment of orchestral and choral music. The lighting inaugurates the 3-week Pageant of Peace, a tremendous holiday celebration with seasonal music, caroling, a Nativity scene, 50 state trees, and a burning Yule log. Call ☎ **202/619-7222** for details. A select Wednesday or Thursday in early December, at 5pm.

- **White House Candlelight Tours.** On 3 evenings after Christmas from 5 to 7pm, visitors can see the president's Christmas holiday decorations by candlelight. String music enhances the tours. Lines are long; arrive early. Call ☎ **202/456-2200** for dates and details.

3 Tips for Travelers with Special Needs

FOR TRAVELERS WITH DISABILITIES

Two helpful travel organizations, **Accessible Journeys** (☎ **800/TINGLES** or 610/521-0339) and **Flying Wheels Travel** (☎ **800/535-6790** or 507/451-5005), offer tours, cruises, and custom vacations worldwide for people with physical disabilities; Accessible Journeys can also provide nurse/companions for travelers. **The Guided Tour Inc.** (☎ **800/783-5841** or 215/782-1370) offers tours for people with physical or mental disabilities, the visually impaired, and the elderly.

Mobility International USA, P.O. Box 10767, Eugene, OR 97440 (☎ **541/343-1284,** TDD 541/343-6812), provides accessibility and resource information to its members. Individual membership costs $25 a year; to receive only the quarterly newsletter, *Over the Rainbow,* is $15.

The **Society for the Advancement of Travel for the Handicapped** (SATH), 347 Fifth Ave., Suite 610, New York, NY 10016 (☎ **212/447-7284;** fax 212/725-8253), offers travel information for people with disabilities, charges $5 for individual requests for information, $45 for adult memberships, and $30 for seniors and studentmemberships.

Visually impaired travelers can obtain large-print and braille atlases of the Washington area (though they're slightly out of date) from **Washington Ear,** 35 University Blvd., E. Silver Spring, MD 20901 (☎ **301/681-6636**).

RECOMMENDED BOOKS A publisher called **Twin Peaks Press,** Box 129, Vancouver, WA 98666 (☎ **800/637-2256** or 360/694-2462; fax 360/696-3210), specializes in books for people with disabilities. Write for their *Disability Bookshop Catalog,* enclosing $5. Books include *Travel for the Disabled* for $19.95, a directory of travel agencies for travelers with disabilities at $19.95, and a directory of accessible van rentals at $9.95 (shipping is an extra $3.50).

SIGHTSEEING ATTRACTIONS Washington, D.C., is one of the most accessible cities in the world for travelers with disabilities. The northeast gate visitor's entrance at the **White House** is equipped for visitors arriving in wheelchairs who, by the way, do not need tickets. For details, call ☎ **202/456-2322.**

All **Smithsonian museum buildings** are accessible to wheelchair visitors. A comprehensive free publication called *Smithsonian Access* lists all services available to visitors with disabilities, including parking, building access, and more. To obtain a copy, contact the VIARC, SI Building, Smithsonian Institution, Washington, DC 20560 (☎ **202/357-2700** or TTY 202/357-1729). You can also use the TTY number to obtain information on all Smithsonian museums and events.

The **Lincoln, Jefferson, and Vietnam Memorials** and the **Washington Monument** are also equipped to accommodate visitors with disabilities and keep wheelchairs on the premises. There's limited parking for visitors with disabilities on the south side of the Lincoln Memorial. Call ahead to other sightseeing attractions for accessibility information and special services.

Call your senator or representative to arrange wheelchair-accessible tours of the **Capitol;** they can also arrange special tours for the blind or deaf. If you need further information on these tours, call ☎ **202/224-4048.**

SHOPPING   For shoppers, places well equipped with wheelchair ramps and other facilities for visitors with disabilities include the Shops at National Place, the Pavilion at the Old Post Office, and Georgetown Park Mall.

THEATER   The **John F. Kennedy Center for the Performing Arts** provides headphones to hearing-impaired patrons at no charge, allowing them to adjust the volume as needed. All theaters in the complex (except the Terrace) are wheelchair accessible. For details, call ☎ **202/416-8340;** for other questions regarding patrons with disabilities, call ☎ **202/416-8727.** The TTY number is ☎ **202/416-8524** for tickets.

The **Arena Stage** (☎ **202/554-9066**) has a wheelchair lift and is otherwise accessible. It offers audio description and sign interpretation at designated performances as well as infrared and audio loop assisted-listening devices for the hearing-impaired; program books in braille, large-print, and (by advance request) on audiocassette. The TTY box office line is ☎ **202/484-0247.**

Ford's Theatre is wheelchair-accessible and offers listening devices as well as special signed and audio-described performances. Call ☎ **202/347-4833** for details. The TTY number is ☎ **202/347-5599.**

The **National Theatre** is wheelchair-accessible and features special performances of its shows for visually and hearing-impaired theatergoers. To obtain earphones for narration, simply ask an usher before the performance. The National also offers a limited number of half-price tickets to patrons with disabilities. For details, call ☎ **202/628-6161.**

GETTING AROUND TOWN   Each **Metro** station is equipped with an elevator (complete with braille number plates) to train platforms, and rail cars are fully accessible. Conductors make station and on-board announcements of train destinations and stops. Most of the District's Metrobuses have wheelchair lifts and kneel at the curb (this number will increase as time goes on). The TDD number for Metro information is ☎ **202/628-8973.** For other questions about Metro services for travelers with disabilities, call ☎ **202/962-1100.**

Regular **Tourmobile** trams are accessible to visitors with disabilities. The company also operates special vans for immobile travelers, complete with wheelchair lifts. For information, call ☎ **202/554-5100.**

TRAVELING BY BUS, TRAIN & PLANE   A companion can accompany a person with a disability at no charge aboard a **Greyhound** bus (you must inform Greyhound in advance); call ☎ **800/231-2222** for details. Call ☎ **800/752-4841** at least 24 hours in advance to discuss other special needs. Greyhound's TDD number is ☎ **800/345-3109.**

Amtrak (☎ **800/USA-RAIL**) provides redcap service for Washington and at many stations, wheelchair assistance, and special seats with 24 hours' notice. Passengers with disabilities are also entitled to a discount of 15% off the lowest available rail fare. Documentation from a doctor or an ID card proving your disability is required. Amtrak also provides wheelchair-accessible sleeping accommodations on long-distance trains, and service animals are permitted and travel free of charge. Write for a free booklet called *Amtrak Travel Planner* from Amtrak Distribution Center, P.O. Box 7717, Itasca, IL 60143, which has a section detailing services for passengers with disabilities. Amtrak's TDD number is ☎ **800/523-6590.**

When making your flight reservations, ask the airline or travel agent where your wheelchair will be stowed on the plane and if seeing or hearing guide dogs can accompany you.

FOR SENIORS

Bring some form of photo ID that includes your birth date since many city attractions, theaters, transportation facilities, hotels, and restaurants grant special senior discounts.

Contact the **D.C. Office on Aging,** 441 4th St. NW (☎ **202/289-1510**) to request its free directory, *Golden Washingtonian Club Gold Mine.* It lists numerous establishments offering 10% to 20% discounts to seniors on goods and services.

If you haven't already done so, consider joining the **American Association of Retired Persons** (AARP), 601 E St. NW, Washington, DC 20049 (☎ **800/ 424-3410** or 202/434-2277). Annual membership costs $8 per person or per couple. You must be at least 50 to join. Membership entitles you to many discounts. Write to Purchase Privilege Program, AARP Fulfillment, 601 E St. NW, Washington, DC 20049, to receive AARP's *Purchase Privilege* brochure—a free list of nationwide hotels, motels, and car-rental firms that offer discounts to AARP members.

Elderhostel, a national organization that offers low-cost educational programs for people 55 or older and their adult companions, sponsors frequent week-long residential programs in Washington. Some of these focus on government and American history, others on art, literature, and other subjects. Cost averages about $460 per person, including meals, room, and classes. For information, call ☎ **410/830-3437** or contact Elderhostel headquarters at 75 Federal St., Boston, MA 02110 (☎ **617/ 426-7788**).

Saga International Holidays, 222 Berkeley St., Boston, MA 02116 (☎ **800/ 343-0273**), offers tours in the United States and abroad designed for travelers over 50. In Washington, D.C., their 5-night, 6-day Smithsonian Odyssey Tours program offers a behind-the-scenes look at several museums and other major D.C. institutions. For this specific program, call ☎ **800/258-5885.** Prices are moderate.

Amtrak (☎ **800/USA-RAIL**) offers a 15% discount off the full, one-way coach fare (with certain travel restrictions) to people 62 or older.

Greyhound also offers discounted fares for senior citizens. Call your local Greyhound office for details.

FOR GAYS & LESBIANS

The complete source for the gay and lesbian community is *The Washington Blade,* a comprehensive weekly newspaper distributed free at about 700 locations in the District. Every issue provides an extensive events calendar and a list of hundreds of resources, such as crisis centers, health facilities, switchboards, political groups, religious organizations, social clubs, and student activities; it puts you in touch with everything from groups of lesbian bird-watchers to the Asian Gay Men's Network. Gay restaurants and clubs are, of course, also listed and advertised. You can subscribe to the *Blade* for $45 a year or pick up a free copy at: **Olsson's Books/Records,** 1307 19th St. NW; **Borders,** 18th and L sts.; **Annie's Paramount Steak House,** 1609 17th St. NW; **Kramerbooks,** 1517 Connecticut Ave. NW, at Dupont Circle; and **Chesapeake Bagel Bakery,** 215 Pennsylvania Ave. SE, on Capitol Hill. Call the *Blade* office at ☎ **202/797-7000** for other locations. One final source: Washington's gay bookstore, **Lambda Rising,** 1625 Connecticut Ave. NW (☎ **202/462-6969**), also informally serves as an information center for the gay community, which centers in the Dupont Circle neighborhood.

FOR FAMILIES

Field trips during the school year and family vacations during the summer keep Washington, D.C., crawling with kids all year long. As the nation's capital,

Washington is a natural place for families to visit. Still, you may be surprised at just how much there is to do. More than any other city, perhaps, Washington is crammed with historic buildings, arts and science museums, parks, and recreational outlets to interest young and old alike. Some of the museums, like the National Museum of Natural History and the Daughters of the American Revolution (DAR) Museum, have hands-on exhibits for children. Many more sponsor regular, usually free, family-oriented events, such as the Corcoran Gallery of Art's "Family Days" and the Folger Shakespeare Library's seasonal activities. It's worth calling or writing in advance for schedules from the sites you're thinking of visiting (see chapter 7 for addresses and phone numbers). Truly, there is something here for everyone, and the fact that so many attractions are free is a boon to the family budget.

Hotels, more and more, are doing their part to make family trips affordable, too. At many of the hotels, children under a certain age (usually 12) sleep free in the same room with their parents. Hotel weekend packages often offer special family rates. An excellent resource for family travel, including information about deals that chains and other hotels offer to families, is **Family Travel Times,** a quarterly newsletter published by TWYCH, Travel With Your Children. To subscribe or get information, contact TWYCH, 40 Fifth Ave., New York, NY 10011 (☎ 212/477-5524). A subscription rate of $40 per year entitles you to four issues of the newsletter, discounts on other publications and back issues, and weekly call-in service for advice. If you want to get an idea of the kinds of family promotion packages hotels sometimes offer, ask for a back issue of the Winter/Spring 1997 newsletter, which included a "Hotel Happenings" article.

Restaurants throughout the Washington area are growing increasingly family-friendly, as well: many provide kids menus or charge less for children's portions. The best news, though, is that families are welcome at all sorts of restaurants these days and need no longer seek out the hamburger/french fries eateries.

Washington, D.C., is easy to get around with children. The Metro covers the city, taking you nearly anywhere you'd want to go, and it's safe. Children under 4 ride free. Remember, however, that eating or drinking on the subway or in the station is prohibited.

Once you arrive, get your hands on a copy of the most recent *Washington Post* "Weekend" section, published each Friday. The section covers all possible happenings in the city, with a weekly feature, called "Saturday's Child," and a column, called "Carousel," devoted to children's activities.

4 Getting There

BY PLANE

D.C.'s AREA AIRPORTS

Washington, D.C., has three airports serving the area—two of which, Washington National and Baltimore-Washington International, have recently undergone superb renovations. Dulles International, meanwhile, is in the midst of a grand expansion, to be completed in stages by 2010; a new midfield terminal opened in the summer of 1997.

Washington National Airport (National) lies across the Potomac River in Virginia, about 20 minutes from downtown in non-rush hour traffic. Eleven airlines service this airport. If you are arriving from a city that is within 1,250 miles of National, this may be your airport; by law only short- and medium-haul flights use National.

Built in 1941, National was long due for an overhaul, and the recently completed, $1-billion project has improved, though not enlarged, the airport. Enhancements include a new, three-level terminal with 35 gates and a large window overlooking the city; ticket counters that provide access to passengers with disabilities; several new gift shops and restaurants; more parking space; and climate-controlled pedestrian bridges that connect the terminal directly to the Metro station, whose Blue and Yellow lines stop here. For airport information, call ☎ **703/419-8000.** For Metro information, call ☎ **202/637-7000.**

Washington Dulles International Airport (Dulles) lies 26 miles outside the capital, in Chantilly, VA, a 35- to 45-minute ride to downtown in non-rush hour traffic. The expansion, to be finished in 2010, will eventually add an underground "people mover" system to replace the inconvenient and unwieldy mobile lounges that, for now, transport travelers to and from the main and midfield terminals. This airport handles domestic and international flights. Call ☎ **703/419-8000** for airport information.

Last but not least is **Baltimore-Washington International Airport** (BWI), which is located about 45 minutes from downtown, a few miles outside of Baltimore. Often overlooked by Washingtonians, BWI's bargain fares make it worth considering. Its renovation has added a two-level observation gallery, a Smithsonian Museum Shop, and even Starbucks. Call ☎ **410/859-7111** for airport information.

THE MAJOR AIRLINES

Scheduled domestic airlines flying into Washington's three airports include **American** (☎ 800/433-7300); **America West** (☎ 800/235-9292); **Continental** (☎ 800/525-0280); **Delta** (☎ 800/221-1212); **Northwest** (☎ 800/225-2525); **TWA** (☎ 800/221-2000); **United** (☎ 800/241-6522); and **US Airways** (☎ 800/428-4322). Scheduled international flights flying into Baltimore-Washington International and/or Dulles International Airports include **Air Canada** (☎ 800/776-3000); **Air France** (☎ 800/237-2747); **All Nippon Airways** (☎ 800/235-9262); **British Airways** (☎ 800/247-9297); **KLM** (☎ 800/374-7747); **Lufthansa** (☎ 800/645-3880); **Saudi Arabian Airlines** (☎ 800/472-8342); **Swissair** (☎ 800/221-4750); and **Virgin Atlantic** (☎ 800/862-8621).

For a quarterly guide to flights in and out of National and Dulles, write to: **Metropolitan Washington Airports Authority,** P.O. Box 17045, Washington Dulles International Airport, Washington, DC 20041. For a BWI flight guide, write to: **Maryland Aviation Administration,** Marketing and Development, P.O. Box 8766, BWI Airport, MD 21240-0766.

BEST-FOR-THE-BUDGET FARES   Fare wars, the Internet, the rise of low-fare airlines, and the use of a smart travel agent will all help to get you a deal on flight fare. Travel agents and airlines offer greatly varying rates, so shop around. And closely scan the newspaper and airline informational packets to cash in on flash promotions and airline discounts. Read the Sunday travel sections of *The New York Times* and the *Washington Post;* their weekly columns ("Fly Buys" in the *Post* and "Lowest Air Fares for Popular Routes" in the *Times*) highlight bargain airfares.

Contact all the airlines flying into Washington and inquire about charters and specials. When you call, ask about reduced rates for seniors, children, and students, as well as money-saving packages that include such essentials as hotel accommodations, car rentals, and tours with your airfare. Coupon books, such as the **"Golden Opportunities"** booklet sold by US Airways, give seniors savings options on four one-way tickets, good in the U.S., Canada, Mexico, and Puerto Rico. The Delta Shuttle's **"Family A-Fare"** program allows children under 12 to fly free for each paying adult, on Saturday and Sunday, between Washington National and New York's LaGuardia airports. **Delta Dream Vacations** offers some of the best packages—call ☎ **800/ 872-7786** for details; your local travel agency may be able to suggest others.

If you can, be flexible: The best rates are usually available on off-peak days (mid-week) and seasons (winter and August, for flights into Washington). Think about fly-ing into Baltimore-Washington International Airport (see below). The airport lies closer to Baltimore than Washington, but the inconvenience of adding about 20 more minutes to get into Washington may be well outweighed by the savings you receive in booking seats on the low-cost airlines that fly into BWI: **Southwest Airlines** (☎ **800/435-9792**) is the main one.

If you can do without frills, find out whether your city is served by any of the other low-cost airlines that serve Washington: **Carnival Air Lines** (☎ **800/824-7386**), **Delta Express** (☎ **800/325-5205**), **Midway Airlines** (☎ **800/446-4392**), **ValuJet** (☎ **800/825-8538**), and **Western Pacific Airlines** (☎ **800/930-3030**). All but Midway use Washington Dulles International Airport; Midway uses National.

If you are booking your airline through a travel agent, ask about consolidator tick-ets. Consolidators, such as **Euram Flight Center,** located here in Washington at (☎ **202/789-2255**), buy up blocks of unsold seats from airlines and re-sell them at reduced rates to agents and consumers. Look for their ads in the Sunday travel sec-tions of the larger newspapers. And while you're at it, ask your agent about hotel con-solidators, as well.

Finally, if you're at home in the cyberworld, check out last-minute discounted fares posted by airlines on the Internet. Such major airlines as American, Continental, Delta, Northwest, TWA, and US Airways have their own Web sites and will e-mail you notices of bargain fares. For specific Internet addresses, consult the "Useful Toll-Free Numbers & Web Sites" Appendix at the back of this book.

SHUTTLES TO & FROM NEW YORK   The **Delta Shuttle** (☎ **800/ 221-1212**), which runs between its own terminal at New York's LaGuardia Airport and Washington's National Airport, departs New York every hour on the half hour Monday to Friday, 6:30am to 8:30pm, plus an extra 9pm flight; Saturday from 7:30am to 8:30pm; and Sunday from 8:30am to 8:30pm, plus an extra 9pm flight. Weekdays the first flight leaves Washington at 6:45am, with flights every hour on the half hour after that until 9:30pm; on Saturday hourly on the half hour from 7:30am to 8:30pm; and on Sunday, from 8:30am to 9:30pm. The **US Airways Shuttle** (☎ **800/428-4322**) flies from the US Airways terminal at LaGuardia Air-port in New York to Washington National Airport. Weekday and Saturday depar-tures from LaGuardia Airport are hourly from 7am to 9pm and Sunday from 9am to 9pm. Washington to New York hourly departures weekdays and Saturday are 7am to 9pm and Sunday 9am to 9pm. Ask about student (12 to 24) and senior (62 and older) discounts.

FLIGHTS TO & FROM BOSTON   Both **Delta (Business Express)** and **US Air-ways** offer frequent service weekdays between Boston and Washington; the least expensive tickets must be purchased in advance and entail certain restrictions.

FLIGHTS TO & FROM CHICAGO   **Southwest Airlines** (☎ **800/435-9792**) offers hourly service between Chicago's Midway Airport and Washington's BWI Airport weekdays between 11:10am and 9:25pm.

GETTING DOWNTOWN FROM THE AIRPORT

The cheapest and probably the fastest way to get into town from National Airport is by using the **Metro:** $1.10 and a 15- to 20-minute ride later, and you're there.

Metro is an option at National only. Airport transportation possibilities at the three airports include:

SuperShuttle (☎ **800/258-3826**), whose seven-passenger blue vans provide door-to-door service between National Airport and downtown and suburban locations, and between Baltimore Washington International Airport and destinations in both the Baltimore and Washington areas. (By the time you read this, the service will probably have expanded to include transportation to and from Dulles International Airport, as well.) Fares are based on zip code, so expect to pay anywhere from $6 to $13 to and from downtown, and about $25 for Maryland and Virginia suburbs.

The Washington Flyer (☎ **703/685-1400**) operates buses between the centrally located Airport Terminal Building at 1517 K St. NW and Dulles Airport, and provides transportation between Dulles and National Airports. Fares to/from Dulles are $16 one way, $26 round-trip. Children 6 and under ride free. There are departures in each direction about every 30 minutes. At the K Street Terminal Building, you can board a free loop shuttle that goes to eight Washington hotels: the Sheraton Washington, Omni Shoreham, Washington Hilton, Renaissance Mayflower, Washington Renaissance, Grand Hyatt, J. W. Marriott, and the Capital Hilton.

The Montgomery Airport Shuttle (☎301/990-6000) operates between Montgomery County, MD and all three airports, Union Station, and many other locations, from 5am to 11pm. The fare to any hotel in Montgomery County is $16. Call at least 2 hours ahead to reserve.

The Airport Connection II (☎ **800/284-6066** or 301/441-2345) runs a door-to-door van service between BWI and Washington, D.C., Prince George's County, MD, and Montgomery County, MD; a minimum of 24 hours' notice is required. Fares run between $18 and $30 for one person, $26 and $37 for two people. Children 5 and younger ride free. Train service is available daily on Amtrak (☎ **800/USA-RAIL**) and weekdays on Maryland Rural Commuter System (MARC) (☎ **800/325-RAIL**) at the BWI Rail Station, 5 minutes from the airport. A courtesy shuttle runs between the airport and the train station.

Taxi fares come to about $9 or $10 between National Airport and the White House, $42 to $45 between the White House and Dulles or BWI.

Note: There have been price-gouging incidents in which tourists going from the airports into town have been overcharged by taxi drivers. If you think you're being ripped off, make sure to write down the company name and number of the cab (they're on the door), get an accurate receipt for the fare, and, if possible, the license plate number of the cab and the driver's name. Call ☎ **202/331-1671** to report any problems.

BY TRAIN

Amtrak offers daily service to Washington from New York, Boston, Chicago, and Los Angeles (you change trains in Chicago). Amtrak trains arrive at historic **Union Station,** 50 Massachusetts Ave. NE, a turn-of-the-century beaux arts masterpiece that was magnificently restored in the late 1980s at a cost of more than $180 million. Offering a three-level marketplace of shops and restaurants, this stunning depot is conveniently located and connects with Metro service. There are always taxis available there. For rail reservations, contact Amtrak (☎ **800/USA-RAIL**). (For more on Union Station, see chapters 7 and 9.)

Like the airlines, Amtrak offers several discounted fares; although not all are based on advance purchase, you have more discount options by reserving early. The discount fares can be used only on certain days and hours of the day; be sure to find out exactly what restrictions apply. Tickets for children ages 2 to 12 cost half the price of a regular coach fare. At this writing, the lowest round-trip coach fares are as follows between Washington's Union Station and five selected cities:

Lowest Round-Trip Coach Fares on Amtrak

Route	Discount Fare
N.Y.–D.C.	$120
Chicago–D.C.	$141
Atlanta–D.C.	$136
L.A.–D.C.	$266
Boston–D.C.	$122

I also suggest that you inquire about money-saving packages that include hotel accommodations, car rentals, tours, and so on with your train fare. Call ☎ **800/ 321-8684** for details about these "Amtrak Vacations" packages.

Metroliner service—which costs a little more but provides faster transit and roomier, more comfortable seating—is available between New York and Washington, D.C., and points in between. The round-trip Metroliner fare between New York and D.C. at this writing is $218. *Note:* Metroliner fares are substantially reduced on weekends.

The most luxurious way to travel is **First Class Club Service,** available on all Metroliners and some other trains, as well. For an additional $72 each way, passengers enjoy roomier, more upscale seating in a private car; complimentary meals and beverage service; and Metropolitan Lounges (in New York, Chicago, Philadelphia, and Washington) where travelers can wait for trains in a comfortable, living room–like setting while enjoying free snacks and coffee.

BY BUS

Greyhound buses connect almost the entire United States with Washington, D.C. They arrive at a terminal at 1005 1st St. NE at L Street (☎ **800/231-2222**). The closest Metro stop is Union Station, 4 blocks away. The bus terminal area is not what you'd call a showplace neighborhood, so if you arrive at night, it's best to take a taxi. If you're staying in the suburbs, you should know that Greyhound also has service to Silver Spring, MD, and Arlington and Springfield, VA.

The fare structure on buses is not necessarily based on distance traveled. The good news is that when you call Greyhound to make a reservation, the company will always offer you the lowest fare options. Call in advance and know your travel dates, since some discount fares require advance purchase. In the spring of 1997, the lowest discounted round-trip fare between New York City and Washington was $50.

BY CAR

Major highways approach Washington, D.C., from all parts of the country. Specifically, these are I-270, I-95, and I-295 from the north; I-95, Route 1, and Route 301 from the south; Route 50/301 and Route 450 from the east; and Route 7, Route 50, I-66, and Route 29/211 from the west. No matter what road you take, you are going to have to navigate the Capital Beltway (I-495 and I-95) to gain entry to D.C. The Beltway girds the city, 66 miles around, with 56 interchanges or exits, and is nearly always congested, but especially weekdays, during the morning and evening rush hours, roughly between 7 to 9am and 3 to 7pm. Commuter traffic on the Beltway now rivals that of major LA freeways, and drivers can get a little crazy, weaving in and out of traffic.

If you're planning to drive to Washington, get yourself a good map before you do anything else. The **American Automobile Association (AAA)** (☎ **800/222-4357** or 703/222-6000) provides its members with maps and detailed Trip-Tiks that give travelers precise directions to a destination, including up-to-date information about areas of construction along the nation's highways and within city boundaries. If you are driving to a hotel in D.C. or its suburbs, contact the establishment and talk to the concierge or receptionist to find out the best route to the hotel's address, and other crucial details concerning parking availability and rates. See chapter 4 for information about driving in D.C.

The District is 240 miles from New York City, 40 miles from Baltimore, 700 miles from Chicago, nearly 500 miles from Boston, and about 630 miles from Atlanta.

3 For Foreign Visitors

This is a city that is used to receiving foreign visitors. The latest figures from the Washington, D.C., Convention and Visitors Association show that more than 1.5 million international visitors tour the capital annually. As the nation's capital and a world center, Washington is well equipped to handle the specific needs of foreign visitors. This section provides information on getting to the United States and facts that should help you understand Washington ways once you're here.

1 Preparing for Your Trip

In Washington, D.C., several major attractions (the White House, the Kennedy Center, the Library of Congress, and the Smithsonian Institution) all offer free brochures in several languages. The Smithsonian also welcomes international visitors at its Information Center with a multilingual slide show and audio phones. You can obtain Metro maps in French, German, Japanese, and Spanish by calling ☎ 202/637-1261. And the **Washington, D.C., Convention and Visitors Association** (☎ 202/789-7000) can provide sightseeing and hotel information in those same languages.

The **Meridian International Center** (☎ 202/939-5544), a nonprofit institution dedicated to the promotion of international understanding, extends its special services to D.C.'s many visitors from abroad. Visitors can call the center from 7am to 11pm daily for language assistance with sightseeing and other tourist needs. The center has on call a bank of volunteers who, together, speak more than 60 languages.

ENTRY REQUIREMENTS

DOCUMENT REGULATIONS Citizens of Canada and Bermuda may enter the United States without visas, but they will need to show proof of nationality (commonly a passport).

Citizens of the United Kingdom, New Zealand, Japan, Australia, Argentina, and most Western European countries traveling on valid passports may not need a visa for fewer than 90 days of holiday or business travel to the United States, provided that they hold a round-trip or return ticket and enter the United States either on an airline or cruise line that participates in the visa-waiver program, or cross the land border from Canada or Mexico. Citizens of these visa-exempt countries who first enter the United States may subsequently visit Bermuda and/or the Caribbean islands and then reenter the United States, by any mode of transportation, without needing a visa. (Additional information is available from the U.S. embassy or consulate in your home country. Your travel agency or airline office may also be able to provide additional information.)

Citizens of countries other than those specified above, or those traveling to the U.S. for reasons or length of time outside the restrictions of the visa waiver program, or those who require waivers of inadmissibility, must have two documents:

- a valid **passport,** with an expiration date at least 6 months later than the scheduled end of the visit to the United States (Some countries are exceptions to the 6-month validity rule. Contact any U.S. embassy or consulate for complete information.); and
- a **tourist visa,** available from the nearest U.S. consulate. To obtain a visa, the traveler must submit a completed application form (either in person or by mail) with a $1^1/_2$-inch square photo and the required application fee. There may also be an issuance fee, depending on the type of visa and other factors.

Usually you can obtain a visa right away or within 24 hours, but it may take longer during the summer rush period (June to August). If you cannot go in person, contact the nearest U.S. embassy or consulate for directions on applying by mail. Your travel agent or airline office may also be able to provide you with visa applications and instructions.

The U.S. consulate or embassy that issues your visa will determine whether you will be issued a multiple- or single-entry visa. The Immigration and Naturalization Service officers at the port of entry in the U.S. will make an admission decision and determine your length of stay.

MEDICAL REQUIREMENTS   No inoculations are needed to enter the United States unless you are coming from, or have stopped over in, areas known to be suffering from epidemics, particularly cholera or yellow fever.

If you have a condition requiring treatment with medications containing narcotics or drugs requiring a syringe, carry a valid signed prescription from your physician to allay any suspicions that you might be smuggling drugs.

CUSTOMS REQUIREMENTS   Every adult visitor may bring in free of duty and internal revenue tax, not more than 1 liter of wine, beer, or hard liquor, for personal use. Be aware that you are subject to the alcoholic beverage laws of the state in which you arrive. You may also bring in no more than 200 cigarettes, 50 cigars (but no cigars from Cuba), or 2 kilograms (4.4 pounds) of smoking tobacco.

A gift exemption allows you to bring in up to $100 worth of gifts for other people, including 100 cigars, but not including alcoholic beverages. These exemptions are offered to travelers who spend at least 72 hours in the United States and who have not claimed them within the preceding 6 months.

Certain food products, such as bakery items and all cured cheeses, are admissible. Fruits, vegetables, plants, cuttings, seeds, unprocessed plant products, and certain endangered plant species are either prohibited from entering the country or require an import permit. The only meat you may bring in is canned meat that the inspector can determine has been commercially canned, cooked in the container, hermetically sealed, and can be kept without refrigeration; all other meat, livestock, poultry, and their by-products are either prohibited or restricted from entering the country.

Foreign tourists may bring in or take out up to $10,000 in U.S. or foreign currency with no formalities; larger sums must be declared to Customs on entering or leaving the country.

For more information, contact any U.S. embassy or consulate. Various agencies of the U.S. government provide free leaflets of information about travel tips for nonresidents. These include "United States Customs Hints for Visitors (Nonresidents)," produced by the U.S. Customs Service, within the Department of the Treasury, and "Traveler's Tips," published by the U.S. Department of Agriculture Animal and Plant Health Inspection Service.

INSURANCE

There is no national health system in the United States. Because the cost of medical care is extremely high, I strongly advise every traveler to secure health insurance coverage before setting out.

You may want to take out a comprehensive travel policy that covers (for a relatively low premium) sickness or injury costs (medical, surgical, and hospital); loss or theft of your baggage; trip-cancellation costs; guarantee of bail in case you are arrested; and costs of accident, repatriation, or death. Such packages (for example, "Europe Assistance" in Europe) are sold by automobile clubs at attractive rates, as well as by insurance companies and travel agencies.

MONEY

CURRENCY & EXCHANGE   The U.S. monetary system has a decimal base: one American **dollar** ($1) = 100 **cents** (100¢).

Dollar bills commonly come in $1 ("a buck"), $5, $10, $20, $50, and $100 denominations (the last two are not welcome when paying for small purchases and are not accepted in taxis or at subway ticket booths). There are also $2 bills (seldom encountered).

There are six denominations of coins: 1¢ (one cent or "a penny"); 5¢ (five cents or "a nickel"); 10¢ (ten cents or "a dime"); 25¢ (twenty-five cents or "a quarter"); 50¢ (fifty cents or "a half dollar"); and the rare $1 piece.

TRAVELER'S CHECKS   Traveler's checks denominated in U.S. dollars are readily accepted at most hotels, motels, restaurants, and large stores. But the best place to change traveler's checks is at a bank. Do not bring traveler's checks denominated in other currencies. American Express, Barclay's Bank, and Thomas Cook traveler's checks are the ones most accepted.

CREDIT & CHARGE CARDS   The most widely used method of payment is the credit card: Visa (BarclayCard in Britain), MasterCard (Eurocard in Europe, Access in Britain, Diamond in Japan, Chargex in Canada), American Express, Discover, Diners Club, Carte Blanche, Japan Credit Bank, and enRoute. You can save yourself trouble by using "plastic" rather than cash or traveler's checks in most hotels, motels, restaurants, and retail stores (many food and liquor stores now accept credit/charge cards). You must have a credit or charge card to rent a car. It can also be used as proof of identity or as a "cash card," enabling you to withdraw money from banks and automated teller machines (ATMs) that accept it.

You can telegraph money or have it wired to you very quickly using the **Western Union** system (☎ **800/325-6000**), which is linked to thousands of locations throughout more than 100 countries.

Note: The "foreign-exchange bureaus" so common in Europe are rare even at airports in the United States and nonexistent outside major cities. It is best not to change foreign money (or traveler's checks denominated in a currency other than U.S. dollars) at a small-town bank, or even a branch in a big city; in fact, leave any currency other than U.S. dollars at home—it may prove a greater nuisance to you than it's worth.

SAFETY

GENERAL   Though Washington, D.C., has a reputation as a high-crime city, most of that crime occurs far from tourist areas. The attractions, hotels, and restaurants listed in this book are in reasonably safe areas of town. Nevertheless, as in any big city, keep an eye on your purse, wallet, camera, and other belongings in public places, and, in your hotel, keep your door locked. Many hotels these days offer in-room safes; if yours doesn't, and you are traveling with valuables, put them in a safety-deposit box at the front desk.

Try not to "look" like a tourist, if you can help it. That is, get a sense of where you are headed before you leave your hotel and, if you're walking, pay attention to who is near you as you walk. In general, it's better to avoid direct eye contact with people, especially panhandlers, who can be aggressive. If you are attending a convention or an event where you wear a name tag, remove it before venturing outside.

DRIVING   Safety while driving is particularly important. Question your rental agency about personal safety, or ask for a brochure of traveler safety tips when you pick up your car. Obtain written directions, or a map with the route marked in red, from the agency showing how to get to your destination. If possible, arrive and depart during daylight hours.

If you see someone on the road who indicates a need for help, do *not* stop. Take note of the location, drive on to a well-lighted area, and telephone the police by dialing ☎ **911.**

Park in well-lighted, well-traveled areas if possible. Always keep your car doors locked, whether attended or unattended. Look around you before you get out of your car, and never leave any packages or valuables in sight. If someone attempts to rob you or steal your car, do *not* try to resist him—report the incident to the police department immediately.

You may wish to contact the local tourist information bureau in Washington, D.C., before you arrive. They may be able to provide you with a safety brochure.

2 Getting To & Around the United States

A number of U.S. airlines offer service from Europe to the United States. If they don't have direct flights from Europe to Washington, they can book you straight through on a connecting flight. You can make reservations by calling the following numbers in the U.K.: **American** (☎ **0181/572-5555**), **Continental** (☎ **04412/9377-6464**), **Delta** (☎ **0800/414-767**), and **United** (☎ **0181/990-9900**). For a more extensive listing of airlines that fly into the Washington area, see "Getting There" in chapter 2. Travelers from overseas can take advantage of the **APEX (advance purchase excursion) fares** offered by all the major U.S. and European carriers. Aside from these, attractive values are offered by **Virgin Atlantic Airways** (☎ **800/862-8621**), which flies direct from London to Washington Dulles International Airport, as well as from London to New York/Newark.

Some large American airlines (for example, TWA, American Airlines, Northwest, United, and Delta) offer travelers on their trans-Atlantic or trans-Pacific flights special discount tickets allowing travel between any U.S. destinations at minimum rates. (Two such programs are American's **Visit USA** and Delta's **Discover America.**) These tickets are not on sale in the United States and must, therefore, be purchased before you leave your foreign point of departure. This arrangement is the best, easiest, and fastest way to see the United States at low cost. You should obtain information well in advance from your travel agent or the office of the airline concerned, since the conditions attached to these discount tickets can be changed without advance notice.

The visitor arriving by air should make very generous allowance for delay in planning connections between international and domestic flights—an average of 2 to 3 hours at least.

In contrast, travelers arriving by car or by rail from Canada will find border-crossing formalities streamlined to the vanishing point. And air travelers from Canada, Bermuda, and some places in the Caribbean can sometimes go through Customs and Immigration at the point of departure, which is much quicker and less painful.

International visitors, except Canadians and Mexicans, can buy a **USA Railpass**, good for 15 or 30 days of unlimited travel on **Amtrak** trains throughout the United States and Canada. The pass is available through many foreign travel agents. At press time, prices for a nationwide 15-day adult pass were $260 off-peak, $375 peak; a 30-day pass costs $350 off-peak, $480 peak. (With a foreign passport, you can also buy passes at some Amtrak offices in the United States, including locations in San Francisco, Los Angeles, Chicago, New York, Miami, Boston, and Washington, D.C.) Even cheaper are **regional USA Railpasses** allowing unlimited travel through a specific section of the United States. Reservations are generally required and should be made as early as possible for each part of your trip. Also available through Amtrak is an **Airail pass,** a joint venture of United Airlines and Amtrak that's available as part of **Amtrak Vacations packages** (☎ **800/321-8684**). The pass allows you to arrive in Washington (from a location within the U.S.) by one mode, plane or rail, and return via the other. During the train portion of your trip, you can make up to three stops along the way at no extra charge.

With a few notable exceptions (for instance, the Northeast Corridor line between Boston and Washington, D.C.), train service is rarely up to European standards: Delays are common, routes are limited and often infrequently served, and fares are rarely significantly lower than discount airfares. Thus, cross-country train travel should be approached with caution.

Bus travel in the United States can be both slow and uncomfortable; however, it can also be quite inexpensive. **Greyhound,** the sole nationwide bus line, offers an **Ameripass** for unlimited travel throughout the United States. At press time, prices were $179 for 7 days, $289 for 15 days, and $399 for 30 days.

FAST FACTS: For the Foreign Traveler

Automobile Organizations   Auto clubs will supply maps, suggested routes, guide-books, accident and bail-bond insurance, and emergency road service. The major auto club in the United States, with 983 offices nationwide, is the **American Automobile Association (AAA).** Members of some foreign auto clubs have reciprocal arrangements with AAA and enjoy its services at no charge. In Washington, AAA offers American Express traveler's checks free to members. The D.C. office, at 701 15th St. NW (☎ **202/331-3000**), also provides translation services in more than 24 languages. If you belong to an auto club, inquire about AAA reciprocity before you leave home.

AAA can provide you with an **International Driving Permit** validating your foreign license. You may be able to join AAA even if you are not a member of a reciprocal club. To inquire, call ☎ **800/763-9900** or the number listed above for the D.C. office. In addition, some automobile-rental agencies now provide these services, so you should inquire about their availability when you rent your car.

Business Hours   Banks are open weekdays from 9am to 2 or 3pm, with some open on Friday until 6pm and on Saturday morning. Most banks provide 24-hour access to their automatic teller machines (ATMs), usually set in the bank's outside wall; other ATM locations include grocery stores and shopping malls.

Generally, public and private offices are open weekdays 9am to 5pm. Stores are open 6 days a week, with many open on Sunday, too; department stores usually stay open until 9pm at least 1 day a week. Some grocery stores and drugstores are open for 24 hours.

Climate   See "When to Go" in chapter 2.

Currency Exchange   You will find currency exchange services in major airports with international service. Elsewhere, they may be quite difficult to come by. A reliable choice in both Washington and New York (should you arrive in Washington via New York) is **Thomas Cook Currency Services, Inc.** The agency sells commission-free foreign traveler's checks and U.S. traveler's checks at a 1% commission, as well as drafts and wire transfers; Thomas Cook also does check collections (including Eurochecks) and purchases and sells foreign banknotes, gold, and silver. Rates are competitive and the service excellent. Call ☎ **800/CURRENCY** for Manhattan locations and office hours, and ☎ **718/656-8444** to reach the office at JFK Airport International Arrivals Terminal. In Washington, there are Thomas Cook offices at all three major airports, at 1800 K St. NW, and at Union Station opposite Gate G on the train concourse, all of which may be reached at (☎ **800/CURRENCY**).

Drinking Laws   See "Liquor Laws" in "Fast Facts: Washington, D.C." in chapter 4.

Electricity   The United States uses 110–120 volts, 60 cycles, as opposed to 220–240 volts, 50 cycles, as in most of Europe. In addition to a 100-volt converter, small appliances of non-American manufacture, such as hair dryers or shavers, will require a plug adapter, with two flat, parallel pins.

Embassies/Consulates   All embassies are located in Washington, D.C., since it's the nation's capital, and many consulates are located here, as well. Here are several embassy addresses: **Australia,** 1601 Massachusetts Ave. NW (☎ **202/797-3000**); **Canada,** 501 Pennsylvania Ave. NW (☎ **202/682-1740**); **France,** 4101 Reservoir Rd. NW (☎ **202/944-6000**); **Germany,** 4645 Reservoir Rd. NW (☎ **202/298-4000**); **Ireland,** 2234 Massachusetts Ave. NW (☎ **202/462-3939**); **Netherlands,** 4200 Linnean Ave. NW (☎ **202/244-5300**); **New Zealand,** 37 Observatory Circle, NW (☎ **202/328-4800**); and the **United Kingdom,** 3100 Massachusetts Ave. NW (☎ **202/462-1340**). You can obtain the telephone numbers of other embassies and consulates by calling information in Washington, D.C. (dial **411** within D.C. and its metropolitan area). Or consult the phone book in your hotel room.

Emergencies   In all major cities, you can call the police, an ambulance, or the fire brigade through the single emergency telephone number ☎ **911.**

If you encounter such travelers' problems as sickness, accident, or lost or stolen baggage, call the **Travelers Aid Society,** 512 C St. NE (☎ **202/546-3120**), an organization that specializes in helping distressed travelers, whether American or foreign. See "Orientation" in chapter 4 for further details.

U.S. hospitals have emergency rooms, with a special entrance where you will be admitted for quick attention. The closest hospital to the downtown area is the **George Washington University Medical Center,** located at 901 23rd St. NW, at

Washington Circle, ☎ **202/994-3211;** the hospital is a major trauma center with a built-in minor emergency care area and 24-hour medical advice line.

Late-night pharmacies include CVS Pharmacy, open 24 hours, at 14th St. NW and Thomas Circle NW ☎ **202/628-0720,** and at 7 Dupont Circle NW, ☎ **202/ 785-1466.**

Gasoline (Petrol)   One U.S. gallon equals 3.75 liters, while 1.2 U.S. gallons equal 1 Imperial gallon. You'll notice there are several grades (and price levels) of gasoline available at most gas stations. And you'll also notice that their names change from company to company. The unleaded ones with the highest octane are the most expensive (most rental cars take the least expensive "regular" unleaded), and leaded gas is the least expensive; but only older cars can take leaded gas now, so check if you're not sure.

Holidays   On the following legal national holidays, banks, government offices, post offices, and many stores, restaurants, and museums are closed: January 1 (New Year's Day); third Monday in January (Martin Luther King, Jr. Day); third Monday in February (Presidents' Day, Washington's Birthday); last Monday in May (Memorial Day); July 4 (Independence Day); first Monday in September (Labor Day); second Monday in October (Columbus Day); November 11 (Veterans' Day/ Armistice Day); fourth Thursday in November (Thanksgiving Day); and December 25 (Christmas).

Finally, the Tuesday following the first Monday in November is Election Day and is a legal holiday in presidential-election years.

Languages   Major hotels often have multilingual employees. Unless your language is obscure, they can usually supply a translator on request. Also, remember the assistance available from Meridian House International and from AAA, whose addresses and phone numbers are listed earlier in this chapter.

Legal Aid   If you are stopped for a minor infraction (for example, of the highway code, such as speeding), never attempt to pay the fine directly to a police officer; you may wind up arrested on the much more serious charge of attempted bribery. Pay fines by mail or directly into the hands of the clerk of the court. If you are accused of a more serious offense, it's wise to say and do nothing before consulting a lawyer. Under U.S. law, an arrested person is allowed one telephone call to a party of his or her choice. Call your embassy or consulate.

Mail   If you want your mail to follow you on your vacation and you aren't sure of your address, your mail can be sent to you, in your name, **c/o General Delivery** at the main post office of the city or region where you expect to be. The addressee must pick it up in person and produce proof of identity (for example, driver's license, credit or charge card, or passport). In Washington, the **main post office** is located at 900 Brentwood Rd. NE, Washington, DC 20066-9998, USA (☎ **202/ 636-1532**). It's open Monday to Friday 8am to 8pm, Saturday 10am to 6pm, and Sunday noon to 6pm.

Generally to be found at intersections, mailboxes are blue with a red-and-white stripe and carry the inscription U.S. MAIL. If your mail is addressed to a U.S. destination, don't forget to add the five-digit postal code, or zip code, after the two-letter abbreviation of the state to which the mail is addressed (CA for California, NY for New York, and so on).

Medical Emergencies   See "Emergencies," above.

Newspapers/Magazines   National newspapers include *The New York Times, USA Today,* and *The Wall Street Journal.* There are also a great many national newsweeklies including *Newsweek, Time,* and *U.S. News and World Report.* For information on local Washington, D.C., periodicals, see "Newspapers/Magazines" in "Fast Facts: Washington, D.C." in chapter 4.

Post   See "Mail," above.

Safety   See "Safety" in "Preparing for Your Trip," above.

Taxes   In the United States, there is no VAT (value-added tax) or other indirect tax at a national level. Every state, and each city in it, has the right to levy its own local tax on all purchases, including hotel and restaurant checks, airline tickets, and so on.

The sales tax on merchandise is 5.75% in the District, 5% in Maryland, and 4.5% in Virginia. The tax on restaurant meals is 10% in the District, 5% in Maryland, and 4.5% in Virginia.

In the District, in addition to your hotel rate, you pay 13% sales tax and $1.50 per night occupancy tax. The state sales tax on a hotel room is 9.75% in suburban Virginia and 10% in Maryland (where you can expect an additional 5% to 7% in city or local taxes).

Telephone/Telegraph/Fax   The telephone system in the United States is run by private corporations, so the rates, especially for long-distance service, can vary widely, even on calls made from public telephones. Local calls in the United States usually cost 25¢.

In the past few years, many American companies have installed voice-mail systems, so be prepared to deal with a machine instead of a receptionist if you're calling a business number.

Generally, hotel surcharges on long-distance and local calls are astronomical. Always ask the hotel operator about these charges before making a call from your room. You are usually better off using a **public pay telephone,** which you will find clearly marked in most public buildings and private establishments as well as on the street. Outside metropolitan areas, public telephones are more difficult to find. Stores and gas stations are your best bet.

Most **long-distance** and **international** calls can be dialed directly from any phone. It's most economical to charge the call to a telephone charge card or a credit card, or you can use a lot of change (while phone cards are catching on in the U.S., they are not nearly as common as they are in Europe). The pay phone will instruct you how much to deposit into the slot box and when. For calls to Canada and other parts of the United States, dial **1** followed by the area code and the seven-digit number. For international calls, dial **011** followed by the country code, city code, and the telephone number of the person you wish to call. It's helpful to write down these codes before you leave your own country.

For **reversed-charge or collect calls,** and for **person-to-person calls,** dial **0** (zero, *not* the letter "O") followed by the area code and number you want; when an operator comes on the line, you should specify that you are calling collect, or person-to-person, or both. If your operator-assisted call is international, ask for the overseas operator.

For local **directory assistance** ("information"), dial **411;** for **long-distance information,** dial **1,** then the appropriate area code and **555-1212.**

Like the telephone system, **telegraph** services are provided by private corporations like ITT, MCI, and most commonly, Western Union. You can bring your telegram in to the nearest Western Union office (there are hundreds across the country), or dictate it over the phone (☎ **800/325-6000**). You can also telegraph money, or have it telegraphed to you, very quickly over the Western Union system.

Most hotels have **fax machines** available for their customers and usually charge to send or receive a facsimile. You will also see signs for public faxes in the windows of small shops.

Telephone Directory   There are two kinds of telephone directories available to you. The general directory is the so-called **white pages,** in which businesses and personal residences are listed separately, in alphabetical order. The inside front cover lists the emergency numbers for police, fire, ambulance, the Coast Guard, poison-control center, crime-victims hotline, and so on. The first few pages are devoted to community-service numbers, including a guide to long-distance and international calling, complete with country codes and area codes.

The second directory, printed on yellow paper (hence its name, **yellow pages**), lists all local services, businesses, and industries by type of activity, with an index at the back. The yellow pages also include city plans or detailed area maps, often showing postal zip codes and public transportation routes.

Time   The United States is divided into four **time zones** (six, if Alaska and Hawaii are included). From east to west, these are: eastern standard time (EST), which includes Washington; central standard time (CST); mountain standard time (MST); Pacific standard time (PST); Alaska standard time (AST); and Hawaii standard time (HST). Always keep the changing time zones in mind if you are traveling (or even telephoning) long distances in the United States. For example, noon in Washington, D.C. (EST) is 11am in Chicago (CST), 10am in Denver (MST), 9am in Los Angeles (PST), 8am in Anchorage (AST), and 7am in Honolulu (HST).

Daylight saving time is in effect from the first Sunday in April through the last Saturday in October, except in Arizona, Hawaii, part of Indiana, and Puerto Rico. Daylight saving time moves the clock 1 hour ahead of standard time.

To find out the time, call ☎ **202/844-2525.**

Tipping   Some rules of thumb: bartenders, 10% to 15%; bellhops, at least 50¢ per piece of luggage ($2 to $3 for a lot of baggage); cab drivers, 15% of the fare; cafeterias, fast-food restaurants, no tip; chambermaids, $1 a day; checkroom attendants (restaurants, theaters), $1 per garment; cinemas, movies, theaters, no tip; doormen (hotels or restaurants), not obligatory; gas-station attendants, not obligatory; hairdressers, 15% to 20%; redcaps (airport and railroad station), at least 50¢ per bag ($2 to $3 for a lot of luggage); restaurants, nightclubs, 15% to 20% of the check; sleeping-car porters, $2 to $3 per night to your attendant; valet parking attendants, $1.

Toilets   Visitors can usually find a rest room in a bar, restaurant, hotel, museum, department store, service station (though for cleanliness reasons, this should be your last choice), or train station.

Getting to Know Washington, D.C.

Washington is a compact city and easy to get around—but there's so much crammed into its 67 square miles, you'll have to pick and choose the parts you'll most want to discover. This section should help you in that endeavor. Below you'll find a discussion of the city's layout, neighborhoods, transportation, and general ways and means.

1 Orientation

VISITOR INFORMATION

If you haven't already called ahead for information from the **Washington, D.C., Convention & Visitors Association** (☎ 202/ 789-7038), stop in at their headquarters, 1212 New York Ave. NW, Monday through Friday, 9am to 5pm.

There are two other excellent tourist information centers in town, and though each focuses on a specific attraction, they can also provide information about other popular Washington sights.

The **White House Visitors Center,** on the first floor of the Herbert Hoover Building, Department of Commerce, 1450 Pennsylvania Ave. NW (between 14th and 15th streets) (☎ 202/ 208-1631, or 202/456-7041 for recorded information), is open daily 7:30am to 4pm.

The **Smithsonian Information Center,** in the "Castle," 1000 Jefferson Dr. SW (☎ 202/357-2700, or TTY 202/357-1729), is open every day but Christmas, 9:00am to 5:30pm. For a free copy of the Smithsonian's "Planning your Smithsonian Visit," which is full of valuable tips, write to Public Inquiry Mail, Smithsonian Institution Building, MRC 010, Smithsonian Institution, Washington, DC 20560, or stop at the Castle for a copy. A calendar of Smithsonian exhibits and activities for the coming month appears the third Friday of each month in the *Washington Post*'s "Weekend" section.

Try to visit both facilities when you're in town to garner information and see interesting on-site exhibits. Further details are provided in chapter 7.

The **American Automobile Association (AAA)** has a large central office near the White House, at 701 15th St. NW, Washington, DC 20005-2111 (☎ 202/331-3000). Hours are 9am to 6pm, Monday through Friday.

Washington, D.C., at a Glance

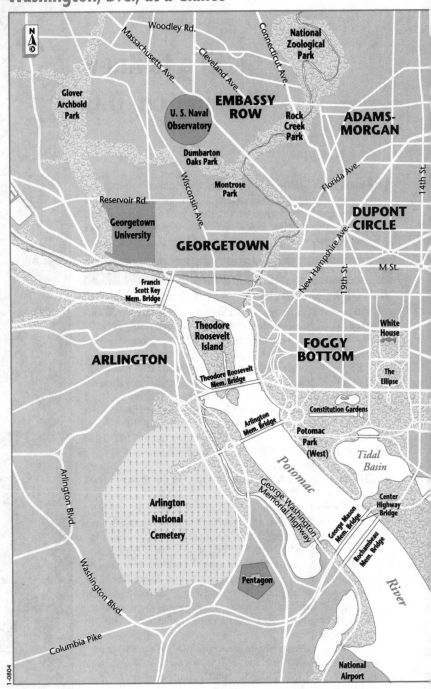

N

Woodley Rd.

Massachusetts Ave.

Cleveland Ave.

Connecticut Ave.

National
Zoological
Park

Glover
Archbold
Park

U. S. Naval
Observatory

EMBASSY
ROW

Rock
Creek
Park

ADAMS-
MORGAN

14th St.

Dumbarton
Oaks Park

Florida Ave.

Montrose
Park

DUPONT
CIRCLE

Reservoir Rd.

Wisconsin Ave.

Georgetown
University

GEORGETOWN

New Hampshire Ave.

19th St.

M St.

Francis
Scott Key
Mem. Bridge

Theodore
Roosevelt
Island

White
House

ARLINGTON

Theodore Roosevelt
Mem. Bridge

FOGGY
BOTTOM

The
Ellipse

Arlington
Mem. Bridge

Constitution Gardens

Potomac
Park
(West)

Tidal
Basin

Potomac

George Washington
Memorial Highway

Center
Highway
Bridge

Arlington Blvd.

Arlington
National
Cemetery

George Mason
Mem. Bridge

Rochambeau
Mem. Bridge

Washington Blvd.

Pentagon

River

Columbia Pike

National
Airport

1-0804

42

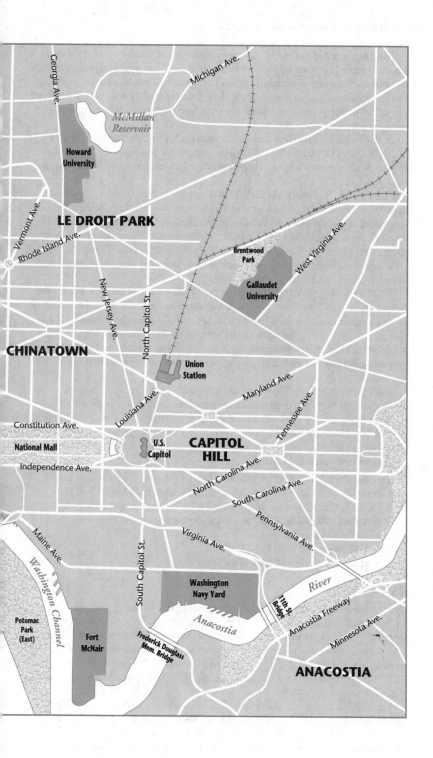

Georgia Ave.

Michigan Ave.

McMillan Reservoir

Howard University

Vermont Ave.

Rhode Island Ave.

LE DROIT PARK

Brentwood Park

West Virginia Ave.

Gallaudet University

New Jersey Ave.

North Capitol St.

CHINATOWN

Louisiana Ave.

Union Station

Maryland Ave.

Tennessee Ave.

Constitution Ave.

National Mall

U.S. Capitol

CAPITOL HILL

Independence Ave.

North Carolina Ave.

South Carolina Ave.

Pennsylvania Ave.

Maine Ave.

Virginia Ave.

South Capitol St.

Washington Channel

Potomac Park (East)

Fort McNair

Frederick Douglass Mem. Bridge

Washington Navy Yard

Anacostia

11th St. Bridge

River

Anacostia Freeway

Minnesota Ave.

ANACOSTIA

The **Travelers Aid Society** is a nationwide network of volunteer nonprofit social-service agencies providing help to travelers in difficulty. This might include anything from crisis counseling to straightening out ticket mix-ups, not to mention reuniting families accidentally separated while traveling, locating missing relatives (sometimes just at the wrong airport), and helping retrieve lost baggage (also sometimes at the wrong airport).

In Washington, **Travelers Aid** has a central office in the Capitol Hill area at 512 C St. NE (☎ **202/546-3120**), where professional social workers are available to provide assistance. It's open only on weekdays 9am to 4pm for walk-ins; you can call up to 5pm.

There are also **Travelers Aid** desks at Washington National Airport (open weekdays 9am to 9pm, Saturday and Sunday 9am to 6pm; ☎ **703/417-3972**); at Dulles International Airport (open Monday to Friday 10am to 9pm, Saturday and Sunday 10am to 6pm; ☎ **703/661-8636**); and at Union Station (open Monday to Saturday 9:30am to 5:30pm, Sunday 12:30 to 5:30pm; ☎ **202/371-1937,** ext. 25); TDD (telecommunications device for the deaf) is provided at all the above-mentioned locations except the main office on C Street.

Washington has two daily newspapers: the *Washington Post* and the *Washington Times.* The Friday "Weekend" section of the *Post* is essential for finding out what's going on, recreation-wise. *City Paper,* published every Thursday and available free at downtown shops and restaurants, covers some of the same material but is a better guide to the club and art gallery scene. If you're staying in the suburbs, the Friday *Journal* papers (one for each area county) provide comprehensive coverage of activities beyond the downtown.

Also on newsstands is *Washingtonian,* a monthly magazine with features, often about the "100 Best" this or that (doctors, restaurants, and so on) to do with Washington; the magazine also offers a calendar of events, restaurant reviews, and profiles of Washingtonians. Available at the airport for free is *Washington Flyer,* a magazine geared to tourists.

Visitor Information lines include:

- **National Park Service** (☎ **202/619-7222**). By the way, National Park Service information kiosks are located near the Jefferson, Lincoln, Vietnam Veterans, and Korean War memorials, and at several other locations in the city.
- **Dial-A-Park** (☎ **202/619-7275**). This is a recording of information regarding park service events and attractions.
- **Dial-A-Museum** (☎ **202/357-2000**).
- **Recreation and Parks** (☎ **202/673-7660**).

CITY LAYOUT

Pierre Charles L'Enfant designed Washington's great sweeping avenues crossed by numbered and lettered streets. At key intersections he placed spacious circles. Although the circles are enhanced with monuments, statuary, and fountains, L'Enfant also intended them to serve as strategic command posts to ward off invaders or marauding mobs. After what had happened in Paris during the French Revolution— and remember, that was current history at the time—his design views were quite practical.

The U.S. Capitol marks the center of the city, which is divided into quadrants: **northwest (NW), northeast (NE), southwest (SW),** and **southeast (SE).** If you look at your map, you'll see that some addresses—for instance, the corner of G and 7th streets—appear in four different places. There's one in each quadrant. Hence you must observe the quadrant designation (NW, NE, SW, or SE) when looking for an address.

MAIN ARTERIES & STREETS   From the Capitol, North Capitol Street and South Capitol Street run north and south, respectively. East Capitol Street divides the city north and south. The area west of the Capitol is not a street at all, but the National Mall, which is bounded on the north by Constitution Avenue and on the south by Independence Avenue.

The primary artery of Washington is **Pennsylvania Avenue,** scene of parades, inaugurations, and other splashy events. Pennsylvania runs northwest in a direct line between the Capitol and the White House—if it weren't for the Treasury Building, the President would have a clear view of the Capitol—before continuing on a northwest angle to Georgetown.

Since May 1995, Pennsylvania Avenue between 15th and 17th streets NW has been closed to cars, for security reasons. H Street is now one-way eastbound between 19th and 13th streets N; I Street is one-way westbound between 11th and 21st streets NW.

Constitution Avenue, paralleled to the south most of the way by **Independence Avenue,** runs east-west flanking the Capitol and the Mall. If you hear Washingtonians talk about the "House" side of the Hill, they're referring to the part of the Capitol that holds Congressional House offices and the House Chamber, on the Independence Avenue side, in other words; the "Senate" side is the part of the Capitol that holds Senate offices and the Senate Chamber, on the Constitution Avenue side.

Washington's longest avenue, **Massachusetts Avenue,** runs north of and parallel to Pennsylvania. Along the way, you'll find Union Station and then Dupont Circle, which is central to the area known as Embassy Row. Farther out are the Naval Observatory (the vice-president's residence is on the premises), Washington National Cathedral, American University, and eventually, Maryland.

Connecticut Avenue, which runs more directly north, starts at Lafayette Square, intersects Dupont Circle, and eventually takes you to the National Zoo, on to the charming residential neighborhood known as Cleveland Park, and into Chevy Chase, Maryland, where you can pick up the Beltway to head out of town. (If you are driving to Washington and want a straightforward, albeit traffic-laden, way into town, reverse these instructions, following the Beltway to the Connecticut Ave. exit, and turn south—left off the ramp—toward Chevy Chase.) Connecticut Avenue, with its posh shops and clusters of restaurants, is a good street to stroll.

Wisconsin Avenue originates in Georgetown and intersects with M Street to form Georgetown's hub. Antique shops, trendy boutiques, discos, restaurants, and pubs all vie for attention. Wisconsin Avenue basically parallels Connecticut Avenue; one of the few irritating things about the city's transportation system is that the Metro does not connect these two major arteries in the heart of the city. (Buses do, and, of course, you can always walk or take a taxi from one avenue to the other.) In fact, Metro's first stop on Wisconsin Ave. is in Tenleytown, a residential part of town. Follow the avenue north, and you land in the affluent Maryland cities, Chevy Chase and Bethesda.

FINDING AN ADDRESS   Once you understand the city's layout, it's easy to find your way around. As you read this, have a map handy.

Each of the four corners of the District of Columbia is exactly the same distance from the Capitol dome. The White House and most government buildings and important monuments are west of the Capitol (in the northwest and southwest quadrants), as are important hotels and tourist facilities.

Numbered streets run north-south, beginning on either side of the Capitol with First Street, northeast (NE) and southeast (SE). **Lettered streets** run east-west and are named alphabetically, beginning with A Street. (Don't look for a B, a J, an X, Y, or Z Street, however.) After W Street, one-syllable, two-syllable, and three-syllable street names come into play; the more syllables in a name, the farther the street will lie from the Capitol.

Avenues, named for U.S. states, run at angles across the grid pattern and often intersect at traffic circles. For example, New Hampshire, Connecticut, and Massachusetts avenues intersect at Dupont Circle.

With this in mind, you can easily find an address. On **lettered streets,** the address tells you exactly where to go. For instance, 1776 K St. NW is between 17th and 18th streets (the first two digits of 1776 tell you that) in the northwest quadrant (NW). *Note:* I Street is often written Eye Street to prevent confusion with 1st Street.

To find an address on **numbered streets,** you'll probably have to use your fingers. For instance, 623 8th St. SE is between F and G streets (the sixth and seventh letters of the alphabet; the first digit of 623 tells you that) in the southeast quadrant (SE). One thing to remember: You count B as the second letter of the alphabet even though no B Street exists today (Constitution and Independence avenues were the original B streets), but since there's no J Street, K becomes the 10th letter, L the 11th, and so on.

NEIGHBORHOODS IN BRIEF

Adams-Morgan   This increasingly trendy, multiethnic neighborhood is about a minute long, centered around 18th Street and Columbia Road NW. Forget parking—it's impossible. But walk (and be alert; the neighborhood is edgy) or taxi here for a taste of Malaysian, Ethiopian, Spanish, or some other international cuisine. Friday and Saturday nights it's a hot nightlife district, rivaling Georgetown and Dupont Circle.

Capitol Hill   Everyone's heard of "the Hill," the area crowned by the Capitol. When people speak of Capitol Hill, they refer to a large section of town, extending from the western side of the Capitol to the D.C. Armory going east, bounded by H Street NE and the Southwest Freeway north and south. It contains not only the chief symbol of the nation's capital, but the Supreme Court building, the Library of Congress, the Folger Shakespeare Library, Union Station, and the U.S. Botanic Garden. Much of it is a quiet residential neighborhood of tree-lined streets and Victorian homes. There are many restaurants in the vicinity.

Downtown   The area roughly between 7th and 22nd streets NW going east to west, and P Street and Pennsylvania Avenue going north to south is a mix of the Federal Triangle's government office buildings, K Street and Connecticut Avenue restaurants and shopping, and historic hotels. Within its boundaries lie the White House and lovely Lafayette Park, an ever expanding Chinatown, the theater district, the MCI Center and the vibrant coming-to-life streets surrounding it, and many sightseeing

---

Impressions

If Washington should ever grow to be a great city, the outlook from the Capitol will be unsurpassed in the world. Now at sunset I seemed to look westward far into the heart of the continent from this commanding position.

—Ralph Waldo Emerson

attractions. Because of its great diversity and size, I've divided discussions of accommodations (chapter 5) and dining (chapter 6) into two sections: "Downtown, 16th Street NW and west," and "Downtown, east of 16th Street NW"; 16th Street and the White House form a natural point of separation.

Dupont Circle   My favorite part of town, the Dupont Circle area is a fun place to be any time of day or night. It takes its name from the traffic circle minipark, where Massachusetts, New Hampshire, and Connecticut avenues collide. The streets extending out from the circle are lively with all-night bookstores, really good restaurants, wonderful art galleries and art museums, nightspots, movie theaters, and Washingtonians at their loosest. It is also the hub of D.C.'s gay community.

Foggy Bottom   The area west of the White House to the edge of Georgetown, Foggy Bottom was Washington's early industrial center. Its name comes from the foul fumes emitted in those days by a coal depot and gasworks, but its original name, Funkstown (for owner Jacob Funk), is perhaps even worse. There's nothing foul about the area today. The Kennedy Center and George Washington University are located here. Constitution and Pennsylvania avenues are Foggy Bottom's southern and northern boundaries, respectively.

Georgetown   This historic community dates from colonial times. It was a thriving tobacco port long before the District of Columbia was formed, and one of its attractions, the Old Stone House, dates from pre-Revolutionary days. Georgetown action centers on M Street and Wisconsin Avenue NW, where you'll find numerous boutiques (see chapter 9 for details), chic restaurants, and popular pubs (lots of nightlife here). But get off the main drags and see the quiet tree-lined streets of restored colonial row houses, stroll through the beautiful gardens of Dumbarton Oaks, and check out the C&O Canal. One of the reasons so much activity flourishes in Georgetown is because of Georgetown University and its students.

Glover Park   Mostly a residential neighborhood, this section of town, just above Georgetown and just south of the Washington National Cathedral, is worth mentioning because of the increasing number of good restaurants opening along its main stretch, Wisconsin Avenue NW. Glover Park sits between the campuses of Georgetown and American Universities, so there's a large student presence here.

The Mall   This lovely tree-lined stretch of open space between Constitution and Independence avenues, extending for $2^1/_2$ miles from the Capitol to the Lincoln Memorial, is the hub of tourist attractions. It includes most of the Smithsonian Institution museums and many other nearby visitor attractions. The 300-foot-wide Mall is used by natives as well as tourists—joggers, food vendors, kite-flyers, and picnickers among them.

U Street Corridor   D.C.'s newest nightlife neighborhood between 12th and 15th streets NW is rising from the ashes of nightclubs and theaters frequented decades ago by African Americans. At the renovated Lincoln Theater, where legends like Duke Ellington, Louis Armstrong, and Cab Calloway once performed, patrons today can enjoy performances by popular though less famous black artists. The corridor offers at least six alternative rock and contemporary music nightclubs and several restaurants (see chapter 10 for details).

Woodley Park   Home to Washington's largest hotel (the Sheraton Washington) and another really big one (the Omni Shoreham), Woodley Park also is the site of the National Zoo, many good restaurants, and some antique stores. Washingtonians are used to seeing conventioneers wandering the neighborhood's pretty residential streets with their name tags still on.

2 Getting Around

Washington is one of the easiest U.S. cities in which to get around. Only New York rivals its comprehensive transportation system, but Washington's clean, efficient subways put the Big Apple's underground nightmare to shame. A complex bus system covers all major D.C. arteries, as well, and it's easy to hail a taxi anywhere at any time. But because Washington is of manageable size and marvelous beauty, you may find yourself shunning transportation and getting around on foot.

BY METRO

Metrorail stations are immaculate, cool, and attractive. Cars are air-conditioned and fitted with upholstered seats; tracks are rubber-cushioned so the ride is quiet; service is frequent enough so you usually get a seat, at least during off-peak hours (basically weekdays 10am to 3pm, weeknights after 8pm, and all day weekends); and the system is so simply designed that a 10-year-old can understand it. As mentioned earlier, eating, drinking, and smoking are strictly prohibited on the Metro and in the station.

Metrorail's 75 stations and 92.3 miles of track (83 stations and 103 miles of track are the eventual goal) include locations at or near almost every sightseeing attraction and extend to suburban Maryland and northern Virginia. If you're in Washington even for a few days, you'll probably have occasion to use the system; but if not, create an excuse. The Metro is a sightseeing attraction in its own right.

There are five lines in operation—**Red, Blue, Orange, Yellow,** and **Green**—with extensions planned for the future. The lines connect at several points, making transfers easy. All but Yellow and Green Line trains stop at Metro Center; all except Red Line trains stop at L'Enfant Plaza; all but Blue and Orange Line trains stop at Gallery Place/Chinatown.

Metro stations are indicated by discreet brown columns bearing the station's name and topped by the letter M. Below the M is a colored stripe or stripes indicating the line or lines that stop there. When entering a Metro station for the first time, go to the kiosk and ask the station manager for a free "Metro System Pocket Guide" (available in six languages). It contains a map of the system, explains how it works, and lists the closest Metro stops to points of interest. The station manager can also answer questions about routing or purchase of fare cards.

To enter or exit a Metro station, you need a computerized **fare card,** available at vending machines near the entrance. The minimum fare to enter the system is $1.10, which pays for rides to and from any point within 7 miles of boarding during nonpeak hours; during peak hours (Monday to Friday from 5:30 to 9:30am and 3 to 8pm), $1.10 takes you for only 3 miles. The machines take nickels, dimes, quarters, and bills from $1 to $20; they can return up to $4.95 in change (coins only). If you plan to take several Metrorail trips during your stay, put more value on the fare card to avoid having to purchase a new card each time you ride. There's a 10% discount on all fare cards of $20 or more. Up to two children under 5 can ride free with a paying passenger. Senior citizens (65 and older) and people with disabilities (with valid proof) ride Metrorail and Metrobus for a reduced fare.

Discount passes, called "One-Day Rail passes," cost $5 per person and allow you unlimited passage for 1 day. You can buy them at Washington Metropolitan Transit Authority, 600 5th St. NW (☎ 202/637-7000) at Metro Center, 12th and G streets NW, or at a Giant or Safeway grocery store.

When you insert your card in the entrance gate, the time and location are recorded on its magnetic tape, and your card is returned. Don't forget to snatch it up and keep

---

Travel Tip

If you're on the subway and plan to continue your travel via Metrobus, pick up a **transfer** *at the station where you enter the system* (not your destination station). Transfer machines are on the mezzanine levels of most stations. It's good for a discount on bus fares in D.C. and Virginia. There are no bus-to-subway transfers.

---

it handy; you have to reinsert it in the exit gate at your destination, where the fare will automatically be deducted. The card will be returned if there's any value left on it. If you arrive at a destination and your fare card doesn't have enough value, add what's necessary at the Addfare machines near the exit gate.

Metrorail operates Monday to Friday from 5:30am to midnight, weekends and holidays from 8am to midnight. Call ☎ **202/637-7000** for information on Metro routes. *Warning:* the line is often busy, so just keep trying.

BY BUS

While a 10-year-old can understand the Metrorail system, the Metrobus system is considerably more complex. The 15,800 stops on the 1,489-square-mile route (it operates on all major D.C. arteries as well as in the Virginia and Maryland suburbs) are indicated by red, white, and blue signs. However, the signs tell you only what buses pull into a given stop, not where they go. For **routing information,** call ☎ 202/637-7000. Calls are taken Monday to Friday from 6am to 10:30pm, weekends and holidays from 8am to 10:30pm. This is the same number you call to request a free map and time schedule, information about parking in Metrobus fringe lots, and for locations and hours of those places where you can purchase bus tokens.

Base fare in the District is $1.10; bus transfers cost 10¢. There are additional charges for travel into the Maryland and Virginia suburbs. Bus drivers are not equipped to make change, so be sure to *carry exact change or tokens.* If you'll be in Washington for a while and plan to use the buses a lot, consider buying a $20 2-week pass, also available at the Metro Center station and other outlets.

Most buses operate daily almost around the clock. Service is quite frequent on weekdays, especially during peak hours. On weekends and late at night, service is less frequent.

Up to two children under 5 ride free with a paying passenger on Metrobus, and there are reduced fares for senior citizens (☎ **202/962-7000**) and people with disabilities (☎ **202/962-1245** or 202/962-1100). If you should leave something on a bus, train, or in a station, call Lost and Found at ☎ **202/962-1195.**

BY CAR

More than half of all visitors to the District arrive by car. If you're one of them, you should know that traffic is always thick during the week, parking spaces often hard to find, and parking lots ruinously expensive.

Even if you don't drive in D.C., you will want a car to get to most attractions in Virginia and Maryland. All the major car-rental companies are represented here. Here are the phone numbers for those rental companies with locations at all three airports: **Budget** (☎ **800/527-0700**), **Hertz** (☎ **800/654-3131**), **Thrifty** (☎ **800/ 367-2277**), **Avis** (☎ **800/331-1212**), and **Alamo** (☎ **800/327-9633**).

If you do drive in the District, watch out for the traffic circles. Traffic law states that the circle traffic has the right of way. No one pays any attention to this rule, however, which can be frightening (cars zoom into the circle without a glance at the cars already there). The other thing you will notice is that while some circles are easy to figure out (Dupont Circle, for example), others are nervewrackingly confusing (Thomas Circle, where 14th Street NW, Vermont Avenue NW, and Massachusetts Avenue NW come together, is to be avoided at all cost).

Also, sections of certain streets in Washington become one-way during rush hour: Rock Creek Parkway, Canal Road, and 17th Street NW are three examples. Other streets during rush hour change the direction of some of their traffic lanes: Connecticut Avenue NW is the main one. In the morning, traffic in four of its six lanes travels south to the downtown and in late afternoon/early evening, downtown traffic in four of its six lanes heads north; between the hours of 9am and 3:30pm, traffic in either direction keeps to the normally correct side of the yellow line. Lit-up traffic signs alert you to what's going on, but pay attention.

BY TAXI

District cabs operate on a zone system instead of meters. By law, basic rates are posted in each cab. If you take a trip from one point to another within the same zone, you pay just $4.00, regardless of the distance traveled. So it would cost you $4.00 to travel a few blocks from the U.S. Botanic Garden to the Museum of American History, but the same $4.00 could take you from the Botanic Garden all the way to Dupont Circle. They're both in Zone 1. Also in Zone 1 are most other tourist attractions: the Capitol, the White House, most of the Smithsonian, the Washington Monument, the FBI, the National Archives, the Supreme Court, the Library of Congress, the Bureau of Engraving and Printing, the Old Post Office, and Ford's Theatre. If your trip takes you into a second zone, the price is $5.50, $6.90 for a third zone, $8.25 for a fourth, and so on.

So far, the fares seem modest. But here's how they could add up: There's a $1.50 charge for each additional passenger after the first, so a $4.00 Zone 1 fare can become $8.50 for a family of four (though one child under 5 can ride free). There's also a rush-hour surcharge of $1 per trip between 7 and 9:30am and 4 and 6:30pm weekdays. Surcharges are also added for large pieces of luggage and for arranging a pickup by telephone ($1.50).

The zone system is not used when your destination is an out-of-District address (such as an airport); in that case, the fare is based on mileage covered—$2 for the first half mile or part thereof and 70¢ for each additional half mile or part. You can call ☎ 202/331-1671 to find out the rate between any point in D.C. and an address in Virginia or Maryland. Call ☎ 202/645-6018 to inquire about fares within the District.

It's generally easy to hail a taxi, although the *Washington Post* has reported that taxi cabs, even those driven by black cabbies, often ignore African Americans to pick up white passengers; African-American friends corroborate that this is so. Unique to the city is the practice of allowing drivers to pick up as many passengers as they can comfortably fit, so expect to share (unrelated parties pay the same as they would if they were not sharing). You can also call a taxi, though there's that $1.50 charge. Try **Diamond Cab Company** (☎ 202/387-6200), **Yellow Cab** (☎ 202/544-1212), or **Capitol Cab** (☎ 202/546-2400). To register a complaint, note the cab driver's name and cab number and call the Taxicab Complaint Office (☎ 202/727-5401).

Impressions

Like a city in dreams, the great white capital stretches along the placid river from Georgetown on the west to Anacostia on the east.

—Allen Drury

Taxicab Zones

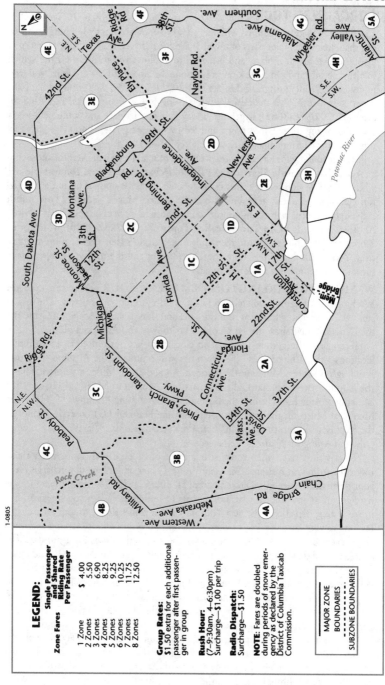

LEGEND:

Zone Fares	Single Passenger and Shared Riding Rate Per Passenger
1 Zone	$ 4.00
2 Zones	5.50
3 Zones	6.90
4 Zones	8.25
5 Zones	9.25
6 Zones	10.25
7 Zones	11.75
8 Zones	12.50

Group Rates:
$1.50 extra for each additional passenger after first passenger in group

Rush Hour:
(7-9:30am, 4-6:30pm)
Surcharge—$1.00 per trip

Radio Dispatch:
Surcharge—$1.50

NOTE: Fares are doubled during periods of snow emergency as declared by the District of Columbia Taxicab Commission.

MAJOR ZONE BOUNDARIES

SUBZONE BOUNDARIES

1-0805

BY ORGANIZED TOUR

The best way to get acquainted with any city, I'm convinced, is by hopping on a tour bus that circles the major parts of town, as a guide narrates. It's a relaxing way to pick up some facts about a place, and usually a tour allows you to jump off the vehicle to visit one site, and jump back on to continue the circuit. In Washington, you have many choices, including **DC Ducks** (☎ 202/966-3825), a 90-minute land and water tour focusing on the capital's historic and military landmarks, and **Bike the Sites** (☎ 202/966-8662), which provides you bikes, helmets, and equipment to use on tours lasting from 1 to 4 hours and led by licensed guides. For a complete listing of organized tours of all sorts, see chapter 7.

If you're looking for an easy-on/easy-off tour of major sites, consider the more conventional **Tourmobile Sightseeing** (☎ 202/554-5100), whose comfortable red, white, and blue sightseeing trams travel to as many as 16 sites, as far out as Arlington National Cemetery and even (with coach service) Mount Vernon. (**Tourmobile** is the only narrated sightseeing shuttle tour authorized by the National Park Service.) Another standard is **Old Town Trolley Tours** (☎ 202/832-9800), which offers 2-hour narrated tours aboard green-and-orange trolleys that stop at more than 18 sites. You should know that both the Tourmobiles and the trolleys are open-air in summer—meaning not air-conditioned.

WASHINGTON/ARLINGTON CEMETERY TOUR You can take the Washington/Arlington Cemetery tour or tour only Arlington Cemetery. The former stops at 14 different sites on or near the Mall and three sights at Arlington Cemetery: the Kennedy grave sites, the Tomb of the Unknown, and Arlington House.

Here's how the system works: You can board a Tourmobile at 15 different locations—the White House, the Washington Monument, the Arts and Industries Building/Hirshhorn Museum, the National Air and Space Museum, Union Station, the Capitol, the National Gallery of Art, the Museum of Natural History, the Museum of American History, the Bureau of Engraving and Printing/U.S. Holocaust Memorial Museum; the Jefferson Memorial; the Franklin D. Roosevelt Memorial, the Kennedy Center, the Lincoln/Vietnam Veterans/Korean War Veterans Memorials, and Arlington National Cemetery.

You pay the driver when you first board the bus (you can also purchase a ticket inside the Arlington National Cemetery Visitor Center or, for a small surcharge, order your ticket in advance from Ticketmaster (☎ 800/551-SEAT). Along the route, you may get off at any stop to visit monuments or buildings. When you finish exploring each area, step aboard the next Tourmobile that comes along without extra charge (as long as you can show your ticket). The buses travel in a loop, serving each stop about every 30 minutes. One **fare** allows you to use the buses for a full day. The charge for the Washington/Arlington Cemetery tour is $12 for anyone 12 and older, $6 for children 3 to 11. For Arlington Cemetery only, those 12 and older pay $4, children $2. Children under 3 ride free. Buses follow figure-eight circuits from the Capitol to Arlington Cemetery and back. You can also buy a regular-price ticket after 2pm that is valid for the rest of the afternoon plus the following day. Well-trained narrators give commentaries about sights along the route and answer questions.

Tourmobiles operate daily year-round. From June 15 to Labor Day, they ply the Mall between 9am and 6:30pm. After Labor Day, the hours are 9:30am to 4:30pm. In Arlington Cemetery, between November and March, they start at 8:30am and end at 4:30pm. April through October, the hours are 8:30am to 6:30pm.

OTHER TOURMOBILE TOURS April through October, Tourmobiles also run round-trip to **Mount Vernon.** Coaches depart from the Arlington National

Tourmobile

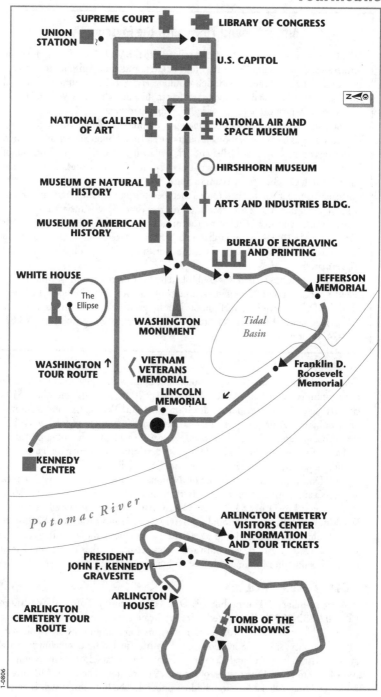

SUPREME COURT

LIBRARY OF CONGRESS

UNION STATION

U.S. CAPITOL

NATIONAL GALLERY OF ART

NATIONAL AIR AND SPACE MUSEUM

HIRSHHORN MUSEUM

MUSEUM OF NATURAL HISTORY

ARTS AND INDUSTRIES BLDG.

MUSEUM OF AMERICAN HISTORY

BUREAU OF ENGRAVING AND PRINTING

WHITE HOUSE

The Ellipse

JEFFERSON MEMORIAL

WASHINGTON MONUMENT

Tidal Basin

WASHINGTON TOUR ROUTE ↑

VIETNAM VETERANS MEMORIAL

Franklin D. Roosevelt Memorial

LINCOLN MEMORIAL

KENNEDY CENTER

Potomac River

ARLINGTON CEMETERY VISITORS CENTER INFORMATION AND TOUR TICKETS

PRESIDENT JOHN F. KENNEDY GRAVESITE

ARLINGTON HOUSE

ARLINGTON CEMETERY TOUR ROUTE

TOMB OF THE UNKNOWNS

1-0806

53

Motor Around Town with the Museum Bus

While a slew of organized tour vehicles take you to the Mall and various sightseeing attractions, the **Museum Bus** is the only dedicated museum transportation system in the city. The minibuses provide door-to-door service to 22 museums—some well known, like the National Gallery, others less so, like the Woodrow Wilson House, and many of which do not have adequate public parking.

The specially marked buses wend their way in intersecting loops throughout the city, traveling as far as the National Zoo at one end and Union Station at the other, with stops at the Corcoran Gallery of Art, Octagon House, National Museum of Women in the Arts, National Portrait Gallery, and 20 other sites. They operate June through October, from 10am to 5pm.

Passage is free if you happen to be a member of a participating museum; otherwise, you can purchase a low-cost pass (at press time, $5 was the starting price), which entitles you to bus rides, free admission to museums that charge a fee or donation, and a 10% discount in all museum shops and restaurants, the Smithsonian included. You can purchase passes at museum shops, hotels, TICKETplace and Ticketmaster.

The Museum Bus system was established by the Corcoran Gallery, who coordinated a consortium of 22 museum-participants, as well as the National Park Service, the D.C. Committee to Promote Washington, and the Smithsonian. The Cultural Alliance of Greater Washington administers the program. Call ☎ **202/ 588-7470** for information.

Cemetery Visitor Center at 10am, noon, and 2pm, with a pickup at the Washington Monument shortly thereafter. The price is $20 for those 12 and older, $10 for children ages 3 to 11, including admission to Mount Vernon. A combination tour of Washington, Arlington Cemetery, and Mount Vernon (good for 2 days) is $32 for anyone 12 and older, $16 for children ages 3 to 11. Another offering (June 15 to Labor Day) is the **Frederick Douglass National Historic Site Tour,** which includes a guided tour of Douglass's home, Cedar Hill, located in southeast Washington. Departures are from Arlington National Cemetery at noon, with a pickup at the Washington Monument shortly thereafter. Those 12 and older pay $6, and children ages 3 to 11 pay $3. A 2-day **Combination Frederick Douglass Tour and Washington/Arlington National Cemetery Tour** is also available at $24 for those 12 and older, $12 for children ages 3 to 11. For both the Mount Vernon and Frederick Douglass tours, you must reserve in person at either Arlington Cemetery or the Washington Monument at least an hour in advance.

BY OLD TOWN TROLLEY

A service similar to Tourmobile's is **Old Town Trolley Tours of Washington** (☎ **202/832-9800**). For a fixed price, you can get on and off these green-and-orange vehicles as often as you like for an entire loop around the city. Following a loop, the trolleys stop at 18 locations in the District, including Georgetown; they also go out to Arlington National Cemetery. They operate daily from 9am to 5pm, Memorial Day to Labor Day; the rest of the year, 9am to 4pm. The cost is $18 for adults, $9 for children 4 to 12, free for children under 4. The full tour, which is narrated, takes 2 hours, and trolleys come by every 30 minutes or so. Stops are made at Union Station, the Hyatt Regency Hotel (near the National Gallery), the Pavilion at the Old

Post Office, Metro Center (near the Convention Center), the Grand Hyatt (China-town), the FBI Building, the J. W. Marriott (near the Renwick and Corcoran), the Hotel Washington (near the White House), the Capital Hilton (near the National Geographic Society), the Washington Hilton (near the Phillips Collection and Adams-Morgan restaurants), the Washington Park Gourmet (near the National Zoo), Washington National Cathedral, the Georgetown Park Mall, Lincoln Memorial, Arlington National Cemetery, the Washington Monument/U.S. Holocaust Memorial Museum, the Smithsonian Castle, the Air and Space Museum, and the Library of Congress. You can board without a ticket and purchase it en route.

Old Town Trolley also offers a 2^1/2-hour "Washington After Hours" tour of illu-minated federal buildings and memorials from mid-March to the end of December. Call the number listed above for details.

FAST FACTS: Washington, D.C.

Airports   See "Getting There" in chapter 2.

American Express   There's an American Express Travel Service office at 1150 Connecticut Ave. NW (☎ **202/457-1300**) and another in upper northwest Washington at 5300 Wisconsin Ave. NW, in the Mazza Gallerie (☎ **202/ 362-4000**). Both function as a full travel agency and currency exchange; of course, you can also buy traveler's checks here.

Area Code   Within the District of Columbia, it's 202. In suburban Virginia, it's 703. In suburban Maryland, it's 301.

Baby-sitters   Most hotels can arrange for sitters. If your hotel does not offer a baby-sitting service, you can contact White House Nannies (☎ **301/652-8088**) your-self. In business since 1985, this company checks their "caregivers'" qualifications, child-care references, and personal histories, including driving and social security records. Each caregiver has been trained in CPR and first aid training. Rates are $8 to $12 per hour (4-hour minimum), depending upon the caregiver's experience and how many children she'll be baby-sitting, plus a one-time booking fee of $25. If the hotel does not pay for her parking, you may have to pay that fee, as well.

Business Hours   See "Fast Facts: For Foreign Visitors" in chapter 3.

Car Rentals   See "Getting Around," earlier in this chapter.

Climate   See "When to Go" in chapter 2.

Congresspersons   To locate a senator or congressional representative, call the Capitol switchboard (☎ **202/224-3121**).

Convention Center   The Washington, D.C., Convention Center, 900 9th St. NW, between H Street and New York Avenue (☎ **202/789-1600**), is a vast multi-purpose facility with 381,000 square feet of exhibition space and 40 meeting rooms.

Crime   See "Safety," below.

Doctors/Dentists   **Prologue** (☎ **800/DOCTORS**) can refer you to any type of doctor or dentist you need. Its roster includes just about every specialty. Hours are Monday through Saturday, 7:30am to 10pm. **Physicians Home Service,** Suite 401, 2311 M St. NW (☎ **202/331-3888**) will come to your hotel if you are staying in the District, or will treat you in its downtown office during regular hours; PHS accepts credit cards, traveler's checks, personal checks with adequate identification, and cash.

Driving Rules   See "Getting Around," earlier in this chapter.

Drugstores   **CVS,** Washington's major drugstore chain (with more than 40 stores), has two convenient 24-hour locations: 14th Street and Thomas Circle NW, at Vermont Avenue (☎ **202/628-0720**), and at Dupont Circle (☎ **202/785-1466**), both with round-the-clock pharmacies. These drugstores also carry miscellaneous goods ranging from frozen food and basic groceries to small appliances. Check your phone book for other convenient locations.

Embassies   See "Fast Facts: For the Foreign Traveler" in chapter 3.

Emergencies/Hotlines   Dial ☎ **911** to contact the police or fire department or to call an ambulance. See also "Hospital Emergency Wards," below. To reach a 24-hour poison control hotline, call ☎ **202/625-3333,** to reach a 24-hour crisis line, call ☎ **202/561-7000,** and to reach the Drug Abuse/Action Health line for alcohol and drug problems, call ☎ **800/234-0420.**

Hospitals   In case of a life-threatening emergency, call ☎ **911.** If you don't require immediate ambulance transportation but still need emergency-room treatment, call one of the following hospitals; be sure to get directions: **Children's Hospital National Medical Center,** 111 Michigan Ave. NW (☎ **202/884-5000** for emergency room and general information); **George Washington University Hospital,** 901 23rd St. NW (entrance on Washington Circle; ☎ **202/994-3211** for emergency room or 202/994-1000 for general information); **Georgetown University Hospital,** 3800 Reservoir Rd. NW (☎ **202/784-2118** for emergency room or 202/687-2000 for general information); **Howard University Hospital,** 2041 Georgia Ave. NW (☎ **202/865-1131** for emergency room or 202/865-6100 for general information).

Laundry/Dry Cleaning   Most hotels provide laundry and dry-cleaning services and/or have coin-operated facilities. Otherwise, try Washtub Laundromat, 1511 17th St. NW (☎ **202/332-9455**), for self-service coin-operated laundering. For complete laundry and dry-cleaning services with pickup and delivery, contact **Bergmann's** (☎ **202/737-5400**). For same-day dry-cleaning service, try **MacDee Quality Cleaners** at 1639 L St. NW (☎ **202/296-6100**), open Monday through Saturday.

Liquor Laws   The minimum drinking age is 21. Establishments can serve alcoholic beverages from 8am to 2am Monday to Thursday, until 2:30am Friday and Saturday, and 10am to 2am Sunday. Liquor stores are closed on Sunday. District gourmet grocery stores, mom-and-pop grocery stores, and 7-Eleven convenience stores often sell beer and wine, even on Sundays.

Luggage Storage/Lockers   Washington National, Dulles, and Baltimore-Washington International airports each have luggage storage facilities, as do most hotels.

Maps   Free city maps are often available at hotels and throughout town at tourist attractions. You can also contact the **Washington, D.C., Convention and Visitors Association,** 1212 New York Ave. NW, Washington, DC 20005 (☎ **202/ 789-7000**).

Newspapers/Magazines   See "Visitor Information," earlier in this chapter.

Police   In an emergency, dial ☎ **911.** For a nonemergency, call ☎ **202/ 727-1010.**

Post Office   If you want your mail to follow you on your vacation and you aren't sure of your address, your mail can be sent to you, in your name, ℅ **General**

Delivery at the main post office of the city or region where you expect to be. The addressee must pick it up in person and produce proof of identity (for example, driver's license, credit or charge card, or passport). In Washington, the **main post office** is located at 900 Brentwood Rd. NE, Washington, DC 20066-9998, USA (☎ **202/636-1532**). It's open Monday to Friday 8am to 8pm, Saturday 10am to 6pm, and Sunday noon to 6pm. Other post offices are located throughout the city, including the one in the **National Postal Museum** building, opposite Union Station at 2 Massachusetts Ave. NE (at G and North Capitol streets) (☎ **202/523-2628**). It's open Monday to Friday 7am to midnight, and on weekends until 8pm.

Religious Services   Every hotel keeps a list of places of worship for all faiths. Inquire at the front desk. Among Washington's notable places of worship are: the **Washington National Cathedral** (the Episcopal church is the sixth largest cathedral in the world), Wisconsin and Massachusetts avenues NW (☎ **202/537-6200**); **Saint John's Church** (also Episcopal, known as the "church of the Presidents"), on Lafayette Square across from the White House (☎ **202/347-8766**); the **Basilica of the National Shrine of the Immaculate Conception** (the nation's largest Catholic church), Michigan Avenue and 4th Street NE (☎ **202/526-8300**); **Adas Israel** (Jewish), Connecticut Avenue and Porter Street NW ☎ **202/362-4433**); and the **Islamic Mosque and Cultural Center** (Muslim), 2551 Massachusetts Ave. NW (☎ **202/332-8343**).

Rest Rooms   Visitors can usually find a rest room in a bar, restaurant, hotel, museum, department store, train station, or service station (frequent cleanliness problems should make this your last choice). You might have to buy a snack or drink in a restaurant/bar to gain bathroom privileges.

Safety   In Washington, you're quite safe throughout the day in all the major tourist areas described in this book, and you can also safely visit the Lincoln Memorial after dark. At nighttime, be alert anywhere you go in Washington. Riding the Metro is quite safe.

Taxes   Sales tax on merchandise is 5.75% in the District, 5% in Maryland, and 4.5% in Virginia. The tax on restaurant meals is 10% in the District, 5% in Maryland, and 4.5% in Virginia.

In the District, in addition to your hotel rate, you pay 13% sales tax and $1.50 per night occupancy tax. The state sales tax on a hotel room is 9.75% in suburban Virginia and 10% in Maryland (where you can expect an additional 5% to 7% in city or local taxes).

Taxis   See "Getting Around," earlier in this chapter.

Tickets   A service called **TICKETplace** (☎ **202/TICKETS**) sells half-price tickets, on the day of performance only, to most major Washington-area theaters and concert halls. It also functions as a Ticketmaster outlet. Same-day half-price ticket booths operate at the Old Post Office Pavilion and at Lisner Auditorium. For advance sale tickets, call **Ticketmaster** (☎ **202/432-SEAT**) or **Protix** (☎ **703/218-6500**). See chapter 10 for details.

Time   Call ☎ **202/844-2525**.

Transit Information   See "Getting There" in chapter 2 and "Getting Around," earlier in this chapter.

Weather   Call ☎ **202/936-1212**.

5 Where to Stay in Washington, D.C.

The city of Washington alone has more than 100 hotels and motels, the total number of guest rooms upwards of 22,000. When you consider suburban Washington (that is, Maryland and Virginia), the number of rooms reaches 65,000. With so many accommodations available, you'll probably always be able to snag a room, even in high season, and even at the last minute. So how to make sure you get the kind of room in the kind of hotel in the location you desire?

To visit Washington in season, reserve well in advance. Peak seasons in Washington roughly correspond to two activities: the sessions of Congress and springtime, starting with the appearance of the cherry blossoms along the Potomac. Specifically, when Congress is "in," from about the second week in September until Thanksgiving, and again from about mid-January through June, hotels are fairly full with guests whose business takes them to Capitol Hill, and with those attending the many meetings and conventions that take place here.

True peak season starts in mid-March, when tourists come to see the cherry blossoms, which might bloom anytime from mid-March to the end of April (their blooms typically last about 7 to 12 days). April is the city's busiest month, with May and June only a little less so. Springtime in Washington *is* something special, hence the crowds.

Conversely, you'll find hotels offering more room options on weekends throughout the year, around holidays, and on weekdays and weekends during the periods of July through the first week of September and late November through January. These are also the times when you'll receive the best rates, but for more on that subject, keep reading.

HOW TO GET THE BEST RATE

As you peruse this chapter, you should keep certain things in mind. First, consider all of the hotels, no matter the rate category. The accepted wisdom is that no one pays the advertised "rack" rate. Even the best and most expensive hotels may be ready to negotiate and often offer bargain rates at certain times or to guests who are members of certain groups, and you may be eligible. If you can be flexible about the time you are traveling, all the better. Second, as a rule, when you call a hotel, you should ask whether there are special promotions or discounts available. Most hotels offer discounts of at least 10% to members of the American Automobile Association

(AAA) and the American Association of Retired Persons (AARP). The magnificent Willard Hotel, for instance, offers 50% off its regular rates for guests older than 65—on a space available basis. Many hotels in Washington, like the State Plaza Hotel, discount rates for government, military, or embassy-related guests. Long-term rates, corporate rates, and holiday rates are also possibilities.

Families often receive special rates, as much as 50% off on a room adjoining the parents' room (Hyatt is one chain that offers this, based on availability), or perhaps free fare in the hotel's restaurant (many Holiday Inns let kids 12 and under eat free from children's menus year-round). Every hotel (but not necessarily inns or bed and breakfasts) included in this chapter allows children under a certain age, usually 12 or 18, to stay free in the parents' room.

Finally, it pays to know what you want and to do some research. Consider the variety of weekend rates for a double that were in effect in early spring of 1997: $100 to $110 at the Holiday Inn Downtown; about $155 at the posh Watergate Hotel; $119 ($60 or so off the regular rate) for a "Weekend Superbe" package available through the Hotel Sofitel, entitling couples to a one-night stay with a continental breakfast of croissants and pastries served in the room; and $89, including continental breakfast served in the restaurant, at the Morrison-Clark Inn.

RESERVATIONS SERVICES   If you don't have time or energy to find yourself the right accommodation, these Washington reservations services will do it for you, for free. Because each of these businesses is Washington-based, you can specify your needs and ask for details about neighborhoods that only local people would know.

Capitol Reservations, 1730 Rhode Island Ave. NW, Suite 1114, Washington, DC 20036 (☎ **800/VISIT-DC** or 202/452-1270; fax 202/452-0537; Internet **www.hotelsdc.com**), will find you a hotel that meets your specific requirements and is within your price range, and they'll do the bargaining for you. "Because of the high volume of room nights we book," explains owner Thom Hall, "many properties offer discounts available only through this service and below public rates." Capitol Reservations listings begin at about $55 a night for a double. The 14-year-old Capitol Reservations works with about 75 area hotels, all of which have been screened for cleanliness, safe locations, and other desirability factors. **Washington D.C. Accommodations,** 2201 Wisconsin Ave. NW, Suite C110, Washington, DC 20007 (☎ **800/554-2220** or 202/289-2220; fax 202/338-4517), has been in business for 13 years, providing the same service. In addition to finding hotel accommodations for you, this service can advise you about transportation and general tourist information.

GROUPS   If you're planning a meeting, convention, or other group function requiring 10 rooms or more, contact **U.S.A. Groups** (☎ **800/872-4777** or 202/861-1900). This free service represents hotel rooms at almost every hostelry in the Washington, D.C., and suburban Virginia–Maryland region—in all price categories.

BED & BREAKFASTS   If a stay in a private home, apartment, or small inn appeals to you, you may want to consider the specific inns I've listed in this chapter, or try calling these two services. The **Bed and Breakfast League/Sweet Dreams and Toast,** P.O. Box 9490, Washington, DC 20016 (☎ **202/363-7767;** fax 202/363-8396), represents more than 70 B&Bs in the District. Through them, you might find a room in a mid-1800s Federal-style Capitol Hill mansion, a Georgetown home with a lovely garden, or a turn-of-the-century Dupont Circle townhouse with Victorian furnishings. The accommodations are screened, and guest reports are given serious consideration. Hosts are encouraged, though not required, to offer such niceties as fresh-baked muffins at breakfast. All listings are convenient to public transportation. Rates for most range from $50 to $120 for a single and $60 to $150 for a double, plus tax, and $10 to $25 per additional person. There's a 2-night minimum-stay requirement and a booking fee of $10 (per reservation, not per night). American Express, Diner's Club, MasterCard, and Visa are accepted.

A similar service, **Bed & Breakfast Accommodations Ltd.,** P.O. Box 12011, Washington, DC 20005 (☎ **202/328-3510;** fax 202/332-3885), has more than 80 homes, inns, guest houses, and unhosted furnished apartments in its files. Most are in historic districts. Its current roster offers, among many others, a Georgian-style colonial brick home on a tree-lined avenue in Tenley Circle and a Dupont Circle Victorian town house with a two-level deck. Rates are $45 to $150 single, $55 to $160 double, $15 for an extra person, and from $65 for a full apartment. At guest houses and inns, rates run the gamut from $68 to $180 single, $78 to $250 double. American Express, Diner's Club, MasterCard, Visa, and Discover are accepted.

PRICE CATEGORIES   The hotels listed in this chapter are grouped first by location, then alphabetically by price. I've used the following guide for per-night prices: **Very Expensive,** more than $215; **Expensive,** $150 to $215; **Moderate,** $100 to $149; and **Inexpensive,** less than $100.

Prices are based on published rates for a standard double room weekdays during high season. As mentioned earlier, you can often do better. Two rates are given, weekday and weekend, since the difference can be enormous. Reduced rates and weekend rates are, generally, subject to availability. Don't forget tax: In the District, in addition to your hotel rate, you'll have to pay 13% in taxes plus $1.50 a night room tax. And keep in mind that parking can cost a bundle, so inquire about parking rates when you make your reservation; some hotels charge more than $20 a night!

1   Best Bets

- **Best Historic Hotel:** The grand dame of Washington hotels is the magnificent **Renaissance Mayflower,** 1127 Connecticut Ave. NW (☎ **800/HOTELS-1** or 202/347-3000), which, when it was built in 1925, was considered not only the last word in luxury and beauty but "the second-best address" in town. Harry S. Truman preferred it even over the White House.
- **Best Location:** The **Willard Inter-Continental,** 1401 Pennsylvania Ave. NW (☎ **800/327-0200** or 202/628-9100), is primely situated within walking distance of the White House, museums, theaters, downtown offices, good restaurants, and the Metro; it's also a quick taxi ride to Capitol Hill.
- **Best Place to Stay During an Inauguration:** For the best views of the inaugural parade, book rooms at the **J.W. Marriott,** 1331 Pennsylvania Ave. NW (☎ **800/228-9290** or 202/393-2000), or the **Hotel Washington,** 15th and Pennsylvania avenues NW (☎ **800/424-9540** or 202/638-5900)—be sure to specify a room with a view of Pennsylvania Avenue. Also, know that the best inaugural parties are inevitably held at the **Willard Inter-Continental** (see "Best Location," above).
- **Best for a Romantic Getaway:** The posh **Jefferson,** 16th and M streets NW (☎ **800/368-5966** or 202/347-2200), is just enough off the beaten track, but still conveniently downtown, to feel like you've really escaped. Because the service, the bar, and the restaurant (see chapter 6 for a review of **The Restaurant at The Jefferson**) are outstanding, you have no need to leave the premises. The restaurant itself has one of the most romantic nooks in the city.
- **Best Moderately Priced Hotel:** The newly renovated **Hotel Lombardy,** 2019 Pennsylvania Ave. NW (☎ **800/424-5486** or 202/828-2600), is now slightly more

than moderately priced but still conveniently located, with spacious and charmingly decorated accommodations, and conciergelike service from the front desk.

- **Best Inexpensive Hotel:** The **Days Inn Premier,** 1201 K St. NW (☎ **800/562-3350** or 202/842-1020), close to the Convention Center, even has a small rooftop pool. If you reserve far in advance, you may be able to get the special $59 per night "Super Saver" rate.

- **Best B&B:** The stunning **Morrison-Clark Inn,** Massachusetts Avenue and 11th Street NW (☎ **800/332-7898** or 202/898-1200), housed in two beautifully restored Victorian town houses, has exquisite rooms and an acclaimed restaurant.

- **Best Service:** The **Four Seasons,** 2800 Pennsylvania Ave. NW (☎ **800/332-3442** or 202/342-0444) pampers you relentlessly, greeting you by name and offering an "I Need It Now" program that delivers any of 100 or more left-at-home essentials (tweezers, batteries, cufflinks, electric hair curlers, and so on) to you in 3 minutes, at no cost.

- **Best Place to Hide If You're Embroiled in a Scandal:** Lovely as it is, the **Normandy Inn,** 2118 Wyoming Ave. NW (☎ **800/424-3729** or 202/483-1350), remains unknown to many Washingtonians—a plus if you need to lay low. Best of all, the neighborhood teems with embassies, in case your trouble is of the I-need-a-foreign-government-to-bail-me-out variety.

- **Best for Business Travelers:** The **Grand Hyatt Washington,** 1000 H St. NW (☎ **800/233-1234** or 202/582-1234), wins for its convenient central location (in the business district between the White House and the Capitol, directly across from the Convention Center, and 3 blocks from the MCI Arena, with direct underground access to the subway); for its ample on-site meeting facilities; and for its inviting, $15-extra "Business Plan," which accommodates travelers in 8th- and 9th-floor rooms equipped with a large desk, fax machine, and computer hookup, with access to printers and other office supplies. Continental breakfast is included in the plan.

- **Best Hotel Restaurant:** The inventive French fare at sumptuous Lespinasse, in **The Carlton** hotel, 923 16th St. NW (☎ **800/325-3535** or 202/638-2626), is the hands-down star. Among the other standouts in this category are: the Jockey Club, in the **Luxury Collection Hotel, Washington, D.C.,** 2100 Massachusetts Ave. (☎ **800/325-3589** or 202/293-2100); the Restaurant at The Jefferson, in **The Jefferson** hotel (see "Best for a Romantic Getaway," above); and Brighton-on-N, in the **Canterbury Hotel,** 1733 N St. NW (☎ **800/424-2950** or 202/393-3000).

- **Best Health Club:** The West End Fitness Center at the **ANA Hotel,** 2401 M St. NW (☎ **800/ANA-HOTELS** or 202/429-2400), is the model against which all other hotels measure their own. The 17,500–square-foot center offers classes in yoga and aerobics; seminars in stress management and weight loss; and equipment that includes virtual reality bike machines, stair climbers with telephones and TV/VCR units, NordicTraks, rowing machines, exercise bikes with telephones, and assorted other torturous machines; as well as squash and racquetball courts, a swimming pool, a steam room, a whirlpool, saunas, and a mini-spa. Personal trainers, fitness evaluation, and workout clothes are available.

- **Best Views:** The **Hay-Adams,** 16th and H streets NW (☎ **800/424-5054** or 202/638-6600), has such a great, unobstructed view of the White House that the 5Secret Service comes over regularly to do security sweeps of the place.

- **Best Hotel Lobby for Pretending You're Rich:** The **Carlton** (see "Best Hotel Restaurant," above), with its plush, oversized sofas and high gilded ceiling, is my first choice in this category; the **Willard Inter-Continental** (see "Best Location," above), though an architectural masterpiece and opulent in its restoration, comes in second, thanks to the hoi polloi milling around.

2 Adams-Morgan/North Dupont Circle

VERY EXPENSIVE

Washington Hilton & Towers

1919 Connecticut Ave. NW (at T St.), Washington, DC 20009. ☎ **800/HILTONS** or 202/483-3000. Fax 202/797-5755. 1,036 rms, 82 suites. A/C MINIBAR TV TEL. Weekdays $230–$270 double, Towers rms $265–$305 double. Weekends (and selected weekdays and holidays) $105 double, Towers rms $135. Extra person $20. Children of any age stay free. AE, CB, DC, DISC, JCB, MC, V. Parking $12. Metro: Dupont Circle.

This is a kind of superhotel/resort, occupying seven acres and offering every imaginable amenity. The Hilton caters to group business travelers and is used to coordinating meetings for thousands. Its vast conference facilities include the largest ballroom on the East Coast between New York and Orlando (accommodates nearly 4,000, theater-style). Besides conventions, the Hilton also hosts inaugural balls, debutante cotillions, and state banquets. Numerous smaller meeting rooms are available, and a business center is open during regular business hours.

Guest rooms are cheerful and attractively furnished; the artwork on the walls was commissioned by local artists. Hair dryers, irons and ironing boards, and cable TVs with pay-movie stations are in each room. From the fifth floor up, city-side, you'll have panoramic views of Washington (as well as a view of the Olympic-size pool). The 10th floor comprises a concierge level called the Towers. Ninth and 10th floors are the executive levels, where rooms have two telephones with data ports and a fax machine.

Dining/Entertainment: The handsome mahogany-paneled **1919 Grill** specializes in steaks, seafood, and pasta dinners. The **Capital Café,** for buffet meals and full restaurant fare, has a wall of windows overlooking the pool. A poolside eatery serves light fare under a striped tent top in season. The clubby **McClellan's** is a handsome brass-railed mahogany bar lounge. **Capital Court,** an elegant lobby lounge, features a nightly piano bar.

Services: Concierge, room service during restaurant hours, transportation/sightseeing desk, paper delivery of your choice upon request (*USA Today, Washington Post,* or *Wall Street Journal*) and express checkout.

Facilities: Extensive health club facilities; Olympic-size, nightlit, and heated outdoor pool; children's pool; three nightlit tennis courts; shuffleboard; lobby shops; comprehensive business center; shoeshine stand.

EXPENSIVE

Hotel Sofitel

1914 Connecticut Ave. NW, Washington, DC 20009. ☎ **800/424-2464** or 202/797-2000. Fax 202/462-0944. 145 rms, including 37 suites. A/C MINIBAR TV TEL. Weekdays $215, weekends $175–$195 for double. Suite rates from $255 weekdays and weekends. Extra person $20. Children under 12 stay free. No-smoking rms available. AE, CB, DC, JCB, MC, V. Valet parking $15. Metro: Dupont Circle.

The front desk greets you with "Bonjour," your room amenities include a bottle of Evian and Nina Ricci toiletries, the hotel's **Trocadero** restaurant serves French bistro food, and you get a fresh baguette at checkout: These are some of the accents that tell you the Sofitel is part of a French hotel chain. The 1906 building is a registered historic property situated on a hill a short walk from lively Dupont Circle; its elevated position allows for great city views from rooms on the upper level, Connecticut Avenue–side of this eight-floor hotel. You're also a short walk away from

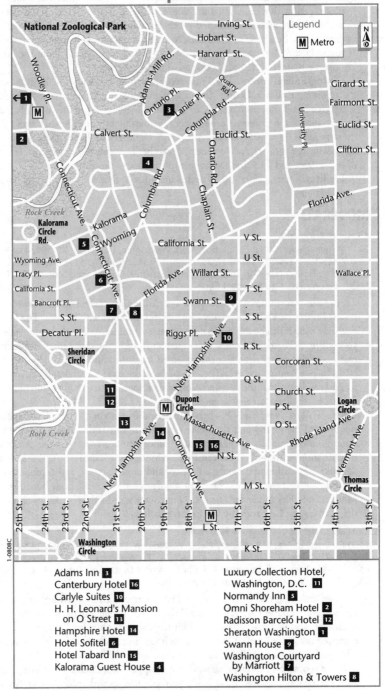

Adams-Morgan &
Dupont Circle Accommodations

National Zoological Park

Legend

M Metro

N

Irving St.
Hobart St.
Harvard St.

Woodley Pl.

Girard St.
Fairmont St.
Euclid St.
Clifton St.

Adams-Mill Rd.
Ontario Pl.
Lanier Pl.
Quarry Rd.
Columbia Rd.

Calvert St.
Euclid St.

Connecticut Ave.

Rock Creek

Kalorama
Circle
Rd.

Kalorama
Wyoming

California St.

V St.
U St.

Florida Ave.

University Pl.

Wyoming Ave.
Tracy Pl.
California St.
Bancroft Pl.
S St.
Decatur Pl.

Florida Ave.
Willard St.
Swann St.
S St.

Wallace Pl.

T St.

Sheridan
Circle

Riggs Pl.

R St.

Corcoran St.

New Hampshire Ave.

Rock Creek

Dupont
Circle

Church St.

Logan
Circle

Q St.

P St.
O St.

Rhode Island Ave.

Vermont Ave.

Massachusetts Ave.

N St.

Connecticut Ave.

M St.

Thomas
Circle

25th St.
24th St.
23rd St.
22nd St.
21st St.
20th St.
19th St.
18th St.
17th St.
16th St.
15th St.
14th St.
13th St.

New Hampshire Ave.

L St.

Washington
Circle

K St.

1-0808C

Adams Inn **3**
Canterbury Hotel **16**
Carlyle Suites **10**
H. H. Leonard's Mansion
  on O Street **13**
Hampshire Hotel **14**
Hotel Sofitel **6**
Hotel Tabard Inn **15**
Kalorama Guest House **4**

Luxury Collection Hotel,
  Washington, D.C. **11**
Normandy Inn **5**
Omni Shoreham Hotel **2**
Radisson Barceló Hotel **12**
Sheraton Washington **1**
Swann House **9**
Washington Courtyard
  by Marriott **7**
Washington Hilton & Towers **8**

trendy Adams-Morgan: cross Connecticut and walk up Columbia Rd. Rooms are spacious, each with a breakfast/study alcove, many with sitting areas, and decorated in muted shades of champagnes and peach. A multilingual staff sees to the needs of an international clientele of diplomats, foreign delegations, and corporate travelers. If you're looking for a romantic getaway at a reasonable rate, ask about the hotel's "Romantic Rendezvous" and "Weekend Superbe" packages.

Dining/Entertainment: The **Trocadero** is open for breakfast, lunch, and dinner; the adjoining **Pullman Lounge** features a pianist weeknights starting at 5:30pm.

Services: Full-service concierge, 24-hour room service, dry cleaning and laundry, major national and European newspapers available in lobby or delivered to your door upon request, nightly turndown, twice daily maid service, baby-sitting, secretarial services including faxing and copying, express checkout, courtesy limo available weekdays 7 to 9am and 5 to 7pm for city jaunts, but not to the airport.

Facilities: Fitness center with Nautilus and other equipment, newly renovated conference rooms.

MODERATE

✪ Normandy Inn

2118 Wyoming Ave. NW (at Connecticut Ave.), Washington, DC 20008. ☎ **800/424-3729** or 202/483-1350. Fax 202/387-8241. 75 rms. A/C TV TEL. Weekdays $118 double. Weekends $79 double. Extra person $10. Children under 18 stay free. One smoking floor. AE, DC, DISC, MC, V. Parking $10. Metro: Dupont Circle.

This gracious small hotel is a real gem. It's situated in a neighborhood of architecturally impressive embassies, many of which fill the hotel with visitors. The French Embassy happens to be the Normandy's largest customer. You may discover this for yourself on a Tuesday evening, when guests gather in the charming Tea Room to enjoy complimentary wine and cheese served from the antique oak sideboard. This is also where continental breakfast is available daily for $5.50, complimentary coffee and tea throughout the day, and cookies after 3pm. In nice weather, you can move outside to umbrella tables on a garden patio.

The six-floor Normandy has pretty twin and queen guest rooms with tapestry-upholstered mahogany and cherrywood furnishings in 18th-century styles, pretty floral-print bedspreads, and gilt-framed botanical prints gracing the walls. Amenities include mini-refrigerators, coffeemakers, remote-control cable TVs, access to the neighboring Washington Courtyard's pool and exercise room, and complimentary *Washington Post* (in lobby). The Normandy is an easy walk from both Adams-Morgan and Dupont Circle. The Irish company that owns the Normandy also owns the Washington Courtyard by Marriott (see below).

Washington Courtyard by Marriott

1900 Connecticut Ave. NW (at Leroy Place), Washington, DC 20009. ☎ **800/842-4211** or 202/332-9300. Fax 202/328-7039. 147 rms. A/C TV TEL. Weekdays $120–$170 double. Weekends $89–$120 double. Extra person $15. Children under 18 stay free. Two smoking floors. AE, DC, DISC, MC, V. Parking $10. Metro: Dupont Circle.

A major renovation in 1994 has given The Courtyard a European feel and a well-heeled look. Those are Waterford crystal chandeliers hanging in the lobby and in the restaurant, and you may hear an Irish lilt from time to time (an Irish management company owns the hotel). Guests tend to linger in the comfortable lounge off the lobby, where coffee is available all day and cookies each afternoon.

Guest rooms, off charming hallways, are equipped with cable TVs (offering HBO and Spectravision), coffeemakers, hair dryers, and phones with modem jacks. Accommodations on the 7th to 9th floors, facing the street, provide panoramic views.

Especially nice are the "executive king" rooms, which are a little larger, with marble baths, a refrigerator, terry robes, pants press, and fax machine.

In addition to an outdoor pool and sundeck, facilities include **Claret's,** serving American fare at breakfast and dinner. (Room service is available during restaurant hours.) **Bailey's,** a clubby bar, adjoins. *USA Today* is available gratis at the front desk. A small exercise room and a meeting room are on site. For a fee, guests can use the, well-equipped Washington Sports Club just across the street.

BED & BREAKFASTS

Adams Inn

1744 Lanier Place NW (between Calvert St. and Ontario Rd.), Washington, DC 20009. ☎ **800/ 578-6807** or 202/745-3600. Fax 202/319-7958. 25 rms (14 with bath). A/C. $55 double without bath, $70–$95 double with bath. Rates include continental breakfast. Extra person $10. Weekly rates available on some rms. AE, CB, DC, DISC, MC, V. Parking $7. Metro: Woodley Park–Zoo (7 blocks away).

Close to Adams-Morgan eateries, shops, and a Safeway supermarket, the homey Adams Inn occupies three turn-of-the-century brick town houses on a residential tree-lined street. Each has a cozy Victorian parlor with decorative fireplace and lace-curtained windows, and books, games, and magazines for guests.

The well-kept accommodations are furnished with flea market and auction finds; many are covered in flowery wallpaper, and some have bay windows or handsome oak paneling. There are no phones or TVs, but you do get a clock radio. Rooms that share baths have in-room sinks. Best deal for families or friends traveling together: two rooms that connect through a bath on the first floor of 1746 Lanier (easily sleeps four, for as little as $115). Rates include a continental breakfast of fresh-baked breads or muffins, and tea, coffee, and doughnuts available throughout the day.

A coin-op washers/dryers is in the basement, a pay phone is in the lobby, and the desk takes incoming messages. Other pluses: a TV lounge, and a refrigerator and microwave oven for communal guest use. Anne Owens is your genial host.

Note: No smoking and no pets, but children are welcome.

Kalorama Guest House

1854 Mintwood Place NW (between 19th St. and Columbia Rd.), Washington, DC 20009. ☎ **202/667-6369.** Fax 202/319-1262. 31 rms (12 with bath). A/C. $45–$75 double with shared bath, $60–$105 double with bath; $95 Two-room suite ($5 each additional occupant). Rates include continental breakfast. AE, CB, DC, DISC, MC, V. Limited parking $7. Metro: Woodley Park–Zoo or Dupont Circle.

This San Francisco–style B&B guest house was so successful, it expanded in a short time from a six-bedroom Victorian town house (at 1854 Mintwood) to include four houses on Mintwood Place and two on Cathedral Avenue NW in Woodley Park (☎ **202/328-0860;** fax 202/328-8730). The Mintwood Place location is near Metro stations, dozens of restaurants, nightspots, and shops. And the Cathedral Avenue houses, even closer to the Metro, offer proximity to Rock Creek Park and the National Zoo.

Common areas and homey guest rooms are furnished with finds from antique stores, flea markets, and auctions. Students, Europeans, and conferees are usually your fellow guests.

Over at 1854 is the cheerful breakfast room with plant-filled windows. The morning meal includes bagels, croissants, and English muffins. There's a garden behind the house with umbrella tables. At each location, you have access to laundry and ironing facilities, a refrigerator, a seldom-used TV, and a phone (local calls are free) for long-distance credit- or charge-card calls (incoming calls are answered around the clock, so people can leave messages for you). It's customary for the innkeepers to put out sherry, crackers, and cheese on Friday and Saturday afternoons. Magazines, games, and current newspapers are available. Some of the houses are nonsmoking.

3 Capitol Hill/The Mall

EXPENSIVE

Capitol Hill Suites

200 C St. SE, Washington, DC 20003. ☎ **800/424-9165** or 202/543-6000. Fax 202/547-2608. 152 suites. A/C TV TEL. Weekdays $159–$199 double. Weekends $99–$119 double. Extra person $20. Rates include continental breakfast. Children under 18 stay free. AE, CB, DC, DISC, MC, V. Valet parking $12. Metro: Capitol South.

This well-run all-suite property (on the House of Representatives side of the Capitol) comprises two contiguous converted apartment houses on a residential street close to the Library of Congress, the Capitol, and Mall attractions—hence its popularity with numerous congresspeople, whose photographs are displayed in the pleasant lobby. Spacious accommodations, ideal for families, offer full kitchens or kitchenettes and dining areas; you'll find complete living and dining rooms in these one-bedroom units. Decor is residential, with 18th-century mahogany reproduction furnishings and museum art prints adorning the walls. Cable TVs offer Showtime and pay-movie options. The hotel provides a helpful guide to local shops and services.

A food market and about 20 nearby restaurants (many of which deliver to the hotel) compensate for the lack of on-premises dining facilities. You get complimentary continental breakfast daily, but it's served up the street at Le Bon Cafe, just across from the Library of Congress. The *Washington Post* is delivered to your door Monday to Saturday. There are coin-op washers/dryers, and guests enjoy free use of extensive facilities at the nearby Washington Sports Club.

Phoenix Park Hotel

520 N. Capitol St. NW, Washington, DC 20001. ☎ **800/824-5419** or 202/638-6900. Fax 202/393-3236. 150 rms, including 9 suites. A/C MINIBAR TV TEL. Weekdays $189–$219 double. Weekends starting from $88 double. Suites $225–$750. Extra person $20. Children under 16 stay free. No-smoking rms available. AE, DC, DISC, MC, V. Parking $15. Metro: Union Station.

The Phoenix Park is one of a cluster of hotels situated across from Union Station and 2 blocks from the Capitol. What distinguishes the Phoenix Park is its popular and authentic Irish pub, **The Dubliner,** which attempts to set the tone for the entire property. Thanks to this well-worn, wood-paneled pub, which offers Irish fare, ale, and entertainment, the hotel attracts a number of Irish and Irish-American guests, stages a number of Ireland-related events in its ballroom, and attempts an Irish air of hospitality—which, frankly, fails outside the doors of the pub. The rooms are attractive but rather cramped with furnishings. Irish linens and toiletries are in the bath, along with coffeemakers and hair dryers. Cable TV with complimentary HBO and Showtime channels, room service until 11pm, voice mail, in-room computer connections, and some secretarial services (faxing, copying) are additional amenities. A small fitness center is on-site.

MODERATE

Channel Inn

650 Water St. SW (at 7th St. and Maine Ave.), Washington, DC 20024. ☎ **800/368-5668** or 202/554-2400. Fax 202/863-1164. 100 rms. A/C TV TEL. Weekdays $110–$125 double. Weekends $85–$95 double. Extra person $10. Children under 12 stay free. Call toll-free number for best rates. AE, CB, DC, DISC, JCB, MC, V. Free parking. Metro: Waterfront.

Family-Friendly Hotels

Channel Inn *(see p. 66)* This hotel has a swimming pool, and adults will love the rooms that overlook the boat-filled Washington Channel.

The Premier Hotel, Howard Johnson's *(see p. 89)* Close to the Kennedy Center, this flagship HoJo has a rooftop pool and Ping-Pong area, coin-op washers and dryers, and family-friendly diner. Rooms have small refrigerators and TVs equipped with Nintendo games.

Omni Shoreham *(see p. 93)* Adjacent to Rock Creek Park, close to the zoo, and equipped with two outdoor pools—a large one for swimming laps and a kiddie pool—the Shoreham offers an extensive program of children's activities. Three lighted tennis courts are an additional attraction.

One Washington Circle *(see p. 88)* Great location in a safe neighborhood, bright and airy suites with full kitchens and sofabeds, an outdoor pool, a coin-op washer and dryer, a good restaurant on the premises—and a hospital across the street for emergencies—all for a great price, which, if more than $135, includes continental breakfast.

Washington Hilton & Towers *(see p. 62)* A large, heated outdoor pool, a wading pool, three tennis courts, shuffleboard, and bike rental—what more do you need?

Washington's only pierfront hotel, the Channel Inn caters largely to government employees, but it's also a great choice for leisure travelers, close to a Metro stop, and within walking distance of the Mall. Right across the street is one of Washington's best theaters, Arena Stage (see chapter 10 for details); it would be criminal for you to stay at this hotel without at least finding out what's playing at Arena.

Most rooms offer nice views of the boat-filled Washington Channel. They are decorated with 18th-century–style mahogany furnishings and floral chintz bedspreads and drapes. Some have high cathedral ceilings; all have balconies.

Pier 7, a continental/seafood restaurant with marina views, serves moderately priced fare. A glass-walled coffee shop offers cafeteria-style breakfasts. The **Engine Room** lounge offers a happy hour buffet of free hors d'oeuvres Monday through Friday and live jazz Wednesday through Sunday evenings.

Room service is available during restaurant hours. Guests enjoy complimentary access to the fully equipped Waterside Fitness Club and outdoor pool/sundeck; a golf course and indoor/outdoor tennis courts are within walking distance; and the waterfront is an ideal place for jogging.

4 Downtown, East of 16th Street NW

VERY EXPENSIVE

○ Grand Hyatt Washington

1000 H St. NW, Washington, DC 20001. ☎ **800/233-1234** or 202/582-1234. Fax 202/637-4781. 900 rms, including 60 suites. A/C MINIBAR TV TEL. Weekdays $290 double. Weekends $119–$139 double. Extra person $25. Children under 18 stay free. No-smoking floors available. AE, CB, DC, DISC, MC, V. Parking $12. Metro: Metro Center.

Hotel as circus, that's the Grand Hyatt. There's always something going on in the vast lobby—whose atrium is 12 stories high, enclosed by a glass, mansard-style roof. Between the waterfalls, a baby grand piano floating on its own island in the 7,000-square-foot "lagoon," catwalks, 22-foot-high trees, and an array of bars and restaurants on the periphery, you'll stay permanently entertained. Should you get bored, head to the nearby nightspots and restaurants, or hop on the Metro, to which the Hyatt has direct access. The hotel is across from the Convention Center, between Capitol Hill and the White House.

By contrast to its public areas, guest rooms seem rather tame, which might be a good thing. Each room has a 25-inch cable TV with free HBO service, hair dryers, irons, and ironing boards. One of the best things about the Grand Hyatt is the potpourri of special plans and packages the hotel offers, especially for business travelers. For example, an extra $15 qualifies you for the business plan, which includes an 8th- or 9th-floor room equipped with a large desk, fax machine, computer hookup, and coffeemaker; access to printers and other office supplies on the floor; and complimentary continental breakfast. Tourists should ask about seasonal deals, like the annual winter holiday package.

Dining/Entertainment: The Hyatt offers three restaurants: **The Zephyr Deli,** the informal **Grand Cafe,** and the smaller **Via Pacifica,** which features American, Italian, and Asian cuisine; and three bars, the lobby **Via's Bar,** the large **Grand Slam** sports bar, and **Butler's–The Cigar Bar.**

Services: Concierge, room service (6am to 1am Monday through Thursday, 6am to 2am Friday and Saturday), dry cleaning and laundry service, twice daily maid service, express checkout, and courtesy car available on a first come, first served basis that takes guests within a 2-mile or 10-minute radius of the hotel.

Facilities: Two-story health club with Jacuzzi, lap pool, exercise room, steam and sauna room, and aerobics program; business services that include two large ballrooms, a 102-seat theater, and 40,000 square feet of meeting space; an American Express Travel Center for traveler's checks and ticketing; and direct underground access to the Metro.

✪ Willard Inter-Continental

1401 Pennsylvania Ave. NW, Washington, DC 20004. ☎ **800/327-0200** or 202/628-9100. Fax 202/637-7326. 342 rms, including 37 suites. A/C MINIBAR TV TEL. Weekdays $295–$395 double. Weekends $199 double. Extra person $30. Children under 18 stay free. AE, DC, DISC, JCB, MC, V. Parking $20. Metro: Metro Center.

Billed as the "crown jewel of Pennsylvania Avenue," the Willard is the crown jewel of all Washington hotels. Its designation as a National Landmark in 1974 and magnificent restoration in the 1980s helped to revitalize Pennsylvania Avenue and this part of town.

The historic 1901 beaux-arts–style hotel occupies the site of the City Hotel, built in 1815 (renamed the Willard when that family bought it), and plays the same role it did in the 1860s, when Nathaniel Hawthorne said about it, "You exchange nods with governors of sovereign States; you elbow illustrious men, and tread on the toes of generals. . . ." Lincoln spent the eve of his inaugural here, and it was at the Willard that Julia Ward Howe penned the words to the "Battle Hymn of the Republic."

The main lobby today is again an awesome entranceway, with massive marble columns ascending to a lofty ceiling decorated with 48 state seals and hung with huge globe chandeliers. Alaska and Hawaii seals are located in Peacock Alley, a plush potted-palmed promenade. Artisans were able to incorporate some of the Willard's original plasterwork and scagliola marble into the reborn hotel, along with marble mosaic tile floors, carpeting, and chandeliers.

Rooms are sumptuous, spacious, and furnished in Edwardian and Federal-period reproductions. Because of the large number of foreign visitors, many of whom still smoke, only four of the Willard's 12 floors are nonsmoking. Because of the many heads of state (more than 100 in the last decade) who bunk here, the hotel offers the 6th floor as "Secret Service–cleared." Eight rooms are specially outfitted to accommodate guests with disabilities. The "02" suites on each floor allow a partial look at the White House. But perhaps the best rooms are the ones perched in the curve of the 12th floor's southeast corner—the ones with the round "bull's eye" windows that capture glimpses of the Capitol. Phones have dual lines with voice mail, and cable TVs (with pay-movie channels and video message, data-port plugs, retrieval/checkout) are concealed in armoires. In the marble baths are a hair dryer, scale, phone, and TV speaker.

Dining/Entertainment: The **Willard Room** (the term *power lunch* originated here) is simply stunning (see chapter 6 for a review). The circular **Round Robin Bar** is where Henry Clay mixed the first mint julep in Washington. The **Café Espresso** offers croissant sandwiches, pastas, pastries, and vintage wines by the glass, along with more substantial grilled entrées; full afternoon teas are served here weekday afternoons and in the Willard Room weekends. And the **Nest Lounge** offers live jazz on weekends.

Services: Twice-daily maid service, nightly bed turndown, 24-hour room service, concierge, currency exchange, airline/train ticketing, express checkout, choice of newspaper delivery, fax and cellular phone rental.

Facilities: Full business center, complete fitness center, VCRs in suites, upscale boutiques.

EXPENSIVE

✪ Henley Park

926 Massachusetts Ave. NW (at 10th St.), Washington, DC 20001. ☎ **800/222-8474** or 202/638-5200. Fax 202/638-6740. 78 rms, 18 suites. A/C MINIBAR TV TEL. Weekdays $145–$225 double. Summer and weekends $98 double (including parking and continental breakfast). Junior suite $315, one-bedroom suite $395–$475, Ambassador Suite $725 weekdays and weekends. Senior discounts. Extra person $20. Children under 14 stay free. No-smoking rms available. AE, CB, DC, DISC, MC, V. Parking $16. Metro: Metro Center, Gallery Place, or Mt. Vernon Square.

The Henley Park caters to a high-end corporate clientele who are not put off by its location: It's off by itself in an iffy part of town, though within walking distance of the Convention Center, restaurants, and nightlife. This is an intimate, English-style hotel housed in a converted 1918 Tudor-style apartment house with 119 gargoyles on its facade. The lobby, with its exquisite Tudor ceiling, archways, and leaded windows, is particularly evocative of the period. Luxurious rooms make this a good choice for upscale romantic weekends. They are decorated in the English country house mode, with Hepplewhite-, Chippendale-, and Queen Anne–style furnishings, including lovely period beds. Baths offer phones, cosmetic mirrors, and luxury toiletries, and in-room amenities include terry-cloth robes, cable TVs with pay-movie options, and, in some rooms, fax machines.

Dining/Entertainment: The hotel's posh restaurant, **Coeur de Lion,** serves classic continental cuisine; the menu highlights seafood, and the wine list is excellent. Adjoining the Coeur de Lion, **Marley's,** a delightful cocktail lounge, is the setting for piano bar entertainment (and complimentary hors d'oeuvres) weeknights, live jazz Monday through Saturday, and dancing Friday through Saturday. Afternoon tea is served daily in the octagonal **Wilkes Room,** a charming parlor with a working fireplace.

Services: 24-hour concierge and room service, *Washington Post* delivery each weekday morning, complimentary shoeshine, nightly bed turndown with gourmet chocolate, complimentary weekday 7:30 to 9:30am limo service to downtown and Capitol Hill locations.

Facilities: Access to a fitness room in the Morrison-Clark Inn (see listing below) across the street.

Hotel Washington

15th St. and Pennsylvania Ave. NW, Washington, DC 20004. ☎ **800/424-9540** or 202/638-5900. Fax 202/638-1594. 350 rms, including 16 suites. A/C MINIBAR TV TEL. Weekdays $170–$235 double, $430–$545 suite. Subject to availability, certain bargain rates apply: Weekends $135 single or double; $165 corporate rate, weekdays, double; family plan of $99 for family of 4, with children under 14, including breakfast. Extra person $18. Children under 14 stay free. No-smoking floors available. AE, DC, MC, V. Parking $20. Metro: Metro Center.

Built in 1918, this hotel is the oldest continuously operating hotel in Washington. A major renovation in 1980 restored the hotel to play up the historic angle. The two-story lobby's wooden moldings, crystal chandeliers, and marble floors are reconstructed originals. Guest room decor is traditional, with lots of mahogany furnishings and historically suggestive print fabrics and wall coverings.

The main reasons people choose the Hotel Washington are for its location and views. From its corner perch at Pennsylvania Avenue and 15th Street, the 12-story hotel surveys the avenue, monuments, Capitol, and the White House. No other hotel in town can top the panoramic spectacle that you get from the rooftop Sky Terrace where, late April through October, you can have drinks and light fare. Guest rooms on the Pennsylvania Avenue side have great views, as do the first-floor meeting rooms. Clientele are mostly corporate, often international. The hotel's main restaurant, **The Two Continents,** is on the lobby level and serves American cuisine. The **Corner Bar** is a feature of the lobby, where complimentary coffee is provided daily and free hors d'oeuvres, nuts, and fruit are put out weekdays after 3:30pm during the winter.

Services: Room service (6:30am to 11pm), dry cleaning and laundry, express checkout, valet parking.

Facilities: Business center and meeting rooms, fitness center, sauna, tour desk (for Old Town Trolley), gift shop.

J. W. Marriott

1331 Pennsylvania Ave. NW (at E St.), Washington, DC 20004. ☎ **800/228-9290** or 202/393-2000. Fax 202/626-6991. 738 rms, 34 suites. A/C TV TEL. Weekdays $214 double, $224 concierge level, $234 for concierge-level rm with city view. Weekends $109–$234 (concierge level) double with full breakfast. Extra person free. No-smoking rms and floors available. AE, DC, DISC, JCB, MC, V. Parking $16. Metro: Metro Center.

This flagship Marriott property, which opened in 1984, is adjacent to the National Theater, 1 block from the Warner Theater and 2 blocks from the White House. The best rooms on the 7th, 12th, 14th, and 15th floors overlook Pennsylvania Avenue and the monuments (floors 14 and 15 are concierge levels). Conventioneers make up a lot of the clientele; tourists (including families) and businesspeople traveling on their own, will enjoy the extensive facilities and location.

Public areas bustle with groups checking in and locals cutting through to the shops that adjoin the hotel. Decor of the lobby area combines futuristic architecture with lush plantings. Residential-style rooms are furnished with desks and armoires, many of them cherrywood pieces in traditional styles. You'll find an iron and full-sized ironing board in your room, as well as a cable TV that offers HBO and On-Command videos. The hotel's best value is $89 for a double, part of its "home for the holidays" promotion, effective during the 2 weeks prior to Christmas and into early January. Also available is a "two for breakfast" package: November 21 through December, and during the period July 8 through September 2, you pay $109 for a double, including full breakfast (add $10 for city-view room, $40 for concierge level).

Dining/Entertainment: The hotel's main dining room is **Celadon,** a Chinoiserie setting for American/continental cuisine. **Allie's American Grille** overlooks

Pennsylvania Avenue and serves American fare; "early-bird" dinners here are priced under $15. The skylit **Garden Terrace** offers piano music and nightly jazz.

Services: Concierge and 24-hour room service, laundry and dry cleaning, delivery of *USA Today,* nightly turndown, twice daily maid service, baby-sitting, and express checkout.

Facilities: A connecting mall with 80 shops and restaurants, complete health club (with indoor swimming pool and hydrotherapy pool), video games, full business center, gift shop.

Renaissance Washington, D.C., Hotel

999 9th St. NW (at K St.), Washington, DC 20001. ☎ **800/228-9898** or 202/898-9000. Fax 202/289-0947. 779 rms, 21 suites. A/C MINIBAR TV TEL. Weekdays $209–$229 double; Club Level $249 double; $295–$2,000 suite. Weekends $109 double. Extra person $25. Children under 18 stay free. AE, CB, DC, DISC, MC, V. Parking $15. Metro: Gallery Place.

Directly across the street from the D.C. Convention Center and 1 block away from the MCI Arena, this hotel caters primarily to conventioneers and business travelers, while it also delivers a lot of luxury and convenience to tourists.

A renovation completed in 1997 transformed guest rooms from contemporary to traditional decor, with oak furnishings and earth tones. Rooms offer remote-control TVs (with cable stations, pay-movie options, and video message retrieval/checkout) and phones with voice mail and computer jacks. The hotel has 16 rooms for guests with disabilities, including two with roll-in showers. Thirteen rooms are equipped with computer terminals offering unlimited access to the Internet; you pay an extra $20 above the regular room rate. An entire 15-story tower with 166 rooms constitutes the Renaissance Club, which has concierge-level amenities.

Dining/Entertainment: Mahogany-paneled and crystal-chandeliered, **The Tavern** features American regional cuisine; a bar adjoins. Less formal is the cheerful **Café Florentine,** off the lobby, offering reasonably priced buffets and à la carte meals with a Mediterranean flair. The **Caracalla** prepares classic Italian cuisine. And the **Plaza Gourmet** offers take-out sandwiches, salads, and fresh-baked pastries.

Services: 24-hour room service and concierge; dry cleaning and laundry service; delivery of *USA Today;* express checkout; valet parking.

Facilities: Gift shop; full business center including 72,000 square feet of meeting space; 10,000-square-foot health club ($7 fee to use), including pool, whirlpool, sauna, extensive exercise equipment, and aerobics floor.

MODERATE

Holiday Inn Downtown

1155 14th St. NW (at Massachusetts Ave.), Washington, DC 20005. ☎ **800/HOLIDAY** or 202/737-1200. Fax 202/783-5733. 208 rms. A/C TV TEL. Weekdays $130–$159 double. Weekends $100–$110. Extra person $15. Children under 18 stay free. AE, CB, DC, DISC, JCB, MC, V. Valet parking $10. Metro: McPherson Square.

Just 5 blocks from the White House, this 14-story Holiday Inn is a good family choice in the moderately priced category. There's a fairly large rooftop swimming pool and sundeck offering nice city views. A renovation in 1997 has spruced up guest rooms, the four meeting rooms, and the lobby. Rooms are equipped with cable TVs offering HBO plus On-Command Video, an electronic key system, coffeemakers, and phones that feature call waiting and modem jacks. The best room is the "junior suite"—not really a suite, but the corner room on each of the top 10 floors. They're much larger and airier than other rooms and include two double beds and sofa beds; they're worth the extra $20.

The hotel's restaurant/lounge serves buffet breakfasts and dinners. Other amenities include coin-op washers/dryers and a special parking lot for oversize vehicles.

At this writing, all Holiday Inns are featuring a "Great Rates" promotion, offering discounts of 10% to 50%, depending on the season and space availability. Be sure to inquire when you call the toll-free number given above.

INEXPENSIVE

✪ Days Inn Premier

1201 K St. NW, Washington, DC 20005. ☎ **800/562-3350,** 800/325-2525 or 202/842-1020. Fax 202/289-0336. 219 rms. A/C TV TEL. Weekdays $89–$109 double. Weekends $58–$89 double. Extra person $10. Children under 18 stay free. AE, CB, DC, DISC, MC, V. Parking $12. Metro: McPherson Square, Metro Center.

Proximity to the Convention Center makes this eight-floor Days Inn a perfect choice for visitors attending events there. A small rooftop pool and a video-game arcade will also appeal to families with young children. Newly renovated rooms are cheerfully decorated and equipped with remote-control satellite TVs (with free and pay-movie channels) in armoires, hair dryers, and coffeemakers. On the top two "executive floors," guests get king-size beds, mini-refrigerators, microwaves, views of the Capitol (corner room 919 is probably best), and access to the Executive Club, with its computer, TV, continental breakfast, and kitchen. Rooms are split about 50–50 between smoking and nonsmoking. Four rooms are specially equipped for wheelchair accessibility.

The lobby is crowded with conventioneers checking in all year long, along with families during the summer. The facility has 12,000 square feet of meeting space, a full-service restaurant, and adjoining lounge. Additional amenities include room service, a small fitness center, and a coin-operated laundry; a car-rental agency is just across the street. City tours depart from the lobby. Inquire about special packages when you reserve. Lower "Super Saver" rates (about $59) are sometimes available if you reserve in advance (the earlier the better) via the toll-free number, ☎ **800/ 325-2525**—it's worth a try.

Red Roof Inn

500 H St. NW, Washington, DC 20001. ☎ **800/THE-ROOF** or 202/289-5959. Fax 202/ 682-9152. 197 rms. A/C TV TEL. Weekdays $97.99–$102 double. Weekends $70–$102 double. Children under 18 stay free. No-smoking rms available. AE, CB, DC, DISC, MC, V. Parking $8.50. Metro: Gallery Place.

Reserve early. This popular hotel, with endearingly considerate staff, sits in the heart of Chinatown, within walking distance of many attractions, including two (off the Mall) Smithsonian museums; it's also just 3 blocks from the Convention Center. Red Roof Inns purchased the 10-story property (which used to be a Comfort Inn) in 1996 and renovated the rooms, which are attractively decorated and equipped with cable TVs offering free Showtime and pay-movie options plus Nintendo. There's a reasonably priced cafe open 6:30am to 2pm, and 5:30 to 10pm. On-premises facilities include coin-op washers/dryers and a sunny 10th-floor exercise room with sauna. *USA Today* newspapers are free at the front desk.

BED & BREAKFAST

✪ Morrison-Clark Inn

Massachusetts Ave. at 11th St. NW, Washington, DC 20001. ☎ **800/332-7898** or 202/898- 1200. Fax 202/289-8576. 40 rms (all with bath), 14 suites. A/C MINIBAR TV TEL. Weekdays $155–$185 double. Weekends $99–$129 double. Suites $129–$149 weekdays and weekends. Rates include continental breakfast. Extra person $20. Children under 12 stay free. AE, CB, DC, DISC, MC, V. Parking $15. Metro: Metro Center or Mt. Vernon Square.

This magnificent inn, occupying twin 1865 Victorian brick town houses—with a newer wing in converted stables across an interior courtyard—is on the National Register of Historic Places. Guests enter via a turn-of-the-century parlor, with velvet-lace–upholstered Victorian furnishings and lace-curtained bay windows. The adjoining Club Room is where you eat a delicious continental breakfast; the room is furnished with an original white marble fireplace and 13-foot windows flanking gilded mirrors. In warm weather, you can breakfast in the lovely, two-level, brick-paved courtyard, enclosed by the inn and neighboring buildings.

High-ceilinged guest rooms are individually decorated with original artworks, sumptuous fabrics, and antique or reproduction 19th-century furnishings. Most popular—and the grandest—are the Victorian-styled rooms. Four Victorians have private porches; many other rooms have plant-filled balconies. All have cable TVs, two phones (bed and bath) equipped with computer jacks, and hair dryers.

Room service is available from the inn's highly acclaimed restaurant (see chapter 6 for a review). Other amenities include twice-daily maid service with Belgian chocolates at bed turndown, complimentary *Washington Post,* business services, and fresh flowers in every room. A fitness center is on the premises. Look for ads in *The New York Times* to obtain the best rate of $79.

5 Downtown, 16th Street NW & West

VERY EXPENSIVE

✪ The Carlton

923 16th St. NW, Washington, DC 20006. ☎ **800/325-3535** or 202/638-2626. Fax 202/638-4231. 180 rms, 12 suites. A/C MINIBAR TV TEL. Weekdays $285–$325 double, $450–$2,500 suite. Weekends $265–$285 double. Extra person $15. Children under 10 stay free. AE, CB, DC, DISC, JCB, MC, V. Parking $22. No-smoking rms available. Metro: Farragut West or McPherson Square.

Ah, luxury! Palladian windows dressed in rich damask draperies, elaborately gilded ceilings, Louis XVI chandeliers, plush green oversized sofas, and cozy arrangements of comfortable chairs: This is the lobby of The Carlton, designed to resemble a Milan palazzo. Guest rooms are more quietly opulent and decorated in tastefully coordinated colors (for instance, beigey grays and royal blues), with desks set in alcoves, a mirror-covered armoire, and creamy silk moiré wallcoverings. Amenities in each room include dual telephone lines, voice mail and modem capabilities, personal safes, terry robes, and hair dryers. Guests over the years have included everyone from Queen Elizabeth to the Rolling Stones.

Dining/Entertainment: The Carlton's **Lespinasse** is causing quite a stir in the capital (see chapter 6 for a review). The **Library Lounge** might be the best hotel bar in Washington; it has a working fireplace and paneled walls lined with bookcases. High tea is offered daily in the posh lobby.

Services: 24-hour concierge and room service, pressing service, complimentary transportation each morning within a 5-mile radius, complimentary coffee or tea with wake-up call, complimentary newspaper and shoe shine, complimentary bottled water with turndown service, no charge for credit card calls and local faxes.

Facilities: State-of-the-art fitness room and access to a complete health club (at the University Club), 10,000 square feet of meeting space, ballroom.

✪ Hay-Adams

16th and H sts. NW, Washington, DC 20006. ☎ **800/424-5054** or 202/638-6600. Fax 202/638-3803. 117 rms, 19 suites. A/C MINIBAR TV TEL. Weekdays $265–$450 double. Weekends $170–$310 per rm. Extra person $30. Children under 12 stay free. AE, CB, DC, JCB, MC, V. Parking (valet only) $20. Metro: Farragut West or McPherson Square.

Georgetown & Downtown Accommodations

ANA Hotel **2**
The Capital Hilton **23**
Capitol Hill Suites **36**
The Carlton **24**
Channel Inn **37**
Days Inn Premier **29**
Embassy Inn **20**
Four Seasons **7**
George Washington
  University Inn **10**
The Georgetown Dutch Inn **5**
Georgetown Suites **6**
Grand Hyatt **33**
Hay-Adams **25**
Henley Park **31**
Holiday Inn Downtown **22**
Hotel Lombardy **14**
Hotel Washington **26**
J.W. Marriott **27**
The Jefferson **18**
Latham Hotel **4**
Lincoln Suites Downtown **16**
Morrison-Clark Inn **30**
One Washington Circle Hotel **13**
Park Hyatt **3**
Phoenix Park Hotel **35**
The Premier, Howard
  Johnson's **8**
Red Roof Inn **34**
Renaissance Mayflower **17**
Renaissance Washington, D.C. **32**
Savoy Suites **1**
St. James Hotel **11**
State Plaza Hotel **15**
The Watergate **9**
Willard Inter-Continental **28**
Wyndham Bristol **12**
Windsor Inn **19**

Reserve a room on the fifth through eighth floor, H Street side of the hotel, pull back the curtains from the windows, and enjoy your full frontal view of the White House—with the Washington Monument sticking up high behind it. One block from the President's abode, the Hay-Adams offers the best vantage point in town. In between you and the White House is Lafayette Square, another landmark.

The Hay-Adams is one in the triumvirate of exclusive hotels built by Harry Wardman in the 1920s (the Jefferson and the Carlton are the other two). Its architecture evokes an Italian Renaissance style, whose interior features walnut wainscoting, arched alcoves, and intricate Tudor and Elizabethan ceiling motifs. Among the early guests were Amelia Earhart, Sinclair Lewis, Ethel Barrymore, and Charles Lindbergh. Today's guests tend to be socialites, foreign dignitaries, and powerful business leaders (but the staff won't divulge names).

Rooms are individually furnished with antiques and superior appointments. A typical accommodation might feature 18th-century–style furnishings, silk-covered walls hung with botanical prints and fine art, a gorgeous molded plaster ceiling, and French silk floral-print bedspreads, upholstery, and curtains. Many rooms have ornamental fireplaces. Amenities include fine toiletries, hair dryers, cosmetic mirrors, and phones in the bathrooms; terry-cloth robes; and cable TVs equipped with HBO.

Dining/Entertainment: The sunny **Lafayette Restaurant** (overlooking the White House) is an exquisite dining room; it serves contemporary American/continental fare at all meals, plus afternoon tea. The adjoining lounge features nightly piano-bar entertainment. **Off the Record** is the hotel's newly opened wine and champagne bar.

Services: 24-hour room and concierge service, nightly bed turndown, complimentary shoe shine.

Facilities: Guest access to a local health club, secretarial and business services, in-room fax on request, meeting rooms.

✪ The Jefferson

1200 16th St. NW (at M St.), Washington, DC 20036. ☎ **800/368-5966** or 202/347-2200. Fax 202/223-9039. 70 rms, 30 suites. A/C MINIBAR TV TEL. Weekdays $250–$270 double, $350–$1,000 suite. Weekends $160 double, $225–$275 suite. Extra person $25. Children under 12 stay free. AE, CB, DC, JCB, MC, V. Parking $22. Metro: Farragut North.

Opened in 1923 just 4 blocks from the White House, The Jefferson is one of the city's three most exclusive venues (along with the Hay-Adams and the Carlton), proffering discreet hospitality to political personages, royalty, literati, and other notables. With a very high staff-to-guest ratio, The Jefferson puts utmost emphasis on service; if you like, a butler will unpack your luggage and press clothes wrinkled in transit.

Set foot in the lobby, and you won't want to leave: An inviting sitting room with fireplace at the rear of an extended vestibule draws you past green-velvet loveseats placed back-to-back down the middle, and enclosed terraces opening off each side. A fine art collection, including original documents signed by Thomas Jefferson, graces the public area as well as the guest rooms. You'll hear a Thomas Jefferson–style grandfather clock chime the hour.

Each antique-filled guest room evokes a European feel. Yours might have a four-poster bed with plump eyelet-trimmed comforter and pillow shams (many are topped with canopies), or a cherrywood bookstand from the Napoleonic period filled with rare books. In-room amenities include two-line speaker phones with hold buttons, fax machines (you get your own fax number when you check in), cable TVs with VCRs, CD players, and, in the baths, terry robes, hair dryers, and phones.

Dining/Entertainment: Off the lobby is **The Restaurant at the Jefferson,** one of the city's premier dining rooms (see chapter 6 for a review) and a cozy bar/lounge. In the paneled lounge, whose walls are hung with framed original Thomas Jefferson letters and documents, you can sink into a red leather chair and enjoy a marvelous high tea daily from 3 to 5pm, or cocktails anytime—the bar stocks a robust selection of single-malt scotches and a fine choice of Davidoff cigars.

Services: 24-hour butler service, overnight shoe shine, nightly bed turndown with Godiva chocolate, morning delivery of *Washington Post,* 24-hour room and multilingual concierge service, video and CD rentals, express checkout.

Facilities: Business/secretarial services and meeting rooms; for a fee, guests have access to full health club facilities (including Olympic-size pool) at the University Club across the street.

✪ Renaissance Mayflower

1127 Connecticut Ave. NW (between L and M sts.), Washington, DC 20036. ☎ **800/ HOTELS-1** or 202/347-3000. Fax 202/776-9182. 581 rms. 78 suites. A/C MINIBAR TV TEL. Weekdays $275–$335 double. Weekends $139–$199 double. Extra person $25. Children under 18 stay free. AE, CB, DC, DISC, JCB, MC, V. Parking $12. Metro: Farragut North.

Superbly located in the heart of downtown, the Mayflower is the hotel of choice for guests as varied as Israeli Prime Minister Benjamin Netanyahu and pop group Hootie and the Blowfish. The lobby, which extends an entire block from Connecticut Avenue back to 17th Street, is always active, since Washingtonians tend to use it as a shortcut in their travels.

The hotel is quite historic. Among other things, the Mayflower was the site of Calvin Coolidge's inaugural ball in 1925, the year it opened. (Coolidge didn't actually attend—he was grieving over the death of his son from blood poisoning.) President-elect FDR and family lived in rooms 776 and 781 while waiting to move into the White House—this is where FDR penned the words, "The only thing we have to fear is fear itself." A major restoration in the 1980s uncovered large skylights and renewed the lobby's pink marble bas-relief frieze and spectacular promenade.

Graciously appointed guest rooms feature high ceilings, cream moiré wall coverings, and mahogany reproduction furnishings (Queen Anne, Sheraton, Chippendale, Hepplewhite). Handsome armoires hold 25-inch remote-control TVs. Amenities include ironing board and iron, three phones, a terry robe, hair dryer, and a small color TV in the bathroom. Inquire about "summer value rates."

Dining/Entertainment: Washington lawyers and lobbyists gather for power breakfasts in the **Café Promenade.** Under a beautiful domed skylight, the restaurant is adorned with Edward Laning's murals, crystal chandeliers, marble columns, and lovely flower arrangements. A full English tea is served here afternoons Monday to Saturday.

The clubby, mahogany-paneled **Town and Country** is the setting for light buffet lunches and complimentary cocktail-hour hors d'oeuvres. Bartender Sambonn Lek has quite a following and is famous for his magic tricks and personality. The **Lobby Court,** a Starbucks espresso bar just opposite the front desk, features coffee and fresh-baked pastries each morning, piano bar and cocktails later in the day.

Services: Coffee/tea/hot chocolate and *USA Today* with wake-up call, 24-hour room service, twice-daily maid service, complimentary overnight shoeshine, concierge, courtesy car takes you within 3-mile radius, express checkout, valet parking.

Facilities: Business center, full on-premises fitness center, florist, gift shop, Cartier jeweler.

EXPENSIVE

The Capital Hilton

16th St. NW, between K and L sts. Washington, DC 20036. ☎ **800/HILTONS** or 202/ 393-1000. Fax 202/639-5784. 517 rms, 32 suites. A/C MINIBAR TV TEL. Weekdays $195–$295 double, Tower rms $225–$325. Weekends (including continental breakfast) $133 per rm, Tower rms $155. Extra person $25; children of any age stay free. AE, CB, DC, DISC, JCB, MC, V. Parking $22. Metro: Farragut West, Farragut North, or McPherson Square.

This longtime Washington residence has hosted every American president since FDR, and the annual Gridiron Club Dinner and political roast takes place in its ballroom. The Hilton's central location (2 blocks from the White House) makes it convenient for tourists, while business travelers will appreciate the Tower's concierge floors (10 to 14) and extensive facilities.

During a 5-year, $55-million renovation in the late 1980s, the public areas were upgraded (note the gorgeous cherry paneling in the lobby). And in 1993, the rooms were redecorated in Federal-period motif with Queen Anne– and Chippendale-style furnishings. Each room has three phones equipped with call waiting and a cable TV featuring pay-movie stations. In the bath, you'll find a small TV and hair dryer. Ask about special rates for AAA members, seniors, military, and families.

Dining/Entertainment: Steak and seafood highlight the menu at **Fran O'Brien's Steakhouse,** an upscale sports-themed restaurant named for its owner, a former Redskin. American regional fare is served at the sunny, gardenlike **Twigs** and the more elegant **Twigs Grill,** which adjoins. Weekdays from 5 to 7pm, complimentary hors d'oeuvres are served in **The Bar,** a plush lobby lounge that is later the setting for piano bar entertainment.

Services: 24-hour room service, concierge (7am to 11pm), full business center including 25,000 square feet of conference rooms, morning delivery of *USA Today*, tour and ticket desk.

Facilities: Unisex hairdresser, gift shop, facial salon, shoe-shine stand, airline desks (American, Continental, Northwest), fitness center (in the process of being expanded), ATM with foreign-currency capabilities.

MODERATE

Lincoln Suites Downtown

1823 L St. NW, Washington, DC 20036. ☎ **800/424-2970** or 202/223-4320. Fax 202/223-8546. 99 suites. A/C TV TEL. Weekdays $129–$149 suite for 1 person, extra person $10. Weekends $79–$109 suite for 2, extra person $15. Children under 16 stay free. AE, CB, DC, DISC, MC, V. Parking $9 (in adjoining garage). Metro: Farragut North or Farragut West.

Lots of long-term guests stay at this all-suite, 10-story hotel in the heart of downtown, just 5 blocks from the White House. Its large, comfortable suites were completely refurbished in 1995 during a multimillion-dollar renovation. About 36 suites offer full kitchens; others have refrigerators, wet bars, coffeemakers, and microwaves. Rooms are fairly spacious, well-kept, and attractive, and equipped with such amenities as cable TVs with free HBO, Water Pik shower massagers, hair dryers, and irons and ironing boards. The property also has a coin-op washer and dryer and a small meeting room.

Samantha's, next door (and leased from the hotel), offers reasonably priced American fare. The hotel's own **Beatrice** is a grotto-like Italian restaurant open for all meals. In the lobby are complimentary copies of the *Washington Post* each morning, complimentary milk and homemade cookies each evening, and complimentary continental breakfast Saturday and Sunday mornings; guests enjoy free use of the well-equipped Bally's Holiday Spa nearby.

BED & BREAKFASTS

Embassy Inn

1627 16th St. NW (between Q and R sts.), Washington, DC 20009. ☎ **800/423-9111** or 202/234-7800. Fax 202/234-3309. 38 rms (all with bath). A/C TV TEL. Weekdays $79–$110 double. Weekends $59 double based on availability. Rates include continental breakfast, evening sherry,

Inside Washington: Hotel Stories

Washington hotels have seen a lot of history (not to mention gossip-column fodder), from pre–Civil War days when the **Willard** maintained separate entrances for pro-Union and secessionist factions, to pre-Trump wedding (and divorce) days when Marla Maples flung a shoe (and a $7^1/_2$-carat engagement ring) at The Donald in the lobby of the **Four Seasons.**

Washington "Mayor-for-Life" Marion Barry experienced a brief power outage—in the form of a 6-month jail sentence—when he was lured to the **Vista Hotel** (now known as The Westin City Center) by former girlfriend Rasheeda Moore, arrested for smoking crack cocaine, and led off in handcuffs muttering curses.

FDR lived at the **Mayflower,** the grande dame of Washington hotels, between his election and inauguration, and both Lyndon Johnson and John F. Kennedy called the Mayflower home while they were young congressmen. For 20 years before his death, J. Edgar Hoover ate the same lunch at the same table in the hotel's Grille Room every day—chicken soup, grapefruit, and cottage cheese (one wonders what he ate for dinner to maintain his portly frame). One day he spotted Public Enemy No. 3 at an adjoining table and nabbed him!

Back at the **Willard:** Brought to the capital by her lover and manager, P. T. Barnum, the "Swedish Nightingale" Jenny Lind received a steady stream of visitors during her stay, among them Daniel Webster and Pres. Millard Fillmore. Ulysses S. Grant, who often partook of cigars and brandy at the Willard, coined the term *lobbyists* to describe the people who pestered him there seeking to influence government business. Thomas Marshall, vice president under Woodrow Wilson, also liked to smoke cigars at the Willard, but found the prices scandalous, commenting, "What this country needs is a good 5-cent cigar."

During JFK's inaugural festivities, Frank Sinatra and his Rat Pack cronies took over a dozen rooms on the 10th floor of the **Capital Hilton** so they could visit each other without being bothered by autograph-seekers in the halls.

Speaking of JFK, he courted Jackie over drinks in the Blue Room at the **Shoreham,** a famous nightclub where Rudy Vallee, Lena Horne, Bob Hope, Maurice Chevalier, Judy Garland, and Frank Sinatra performed; today the room is a meeting facility. In its heyday, the Shoreham entertained the rich and the royal. Prominent socialites such as Perle Mesta and Alice Roosevelt Longworth threw private parties here, and Truman held poker games in Room D-106 while his limousine waited outside. But the hotel's most ostentatious guest ever was Saudi Arabian King Ibn-Saud who, traveling with a full complement of armed guards and 32 limos, dispensed solid gold watches as tips.

More recently, Suite 205 at **The Jefferson** served as backdrop for the year-long dalliance between President Bill Clinton's chief political strategist, Dick Morris, and call girl Sherry Rowlands. The scandal broke in August 1996, when Rowlands reported to the *Star* that Morris sometimes allowed her to listen in to telephone conversations he was having with the president as well as read speeches that were to be delivered at the 1996 Democratic National Convention.

and snacks. Smoking rooms on lower level. Extra person $10. Children under 14 stay free. AE, CB, DC, MC, V. Metro: Dupont Circle.

This four-story 1910 brick building, a former inn, was rescued from demolition some years back, spruced up, and transformed once more into a quaint, homey, small hotel. Its Federal-style architecture harmonizes with other town houses on the block, some of which were actually designed by Thomas Jefferson. Accommodations are comfortable, clean, and a little quirky in design: the sink is in the bedroom, not the bath; bathrooms have only shower stalls, no tubs; and middle rooms have no windows. The lobby doubles as a parlor where breakfast (including fresh-baked muffins and croissants) is served daily, and fresh coffee brews all day; tea, cocoa, and evening sherry are also complimentary. You can pick up maps and brochures, read a complimentary *Washington Post,* or request sundries you may have forgotten (toothbrush, razor, and the like). *Note:* There is no elevator, and there's street parking only.

Windsor Inn

1842 16th St. NW (at T St.), Washington, DC 20009. ☎ **800/423-9111** or 202/667-0300. Fax 202/667-4503. 45 rms (all with bath), 2 suites. A/C TV TEL. Weekdays $79–$125 double, $125–$150 suite. Weekends $59 based on availability. Rates include continental breakfast, evening sherry, and snacks. Smoking rms on lower level. Extra person $10. Children under 14 stay free. AE, CB, DC, MC, V. Metro: Dupont Circle.

Under the same ownership and just a couple of blocks north of the above-mentioned Embassy Inn, the Windsor Inn occupies two brick buildings, side by side but with separate entrances. The Windsor annex has slightly larger rooms and more charming features, like the occasional bay window or an arching ceiling; the annex and the main building maintain the old-fashioned feel of the Embassy. Some of the public areas are done up in art deco motif, and hallways are lit by sconces and hung with gilt-framed lithographs. All rooms are neat and comfortable; a few have sofas and/ or decorative fireplaces. Suites offer the greatest value, very roomy and attractively furnished, for much less than you'd usually pay in Washington. Lower-level rooms (the smoking floor) face a skylit terrace with lawn furnishings and colorful murals. Continental breakfast, which includes croissants and muffins, is served in the lobby, as are the complimentary coffee, tea, hot chocolate, and sherry. Ice machines, a refrigerator, and a handsome conference room are available to guests. The very friendly multilingual staff is a big plus. *Note:* There is no elevator, and parking is on the street.

6 Dupont Circle

VERY EXPENSIVE

✪ Luxury Collection Hotel, Washington, D.C.

2100 Massachusetts Ave. NW, Washington, DC 20008. ☎ **800/325-3589** or 202/293-2100. Fax 202/293-0641. 206 rms, including 20 suites. A/C MINIBAR TV TEL. Weekdays $215–$235 double, suites from $350–$2,100 for Presidential Suite. Weekends $195 double, including breakfast. Children under 18 stay free. No-smoking floors available. AE, CB, DC, MC, V. Valet parking $20. Metro: Dupont Circle.

Built in 1924 and totally renovated in 1993, this D.C. haunt of the rich and famous is top-drawer, from its canopied entrance angled on Embassy Row, to its rich, walnut-paneled lobby, to its pristine Oriental-carpeted hallways and lovely rooms. The latter are handsomely appointed with traditional dark-wood pieces, elegant tasseled draperies, and French architectural watercolor renderings. Front-of-the-house rooms overlook Embassy Row. Some 6th- to 8th-floor rooms at the back of the house give you a glimpse of the Washington Monument and Georgetown. In-room amenities include cable TVs (with HBO) concealed in armoires, safes, three phones, and terry robes. Gorgeous marble baths are equipped with hair dryers and upscale toiletries (some also have small black-and-white TVs). The seventh floor of the eight-story hotel is the Club level, with its own lounge, and is where a concierge attends you.

Dining/Entertainment: The **Jockey Club** has long been one of Washington's most prominent restaurants (see chapter 6 for a review). The elegant **Fairfax Club,**

with a working fireplace, is an intimate setting for cocktails, light fare, and piano music. The back room of the bar is an exclusive club and disco for certain wealthy Washingtonians.

Services: Complimentary morning newspaper delivery and shoe shine, nightly turndown with imported chocolates, 24-hour concierge and room service, in-room massage, twice daily maid service, express checkout, dry cleaning and laundry service.

Facilities: Fitness room with sauna, massage, and separate locker areas; meeting rooms and services.

EXPENSIVE

Canterbury Hotel

1733 N St. NW, Washington, DC 20036. ☎ **800/424-2950** or 202/393-3000. Fax 202/785-9581. 99 junior suites. A/C MINIBAR TV TEL. Weekdays $160–$400 suite for 2 (most are under $200). Weekends and off-season weekdays $109–$140 per rm. Rates include continental breakfast served in restaurant. Extra person $20. Children under 12 stay free. No-smoking rms available. AE, CB, DC, DISC, MC, V. Parking $14. Metro: Dupont Circle.

Located on a lovely residential street, this small, European-style hostelry is close to many tourist attractions. It's entered via a graciously appointed lobby hung with British prints that conjure up shades of Jane Austen. Classical music is played in public areas.

Each room is actually a junior suite and differently appointed, although all have a sofa/sitting area, dressing room, and kitchenette or full kitchen. Attractively decorated to make you feel at home, these spacious accommodations sport 18th-century mahogany English-reproduction furnishings (a few have four-poster beds). Among the amenities: cable TVs with CNN and pay-movie stations, coffeemakers, and multifeature phones; baths are supplied with cosmetic mirrors, hair dryers, phones, and baskets of fine toiletries.

Dining/Entertainment: The hotel's wonderful new restaurant, **Brighton-on-N** (see chapter 6 for details), serves American-regional fare at all meals. And the Tudor-beamed **Brighton Lounge,** complete with dart board and a menu featuring fish-and-chips, is the perfect place to relax after a busy day on the town. English beers on tap are served in pint mugs.

Services: Nightly turndown with fine chocolate, room service during restaurant hours, morning delivery of the *Washington Post,* complimentary *Wall Street Journal* available in lobby and restaurant, express checkout, and secretarial services.

Facilities: Meeting space for up to 75 people. Guests enjoy gratis use of the nearby YMCA/National Capital Health Center's extensive workout facilities, including an indoor lap pool.

Radisson Barceló Hotel

2121 P St. NW, Washington, DC 20037. ☎ **800/333-3333** or 202/293-3100. Fax 202/857-0134. 229 rms, 72 suites. A/C TV TEL. Weekdays $155–$180 double. Weekends $69–$109 double. Suites $250–$500 weekdays in season, $120–180 weekends and off-season. Extra person $20. Children under 18 stay free. No-smoking rms available. AE, CB, DC, DISC, MC, V. Parking $13. Metro: Dupont Circle.

The first American venture for a Mallorca-based firm, the 10-story Barceló offers friendly European-style service, an unbeatable location midway between Dupont Circle and Georgetown, and a superb restaurant. Groups of association and government folks here on business often stay here weekdays. On weekends, you'll be in the mix of all sorts of guests. The Barceló's art deco marble-floored lobby is inviting, and its accommodations (formerly apartments) are enormous—the hotel claims these are the largest sleeping rooms in Washington. All offer workspaces with desks and living room areas containing sofas and armchairs. In-room amenities include cable TVs with HBO and more than 200 pay-movie options, three phones with voice-mail and modem jacks, and marble baths with hair dryers. *Note:* Weekend "bed and breakfast" packages can go as low as $89 for a double, Friday and Saturday nights in summer.

Dining/Entertainment: Gabriel features first-rate Latin American/Mediterranean cuisine (see chapter 6 for a review); its simpatico bar/lounge (featuring tapas and sherry) is popular with sophisticated Washingtonians.

Services: Concierge, room service (6:30am to 11pm), complimentary *Washington Post* in the morning at the front desk, nightly turndown, faxing and other secretarial services, express checkout.

Facilities: Rooftop swimming pool and sundeck, sauna, small fitness room, bike rentals, gift shop.

MODERATE

Hampshire Hotel

1310 New Hampshire Ave. NW (at N St.), Washington, DC 20036. ☎ **800/368-5691** or 202/296-7600. Fax 202/293-2476. 82 junior suites. A/C MINIBAR TV TEL. Weekdays $109–$159 suite for 2. Weekends and off-season weekdays $79–$109 per suite. Extra person $20. Children under 12 stay free. No-smoking rms available. AE, CB, DC, DISC, JCB, MC, V. Parking $12. Metro: Dupont Circle.

The Hampshire is within easy walking distance of Georgetown and 2 blocks from Dupont Circle, convenient to numerous restaurants, nightspots, and offices: The Hampshire serves mostly an association, corporate, and government clientele. (Inquire about low summer rates.)

Spacious, junior-suite accommodations are furnished with 18th-century reproductions and offer lots of closet space, big dressing rooms, couches, coffee tables, and desks. Fifty of the 82 rooms have kitchenettes, which come with microwaves and coffeemakers; some have cooking ranges. Balconies at the front of the hotel offer city views. Amenities include a hair dryer; chocolates on arrival; multifeature, data-port–equipped phones; cable TVs; and morning delivery of the *Washington Post*. Guests also receive free passes to a large health club with indoor pool, 10 minutes away.

The hotel's **Peacock Bistro** has an outdoor cafe, a fresh juice bar, and a coffee bar; they serve fresh salads, pastas, grilled meats, and sandwiches. Room service is available during restaurant hours.

INEXPENSIVE

Carlyle Suites

1731 New Hampshire Ave. NW (between R and S sts.), Washington, DC 20009. ☎ **800/964-5377** or 202/234-3200. Fax 202/387-0085. 164 studio suites, 8 one-bedroom suites. A/C TV TEL. Weekdays $79–$149 studio suite for 2; $150–$250 one-bedroom suite. Weekends $79 suite for 2. Extra person $10. Children under 18 stay free. AE, DC, MC, V. Free limited parking. Metro: Dupont Circle.

Spacious accommodations with small but complete kitchens and dining nooks (a huge Safeway is conveniently located 2 blocks away) make Carlyle Suites a good choice for families, and for long-term guests—20% of the clientele book stays of 3 or 4 weeks. The eight-story property occupies a converted art deco landmark building on a quiet residential street near Dupont Circle. The art deco theme is evident in the details, from the stylized chrome room numbers on guest room doors to artwork hanging on walls. I don't know if dim lighting is emblematic of art deco, but the Carlyle's corridors are so dark it's hard to see. Suites are equipped with huge closets, TVs with pay-movie choices, and cozy seating areas with sofas. Most spacious are the rooms whose numbers end in "34" or "36" on each floor.

On the first level are a bar/lounge and a French cafe, newspaper vending machines, and three conference rooms. There are coin-op washers/dryers on the premises, and guests enjoy free access to a well-equipped health club nearby.

BED & BREAKFASTS

✪ H. H. Leonards' Mansion on O Street

2020 O St. NW, Washington, DC 20036. ☎ **202/496-2000.** Fax 202/659-0547. 12 rms, some of them suites, all with private bath. A/C TV TEL. $200–$1,000. Government and nonprofit rates available. No-smoking rms. Rates include breakfast, whatever you want. MC, V. Parking $15. Metro: Dupont Circle.

A legend in her own time, H. H. Leonards operates this three–town house, five-story, Victorian property as an event space, an art gallery, an antiques emporium, and—oh, yeah—a B&B. If you stay here, you may find yourself buying a sweater, a painting, or (who knows?) an antique bed. Everything's for sale. Guest rooms are so creative they'll blow you away; most breathtaking is a log cabin loft suite, with a bed whose headboard encases an aquarium. The Art Deco penthouse takes up an entire floor and has its own elevator, ten phones, and seven televisions. The International Room has a nonworking fireplace and three TVs (one in the bath). All rooms have king-size beds, computer-activated telephones that can hook you up to the Internet, at least one television, and out-of-this-world decor; most have a Jacuzzi, and some have kitchens. Elsewhere on the property are an outdoor pool, eight office/conference spaces, 21 far-out bathrooms, and art and antiques everywhere. Full business services are available, including multiline phones, fax machines, IBM and Mac computers, and satellite feeds.

Hotel Tabard Inn

1739 N St. NW, Washington, DC 20036. ☎ **202/785-1277.** Fax 202/785-6173. 40 rms (13 with shared bath). A/C TEL. Weekdays/weekends $90–$105 with shared bath, $114–$165 with private bath. Extra person $15. $10 for crib. Inquire about reduced summer rates. All rates include continental breakfast. AE, MC, V. Street parking, $13 valet parking, $10 self-parking. Metro: Dupont Circle.

In 1914, three Victorian town houses were joined to form the Tabard Inn, named for the famous hostelry in Chaucer's *Canterbury Tales.* The inn's owners live on the West Coast, but their son manages the Tabard, with the help of a chummy, peace-love-and-understanding sort of staff who clearly love the inn.

At the heart of the ground floor is the dark, paneled lounge, with a wood-burning fireplace and original beamed ceiling and bookcases. This is a favorite place for Washingtonians to come for a drink, especially in winter, or to linger before or after dining in the charming Tabard Inn restaurant, which adjoins (see chapter 6 for a review).

From there, the inn leads you through nooks and crannies to guest rooms: Can you dig chartreuse? How about aubergine? Rooms are painted in these unconventional colors and decorated in similar style. Each is different, though N Street–facing rooms are largest and brightest, and some have bay windows. Furnishings are a mix of antiques and flea-market finds. Perhaps the most eccentric room is the top floor "penthouse," which has skylights, exposed brick walls, its own kitchen, and a deck accessible by climbing out a window.

✪ Swann House

1808 New Hampshire Ave. NW, Washington, DC 20009. ☎ **202/265-7677.** Fax 202/265-6755. 4 rms, 1 suite (all with bath). A/C TV TEL. $75–$200 depending on rm and season. Extra person $20. Rates include breakfast, complimentary beer and wine. Limited off-street parking. No smoking. No pets. MC, V. Metro: Dupont Circle.

This stunning 1883 mansion angled prominently on a Dupont Circle corner holds five exquisite guest rooms, two with private entrances. The coolest is the Blue Sky Suite, which has the original rose-tiled (working) fireplace, queen bed and sofa bed, a gabled ceiling, corner kitchen, and its own roof deck. The "Jennifer Green" Room features a queen-size bed, another working fireplace, an oversized marble steam shower, and a private deck overlooking the pool area and garden. The Regent Room has a king-size bed in front of a carved working fireplace, a Jacuzzi, double shower, outdoor hot tub, TV, VCR, and stereo. The beautiful window treatments and bed coverings are the handiwork of innkeeper Mary Ross. You'll want to spend some time on the main floor of the mansion, which has 12-foot ceilings, fluted woodwork, in-laid wood floors, a turreted living room, columned sitting room, and a sunroom (where breakfast is served) leading through three sets of French doors to the garden and pool. Laundry facilities, meeting space, and business services are available.

7 Foggy Bottom/West End

VERY EXPENSIVE

✪ ANA Hotel

2401 M St. NW, Washington, DC 20037. ☎ **800/ANA-HOTELS** or 202/429-2400. Fax 202/457-5010. 415 rms, including 9 suites. A/C MINIBAR TV TEL. Weekdays $270 double. Weekends $129 double. Weekdays and weekends $660–$1,630 suite. Extra person $30. Children under 18 stay free. No-smoking floors available. AE, CB, DC, DISC, ER, JCB, MC, V. Valet parking $16. Metro: Foggy Bottom.

The ANA is famous for its West End Executive Fitness Center, whose 17,500 square feet include pool and spa facilities, squash and racquetball courts, and every kind of exercise equipment. When in town, this is where Arnold Schwarzenegger stays, and where other visiting celebrities come to work out, even if they don't stay here. Guests pay $10 a day to use exercise equipment or to take aerobics classes but may use the pool, sauna, steam room, and whirlpool for free.

The ANA's lobby and public areas are especially pretty, thanks to the central interior garden courtyard. The 146 guest rooms that overlook this courtyard are probably the best. An $8 million renovation in late 1997 renovated all guest rooms and the lobby. Amenities in guest rooms include large writing desks, terry robes, three phones (one in the bath) with voice mail, safes, remote-controlled TVs, and Caswell Massey toiletries. The ninth floor is a secured executive club level, popular with many of the business travelers who stay here.

Dining/Entertainment: *Washingtonian* magazine's readers' poll named ANA's Sunday brunch the best in Washington; it's served in the lovely **Colonnade,** which is also a popular wedding reception site. **The Bistro** serves American cuisine with a Mediterranean flair; for Japanese guests (the Japanese-owned hotel is named for its owners, All Nippon Airways, and draws a fair number of travelers from Japan), the Bistro offers an authentic Japanese breakfast daily. Cocktails, coffee, and pastries are available in the **Lobby Lounge.**

Services: 24-hour room and concierge service, dry cleaning and laundry service, nightly turndown, twice daily maid service, express checkout, valet parking, complimentary shoe shine.

Facilities: Besides the fitness center, the ANA offers a full business center, 5,500-square-foot ballroom, 186 fixed-seat auditorium, and more than 29,000 square feet of meeting space.

✪ Park Hyatt

1201 24th St. NW, Washington, DC 20037. ☎ **800/922-PARK** or 202/789-1234. Fax 202/457-8823. 224 rms, including 120 suites. A/C MINIBAR TV TEL. Weekdays $249–$299 double, $274–$324 suite. Weekends $169 double, $184 suite. Extra person $25. Children under 17 free. Family plan offered, based on availability: 2nd rm for children under 17 is half price. No-smoking floors available. AE, CB, DC, DISC, JCB, MC, V. Valet parking $20 weekdays, $8 weekends. Metro: Foggy Bottom or Dupont Circle.

At this luxury hotel, museum-quality modern art hangs on the walls of the handsome public areas (including a David Hockney lithograph) and the framed reproductions in guest rooms are of works hanging in the National Gallery and other museums in town. Each room has an iron and ironing board, and each bathroom has a TV and radio, telephone, hair dryer, and makeup mirror. You won't see maid carts in the hallways because housekeeping staff use handheld baskets. The 10-year-old, 10-story hotel prides itself on going the extra mile to please a customer, even if it means taking out a wall to enlarge a suite, as the Park Hyatt did for Lily Tomlin, right after the hotel opened. Guests include big names, royal families (who use the Presidential Suite, with its fireplace and grand piano), lobbyists, and tour bus travelers. Executive suites have separate living and dining areas, fax machines, and a second TV. Rooms are handsome, service superb.

Dining/Entertainment: Melrose's bright and lovely dining room offers four-star cuisine with an emphasis on seafood (see chapter 6 for a review); look for the amiable chef Brian McBride, who's been known to pop into the dining room from time to time to make sure all is well. Afternoon tea is served in the lounge (traditional $14.95, with champagne cocktail $18) Thursday through Sunday and includes finger sandwiches, scones, Devon cream, and pastries, plus the services of a palmist ($10 extra). Adjoining Melrose is a bar; outdoors is a smashingly beautiful cafe.

Services: 24-hour concierge, room service, business center, and valet/laundry service; foreign currency exchange, shoe shine, twice-daily maid service, delivery of *Washington Post* weekdays, nightly turndown, express checkout, gift shop.

Facilities: Hair and skin salon, health club including indoor pool, heated whirlpool, sauna and steam rooms, and extensive exercise room.

✪ The Watergate Hotel

2650 Virginia Ave. NW, Washington, DC 20037. ☎ **800/424-2736** or 202/965-2300. Fax 202/337-7915. 231 rms, including 185 suites. A/C MINIBAR TV TEL. Weekdays $230–$320 double. Weekends $155 double. Suites from $420 double, with greatly reduced weekend rates. Extra person $25. Children under 17 stay free. AE, CB, DC, DISC, JCB, MC, V. Parking $20 (valet only). Metro: Foggy Bottom.

Don't confuse the immense Watergate condo and office complex—site of the notorious 1972 break-in that brought down the Nixon administration—with the elegantly intimate hotel housed within the complex. This was the hotel of choice for many stars attending 1997 inaugural bashes, including Jimmy Smits, Gloria Estefan, and Stevie Wonder, who gave an impromptu performance in the hotel's sumptuous lobby after one of the balls. Year-round, the Watergate's clientele comprises high-level diplomats, business travelers, and Kennedy Center performers (the Kennedy Center is adjacent). Its spa facilities, indoor lap pool and sundeck, state-of-the-art health club, entertainment options, and dozens of adjacent shops also make it a fabulous choice for sophisticated travelers, including couples in search of a romantic weekend.

Rooms and suites are spacious—suites are said to be the largest in the city. River-facing rooms give splendid views of the Potomac, and of these, all but the 8th- and 14th-floor rooms have balconies. All rooms have writing desks and fax machines, and most have wet bars; most executive suites have kitchenettes. TVs offer Showtime movies and more than 50 cable stations. In your bath you'll find Gilchrist & Soames toiletries, a cosmetic mirror, hair dryer, phone, and terry robes.

Dining/Entertainment: Chef Robert Wiedemaier (who ran the Four Seasons's premier restaurant for 7 years) presides over **Aquarelle,** winning accolades for his Euro-American cuisine. The elegant **Potomac Lounge** serves British-style afternoon teas Tuesday through Sunday and features special early evening events (with live music varying from piano bar to Spanish guitar) such as caviar tastings, sushi/ Japanese beer nights, and salmon nights.

Services: 24-hour room service, concierge (7am to 11pm), full business services, nightly turndown, complimentary shoeshine, daily newspaper of your choice, complimentary weekday morning limo to downtown, complimentary coffee in Potomac Lounge.

Facilities: Jacuzzi, steam, sauna, massage and spa treatments, barber/beauty salon (Zahira's, the stylist to three Presidents), 10 meeting rooms, gift shop, ballroom overlooking the Potomac, and, in the adjacent complex, dozens of shops including jewelers, designer boutiques, a supermarket, drugstore, and post office.

EXPENSIVE

St. James Hotel
950 24th St. NW (off of Washington Circle), Washington, DC 20037. ☎ **800/852-8512** or 202/457-0500. Fax 202/466-6484. 195 suites. A/C MINIBAR TV TEL. Weekdays $165–$185. Weekends $89–$129. Rates include breakfast. Extra person $20. Children under 17 stay free. No-smoking rms available. AE, DC, DISC, MC, V. Parking $16. Metro: Foggy Bottom.

The St. James is a home-away-from-home for many of its guests, about one-third of whom book these luxury suites for more than 30 days at a time. The suites are all one-bedrooms, with separate living and sleeping areas, marble bathrooms, and kitchens equipped with everything from china and flatware to cooking utensils. Each living room includes a queen-size pullout sofa. Unlike other hotels in this residential neighborhood of old town houses, the St. James is fairly new (only 10 years old), which means accessibility was a factor in its design: A ramp in the lobby leads to the reception area, and 10 suites are available for travelers with disabilities. The St. James is primely located near Georgetown, George Washington University, and the Kennedy Center. Corporate club members receive extra perks, like evening cocktails and hors d'oeuvres served in the club's pleasant second-floor quarters.

Services: Room service (11am to 11pm), dry cleaning, laundry service, *Washington Post, The New York Times, Wall Street Journal, USA Today* available in breakfast room or delivered to room on request, nightly turndown on request, baby-sitting, business services including faxing and courier service, daily shoe shine.

Facilities: Full kitchens, outdoor pool, 24-hour state-of-the-art fitness center, nearby tennis courts and jogging/biking paths, conference rooms.

Wyndham Bristol Hotel
2430 Pennsylvania Ave. NW, Washington, DC 20037. ☎ **800/955-6400** or 202/955-6400. Fax 202/955-5765. 205 rms, 34 suites. A/C MINIBAR TV TEL. Weekdays $145–$199 double. Weekends $89–$119 double. Year-round weekday and weekend rates for one-bedroom suite $225, Ambassador Suite $450, Presidential Suite $800. Extra person $20 in double rms and one-bedroom suites. Children under 18 stay free. No-smoking rms and floors available. AE, CB, DC, DISC, JCB, MC, V. Valet parking $16 (no self-parking unless you street-park). Metro: Foggy Bottom.

Location is the key selling point for this eight-floor hotel within walking distance of Georgetown, the White House, the Kennedy Center, and the Metro. The well-run establishment's clientele is about 70% international business travelers, who appreciate the multilingual staff (21 languages represented), two-line telephones with data ports, a voice message system, and complimentary coffeemakers and coffee in each room. Flags flying over and under the marquee entrance enhance the international feel, as does the elegant lobby, whose little sitting areas are often occupied by guests speaking foreign languages. The Wyndham has been a hotel since 1983, but it began as an apartment building in 1940, which explains the generously sized rooms. Decor is tasteful: Each room has a sitting area, furnished with at least a table and two chairs, and more than half have a sofabed and desk. Fourth- through eighth-floor rooms at the front of the hotel have the best outlooks, surveying Pennsylvania Avenue. Ask for corner suites 425, 525, 625, 725, or 825 to get an angled view of the avenue as it heads to Georgetown. Weekend travelers should inquire about "special value rates." Seniors and members of AAA and AARP may be eligible for bargains.

Dining/Entertainment: The **Bristol Grill** is open from 6:30am to 11pm and is known for its weekday pasta bar and Sunday brunch, which includes complimentary champagne.

Services: Concierge service (7am to 11pm) and room service (24-hour), same-day dry cleaning, weekday newspaper delivery, daily maid service, 24-hour bell service, express checkout, valet parking.

Facilities: Kitchenettes in the suites, VCRs but not videos for rent, Spectravision pay-per-view movie channels, modest exercise room, seven meeting rooms totaling 4,000 square feet, rentable audiovisual equipment, and sundries shop.

MODERATE

The George Washington University Inn

824 New Hampshire Ave. NW, Washington, DC 20037. ☎ **800/426-4455** or 202/337-6620. Fax 202/298-7499. 48 rms, 16 efficiencies, 31 one-bedroom suites. A/C TV TEL. Weekdays $120–$155 double, $130–$175 efficiency, $145–$195 one-bedroom suite. Weekends $99–$135 double, $110–$155 efficiency, $125-$170 one-bedroom suite. Children under 18 stay free. AE, DC, MC, V. Limited parking $14. Metro: Foggy Bottom.

This eight-story, whitewashed brick inn, another former apartment building, became a hotel in 1968 and, rumor has it, was a favorite spot for clandestine trysts for high-society types. These days you're more likely to see Kennedy Center performers and visiting professors. The university purchased the hotel (formerly known as "The Inn at Foggy Bottom") in 1994 and renovated it.

Rooms are a little larger and corridors a tad narrower than your typical hotel's, and each room includes a dressing chamber. One-bedroom suites are especially spacious, with living rooms that hold a sleeper sofa and an armoire-hidden TV (there's another in the bedroom). Guest rooms are equipped with a mini-refrigerator, a microwave oven, and a coffeemaker; efficiencies and suites have kitchens. The roominess and the kitchen facilities make this a popular choice for families and for long-term guests, and if it's not full, the inn may be willing to offer reduced rates. Mention prices quoted in the inn's *New York Times* ad, if you've seen it, or your affiliation with George Washington University, if you can. This is a fairly safe and lovely neighborhood, with easy walking to Georgetown, the Kennedy Center, and downtown. But keep an eye peeled—you must pass through wrought iron gates down into a kind of cul-de-sac to find the inn.

Dining/Entertainment: Off the lobby is the well-received restaurant, **Zuki Moon,** designed to reflect a Japanese tea garden. The menu features low-fat, healthy, and inexpensive dishes, mostly Japanese, but some American.

Services: Complimentary newspaper delivered daily, 24-hour message service, same-day laundry/valet service.

Facilities: Coin-operated laundry on the premises, five rooms designed for guests with disabilities, meeting room for 50.

✪ Hotel Lombardy

2019 Pennsylvania Ave. NW, Washington, DC 20006. ☎ **800/424-5486** or 202/828-2600. Fax 202/872-0503. 87 rms, 38 suites. A/C MINIBAR TV TEL. Weekdays $140–$180 double; $160–$180 suite for 2. Weekends (and sometimes off-season weekdays) $69–$99 double; $119–$140 suite for 2.

From its handsome walnut-paneled lobby with carved Tudor ceilings to its old-fashioned nonautomatic elevator (the hotel is not well suited for travelers with disabilities), the 11-story Lombardy offers a lot of character and comfort for the price and the location (about 5 blocks west of the White House). George Washington University's campus is just across Pennsylvania Avenue, which means this part of town remains vibrant at night, when other downtown neighborhoods have shut down. Peace Corps, World Bank, and corporate guests make up a large part of its clientele, but other visitors will also appreciate the Lombardy's warmly welcoming ambience and the attentive service of the multilingual staff.

Spacious rooms, entered via pedimented louver doors, have undergone a recent redecoration, and each one is slightly different, though all share a 1930s northern Italian motif. Large desks, precious dressing rooms, and roomy walk-in closets are other assets.

Dining/Entertainment: Moderately priced and open for all meals, The **Café Lombardy,** a sunny glass-enclosed restaurant, serves authentic northern Italian fare. The **Venetian Room,** the hotel's bar/lounge, is slated to open in late 1997, and will feature local jazz and other musicians.

Services: Complete concierge and room services (7am to 9:30pm), same-day laundry and dry cleaning, weekday delivery of the *Washington Post,* nightly bed turndown, twice-daily maid service, express checkout; terry robes are supplied; shoes are shined gratis overnight.

Facilities: Fully equipped kitchens and dining nooks in all but 20 rooms, Spectravision pay-per-view movie channel, access to health club 1 block away ($10 per visit), two small meeting rooms.

One Washington Circle Hotel

1 Washington Circle NW, Washington, DC 20037. ☎ **800/424-9671** or 202/872-1680. Fax 202/887-4989. 151 suites. A/C TV TEL. Weekdays $115–$155 for smallest suite, $155–$195 for largest suite. Weekends $59–$99 for smallest suite, $109–$149 for largest. Extra person $15. Guests paying rates of $135 or higher receive free continental breakfast weekdays and cocktails/hors d'oeuvres Mon–Thurs. Children under 18 stay free. AE, CB, DC, MC, V. Underground valet parking $8–$15. No-smoking rms available. Metro: Foggy Bottom.

Built in 1960, this building was converted into a hotel in 1976, making it the city's first all-suite hotel property. Five types of suites are available, ranging in size from 390 to 710 square feet. Every suite has a comfortable decor that includes a sofa bed and dining area, kitchens, and walk-out balconies, some overlooking the circle with George Washington's statue upon it. But keep in mind that across the circle is George Washington University Hospital's emergency room entrance, kept busy with ambulance traffic; though the hotel is well insulated, you may want to ask for a suite on the L Street side. President Nixon liked to stay here on his visits to Washington after Watergate; he preferred suite 615. Clientele is mostly corporate, but families like the outdoor pool, in-house restaurant, prime location near Georgetown and the Metro, and the kitchens. Ask about bargain room rates available to groups, AAA members, and seniors, or through a special value ad for the hotel in *The New York Times.*

Dining/Entertainment: The well-reviewed **West End Cafe** features contemporary American cuisine in a garden room/greenhouse setting. Locals frequently dine here, but guests sometimes benefit from special rates—you pay half the $15.95 price for Sunday brunch, for example. A pianist plays jazz Tuesday through Saturday nights.

Services: 24-hour concierge, room service (7am to 11pm), dry cleaning and laundry service, morning delivery of *The Washington Post,* nightly turndown, secretarial services (faxing, typing), valet parking, courtesy shuttle to the Kennedy Center when you dine at the West End Cafe.

Facilities: Fully equipped kitchens stocked with fresh coffee beans, grinder, and coffeemaker; outdoor pool with complimentary passes to nearby health club equipped with an indoor pool, racquetball court, bikes, Stairmaster, weights, and other features; a 925-square-foot conference center; coin-operated washer and dryer; complimentary shoe-shine service.

State Plaza Hotel

2117 E St. NW, Washington, DC 20037. ☎ **800/424-2859** or 202/861-8200. Fax 202/659-8601. 221 suites. A/C MINIBAR TV TEL. Weekdays $125–$150 efficiency suite for 1 or 2 people; $175–$225 for a large one-bedroom suite (with dining rm) for up to 4 people. Weekend (and off-season weeknights, subject to availability) $69–$109. Rates include continental breakfast. Extra person $20. Children under 18 stay free. AE, DC, MC, V. Parking $12. Metro: Foggy Bottom.

This eight-floor, all-suite hotel is actually two buildings, known as the North Tower and the South Tower, connected through the garage. They are identical. South Tower suites overlook the Mall, the Washington Monument, and other sights, the higher up you go; the North Tower overlooks downtown Washington and holds the dining room, where complimentary continental breakfast is served in the morning and free hors d'oeuvres are available each evening during happy hour.

Many guests are affiliated with the nearby State Department, World Bank, or George Washington University; if you are too, inquire about special rates. Suites are pleasant, clean, and fairly spacious; ask for a plaza suite if you want the largest. Each suite has cable TV, iron and ironing board, hair dryer, and full kitchen, including a microwave. On-premises facilities offer 15 suites for guests with disabilities, a small fitness center, three conference rooms, the **Garden Cafe,** self-service laundry, a sundeck, and tennis courts right next door. Among the amenities are room service during restaurant hours, valet parking, complimentary shoe shine, free local phone calls and no-fee long-distance access, and weekday delivery of the *Washington Post.*

INEXPENSIVE

✪ The Premier Hotel, Howard Johnson's

2601 Virginia Ave. NW (at New Hampshire Ave.), Washington, DC 20037. ☎ **800/965-6869** or 202/965-2700. Fax 202/337-5417. 192 rms. A/C TV TEL. Weekdays and weekends $89–$139 double, concierge floor $30 additional. Extra person $10. Children under 18 stay free. AE, DC, DISC, JCB, MC, V. Parking $9 (maximum height 6'2"). Metro: Foggy Bottom.

A short walk from the Kennedy Center, with a nicely landscaped porte cochere entrance, this flagship HoJo property—the first of its more upscale "Premier" group—recently underwent a $3.5 million renovation. Not only is it looking very spiffy, it now offers many assets unusual in its price range, including a concierge and a business center. Pluses include a large L-shaped rooftop pool with a sundeck and adjoining Ping-Pong area, a 24-hour workout room, secured underground parking, coin-op washers and dryers, sightseeing bus tours, and a gift shop. Rooms, attractively decorated in rich earth tones (half with balconies overlooking the Potomac) offer refrigerators, coffeemakers, safes, and cable TVs with HBO, pay-movie options, and Nintendo. Rooms on the executive floor (the seventh) are larger and have either a sofa bed or chair with ottoman. Local calls are free. **America's Best,** a contemporary diner with an exhibition kitchen, serves all meals and provides room service 6am to 11pm weekdays, 6am to midnight weekends.

8 Georgetown

VERY EXPENSIVE

✪ The Four Seasons

2800 Pennsylvania Ave. NW, Washington, DC 20007. ☎ **800/332-3442** or 202/342-0444. Fax 202/944-2076. 166 rms, 30 suites. A/C MINIBAR TV TEL. Weekdays $345–$390 double, $725–$2,350 suite. Weekends $260–$280 double, starting at $475 for suites. Extra person $30. Children under 16 stay free. AE, DC, JCB, MC, V. Parking $22. Metro: Foggy Bottom.

Since it opened in 1979, this most glamorous of Washington's haute hotels has hosted everyone from Jon Bon Jovi to King Hussein of Jordan. Open the front door, and you enter a plush setting where thousands of plants and palm trees grow, and large floral arrangements enhance the gardenlike ambience.

Service is what sets this hotel apart. Staff are trained to know the names, likings, even allergies of guests, and repeat clientele have come to rely on this attention. Accommodations, many of them overlooking Rock Creek Park or the C&O Canal, have walls hung with gilt-framed antique prints, down feather-filled bedding embellished with dust ruffles and scalloped spreads, and large desks and plump cushioned armchairs with hassocks to drive home the residential atmosphere. In-room amenities include cable TVs with free HBO and Spectravision movie options, VCRs (movies and video games are available), CD players (the concierge stocks CDs), bathrobes, and, in the baths, hair dryers, lighted cosmetic mirrors, and upscale toiletries. Under construction now, in an adjoining building, are 40 high-luxury suites for clients who want state-of-the-art business amenities (each suite will have an office equipped with fax machine, printer, and shredder).

Dining/Entertainment: The elegant and highly acclaimed **Seasons** is reviewed in chapter 6. The delightful **Garden Terrace** is bordered by tropical plants, ficus trees, and flower beds and has a wall of windows overlooking the canal. It's open for lunch, a lavish Sunday jazz brunch, and classic English-style afternoon teas.

Services: Twice-daily maid service, 24-hour room service and concierge, complimentary sedan service weekdays within the District, gratis newspaper of your choice, car windows washed when you park overnight, complimentary shoe shine.

Facilities: Beauty salon, gift shop, jogging trail, business facilities, children's programs, extensive state-of-the-art fitness club that includes personal trainers, and a spa that offers a Vichy shower, hydrotherapy, and synchronized massage (two people work on you at the same time).

EXPENSIVE

✪ The Latham

3000 M St. NW, Washington, DC 20007. ☎ **800/528-4261** or 202/726-5000. Fax 202/337-4250. 121 rms, 22 suites. A/C TV TEL. Weekdays $155–$175 double. Weekends $119–$139. $175–$290 suite. Extra person $20. Children under 18 stay free. Two-thirds are no-smoking rms. AE, DC, DISC, MC, V. Valet parking $14.

The Latham is at the very hub of Georgetown's trendy nightlife/restaurant/shopping scene, but since its accommodations are set back from the street, none of the noise of nighttime revelers will reach your room. It's also the only Georgetown hotel with a swimming pool. Charming earth-toned rooms are decorated in French-country motif, with pine furnishings and multipaned windows; cable TVs (offering cable and pay-per-view Spectravision movie selections) are housed in forest-green armoires. All rooms are equipped with large desks, hair dryers, terry robes, irons, and ironing boards. Tenth-floor rooms offer gorgeous river views; third-floor accommodations, all two-room suites, have windows facing a hallway designed to replicate a quaint Georgetown street. Most luxurious are two-story carriage suites with cathedral ceilings, full living rooms, and stocked minibars. Fax printers are in all suites and in one-third of guest rooms; CD players with headphones are in third-floor and carriage suites.

Dining/Entertainment: The highly acclaimed **Citronelle,** one of D.C.'s hottest restaurants, is on the premises (see chapter 6 for a review). And fronting the hotel is the country-French **La Madeleine,** another branch of which is fully described among Alexandria restaurants in chapter 11.

Services: Room service during restaurant hours, concierge, valet parking, nightly turndown, free delivery of *USA Today* or newspaper of your choice, business services, express checkout.

Facilities: Small outdoor pool and bilevel sundeck; guests enjoy free use of an adjacent fully equipped health club; jogging and bike path along the C&O Canal, next to hotel; meeting rooms and audiovisual services.

MODERATE

✪ The Georgetown Dutch Inn

1075 Thomas Jefferson St. NW (just below M St.), Washington, DC 20007. ☎ **800/388-2410** or 202/337-0900. Fax 202/333-6526. 47 suites. A/C TV TEL. Weekdays $125–$195 one-bedroom suite for 2, $195–$300 two-bedroom duplex penthouse (sleeps 6). Weekends $105 one-bedroom suite for 2, $180–$250 penthouse suite. Rates include continental breakfast. Extra person $20. Children under 14 stay free. AE, CB, DC, DISC, MC, V. Free parking. Metro: Foggy Bottom. Bus: M Street buses go to all major Washington tourist attractions.

Many European and South American guests, usually embassy folks, stay at this inn. It's also a favorite for families here to celebrate weddings or graduations; they book several suites, or maybe a whole floor. Personalized service is a hallmark of the hotel, whose staff greet you by name and protect your privacy, should you be a celebrity of some sort—which many guests are.

Accommodations are spacious one- and two-bedroom, apartmentlike suites, nine of them duplex penthouses with $1^1/2$ baths. Amenities include cable TVs with HBO, irons and ironing boards, coffeemakers, and three phones (bedside, living room, and bath). You'll also find a cosmetic mirror and a hair dryer in the bath.

Though there's no on-premises restaurant, an extensive room-service menu is available. Complimentary continental breakfast is served in the lobby each morning. Guests also enjoy free use of nearby state-of-the-art health clubs. The C&O Canal towpath, just down the block, is ideal for jogging and cycling, though be wary of going at night.

Georgetown Suites

1000 29th St. NW (between K and M sts.), Washington, DC 20007. ☎ **800/348-7203** or 202/298-1600. Fax 202/333-2019. 78 suites. A/C TV TEL. $139 studio suite (for 2), $149 one-bedroom suite (for up to 4). Weekends $99 studio suite, $109 one-bedroom suite. Rates include extended continental breakfast. Rollaways or sleeper sofa $10 extra. AE, DC, MC, V. Limited parking $12. Metro: Foggy Bottom.

This property, in the heart of Georgetown, was designed to meet the needs of business travelers making extended visits, but it works well for families, too. You enter the hotel via a brick courtyard with flowering plants in terra-cotta pots and Victorian white wooden benches. You'll find yourself in a large lobby area that seems much like a student lounge. The TV's going; games, books, magazines, and daily newspapers lay scattered across table tops in front of loveseats and chairs; and a cappuccino machine rests on the counter. Tea and coffee are available throughout the day, and a substantial continental breakfast is served daily.

Accommodations sport fully equipped kitchens, living rooms, and dining areas, and are furnished with large desks, cable TVs with HBO, hair dryers, and irons and ironing boards. The biggest, if not the best, suite is probably the two-level, two-bedroom town house, which has its own entrance on 29th Street; this goes for $250 a night. Among the on-premises facilities are an outdoor barbecue grill for guest use, coin-op washers/dryers, and a small exercise room. Hotel services include complimentary grocery shopping and food delivery from nearby restaurants. M Street buses (a block away) will take you to most major D.C. attractions.

Georgetown Suites maintains another 136 suites (same phone number, rates, and amenities) close by at 1111 30th St. NW, between K and M streets.

INEXPENSIVE

Savoy Suites Georgetown

2505 Wisconsin Ave. NW (above Calvert St.), Washington, DC 20007. ☎ **800/944-5377** or 202/337-9700. Fax 202/337-3644. 150 rms. A/C TV TEL. Weekdays $65–$165 double. Weekends $68.69 double. Extra person $10. Children under 18 stay free. AE, DC, MC, V. Free parking. Metro: Shuttle buses travel between the hotel and the Woodley Park–Zoo Metro stop continuously from 6:30am–10:30pm. Even-numbered buses stop in front of the hotel and connect to Georgetown, Dupont Circle, and the Mall.

The Savoy lies in the neighborhood known as "Upper Georgetown," but it's really Glover Park, just 5 minutes from the heart of Georgetown by bus or car. Head down the hill, and you'll find some really great restaurants (see the Glover Park dining section in chapter 6). A 10-minute walk up the hill is Washington National Cathedral. You won't feel like you're in the heart of the city, but you won't be paying center-city prices, either.

The Savoy calls itself a "suites" hotel, but its accommodations are all one-room—though about 25 of these have fully stocked kitchens, and some with dining areas. Decor includes French provincial pieces and grass-cloth–covered walls that are hung with gilt-framed 18th-century color lithographs. All rooms offer satellite TV service. All eighth floor (top floor) rooms have a big, orange Jacuzzi right there in the room, on a platform just beside the bed. Another startling thing about the Savoy is its panoramic city views, available from about half of the rooms.

Its restaurant, **On Wisconsin,** features reasonably priced American/continental fare. In warm weather, the Savoy also has a tree-shaded outdoor cafe serving light fare. Other on-premises amenities include a small sundeck, coin-op washers/dryers, and meeting space for 200. Guests enjoy free use of a well-equipped nearby health club with an Olympic-size pool.

By the way, note the ornate fence fronting the Savoy Suites. Made in 1890, it's from the original lion's cage of the National Zoo.

9 Woodley Park

EXPENSIVE

Omni Shoreham

2500 Calvert St. NW (at Connecticut Ave.), Washington, DC 20008. ☎ **800/228-2121** or 202/234-0700. Fax 202/265-5333. 745 rms, 55 suites. A/C TV TEL. Weekdays $155–$225 double. Off-season and weekends $109 double. Extra person $20. Children under 18 stay free. AE, CB, DC, DISC, JCB, MC, V. Parking $14. Metro: Woodley Park–Zoo.

D.C. with Dogs

If you take your dog along when you travel, you're always grateful to find a hotel that accepts pets, let alone one that actually welcomes them with open arms. Well, Fido has a home in Washington at the **Loew's L'Enfant Plaza Hotel,** 480 L'Enfant Plaza SW, Washington, DC 20024 (☎ **202/484-1000**). It's conveniently located for a game of fetch on the Mall (and for you to do some sightseeing at the Smithsonian). Actually, it's a wonderful choice for anyone: Its rooms are comfortable and have nice views; there are terrific amenities for kids and for business travelers; and the hotel restaurant is first-rate. During my recent stay here, the doorman took a shine to my dog and remembered us each time we came and went, offering tips on where she was welcome and grabbing up extra towels to protect my car seat when she headed off for a swim.

So what's a good outing for you and your dog? My recommendation is to head for the C&O Canal. I had a wonderful scenic stroll here with Lucy, my Golden Retriever (I walked along the towpath, and she swam alongside me up the canal). After your walk, you can head for Georgetown, where there are lots of outdoor cafes that don't mind having a well-behaved dog tied up at your sidewalk table. We also enjoyed Rock Creek Park, though Lucy had to be leashed there for much of the time.

Two terrific resources for your trip are *Frommer's America on Wheels: Mid-Atlantic Region* (Macmillan Travel), which uses easily spotted dog icons to indicate which accommodations throughout the region accept pets; and *Frommer's On the Road Again with Man's Best Friend: Mid-Atlantic States* (Macmillan Travel), which has extensive reviews of select dog-friendly hotels and inns.

—Lisa Renaud

A massive, $60-million renovation of all guest rooms and the lobby is underway at the Omni, scheduled for completion by the end of 1998. The spacious guest rooms will remain twice the size of normal hotel rooms, but their new decor will restore a traditional, elegant look through the use of chintz fabrics, mahogany furnishings, and porcelain fixtures. In the meantime, the hotel continues to operate as, primarily, a meeting and convention venue, though leisure travelers should consider the Shoreham for its numerous recreational facilities: three tennis courts, an Olympic-size swimming pool and a kiddie pool, and an excellent health club. Its 11-acre location on Rock Creek Park is also an asset, for the spectacular views it affords, and for immediate access to bike and jogging paths. An extensive children's activity program is a plus for families. Built in 1930, the Shoreham has been the scene of inaugural balls for every president since FDR. Do you believe in ghosts? Ask about Room 800G, the haunted suite (available for $2,000 a night).

Dining/Entertainment: The elegant **Monique Café et Brasserie,** reminiscent of the famed La Coupole in Paris, specializes in continental/American fare with an emphasis on steak and seafood. Rock Creek Park provides a fitting backdrop for the lushly planted **Palm Court,** a popular cocktail lounge under a 35-foot vaulted ceiling.

Services: Room service (6am to 11pm), concierge, dry cleaning and laundry service, express checkout.

Facilities: Shops; travel/sightseeing desk; business center and conference rooms; 10 miles of jogging, hiking, and bicycle trails, health and fitness center, plus a 1^{1}/$_{2}$-mile Perrier parcourse with 18 exercise stations.

Sheraton Washington

2660 Woodley Rd. NW (at Connecticut Ave. NW), Washington, DC 20008. ☎ **800/325-3535** or 202/328-2000. Fax 202/234-0015. 1,350 rms, including 125 suites. A/C TV TEL. Weekdays $149–$229 double, weekends $109–$139 double; suites $350–$1,200. Extra person $30. Children under 17 stay free. No-smoking rms available. AE, CB, DC, DISC, MC, V. Valet parking $17, self-parking $14. Metro: Woodley Park–Zoo.

This is Washington's biggest hotel, resting on 16 acres just down the street from the National Zoo and from several excellent restaurants. Its size and location (the Woodley Park–Zoo Metro station is literally at its doorstep) makes it a good choice for large and small conventions, tour groups, and individual travelers. The Sheraton feels like a college campus: There's an old part, whose entrance is overhung with stately trees, and a new part, whose entrance is preceded by a great green lawn. The hotel has its own post office, barber shop, florist, and jewelry store, two pools, and two restaurants.

The oldest part of the Sheraton is the nicest. The 80-year-old, redbrick Wardman Tower houses 201 guest rooms, each featuring high ceilings, ornate crown moldings, and an assortment of antique French and English furnishings. This was once an apartment building whose residents ranged from presidents Hoover, Eisenhower, and Johnson, to actor Douglas Fairbanks, Jr., and author Gore Vidal. Wardman rooms, which include 54 suites, offer a few more amenities, such as minibars and terry robes, than the hotel's other, more conventional guest rooms. All rooms have 24-hour room service, voice mail and data ports, hair dryers, and complimentary Starbucks coffee and tea service, and irons and ironing boards. The 10th floor is the club level.

Dining/Entertainment: Americus serves American cuisine, the **Courtyard Cafe** serves more informal fare, **L'Expresso** is a gourmet deli and pastry shop, and the **Lobby Bar** is open for drinks daily.

Services: Multilingual concierge, 24-hour room service, laundry and valet, morning delivery of *USA Today,* express check in and check out, gift shop.

Facilities: 95,000 square feet of exhibit space and 78,000 square feet of meeting space; full business center; outdoor heated pool with sundeck and an indoor pool; fitness room; nearby jogging and bike paths; 61 rooms equipped for guests with disabilities.

BED & BREAKFAST

Kalorama Guest House

2700 Cathedral Ave. NW (entrance on 27th St.), Washington, DC 20008. ☎ **202/667-6369.** Fax 202/319-1262.

This is the Woodley Park location of the bed-and-breakfast based in Adams-Morgan—see listing under "Adams-Morgan/North Dupont Circle," above, for more information.

Where to Dine in Washington, D.C.

6

It's unbelievable that a city situated almost on the Chesapeake Bay and 3 hours from the Atlantic Ocean should have gone for so long without a stable of good seafood restaurants. Sure, you could always count on certain of Washington's fine restaurants for fresh fish entrées. But establishments totally devoted to seafood? Aside from the lone **Sea Catch** in Georgetown and a carryout on the Washington waterfront, our city has been strangely bereft of excellent places to dine on fresh fish.

Until now. Over the past few years, a literal sea change has occurred in downtown Washington. Look around, and you'll count at least seven excellent seafood eateries, including Roberto Donna and Jean-Louis Palladin's collaboration, **Pesce;** local restaurateur Paul Cohn's **Georgetown Seafood Grill, Vincenzo,** which performs an Italian take on seafood; and the remarkable **Kinkead's,** in a class of its own.

Look again and you'll see names that may sound familiar to you: **McCormick & Schmick's, Legal Sea Foods,** and **Grillfish.** Chain restaurants are on the loose in Washington, and these branches of (respectively) the Pacific Northwest, Boston, and Miami-based seafood houses are proving immensely popular.

Washingtonians like fish, but we aren't renouncing red meat anytime soon. **Morton's of Chicago** operates three steakhouses in the area. **The Prime Rib** and **The Palm** are each celebrating 20-something birthdays this year, while French steakhouse **Les Halles** and the Chicago-based Morton's pack full houses daily.

More than anything, Washingtonians like a choice. Because of the cross-cultural mix of people who have settled here, the capital offers a vast array of cuisines, from down-home Southern to Vietnamese, and everything in between. Fusion is big: Chefs more and more are integrating techniques and ingredients from around the world into their particular cuisine, so you have the upscale **Lespinasse** menu described as French food interwoven with Asian touches, and the funky **Xing Kuba** offering dishes that mix Asian, New Mexican, and Cuban flavors.

It makes sense, then, that the current culinary trend encompasses the cooking of several countries: Mediterranean. The term "Mediterranean," after all, covers a lot of territory, namely North Africa, Italy, Provence, and Spain. Whether you dine at the **Café Promenade,** in the Mayflower Hotel, at Dupont Circle's **BeDuCi,** or at two new spots, **Isabella** and **George,** your menu selections will point up the influences of these countries.

A food fad that may have launched the Mediterranean tidal wave are Spanish *tapas,* small dishes of crisp brown ham and cheese croquettes, little beef-filled empanadas, and such. Tapas are popular at elegant **(Taberna del Alabardero)** and casual **(Jaleo)** Spanish restaurants, alike, while versions with Brazilian, Mexican, and Latin roots are served up at eateries such as Coco Loco, Gabriel, and the U St. Bistro.

The Washington restaurant scene has come into its own, at long last. The variety of restaurant prices, menus, and hours entices many Washingtonians, not just the affluent, to dine out often. And because we visit restaurants for more than special occasions, we dress more casually when we eat out—very few restaurants require men to wear jacket and tie anymore; those restaurants in this chapter that do are so noted.

ABOUT THE PRICES

I've tried to present you with a range of menus and prices, in most every Washington neighborhood. The restaurants listed below are grouped first by location, then listed alphabetically by price category. I've used the following price categories: **Very Expensive** (the average main course at dinner is more than $20); **Expensive** ($16 to $20); **Moderate** ($10 to $15); and **Inexpensive** ($10 and under).

Keep in mind that the above categories refer to *dinner* prices, but some very expensive restaurants offer affordable lunches, early-bird dinners, tapas, or bar meals. Starred entries indicate personal favorites.

Note: A Metro station is indicated when it's within walking distance of a restaurant. If you need bus-routing information, call ☎ **202/637-7000.**

1 Best Bets

- **Best Spot for a Romantic Dinner:** Just ask for the "snug" (tables 39 and 40) at **The Restaurant at The Jefferson,** 1200 16th St. NW (at M St.) (☎ **202/ 347-2200**). Two cozy seating areas in alcoves are secluded from the main dining room, complete with banquettes for cuddling. Follow your sumptuous dinner with drinks in front of the fireplace in the adjoining lounge.
- **Best Spot for a Business Lunch:** The upstairs dining room of **The Occidental Grill,** 1475 Pennsylvania Ave. NW (☎ **202/783-1475**), is quiet, with nice-sized booths that guarantee privacy in a restaurant that's centrally located near Capitol Hill and downtown offices. (The food's great, too.)
- **Best Spot for a Celebration: Goldoni,** 1113 23rd St. NW (☎ **202/293-1511**), has a festive air, thanks to the bits of opera bursting through the bubble of conversation in the skylit room. A fun place, and the food is excellent.
- **Best Decor: The Willard Room** (☎ **202/637-7440**), in the Willard Hotel, is simply grand, decorated with paneling, velvet, and silk. (Consider this another contender for most romantic.)
- **Best View:** Washington Harbour is the setting for **Sequoia,** 3000 K St. NW (☎ **202/944-4200**), where a multilevel garden terrace offers a panoramic vista of the Potomac and verdant Theodore Roosevelt Island beyond; if you're dining inside, ask for the bar-level alcove overlooking the Potomac—the best seat in the house.
- **Best Wine List:** At **Seasons,** in The Four Seasons Hotel, 2800 Pennsylvania Ave. NW (☎ **202/944-2000**). For the 10th consecutive year, its wine cellar has been chosen as one of the 100 best worldwide by *Wine Spectator* magazine.

- **Best for Kids:** The **Austin Grill,** 2404 Wisconsin Ave. NW (☎ **202/337-8080**) is a friendly, chattering place with a children's menu and unspillable cups, and an atmosphere to please everyone. Go before 9pm.
- **Best American Cuisine: Kinkead's,** 2000 Pennsylvania Ave. NW (☎ **202/296-7700**) concentrates on seafood, but does offer a meat and poultry item on each menu; at any rate, you could eat here every day and not go wrong.
- **Best Chinese Cuisine: Full Kee,** 509 H St. NW (☎ **202/371-2233**), in the heart of Chinatown, is consistently good and a great value.
- **Best French Cuisine:** For fancy French, **Lespinasse,** in the Carlton Hotel, 923 16th St. NW (**202/879-6900**) is the place to go. The luxuriously decorated dining room is a fitting backdrop for the divinely prepared (and enormously expensive) creations of chef Troy Dupuy. For French staples served with great enthusiasm and charm in a more relaxed setting, head for **Bistrot Lepic,** at 1736 Wisconsin Ave. NW (☎ **202/333-0111**).
- **Best Italian Cuisine:** Roberto Donna's **Galileo,** 1110 21st St. NW (☎ **202/293-7191**), does it best for fine Italian cuisine, preparing exquisite pastas, fish, and meat dishes with savory ingredients like truffles and porcini mushrooms. For more traditional (and affordable) classic Italian fare, Donna's **Il Radicchio,** 1211 Wisconsin Ave. NW (☎ **202/337-2627**) (also at 1509 17th St. NW; ☎ **202/986-2627**) does the trick.
- **Best Seafood: Pesce** offers reasonably priced, perfectly grilled or sautéed seafood in a convivial atmosphere.
- **Best Southern Cuisine: Vidalia,** 1990 M St. NW (☎ **202/659-1990**). Chef Jeff Buben calls his cuisine "provincial American," a euphemism for fancy fare that includes cheese grits and biscuits in cream gravy.
- **Best Southwestern Cuisine:** It doesn't get more exciting than **Red Sage,** 605 14th St. NW (☎ **202/638-4444**), where superstar chef Mark Miller brings contemporary culinary panache to traditional southwestern cookery; keep his **Café and Chili Bar** in mind for Red Sage cuisine and ambience at lower prices.
- **Best Steakhouse:** 22 years old and still going strong, carnivores consider **The Prime Rib,** 2020 K St. NW (☎ **202/466-8811**) the best steak and prime rib place in town despite some awesome competition.
- **Best Tapas:** The elegant **Gabriel,** 2121 P St. NW (☎ **202/293-3100**), where you can graze on chef Greggory Hill's ambrosial little dishes; they range from black figs stuffed with Spanish chorizo to crunchy fried calamari with fiery harissa sauce and lemony thyme aioli.
- **Best Pizza:** At **Pizzeria Paradiso's,** 2029 P St. NW (☎ **202/223-1245**), peerless chewy-crusted pies are baked in an oak-burning oven and crowned with delicious toppings; you'll find great salads and sandwiches on fresh-baked focaccia here, too.
- **Best Desserts:** No frou-frou desserts served at **Café Berlin,** 322 Massachusetts Ave. NE (☎ **202/543-7656**); these cakes, tortes, pies, and strudels are the real thing.
- **Best Diet Meal:** At **Legal Sea Foods,** 2020 K St. NW (☎ **202/496-1111**), follow up a cup of light clam chowder (made without butter, cream, or flour) with an entrée of grilled fresh fish and vegetables and a superb sorbet for dessert.
- **Best Late-Night Dining:** To satisfy a yen for Chinese food, go to **Full Kee,** 509 H St. NW in Chinatown (☎ **202/371-2233**), open until 3am on weekends; for more comfortable surroundings and good old American cuisine, try the **Old Ebbitt Grill,** 675 15th St. NW (☎ **202/347-4801**), whose kitchen stays open until 1am on weekends.

- **Best Outdoor Dining: Les Halles,** 1201 Pennsylvania Ave. NW (☎ **202/ 347-6848**), so much fun inside, carries the party outside in warm weather to its partly covered sidewalk cafe, excellently located on the avenue for people watching and sightseeing (the Capitol lies down the street; the Old Post Office Pavilion is directly across the avenue).
- **Best Afternoon Tea:** With lush plantings and windowed walls overlooking the C&O Canal, the divine **Garden Terrace** at the Four Seasons Hotel (☎ **202/ 342-0444**) provides soothing piano music during afternoon tea Monday through Saturday from 3 to 5pm and Sunday from 3:30 to 5pm. For $13.75 you can enjoy a selection of finger sandwiches, fresh fruit tartlets, assorted English tea breads and biscuits, a Scottish sultana scone with double Devonshire cream and homemade preserves, and a pot of fresh-brewed tea. Vintage ports, sherries, and champagne are also available.
- **Best Brunch:** Combine a Kennedy Center tour or Sunday matinee with a lavish brunch at its on-premises **Roof Terrace Restaurant** (☎ 202/416-8555). This ornate establishment invites guests into the kitchen Sundays, from 11:30am to 2:30pm, where a stunning array of food is laid out. Your meal includes a glass of champagne or a mimosa, and live entertainment while you dine. Price is $25.95.
- **Best for Pre-Theater Dinner:** How could you do better than **701's** $22 three-course bargain and its prime location, right around the corner from the Shakespeare Theater and a few blocks from the National and Warner theaters?
- **Best Teas:** This category differs from the above, which is about British-style afternoon repasts. At the charming **Teaism,** 2009 R St. NW (☎ **202/667-3827**), the Asian "tea list," comprising several dozen varieties, is as lovingly composed as the wine list of the most distinguished French restaurant.
- **Best Spot for a Night on the Town:** For an exuberant evening, dine to a Brazilian beat at **Coco Loco,** 810 7th St. NW (☎ **202/289-2626**), and stay on to dance the night away.

2 Restaurants by Cuisine

AMERICAN

America (Capitol Hill, *M*)
Aquarelle (Foggy Bottom, *VE*)
Ashby Inn (Outside D.C., *VE*)
Brighton-on-N (Dupont Circle, *E*)
Capitol City Brewing Co. (Downtown East, *M*)
Cashion's Eat Place (Adams-Morgan, *M*)
Clyde's (Georgetown, *M*)
Daily Grill (Downtown West, *E*)
Felix (Adams-Morgan, *M–E*)
The Inn at Little Washington (Outside D.C., *VE*)
Martin's Tavern (Georgetown, *M*)
Melrose (Foggy Bottom, *E*)
Mendocino Grille and Wine Bar (Georgetown, *E*)
Mrs. Simpson's (Woodley Park, *E*)

Morrison-Clark Inn (Downtown East, *E*)
Nora (Dupont Circle, *VE*)
Occidental Grill (Downtown East, *VE*)
Old Angler's Inn (Outside D.C., *VE*)
Old Ebbitt Grill (Downtown East, *M*)
Reeve's Restaurant and Bakery (Downtown East, *I*)
Restaurant at The Jefferson (Downtown West, *VE*)
Roof Terrace Restaurant (Foggy Bottom, *VE*)
Rupperts (Downtown East, *VE*)
Seasons (Georgetown, *VE*)
Sequoia (Georgetown, *M*)
1789 (Georgetown, *VE*)
Tabard Inn (Dupont Circle, *E*)

Key to Abbreviations: *E*=Expensive; *I*=Inexpensive; *M*=Moderate; *VE*=Very Expensive

Trio (Dupont Circle, *I*)
The Willard Room (Downtown East, *VE*)
WrapWorks (Dupont Circle, *I*)

ASIAN FUSION

Asia Nora (Foggy Bottom, *E*)
Oodles Noodles (Downtown West, *I*)
Perry's (Adams-Morgan, *M*)
Raku (Dupont Circle, *I*)
Teaism (Dupont Circle, *I*)
Xing Kuba (Glover Park, *M*)

BARBECUE

Old Glory (Georgetown, *I*)

CHINESE

City Lights of China (Dupont Circle, *I*)
Full Kee (Downtown East, *I*)

ETHIOPIAN

Meskerem (Adams-Morgan, *I*)
Zed's (Georgetown, *I*)

FRENCH

Bistrot Lepic (Georgetown, *M*)
Citronelle (Georgetown, *VE*)
The Jockey Club (Dupont Circle, *VE*)
L'Auberge Chez Francois (Outside D.C., *VE*)
La Colline (Capitol Hill, *E*)
La Fourchette (Adams-Morgan, *M–E*)
Le Lion d'Or (Downtown West, *VE*)
Lespinasse (Downtown West, *VE*)
Patisserie Café Didier (Georgetown, *I*)
Provence (Foggy Bottom, *E*)

GERMAN

Café Berlin (Capitol Hill, *M*)

INDIAN

Aditi (Georgetown, *M*)
Bombay Club (Downtown West, *E*)

INTERNATIONAL

Cities (Adams-Morgan, *E*)
New Heights (Woodley Park, *E*)
701 (Downtown East, *E*)

ITALIAN

Bice (Downtown East, *E*)
Cafe Parma (Dupont Circle, *M*)

Coppi's (U Street Corridor, *I–M*)
Galileo (Downtown West, *VE*)
Goldoni (Foggy Bottom, *E*)
Il Radicchio (Dupont Circle, *I*)
Luigino (Downtown East, *E*)
Obelisk (Dupont Circle, *E*)
Paolo's (Georgetown, *M*)
Petitto's (Woodley Park, *M*)
Pizzeria Paradiso (Dupont Circle, *I*)
Vincenzo (Dupont Circle, *E*)

JAPANESE

Sushi-Ko (Glover Park, *M*)

LATIN

Café Atlantico (Downtown East, *M*)
Gabriel (Dupont Circle, *E*)

LEBANESE

Lebanese Taverna (Woodley Park, *M*)

MEDITERRANEAN

BeDuCi (Dupont Circle, *M*)
George (Downtown West, *E*)
Isabella (Downtown East, *E*)

MEXICAN

Coco Loco (Downtown East, *M*)
Mixtec (Adams-Morgan, *I*)

SEAFOOD

Georgetown Seafood Grill on 19th Street (Downtown West, *E*)
Kinkead's (Foggy Bottom, *E*)
Legal Sea Foods (Downtown West, *E*)
McCormick & Schmick's (Downtown West, *E*)
Pesce (Dupont Circle, *M*)
The Sea Catch (Georgetown, *E*)

SOUTHERN/ SOUTHWESTERN/ AMERICAN

Austin Grill (Glover Park, *I*)
B. Smith's (Capitol Hill, *E*)
Georgia Brown's (Downtown East, *E*)
Music City Roadhouse (Georgetown, *I*)
Red Sage (Downtown East, *VE*)
Roxanne (Adams-Morgan, *M*)
Vidalia (Downtown West, *E*)

SPANISH

Jaleo (Downtown East, *M*)
Taberna del Alabardero (Downtown West, *VE*)

U St. Wine Bar and Tapas Bistro
(U Street Corridor, *I–M*)

STEAKHOUSES

Les Halles (Downtown East, *E*)
Morton's of Chicago
(Georgetown, *VE*)
The Palm (Downtown West, *E*)
Prime Rib (Downtown West, *VE*)

THAI

Bua (Dupont Circle, *I*)
Busara (Glover Park, *M*)
Haad Thai (Downtown East, *I*)

VIETNAMESE

Miss Saigon (Adams-Morgan, *M*)

3 Adams-Morgan

Though the action centers on just 2 or 3 blocks, Adams-Morgan is one of D.C.'s live-liest neighborhoods, filled with ethnic and trendy restaurants and happening night-clubs. It's best to come here via taxi, since parking is difficult and the closest Metro stop is a bit of a hike. If you do take the Metro, you can get off at Dupont Circle (the Q Street exit) and walk uphill on Connecticut Avenue until you reach the Columbia Road fork, which you follow to Adams-Morgan. Or take Metro to the Woodley Park–Zoo stop, walk south on Connecticut Avenue to Calvert Street, turn left, and cross the Calvert Street bridge to Adams-Morgan. Don't wander too far from the areas described here and in chapter 10; some of the side streets can be dangerous.

EXPENSIVE

Cities

2424 18th St. NW (near Columbia Rd.). ☎ **202/328-7194.** Reservations recommended. Main courses $12.95–$22.95. AE, DC, MC, V. Mon–Thurs 6–11pm, Fri–Sat 6–11:30pm. Bar open Mon–Thurs 5pm–2am, Fri–Sat 5pm–3am. INTERNATIONAL.

Housed in a century-old former five-and-dime store, Cities is a restaurant-cum-travelogue. Once a year, the restaurant is revamped to reflect the cuisine, character, and culture of a different city. Even the music reflects the city under consideration, and waiters are in native dress or some facsimile thereof. For instance, if the city is Paris, decor and cuisine might suggest a Montparnasse-style brasserie. More recently, Cities offered the cuisine of Istanbul, in keeping with the current "Mediterranean" trend. The wine and champagne list is small but expertly conceived, and premium wines are offered by the glass.

The adjoining bar was completely remodeled in 1997, making it upscale and loungey (the upstairs dance hall and bar is more low-key and open only on weekends). The bar menu features light-fare specialties of the highlighted city in the $3.95 to $6.95 range.

MODERATE TO EXPENSIVE

Cashion's Eat Place

1819 Columbia Rd. NW (between 18th St. and Mintwood Place). ☎ **202/797-1819.** Reservations recommended. Main courses $6–$9 at brunch, $11–$17 at dinner. MC, V. Tues and Sun 5:30–10pm, Wed–Sat 5:30–11pm; Sun brunch 11:30am–2:30pm. AMERICAN WITH EUROPEAN INFLUENCES.

A curving bar lies at the center of the agreeable Cashion's Eat Place, up a couple of steps from the main room; people sitting at tables inside the curve tend to prop their arms comfortably upon the half-wall and converse from time to time with the patrons seated in the dining area below.

Owner/chef Ann Cashion has gained renown for her stints at Nora, Austin Grill, and Jaleo. Her menu includes about eight entrées, split between seafood and meat—for example, grilled wild Chesapeake rockfish, or rabbit loin sautéed with prunes and Armagnac. The side dishes that accompany each entrée, such as spiced red cabbage and chestnuts and sautéed foie gras, are worth as much attention. Cashion's has snagged Washington's best pastry chef, Ann Amernick, who turns out four or five temptations nightly, like lemon caramel tart or banana croissant bread pudding.

The glass-fronted Cashion's opens invitingly to the sidewalk in warm weather. But we were there on a frigid January day when each opening of the door blew a blast of cold over those of us seated at the front of the restaurant. A double door would take care of the problem. Go to Cashion's, but if it's a wintry day, ask for a table at the back.

Felix

2406 18th St. NW. ☎ **202/483-3549.** Reservations recommended. Main courses $7–$10 at brunch, $12–$18 at dinner, $22.50 for pre-theater dinner. AE, DC, DISC, MC, V. Tues–Thurs 5:30–10pm, Fri–Sat 5–11pm, Sun 11am–2:30pm; Tues–Sun 5:30–7:30pm. Live music Thurs 11pm–1:30am, Fri–Sat 11pm–2:30am. AMERICAN.

Felix and its patrons try hard to be hip. Customers down martinis at the bar and sometimes crush up against dining tables (the areas adjoin on the first floor). Despite an attractive decor that includes a three-dimensional mural of international landmark buildings and a celestially painted ceiling, the scene at Felix feels like a party in a group house, an impression reinforced by the dimly lit living room setups in the back room and upstairs. (You're afraid to peer too closely at what that couple in the corner is doing.)

But that's just the atmosphere at this bar-cum-bistro. The food is quite good: Cream of mushroom soup is seasoned just right and delicately creamy; the pork chop, by contrast, is huge and hearty, not at all fatty, and served with upright square pillows of crusted milky mashed potatoes. The lamb shank osso buco is meaty and tender. Chocolate lovers will go for the decadent Sundae-upon-a-brownie, but anyone would like the strawberry mousse parfait.

La Fourchette

2429 18th St. NW. ☎ **202/332-3077.** Reservations recommended on weekends. Prix-fixe menu $14.95. Main courses $8.95–$21.95 at lunch and dinner. Mon–Fri 11:30am–4pm; Mon–Thurs 4–10:30pm, Fri–Sat 4–11pm, Sun 4–10pm. AE, DC, MC, V. FRENCH.

Upstairs is non-smoking, but downstairs is where you want to be, among the French-speaking clientele and Adams-Morgan regulars. The waiters are suitably crusty and the ambience is as Parisian as you'll get this side of the Atlantic. So is the food. The menu lists escargots, onion soup, bouillabaisse, and mussels provencale, along with specials like the grilled salmon on spinach mousse, and the shrimp Niçoise, ever-so-slightly crusted and sautéed in a tomato sauce touched lightly with anchovy. A colorful mural covers the high walls; wooden tables and benches push up against bare brick walls. La Fourchette is Washington's Paris cafe.

MODERATE

Miss Saigon

1847 Columbia Rd. NW (at Mintwood Place). ☎ **202/667-1900.** Reservations recommended, especially weekend nights. Main courses $5.50–$7.95 at lunch, $6.95–$14.95 at dinner. AE, DISC, MC, V. Mon–Thurs noon–10:30pm, Fri–Sat noon–11pm, Sun noon–10pm. VIETNAMESE.

This is a charming restaurant, with tables scattered amid a "forest" of potted palms, ferns, and other tropical foliage. When the weather is warm, umbrella tables on the walled terrace are the more popular seating choice. The Georgetown location (3057 M St. NW; ☎ **202/333-5545**) is equally attractive.

The food here is delicious and authentic, though the service can be a trifle slow when the restaurant is busy. To begin, there are crispy spring rolls stuffed with cellophane noodles, mushrooms, pork, onions, and vegetables; wrap them in lettuce leaves with coriander and dip the whole thing in fish sauce. Also excellent is the shaking beef: crusty cubes of tender beef, marinated in wine, garlic, butter, and soy sauce, then sautéed with onions and potatoes and served with rice and salad. There's a full bar. Desserts range from bananas flambé au rhum to ice cream with Godiva liqueur. Not to be missed is drip pot coffee, brewed tableside and served iced over sweetened condensed milk.

Roxanne

2319 18th St. NW (between Belmont and Kalorama rds.). ☎ **202/462-8330.** Reservations recommended. Main courses $4.95–$9.95 at brunch, $7.95–$14.95 at dinner; sandwiches, salads, and burgers $3.95–$8.95. AE, MC, V. Mon–Fri 5–11pm, Sat–Sun 11:30am–midnight. Bar, Sun–Thurs to 2am, Fri–Sat to 3am. SOUTHWESTERN.

If you want simple tacos and burritos in a smoky bar setting, go downstairs to Peyote Cafe. Roxanne, under the same ownership, offers "cuisine" rather than "eats," says the waitress—which means the atmosphere's still laid-back, but the menu describes things like pepita salmon (baked in a pumpkin seed crust, served over spiced black beans, with chile-grilled shrimp and corn-tomato salsa). You can order from Roxanne's menu if you're in the Peyote Cafe, but not vice versa. (The rooftop On the Rox serves the same menu as Roxanne and is open spring through fall.) If you want a *real* margarita, specify the tequila you want from Roxanne's list of 34 (LARGEST TEQUILA SELECTION IN ADAMS-MORGAN, the sign says); otherwise, you'll end up with the wimp version served in a short highball glass.

INEXPENSIVE

Meskerem

2434 18th St. NW (between Columbia and Belmont rds.). ☎ **202/462-4100.** Main courses $5–$10.50 at lunch, $8.50–$11.50 at dinner. AE, DC, MC, V. Mon–Fri noon–midnight, Sat–Sun noon–2am. ETHIOPIAN.

Washington has a number of Ethiopian restaurants, but this is probably the best. It's certainly the most attractive; the three-level, high-ceilinged dining room (sunny by day, candlelit at night) has an oval skylight girded by a painted sunburst and walls hung with African art and musical instruments. On the mezzanine level, you sit at *messobs* (basket tables) on low carved Ethiopian chairs or upholstered leather poufs. Ethiopian music (including live bands after midnight on weekends) enhances the ambience.

Diners share large platters of food, which are scooped up with a sourdough crepelike pancake called *injera*. Items listed as *watt* are hot and spicy; *alitchas* are milder and more delicately flavored. You might also share an entrée—perhaps *yegeb kay watt* (succulent lamb in thick, hot berbere sauce)—along with a combination platter of five vegetarian dishes served with tomato and potato salads. There are combination platters comprising an array of beef, chicken, lamb, and vegetables. There's a full bar, and the wine list includes Ethiopian wine and beer.

Mixtec

1792 Columbia Rd. (just off 18th St.). ☎ **202/332-1011.** Main courses $2.95–$9.95. MC, V. Sun–Thurs 11am–10:30pm, Fri–Sat 11am–11pm. MEXICAN REGIONAL.

This cheerful Adams-Morgan eatery attracts a clientele of Hispanics, neighborhood folks, and D.C. chefs, all of whom appreciate the delicious authenticity of its regional Mexican cuisines. The kitchen is open, the dining room colorfully decorated, and the music is lively salsa.

Queens for a Day

A drag brunch in conservative, staid D.C.? Only in Adams-Morgan at the whimsically urban-hip **Perry's,** 1811 Columbia Rd. NW (☎ **202/234-6218**). Its funky-elegant art-deco interior features lime-green walls, mirrored columns, French windows (open in warm weather) framed by imposing floor-to-ceiling red curtains, and a chandelier that looks like an alien octopus suspended from a fire engine–red plastic cushion. A weird black metal cagelike structure serves as a room divider, and seating includes gold brocade sofas at 1950s blond-wood coffee tables. During Sunday brunch, drag queens in over-the-top outfits (one slinks around the room in a black vinyl cat costume) appear every 15 minutes or so; they dance, flirt with male customers, camp it up, and lip synch to the music. The crowd is about one-quarter hip straight folks, the rest gay men, and everyone has a great time. Brunch ($15.95, including coffee or tea) consists of an extensive buffet, including paella, French toast, sushi, smoked salmon, eggs and breakfast meats, sesame noodles, grilled vegetables, cold cuts, cheeses, desserts, and more. It's served from 11:30am to 3pm, and you can't make reservations; arrive early to avoid a wait. Also consider Perry's for moderately priced al fresco Asian-fusion dinners; its lovely rooftop deck, festively strung with yellow lights, opens nightly at 6pm.

Delicious made-from-scratch corn and flour tortillas enhance whatever they're stuffed with. Small dishes called *antojitos* ("little whims") are in the $2.50 to $4.95 range, including *queso fundido* (a bubbling hot dish of broiled Chihuahua cheese topped with shredded spicy chorizo sausage and flavored with jalapeños and cilantro). The freshly prepared guacamole is excellent. The house specialty, a full entrée served with rice and beans, is mole Mexicano—broiled chicken in a rich sauce of five peppers (the kitchen uses some 200 different spices!), sunflower and sesame seeds, onions, garlic, almonds, cinnamon, and chocolate. Choose from 30 kinds of tequila, tequila-mixed drinks, Mexican beers, and fresh fruit juices.

4 Dupont Circle

VERY EXPENSIVE

The Jockey Club

In the Luxury Collection Hotel, Washington, D.C., 2100 Massachusetts Ave. NW. ☎ **800/ 325-3589.** Reservations required. Main courses $5–$12 at breakfast, $12–$23 at lunch, $24–$30 at dinner. AE, CB, DC, DISC, MC, V. Daily 6:30–11am, noon–2:30pm, and 6–10:30pm. Jacket and tie required at dinner. Metro: Dupont Circle. FRENCH/CONTINENTAL.

The Jockey Club, Washington's longest-running power-dining enclave, opened in 1961 and immediately became a Kennedy clan favorite (it still is). JFK once quipped that when he wanted to reach a staff member, he first called their office, then their home, then The Jockey Club. Nancy Reagan and Barbara Bush were regulars. It's a moneyed bunch who come here, and you're likely to see more than one whitehaired gentleman squiring about a much younger woman.

The dining room is cheerful and pubby, with red-leather banquettes, a random-plank oak floor, lanterns suspended from a low beamed ceiling (the subdued amber lighting is as cozy as the glow of a fireplace), and walls of stucco or aged oak paneling hung with English equestrian prints.

Executive chef Hidemasa Yamamoto brings Eastern nuance to classic continental cookery. For instance, an appetizer of sautéed quail with California artichokes and

Adams-Morgan & Dupont Circle Dining

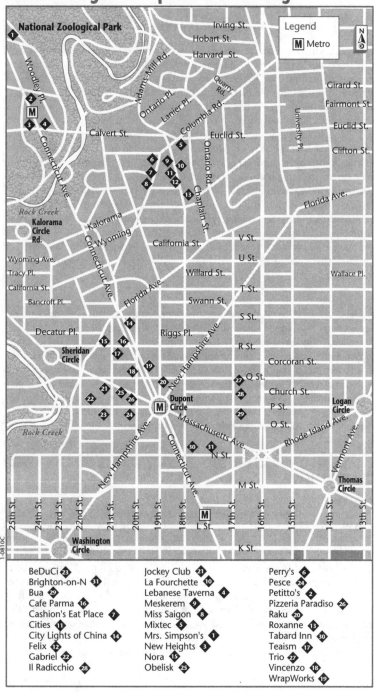

Legend
M Metro

National Zoological Park

Irving St.
Hobart St.
Harvard St.
Girard St.
Fairmont St.
Euclid St.
Clifton St.

Woodley Pl.
Adams-Mill Rd.
Ontario Pl.
Lanier Pl.
Calvert St.
Quarry Rd.
Columbia Rd.
Euclid St.
Ontario Rd.
University Pl.

Connecticut Ave.

Rock Creek
Kalorama
Circle
Rd.
Kalorama
Wyoming
California St.
Chaplain St.
Florida Ave.

V St.
U St.

Wyoming Ave.
Tracy Pl.
California St.
Bancroft Pl.
Willard St.
T St.
S St.
Wallace Pl.

Florida Ave.
Swann St.

Decatur Pl.
Riggs Pl.
R St.
Corcoran St.

Sheridan
Circle
New Hampshire Ave.
Q St.
Church St.
Logan
Circle

Dupont
Circle
M
P St.
O St.
Rhode Island Ave.

Rock Creek
Massachusetts Ave.

New Hampshire Ave.
Connecticut Ave.
N St.

Vermont Ave.
Thomas
Circle

M St.

25th St.
24th St.
23rd St.
22nd St.
21st St.
20th St.
19th St.
18th St.
17th St.
16th St.
15th St.
14th St.
13th St.

Washington
Circle
M
L St.
K St.

1-0810C

BeDuCi 23	Jockey Club 21	Perry's 6
Brighton-on-N 31	La Fourchette 10	Pesce 24
Bua 29	Lebanese Taverna 4	Petitto's 2
Cafe Parma 16	Meskerem 9	Pizzeria Paradiso 26
Cashion's Eat Place 7	Miss Saigon 8	Raku 20
Cities 11	Mixtec 5	Roxanne 13
City Lights of China 14	Mrs. Simpson's 1	Tabard Inn 30
Felix 12	New Heights 3	Teaism 17
Gabriel 22	Nora 15	Trio 27
Il Radicchio 28	Obelisk 25	Vincenzo 18
		WrapWorks 19

104

green lentils is garnished with oba (Japanese basil). However, big fluffy crabcakes meunière comprise the restaurant's signature dish—more than 45,000 are ordered yearly. The pommes souffles side dish has been on the menu since the restaurant opened. The thing to do, though, is to ask for the chef's menu when you reserve a table; Yamamoto will create a four-course sampling dinner for you from the whole menu.

Nora

2132 Florida Ave. NW (at R St.). ☎ **202/462-5143.** Reservations recommended. Main courses $19.95–$24.95. MC, V. Mon–Thurs 6–10pm, Fri–Sat 6–10:30pm. Metro: Dupont Circle. ORGANIC AMERICAN.

Owner-chef Nora Pouillon brings haute panache to healthful organic cookery in this charming restaurant. The skylit main dining room is a converted stable, with a weathered-looking beamed pine ceiling, tables lit by shaded paraffin lamps, and a display of Amish and Mennonite patchwork crib quilts on the walls.

The chemical-free, organically grown, free-range cuisine is extremely healthful, but not brown-rice-and-bean-sprout fare. Nightly varying menus feature entrées such as grilled Copper River king salmon (served with tomato-onion relish, sweet corn succotash, and fiddlehead ferns) and roasted free-range chicken stuffed with goat cheese and toasted pumpkin seeds (served with fresh-baked cornbread and grilled zucchini in ancho chili sauce). Many desserts use fruits and nuts—for instance, warm apple and raspberry cobbler with maple ice cream. An extensive wine list includes, but is not limited to, selections made with organically grown grapes. I promise you won't miss any of the bad-for-you ingredients at Nora, and you will experience the vivid and earthy flavors of natural foods.

EXPENSIVE

✪ Brighton-on-N

In the Canterbury Hotel, 1733 N St. NW. ☎ **202/296-0665.** Reservations recommended. Main courses $10–$13.50 at brunch, $8–$12.50 at lunch, $17.50–$24 at dinner. AE, CB, DC, DISC, MC, V. Mon–Sat 11am–3pm and 6–10pm, Sun brunch 11am–3pm. Metro: Dupont Circle, Farragut North. AMERICAN.

Brighton-on-N lies below street level, in the Canterbury Hotel, and yet it is one of the brightest dining rooms you'll find. (If you want cozy, go upstairs to the Brighton Pub and eat your Brighton-on-N dinner there.) Fabric colors are deep salmon and celery, the carpeting a grassy green, the walls lemon yellow. Little vases of fresh-cut yellow roses decorate each table. Diners tend to be locals more than hotel guests.

The food is sublime. First comes a basket of biscuits, sweet bread, and crusty peasant bread. The appetizers and entrées that follow live up to their dramatically artistic presentation. Steamed carrots, sweet potato, haricots verts, and snap peas arrive piping hot in a pretty bamboo steamer, ready for dipping in the lime cilantro and ginger soy dressings. A romaine heart salad combines caramelized balsamic onions and giant cheese twists with a creamy Caesar dressing. A scale of scalloped red potatoes encloses shrimp mousse layered upon red snapper. The rare tuna entrée is almost sushi, wrapped in a seaweed and coriander crust, with plum soy sauce on the side. Desserts, like trifle, are less spectacular, though tasty.

Gabriel

In the Radisson Barceló Hotel, 2121 P St. NW. ☎ **202/956-6690.** Reservations recommended. Main courses $8–$14 at lunch, $15–$22 at dinner; tapas $2.75–$6.50; Mon–Fri lunch buffet $9.50, Sun brunch buffet $16.75, Wed–Fri happy-hour buffet $7.50. AE, CB, DC, DISC, MC, V. Mon–Thurs 11:30am–10pm, Fri–Sat 11:30am–10:30pm; Sun 11am–9:30pm (brunch 11am–3pm). Tapas and bar daily 11:30am–10:30pm. Metro: Dupont Circle. LATIN AMERICAN/ MEDITERRANEAN.

Glorious Grazing at Gabriel

After work on Wednesday, Thursday, and Friday evenings, Dupont Circle businesspeople head for the bar at Gabriel (details below). The draw: a superb $7.50 happy hour buffet set out from 5:30 to 8pm. It's an all-you-can-eat affair, with a choice of about seven scrumptious tapas, made-to-order quesadillas, and reduced drink prices (including microbrew drafts for $2.50). A more extensive lunch buffet (weekdays 11:30am to 2pm, $9.50), also with a quesadilla station, offers a similar array of tapas plus marvelous salads, cheeses, and entrées such as paella and cassoulet. Even more elaborate is Gabriel's Sunday brunch (11am to 3pm, $16.75), which adds a carving station (for whole suckling pig, roast beef, and leg of lamb), omelets and breakfast meats, pastas, fresh-baked breads, vegetables, and desserts. Every one of these buffets represents sensational value, and the food is first rate.

Like Coco Loco (see below), Gabriel features Latin-accented fare including tapas; while the former is funky/hip, however, this is a sophisticated upscale setting. A large rectangular mahogany bar is the centerpiece of a convivial lounge area; outdoors is a small patio cafe with umbrella tables. Noted Washington chef Greggory Hill spent months studying with major chefs in various parts of Spain and Mexico before creating Gabriel's dazzlingly innovative and ever-changing menu.

Sample a variety of tapas at the bar or begin a meal with them—plump chorizo-stuffed black figs or chili-flavored corn/potato pancakes served with large grilled scallops and spicy chorizo sausage. Entrées might include lamb with mole and sweet potato plantain mash or pork tenderloin with black bean sauce on basmati rice. Crusty-chewy fresh-baked sourdough bread is great dipped in rosemary/garlic-infused olive oil. There's a well-chosen wine list, with several by-the-glass selections including dry and sweet sherries—the ideal complement to tapas. Incredible desserts here include a warm phyllo purse stuffed with papaya, pineapple, berries, and pistachio nuts, poised on cinnamon custard.

✪ Obelisk

2029 P St. NW. ☎ **202/872-1180.** Reservations recommended. Prix-fixe 5-course dinners only: $40. DC, MC, V. Mon–Sat 6–10pm. Metro: Dupont Circle. ITALIAN.

In this pleasantly spare room decorated with 19th-century French botanical prints and Italian lithographs, owner/chef Peter Pastan presents his small prix-fixe menus of simply sophisticated Italian cuisine that uses the freshest possible ingredients. Pastan says his culinary philosophy is to "get the best stuff we can and try not to screw it up." Each night's menu offers diners two or three choices for each course. A recent dinner began with an antipasti of peppers with olivada and anchovies, followed by a Provencale sea bass soup seasoned with saffron, and an artfully arranged dish of pan-cooked snapper with artichokes, thyme, and pancetta. Rather than cheese, I enjoyed a dessert of pear spice cake. Pastan's carefully crafted wine list encompasses varied regions of Italy. The $40 prix-fixe menu seems a deal, but the cost of wine and coffees can easily double the price per person.

Tabard Inn

1739 N St. NW. ☎ **202/331-8528.** Reservations recommended. Main courses $2.50–$7.50 at breakfast, $8.50–$12 at lunch, $14–$23 at dinner. AE, MC, V. Mon 7–10am, 11:30am–2:30pm, and 6–10pm; Tues–Fri 7–10am, 11:30am–2:30pm, and 6–10:30pm; Sat 8–10am, 11am–2:30pm (brunch), and 6–10:30pm; Sun 8–9:30am, 10:30am–2:30pm (brunch), and 6–10pm. Metro: Dupont Circle. AMERICAN.

The restaurant here is only a shade more conventional than the inn in which it resides (see listing in chapter 5). From the cozy lounge, you enter a narrow room, where hanging plants dangle from skylights and a mural of a ponytailed waiter points the way to the kitchen. A small bar hugs one side of the passage, a series of small tables the other, and both lead to the main space. Or you can head up a set of stairs to another dining room and its adjoining courtyard. Restaurant staff, like inn staff, are disarmingly solicitous.

The food is fresh and seasonal, making use of the inn's own homegrown vegetables and herbs. A curried butternut squash and apple soup was thick and smooth, the floating cilantro leaf providing just the right accent. The inn's version of Caesar salad featured an anchovy dressing and slivers of Parmesan cheese over greens peppered with smashed-up croutons. Fresh fish, vegetables, and desserts are your best bets.

Vincenzo

1606 20th St. NW. ☎ **202/667-0047.** Reservations recommended. Main courses $15–$17 at lunch, $15–$21 at dinner. AE, CB, DC, MC, V. Mon–Fri noon–2pm; Mon–Sat 6–10pm. Metro: Dupont Circle. SEAFOOD/ITALIAN.

Alternately known as Vincenzo al Sole, Trattoria al Sole, and now, Vincenzo (or is it Trattoria?), this restaurant is named for its effusive owner, Vince MacDonald, who thinks of himself as Italian, though he is, in fact, American-with-Italian-roots. The menu is Italian, with the emphasis on fish; a sample entrée is the Atlantic cod with breadcrumbs, capers, and olives with sautéed escarole. As soon as soft shell crabs are in season in late spring, this is a good place to try them, lightly breaded and fried. The pastas are excellent—fresh ingredients making all the difference.

At street level is Vincenzo's slate terrace, where you can dine at umbrella tables; you go down a short flight of steps to reach Vincenzo's dining room; it resembles a trattoria with its rosy claytoned walls, arched skylight, and tile floor. Across the long, narrow entry hall from the main dining room are the bar and more tables, where, if you're lucky, you can sit and shoot the breeze with Vince—that is, Vincenzo—himself.

MODERATE

BeDuCi

2100 P St. NW. ☎ **202/223-3824.** Reservations recommended. Main courses $9–$18.95 at lunch, $10–$22.95 at dinner. AE, DC, DISC, MC, V. Mon–Fri 11:30am–2:30pm, Mon–Thurs 5:30–10pm, Fri–Sat 5:30–10:30pm, Sun 5:30–9:30pm. Complimentary valet parking at dinner. Metro: Foggy Bottom. MEDITERRANEAN.

Though Mediterranean cuisine is suddenly trendy in Washington, BeDuCi has been serving it since opening 5 years ago. Entrées range from pastas and couscous to paellas and vegetarian stews. Your best bets are the specials, whether you choose an appetizer (maybe cream of cauliflower soup with rock shrimp), or an entrée (say, the duck breast filled with lemon zest, wrapped with bacon and figs). Desserts, like the pineapple cobbler, are wonderfully rich and made by co-owner Michele Miller. The name BeDuCi refers to the restaurant's location: **Be**low **Du**pont **Ci**rcle. A sun porch fronts the restaurant, turning into a covered outdoor cafe in warm weather. The three inside dining rooms are decorated with paintings and prints on white walls.

Cafe Parma

1724 Connecticut Ave. NW (between R and S sts.). ☎ **202/462-8771.** No reservations. Main courses $8–$14; weekday buffet lunch and daily buffet dinner $9.95, weekend buffet brunch $10.75; pizzas from $6.75; panini (sandwiches) and filoncini (subs) $5–$6.50. AE, DC, DISC, MC, V. Daily 11:30am–10:30pm; bar stays open until 1am Sun–Thurs, 2am Fri–Sat. Metro: Dupont Circle. ITALIAN.

Cafe Parma lures diners inside with an exquisite antipasti display in the front window—about 30 items that might include bean salads, marinated eggplant, snow peas with oil-cured olives, creamy egg salad, pasta salads, escarole and pancetta, home-made potato salad, calamari salad, grilled vegetables, and much more. It's always changing and always fabulous, and if you arrive during weekday happy hour, it's free. Pizzas here are baked on flavorful bread dough that's lightly fried in olive oil before toppings are added (more than 30 choices ranging from grilled chicken breast to sun-dried tomatoes). Besides a selection of pastas, the cafe also serves sandwiches (for example, eggplant parmigiana on baguette with oven-roasted potatoes). Italian wines are reasonably priced and available by the glass. Additional breakfast items such as eggs Benedict are offered at brunch, but you can't beat the lavish all-you-can-eat buffet for value and quality.

The pleasant dining room has pine-wainscoted stucco walls hung with artistic pho-tographs of Washington. A handsome bar and a sunken dining room adjoin. Arrive off-hours to avoid waiting in line.

✪ Pesce

2016 P St. NW. ☎ **202/466-3474.** Reservations accepted for lunch, 6 or more at dinner. Main courses $11.95–$21 at dinner. AE, CB, DC, DISC, MC, V. Mon–Fri 11:30am–2:30pm, Sat noon–3pm; Mon–Thurs 5:30–10pm, Fri–Sat 5:30–10:30pm, Sun 5–9:30pm. Metro: Dupont Circle. SEAFOOD.

Nightly, from about 8:30 until 9:30, a line of people forms inside the cramped wait-ing area of this restaurant, sometimes trailing out the door, just to enjoy the marvel-ous grilled or sautéed fresh fish. If you get there earlier than 8:30, you may still have a wait, but not as long. This small, crowded restaurant has a convivial atmosphere, brought on, no doubt, by the collective anticipation of a pleasant meal. In this simple setting of exposed brick walls adorned with colorfully painted wooden fish, waiters scurry to bring you a basket of crusty bread, your wine selection, and the huge black-board menu. Among the many appetizers are blue point oysters on the half shell and several tasty salads. Entrées always list several pastas along with the differently pre-pared fish. My grilled monkfish entrée was firm but tender, and delicious upon its bed of potato purée and wild mushroom ragoût. Jointly owned by chefs Roberto Donna and Jean-Louis Palladin, Pesce bears their mark of excellence, even though neither actually works in the kitchen.

INEXPENSIVE

Bua

1635 P St. NW. ☎ **202/265-0828.** Reservations suggested. Main courses $5.95–$7.75 at lunch, $7.95–$14.95 at dinner. AE, DC, DISC, MC, V. Mon–Fri 11:30am–2:30pm, Sat–Sun noon–4pm; Sun–Thurs 5–10:30pm, Fri–Sat 5–11pm. Metro: Dupont Circle, with a 10–15 minute walk. THAI.

Walk by on a Friday or Saturday night, and you'll see this two-story restaurant packed (and in summer, tables are full on the second floor outdoor balcony). In spite of its two floors, Bua is not large; it gets mostly a neighborhood crowd, with office people filling the place for weekday lunch. The food is inexpensive and the service gracious and honest; my server steered me away from the "heavenly wings" appetizer, pronouncing them "too crusty." Consider instead the satays, pad thai, and steamed seafood in banana leaves—all house specialties. The peanut sauce accompanying the satays is so good that Bua should sell containers of it for people to stock at home. The spring rolls are very delicate, not greasy.

City Lights of China

1731 Connecticut Ave. NW (between R and S sts.). ☎ **202/265-6688.** Reservations recommended. Main courses $6.95–$11.95 at dinner (a few are pricier). AE, DC, DISC, MC, V. Mon–Thurs 11:30am–10:30pm, Fri 11:30am–11pm, Sat noon–11pm, Sun noon–10:30pm; dinner from 3pm daily. Metro: Dupont Circle. CHINESE.

One of Washington's best Chinese restaurants outside of Chinatown, City Lights keeps getting bigger to accommodate its fans, who range from Mick Jagger to Natalie Cole to Jesse Jackson to Attorney General Janet Reno. White House workaholics frequently order deliveries of City Lights carryout. Favorite dishes prepared by Taiwanese chef (and part owner) Kuo-Tai Soug include crisp-fried Cornish hen prepared in a cinnamon-soy marinade and served with a tasty dipping sauce, garlicky Chinese eggplant with a hot red-pepper tang, stir-fried spinach, crisp fried shredded beef, and the Peking duck. The setting is pretty but unpretentious—a three-tiered dining room with much of the seating in comfortable pale-green leather booths and banquettes. Neat white-linened tables set with peach napkins, cloth flower arrangements in lighted niches, and green neon track lighting complete the picture. There's a full bar.

✪ Il Radicchio

1509 17th St. NW. ☎ **202/986-2627.** Reservations not accepted. Main courses $5.50–$14.50. AE, DC, DISC, MC, V. Mon–Thurs 11:30am–11pm, Fri–Sat 11:30am–midnight, Sun 5–11pm. Metro: Dupont Circle, with a 10–15 minute walk. ITALIAN.

What a great idea: Order a replenishable bowl of spaghetti for the table at a set price of $6.50, and each of you chooses your own sauce from a long list, at prices that range from $1.50 to $4. Most are standards, like the carbonara of cream, pancetta, black pepper, and egg yolk, and the puttanesca of black olives, capers, garlic, anchovies, and tomato. It's a great deal.

The kitchen prepares daily specials, like Saturday's oven-baked veal stew with polenta, as well as sandwiches, and an assortment of 14 wood-baked pizzas, with a choice of 25 toppings. I'd stick with the pizza, pasta, and salad.

Radicchio pops up on one of the thin-crusted pizzas, in salads like the radicchio and pancetta in balsamic vinaigrette, and in a pasta, with sausage, red wine, and tomato, all of which are recommended.

Ingredients are fresh and flavorful, the service quick and solicitous. This branch of the restaurant draws a neighborhood crowd to its long, warm and cozy room decorated with wall murals of barnyard animals and radicchio leaves. The Georgetown Il Radicchio (1211 Wisconsin Ave. NW; ☎ **202/337-2627**) tends to attract college students and families.

Pizzeria Paradiso

2029 P St. NW. ☎ **202/223-1245.** No reservations. Pizzas $6.75–$15.95; sandwiches and salads $3.25–$6.25. DC, MC, V. Mon–Thurs 11am–11pm, Fri–Sat 11am–midnight, Sun noon–10pm. Metro: Dupont Circle. PIZZA AND PANINI.

Peter Pastan, master chef/owner of Obelisk, right next door, owns this classy, often crowded, 16-table pizzeria. Don't think Domino's. An oak-burning oven at one end of the charming room produces exceptionally doughy but light pizza crusts. As you wait, you can munch on the mixed olives placed in a small bowl before you and gaze up at the ceiling painted to suggest blue sky peeking through ancient stone walls. Pizzas range from the plainest Paradiso, which offers chunks of tomatoes covered in melted mozzarella, to the robust Siciliano, which is a blend of 9 ingredients, including eggplant and red onion. Or you can choose your own toppings from a list of 29. You can also order the daily special and be rewarded with an inspired creation, like potatoes roasted with goat cheese, red onions, and chives atop the chewy crust. Two sizes are available, 8-inch and 12-inch, and most toppings cost 75¢ each on the 8-inch, $1.25 each on the 12-inch. As popular as pizza are the panini (sandwiches) of home-made focaccia stuffed with marinated roasted lamb and vegetables and other fillings, and the salads, such as tuna and white bean. Good desserts, but a limited wine list.

Raku

1900 Q St. NW. ☎ **202/265-7258.** No reservations. All menu items $2.25–$8.50. MC, V. Mon–Thurs 11:30am–midnight, Fri–Sat 11:30am–2am, Sun noon–10pm. Metro: Dupont Circle. ASIAN.

Raku's glass-fronted restaurant occupies a prominent, excellent people-watching cor-ner near Dupont Circle. Spring through fall, the scene gets even better, when Raku's windowed walls open to its sidewalk cafe. Inside, you find artfully tied bamboo poles and Japanese temple beams, *shoji* screens, and TV monitors airing campy videos (any-thing from *Godzilla* to instructions for using chopsticks), as background music plays Asian pop. A curvilinear bar overlooks the kitchen, where chefs prepare the street food of China, Japan, Korea, and Thailand. Try the skewers, like the Thai lemongrass chicken and the Saigon satay (soy-glazed minced shrimp and chicken wrapped around sugar cane, served with cucumber salad and piquant peanut sauce) and dumplings, especially Peking duck with scallions and hoisin barbecue. But the noodle dishes are unreliable, bland one day and spicy the next, although the kowloon (roasted pork, shrimps, ham, and Peking duck dumplings in chicken broth full of bok choy, mus-tard greens, pea shoots, and thick noodles) may be worth taking a chance on. The Hunan chicken salad is wildly popular. Staff deliver each dish to your table as it is prepared, whether you're ready or not.

Teaism

2009 R St. NW (between Connecticut and 21st sts.). ☎ **202/667-3827.** No reservations. All menu items 75¢–$7.50. AE, MC, V. Mon–Thurs 8am–10pm, Fri 8am–11pm, Sat 9am–11pm, Sun 9am–10pm. Metro: Dupont Circle. ASIAN TEAHOUSE.

Occupying a turn-of-the-century neoclassic building on a tree-lined street, Teaism has a lovely rustic interior such as you might find at a teahouse in the countryside of China. A display kitchen and tandoor oven dominate the sunny downstairs room, which offers counter seating along a wall of French windows, open in warm weather. Upstairs seating is on banquettes and small Asian stools at hand-crafted mahogany tables.

The tea list, as impressive as the wine list of a top French restaurant, comprises close to 50 aromatic blends, most of them from India, China, and Japan. Many have exotic names: golden water turtle, jasmine pearl. On the menu is light Asian fare served in lacquer lunch boxes (Japanese "bento boxes") or on stainless-steel plates. Items include salmon cured in lapsang souchong served with chopped bok choy, tandoor-baked lamb kebabs, and stir-fried chicken with coconut. Baked goods, coconut ice cream, and lime shortbread cookies are among desserts. At breakfast you might try cilantro eggs and sausage with fresh tandoor-baked onion nan (chewy Indian bread). Everything's available for carryout. Tea pots, cups, and other gift items are for sale.

Trio

1537 17th St. NW (at Q St.). ☎ **202/232-6305.** No reservations. Main courses $5.75–$9.50 at lunch and dinner; burgers and sandwiches $1.75–$5.75; full breakfasts $2.75–$5.95. AE, MC, V. Daily 7:30am–midnight. Metro: Dupont Circle (Q St. exit). AMERICAN.

This art-deco coffee shop's roomy red leather booths (the kind with coathooks) are filled each morning with local residents checking out the *Washington Post* over big platters of bacon and eggs. In warm weather, the awning-covered outdoor cafe is always packed. The four-decades-old Trio is run by George Mallios, son of the original owners, and is something of a Washington legend.

The food is fresh, and you can't beat the prices. The same menu is offered throughout the day, with low-priced lunch and dinner specials, such as crabcakes with tartar sauce and grilled pork chops with applesauce—all served with two side dishes (perhaps roasted new potatoes and buttered fresh carrots). The wine list and à la carte menu are extensive. A full bar offers everything from microbrews to Fuzzy Navels, and a soda fountain turns out hot-fudge sundaes and milkshakes.

Note: If there's no room here, go next door to the **Fox and Hounds,** under the same ownership and offering the same menu.

WrapWorks

1601 Connecticut Ave. NW. ☎ **202/265-4200.** No reservations. Wraps $3.95–$6.75. No credit cards. Sun–Thurs 11am–11pm, Fri–Sat 11am–midnight. Metro: Dupont Circle. TRENDY FUSION AMERICAN.

It's a wrap: an immense tortilla enveloping a meal. Wraps are fast food for health-conscious people in a hurry, so veggies figure prominently. For example, the "Ken and Barbecue" folds a spinach tortilla around spicy barbecue chicken or steak with garlic mashed potatoes, corn and pepper relish, black beans, chipotle slaw, and a splash of lime sour cream. The wraps tend to be unwieldy, so grab plenty of napkins and maybe a fork; you can also order a plate of the same fare, unwrapped. Among the fillings are fish, Kung Pao chicken, and shrimp; other menu items run toward the custom-made salads, black beans and Mexican rice, and smoothies (shakes made with yogurt and fruit). The Dupont Circle WrapWorks has countertops and stools placed before its full-length windows for people-watching. WrapWorks originated in San Francisco and plans to expand to other locations; there's already another branch in Georgetown, at 1079 Wisconsin Ave. NW (☎ **202/333-0220**).

5 Capitol Hill

For information on eating at the Capitol and other government buildings, see "Dining at Sightseeing Attractions," later in this chapter.

EXPENSIVE

B. Smith's

Union Station, 50 Massachusetts Ave. NE. ☎ **202/289-6188.** Reservations recommended. Main courses mostly $8.95–$17.95 at lunch and brunch, $10.95–$21.95 at dinner. AE, CB, DC, DISC, MC, V. Mon–Sat 11:30am–4pm and 5pm–midnight, Sun 11:30am–8pm. Free validated parking for 2 hours. Metro: Union Station. TRADITIONAL SOUTHERN.

Union Station's most upscale restaurant is the creation of former model Barbara Smith; it occupies the room where presidents once greeted visiting monarchs and dignitaries. The dining room has 29-foot ceilings, imposing mahogany doors, white marble floors, gold-leafed moldings, and towering Ionic columns. Background music is mellow (Nat King Cole, Ray Charles, Sarah Vaughan). The restaurant features live jazz on Friday and Saturday evenings and at Sunday brunch. Chef Robert Holmes spent 14 years as head chef in Paul Prudhomme's kitchen at K-Paul's in New Orleans. Hence, his menu offers appetizers such as jambalaya or red beans and rice studded with andouille sausage and tasso (spicy smoked pork). Among the main dishes are Holmes's sautéed Virginia trout piled high with crabmeat/vegetable "stuffing" and served atop mesclun with rice and a medley of roasted vegetables. A basket of minibiscuits, corn and citrus-poppyseed muffins, and sourdough rolls accompanies all dishes. Desserts include pecan sweet potato pie. An almost all-American wine list features many by-the-glass selections.

Power Breakfasts

If you stay at one of Washington's nicer hotels during the week and decide to eat breakfast in the hotel dining room, you won't be alone. Posh hotel restaurants are favorite spots for breakfast meetings among the capital movers and shakers anxious to cut a deal, brief a client, or conduct business—as quickly, sweetly, and discreetly as possible. Washington's stock of fine hotels—the closer to the White House or Capitol Hill the better—are famous for providing quick service and privacy, and, naturally, fabulous breakfast food. The **Hay-Adams** is thought to be the favorite among power brokers, who enjoy a view of the White House along with their soft-scrambled eggs on brioche with smoked fish and scallions. The **Renaissance Mayflower**'s sunny Cafe Promenade serves up omelettes, eggs Benedict, and brioche French toast to both White House and media types (ABC's news studio is right across the street). At the carefully distanced tables in the **Willard Inter-Continental Hotel**'s dining room, most guests munch on items chosen from a breakfast buffet of smoked fish and meat, as well as pastries, fruit, and eggs. Peak time is from about 7–9am, so if you want to dine within that time frame, reserve a table or expect a wait. *A final note:* Hotel restaurants are the main power breakfast spots, but not the only ones. **La Colline,** just off Capitol Hill, has long been open for breakfast; **Galileo** introduced an Italian breakfast in 1997 for early pow-wows.

La Colline

400 N. Capitol St. NW. ☎ **202/737-0400.** Reservations recommended. Main courses $5–$8.75 at breakfast, $8.75–$16.25 at lunch, $18.75–$21 at dinner. AE, CB, DC, MC, V. Mon–Fri 7–10am, 11:30am–3pm, and 6–10pm; Sat 6–10pm. Metro: Union Station. FRENCH.

Mornings, you'll see breakfast fundraisers in progress. Hill people like La Colline for its convenience to the Senate side of the Capitol, the great bar, the high-backed leather booths that allow for discrete conversations, and, last but not least, the food. You'll always get a good meal here. The regular menu offers an extensive list of French standards, like the salade Niçoise, the terrine of foie gras (a deal for under $9), and the fish—poached, grilled, or sautéed. Almost as long is the list of daily specials, which are worth considering—the soft shell crab is superb here in season. The wine list concentrates on French and California wines; wine-by-the-glass choices change with the season to complement the menu. Don't let the dessert cart roll past you; the apple pie is a winner.

MODERATE

America

Union Station, 50 Massachusetts Ave. NE. ☎ **202/682-9555.** Reservations recommended. Main courses $6.95–$17.95; sandwiches, burgers, and salads $3.50–$13.95; brunch $7.25–$13.50. AE, DC, DISC, MC, V. Sun–Thurs 11:30am–midnight, Fri–Sat 11:30am–1am. Metro: Union Station. AMERICAN REGIONAL.

Our helpful waiter gave us the lowdown: Candice Bergen, Justice Clarence Thomas, Martin Sheen, Newt Gingrich, Joe Kennedy, Steven Seagal, and Pete Dominici have all been spotted here at one time or another. People-watching is one reason to come to this vast, four-level restaurant, but sightseeing is another. Ask for a seat in the up-permost Capital Wine Room—if you look out the window, you see the Capitol dome; look the other direction (between the Roman legionnaire statues), and you've got a grand view of Union Station. Walls are decorated with WPA-style murals, a large painting of the American West, and a whimsical frieze depicting surfers, athletes, astronauts, and superheroes in outer space.

A vast American-classic menu comprises hundreds of items, each with the name of the city, state, or region in which the dish supposedly originated: spaghetti and meatballs (Cleveland?), chili dogs (Fort Lee, NJ?). The B.L.T. (Newport) is a safe bet, the nachos (Eagle Pass, TX) too greasy, and you'll definitely find better crabcakes (Ocean City, MD) elsewhere in the city.

Cafe Berlin

322 Massachusetts Ave. NE. ☎ **202/543-7656.** Reservations recommended. Main courses $11.95–$16.95 at lunch and dinner; soups, sandwiches, and salads $2.95–$6.95 at lunch. AE, DC, MC, V. Mon–Thurs 11am–10pm, Fri–Sat 11am–11pm, Sun 4–10pm. Metro: Union Station. GERMAN.

You have to walk past the dessert display on your way to your table at Café Berlin, so forget your diet. These delicious, homemade confections are the best reason to come here. The vast spread might include a dense pear cheesecake, raspberry linzer torte, sour cherry crumbcake, or vanilla custard cake. Entrées feature things like the Rahm Schnitzel, which is a center-cut of veal topped with a light cream and mushroom sauce, or a wurstplatte of mixed sausages. Seasonal items highlight asparagus in spring, game in the fall, and so on. Lunch is a great deal: a simple chicken salad sandwich (laced with tasty bits of mandarin orange), the soup of the day, and German potato salad, all for $5.75. The owners and chef are German; co-owner Peggy Reed emphasizes that their dishes are "on the light side—except for the beer and desserts." The 11-year-old restaurant occupies two prettily decorated dining rooms on the bottom level of a Capitol Hill town house, whose front terrace serves as an outdoor cafe in warm weather.

6 Downtown, East of 16th Street NW

VERY EXPENSIVE

Occidental Grill

1475 Pennsylvania Ave. NW. ☎ **202/783-1475.** Reservations recommended. Main courses $12.95–$19.95 at lunch, $12.95–$27.95 at dinner; sandwiches, soups, and salads $4.95–$16.95; pre-theater $28. AE, CB, DC, DISC, MC, V. Mon–Sat 11:30am–11pm, Sun noon–9:30pm. Metro: Metro Center, Federal Triangle. AMERICAN.

In the same complex as the Willard Hotel, the Occidental Grill was, in fact, opened by the Willard family in 1906. Subsequent owner Gus Bucholz started, in the 1920s, the tradition of displaying autographed photographs of his customers, many of whom were famous. The restaurant closed in 1972, but when it re-opened with the Willard in 1986, its walls in the lower dining room were covered with those photographs of past patrons—military, political, sports, even royalty figures. They're the first thing you notice when you enter.

The upstairs dining room is more formal, with larger booths, a smaller bar, and no photos. The downstairs feels more like a club, with dark wood paneling, a classic bar, walls lined with booths, and leather seats. On both levels you choose from the same menu, which offers traditional meat-and-potatoes fare along with grilled fish and nouvelle cuisine. Certain things are famous: onion crisps, the swordfish club sandwich. And certain things that aren't famous should be: the black bean soup with grilled shrimp and lime cream, the Atlantic salmon grilled on crab and potato hash with saffron-fennel broth. The potato dishes are always good.

Red Sage

605 14th St. NW (at F St.). ☎ **202/638-4444.** Reservations recommended for main dining room, not accepted for chili bar and cafe. Main courses $11–$14 at lunch, $19–$30 at dinner; Cafe/Chili Bar $6–$10. AE, CB, DC, DISC, MC, V. Restaurant Mon–Thurs 11:30am–1:30pm and

Georgetown & Downtown Dining

701 ❸
1789 ❻
America ❻❼
Aditi ❽
Aquarelle ㉑
Asia Nora ㉕
Austin Grill ❶
B. Smith's ㊻
Bice ❻❷
Bistrot Lepic ❺
Bombay Club ❻❾
Busara ❷
Café Atlantico ❻⓪
Café Berlin ❻❺
Capitol City
  Brewing Company ❺❺
Citronelle ⑭
Clyde's ❾
Coco Loco ❺❽
Coppi's ㊺
Daily Grill ㉞
Full Kee ❺❾
Galileo ㉛
George ❸❻
Georgetown Seafood
  Grill on 19th St. ㉝
Georgia Brown's ㊷
Goldoni ㉖
Haad Thai ❺❸
Isabella ㊸
Jaleo ㊼
Kinkead's ㉗
La Colline ❻❹
Le Lion d'Or ㊴⑦
Legal Sea Foods ㉙
Les Halles ❺①
Lespinasse ㊶

Luigino ㊷④
Martin's Tavern ⑪
McCormick &
  Schmick's ㊵
Melrose ㉔
Mendocino Grille
  and Wine Bar ⑲
Morrison-Clark Inn ❺❻
Morton's of Chicago ⑩
Music City Roadhouse ⑱
Occidental Grill ㊿
Old Ebbitt Grill ㊼
Old Glory Barbecue ⑬
Oodles Noodles ㊷②
The Palm ㉟
Paolo's ⑫
Prime Rib ㉘
Patisserie Café Didier ⑯
Provence ㊸③
Red Sage ㊽
Reeve's Restaurant
  and Bakery ㊷②
Restaurant at
  The Jefferson ㊻⑥
Roof Terrace Restaurant ㉒
Ruppers ㊷⑦
The Sea Catch ⑮
Seasons ⑳
Sequoia ⑰
Sushi-Ko ❸
Taberna del Alabardero ㊳⑧
U Street Wine Bar
  and Tapas Bistro ㊸④
Vidalia ㊸③
The Willard Room ㊹⑨
Xing Kuba ❹
Zed's ❼

5:30–9:45pm, Fri 11:30am–1:30pm and 5:30–10:30pm, Sat 5:30–10:30pm, Sun 5–9:45pm. Cafe/Chili Bar Mon–Sat 11:30am–11:30pm, Sun 4:30–11:30pm. Metro: Metro Center. WESTERN/CONTEMPORARY AMERICAN.

Nationally renowned chef Mark Miller has created an elegantly whimsical Wild West fantasy. Downstairs, the main dining room comprises a warren of cozy, candlelit alcoves under a curved ponderosa-log–beamed ceiling. Upstairs are the more casually gorgeous Cafe and high-ceilinged Chili Bar.

When you look at the menu, think spicy. Some examples: an appetizer of citrusy crisp grilled quail rests on a corn husk filled with "drunken" salsa (corn, jalapeños, and smoky-sweet maize mushroom spiked with tequila and ale). A filet mignon–like entrée of oak-grilled rare tuna is glazed with a merlot/habenero chile reduction and served atop pinto beans studded with smoked bacon, chipped garlic, and roasted jalapeños. Red Sage desserts, such as a frozen fudgy mousse made with bittersweet chocolate and layered with chocolate cake, are sublime, and the wine list is extensive and well researched. The Chili Bar and Cafe offer inexpensive light fare ranging from barbecued brisket quesadillas to roasted Virginia trout with smoky potato salad and serrano-garlic brown butter.

✪ Rupperts

1017 7th St. NW. ☎ 202/783-0699. Reservations recommended. Main courses $16–$30 at lunch and dinner. AE, DC, MC, V. Lunch Thurs only, 11:30am–2:30pm; dinner Tues–Thurs 6–10pm, Fri–Sat 6–11pm. Metro: Mount Vernon Square–UDC, Gallery Place–Chinatown. AMERICAN.

Within spitting distance of the DC Convention Center, Rupperts lies in a marginal neighborhood still only intermittently graced by revitalization. Thankfully, a boom in downtown development is rapidly bringing other restaurants and nightlife a little closer.

The restaurant's success is a tribute to the chef's simple but excellent ways with seasonal produce. The chef changes the menu daily, sometimes three times a day, to work with the freshest ingredients. You may see a foie gras and figs dish on the menu in late fall or soft shell crabs and grilled rhubarb in spring. The food is not heavy, nor laden with sauces. With dinner come three different freshly baked breads. The wine list is eclectic, everything from a $210 bottle of Borgogno Riserva Barolo to a $15 Domaine Manoir Beaujolais Noveau. Desserts, however, are too hip; black rice with persimmon left me unimpressed.

This is a one-room, understated restaurant with a casual atmosphere. Patrons don't seem to fall into any identifiable group—say, celebrities of sorts like National Public Radio correspondent Cokie Roberts; most people are in business dress at lunch, less formal attire in the evening.

The Willard Room

In the Willard Inter-Continental Hotel, 1401 Pennsylvania Ave. NW. ☎ **202/637-7440.** Reservations recommended. Main courses $9.75–$16.75 at lunch, $17–$25.50 at dinner; 3-course prix-fixe lunch $24; prix-fixe dinners $36–$45 ($49–$65 with wines); afternoon tea $14.50. AE, DC, DISC, JCB, MC, V. Mon–Fri 7:30–10am and 11:30am–2pm, afternoon tea 2:30–4pm; nightly 6–10pm. Metro: Metro Center. AMERICAN REGIONAL/CLASSIC EUROPEAN.

Like the rest of the hotel (see chapter 5), The Willard dining room has been restored to its original turn-of-the-century splendor, with gorgeous carved oak paneling, towering scagliola columns, brass and bronze torchères and chandeliers, and a faux-bois beamed ceiling. Scattered among the statesmen and diplomats dining here are local couples who have come for romance; the Willard has been the setting for more than one betrothal.

Chef de cuisine Guy Reinbolt trained in Alsace; he added creole and Southern dishes to his repertoire during stints in Memphis and New Orleans. A recent menu (they change seasonally) offered an appetizer of sautéed duck foie gras (served atop a corn-flour tart with a dice of smoked duck breast au jus). Among the entrées was a stunning combination of seared veal medallion and sautéed lobster tail accompanied by a medley of grapes, tiny cocotte potatoes, and chanterelles in cream sauce. And for dessert, a feuilleté of Asian pear (served on crème anglaise marbleized with fruit confit and drizzled with kirsch sauce) was exquisite. A list of more than 250 fine wines mentions Thomas Jefferson's notes from his voyages in the vineyards of France.

EXPENSIVE

✪ Bice
601 Pennsylvania Ave. NW. ☎ **202/638-2423.** Reservations recommended. Main courses $12–$24, light fare $7–$15. AE, MC, V. Mon–Fri 11:30am–2:30pm (light fare 2:30–5pm) and 5:30–10pm, Sat 5:30–10pm. Metro: Archives–Navy Memorial. NORTHERN ITALIAN.

This branch of the Milan-based restaurant draws a cross-section of Washington, from Supreme Court judges to super models, for lunch and dinner. Bice's imaginative menu has a firm grounding in traditional Italian cuisine, but there's a delicacy to the cooking. Pastas are homemade, as is the focaccia; salad dressings are light but tasty; a fresh puréed soup appears daily on the menu. Anyone concerned about diet can put together a sensible meal here. Start with the grilled vegetable antipasto, drizzled with a lemony olive oil, go on to a lightly crumbed and crisped grilled snapper, finish with a robust espresso and tiramisu. On your way out, enjoy an after-dinner drink in the generous-sized bar, a hangout for a young, Euro-Italian bunch late in the evening.

✪ Georgia Brown's
950 15th St. NW. ☎ **202/393-4499.** Reservations recommended. Main courses $9–$19 at lunch and dinner, $22 for brunch. AE, CB, DC, DISC, MC, V. Mon–Thurs 11:30am–11pm, Fri 11:30am–midnight, Sat 5:30pm–midnight, Sun 11:30am–11pm (brunch 11:30am–3pm). Metro: McPherson Square. AMERICAN/SOUTHERN.

In Washington restaurants, seldom do you find such a racially diverse crowd. The harmony may stem from the waitstaff, whose obvious rapport results in gracious service to diners, and certainly extends from the open kitchen, where chef Neal Langerman directs his multicultural staff. But in this large handsome room, whose arched windows overlook McPherson Square, the food may capture all of your attention. A plate of corn bread and biscuits arrives, to be slathered with a butter that's been whipped with diced peaches and honey. The menu is heavily Southern, with the emphasis on the "low country" cooking of South Carolina and Savannah: collards, grits, and lots of seafood, especially shrimp dishes. The Carolina Perlau is a stewlike mix of duck, spicy sausage, jumbo shrimp, and rice, topped with toasted crumbs and scallions—it has bite without being terribly spicy.

Isabella
809 15th St. NW (between H and I sts.). ☎ **202/408-9500.** Reservations recommended. Main courses $5.25–$21.50 at lunch, $12.50–$21.50 at dinner. AE, DISC, MC, V. Mon–Thurs 11:30am–3pm and 5:30–10:30pm, Fri 11:30am–3pm and 5:30–11pm, Sat 5:30–11pm. Metro: McPherson Square. MEDITERRANEAN.

Since it opened in early 1997, Isabella has been getting much attention. Chef Will Greenwood (known for his 5 years at The Jefferson) is preparing classic Mediterranean dishes with a contemporary touch: feta cheese chiffon (*taramasalata*) with Niçoise olive crisps, crusted lamb chops (*kibbeh*) with pomegranate barbecue sauce, and black sea bass with frizzled leeks in a preserved lemon and tomato broth.

The wine list is an interesting mix of Italian, Spanish, French, and California wines. A sidewalk patio fronts Isabella; inside, the restaurant is decorated in shades of purple and gold, has giant palm trees, and two levels of semi-circular banquettes. But watch out; tables are packed too closely together—on a recent visit, I saw a woman, maneuvering between tables to sit down, knock a glass of wine off of one table, then a glass of water off another.

○ Les Halles

1201 Pennsylvania Ave. NW. ☎ **202/347-6848.** Reservations recommended. Main courses $11.75–$20 at lunch, $13.25–$22.50 at dinner. AE, CB, DC, DISC, MC, V. Daily 11:30am– midnight. Metro: Metro Center, Federal Triangle. FRENCH/STEAKHOUSE.

Anyone who believes that red meat is passé should stop here. At lunch and dinner, people are eating the *onglet* (a boneless French cut hangar steak hard to find outside France), steak au poivre, steak tartare, New York sirloin, and other cuts of cow— always accompanied by frites (fries), of course. The menu isn't all beef, but it is classic French: cassoulet, confit de canard, escargots, onion soup, and such. I can never resist the *frisee aux lardons,* a savory salad of chicory studded with hunks of bacon and toasts smeared thickly with Roquefort.

Les Halles is big and charmingly French, with French-speaking waitstaff providing breezy, flirtatious service. The banquettes, pressed tin ceiling, mirrors, wooden floor, and the side bar capture the feel of a brasserie. A vast windowfront overlooks Pennsylvania Avenue and the awning-covered sidewalk cafe, which is a superb spot to dine in warm weather. Les Halles is a favorite hangout for cigar smokers, but the smoking area is well ventilated.

Luigino

1100 New York Ave. NW. ☎ **202/371-0595.** Reservations recommended. Main courses $8.25–$14.50 at lunch, $12.50–$22.50 at dinner; pre-theater $18.50. AE, DC, DISC, MC, V. Mon–Thurs 11:30am–2:30pm and 5:30–10:30pm, Fri 11:30am–2:30pm and 5:30–11:30pm, Sat 5:30–11:30pm, Sun 5–10pm. Pre-theater daily 5:30–7pm. Metro: Metro Center. ITALIAN.

In the same building (an ex-bus station) that houses the Capitol City Brewing Company (see below) is this classy Italian restaurant, where elegance combines amusingly with informality. Starched white cloths lie upon traditional red-checked tablecloths, waiters wear colorful vests atop their classic black pants and white shirts, a line of cushioned chairs (not stools) stretch the length of a bar overlooking the open kitchen, and rock and roll plays softly in the background.

The pizza is a bit greasy, but has a good, chewy thin crust. Grilled fish and meat specials are popular, but we find the fresh pasta dishes satisfying, including the ravioli filled with crabmeat and braised vegetables, and the twists of pasta with diced green beans and potatoes topped with a standard (but fine) basil pesto sauce. Among the wine list offerings are some affordable Italian wines.

Morrison-Clark Inn

Massachusetts Ave. NW (at 11th St.). ☎ **202/898-1200.** Reservations recommended. Main courses $12.50–$14.50 at lunch, $17.50–$23 at dinner; 3-course Sun brunch (including unlimited champagne) $25. AE, CB, DC, MC, V. Mon–Thurs 6–9:30am, Fri–Sat 6–10am, Mon– Fri and Sun 11:30am–2pm, Sun 6–9pm. Metro: Metro Center. AMERICAN REGIONAL.

The Morrison-Clark restaurant is often mentioned as one of the best in the city in such publications as the *Washington Post* and *Gourmet* magazine. The dining room is a Victorian drawing room with ornately carved white marble fireplaces. At night, soft lighting emanates from Victorian brass candelabras, crystal chandeliers, and candles. During the day, sunlight streams in through floor-to-ceiling, mahogany- and gilt-valanced windows. And, weather permitting, you can dine outdoors at courtyard umbrella tables.

In case you want to see the world.

At American Express, we're here to make your journey a smooth one. So we have over 1,700 travel service locations in over 120 countries ready to help. What else would you expect from the world's largest travel agency?

do more ®

Travel

http://www.americanexpress.com/travel

In case you want to be welcomed there.

We're here to see that you're always welcomed at establishments everywhere. That's why millions of people carry the American Express® Card – for peace of mind, confidence, and security, around the world or just around the corner.

do more®

In case you're running low.

We're here to help with more than 118,000 Express Cash locations around the world. In order to enroll, just call American Express before you start your vacation.

do more

Express Cash

And just in case.

We're here with American Express® Travelers Cheques and Cheques *for Two.*® They're the safest way to carry money on your vacation and the surest way to get a refund, practically anywhere, anytime.

Another way we help you...

do more

Travelers Cheques

Chef Susan McCreight Lindeborg's seasonally changing menus are elegant and inspired. An early spring menu may feature potato and leek soup with country ham toasts as a first course and sautéed salmon with risotto cakes and crimini mushroom butter sauce as a main course. The inn is known for its desserts, like the chocolate caramel tart topped with praline-studded whipped cream. Similar fare is available at lunch and brunch. A reasonably priced wine list offers a variety of premium wines by the glass, plus a nice choice of champagnes, dessert wines, and ports.

701

701 Pennsylvania Ave. NW. ☎ **202/393-0701.** Reservations recommended. Main courses $8.50–$18.50 at lunch, $13.50–$22.50 at dinner; pre-theater $22. AE, CB, DC, MC, V. Mon–Fri 11:30am–3pm, Mon–Tues 5:30–10:30pm, Wed–Thurs 5:30–11pm, Fri–Sat 5:30–11:30pm, Sun 5–9:30pm. Metro: Archives–Navy Memorial. AMERICAN/INTERNATIONAL.

This restaurant is literally steps away from the Archives–Navy Memorial Metro stop and a short walk from several theaters. Its plate-glass windows allow you to watch commuters, theatergoers, and tourists scurrying along Pennsylvania Avenue. Walls, glass partitions, and columns in the dining room create pockets of privacy throughout.

701 has gained renown for its extensive caviar and vodka selections. But don't disregard the main menu, which features sophisticated American fare and always includes a few vegetarian items like the Yukon Gold potato-and-mushroom cake. A signature soup with great texture and flavor is Iowa corn and shrimp chowder, with dry sack sherry and chives; another to recommend is the roasted mushroom melange on creamy polenta in a delicious Madeira wine broth. Artful presentation makes the food all the more enticing. Portions are generous, and service is marvelous.

MODERATE

✪ Café Atlantico

405 8th St. NW. ☎ **202/393-0812.** Reservations are a must. Main courses $9.50–$14.50 at lunch, $13.95–$16.50 at dinner; light fare $4.50–$7.50. AE, DC, MC, V. Mon–Tues 11:30am–2:30pm and 5:30–10pm, Wed–Thurs 11:30am–2:30pm and 5:30–11pm, Fri 11:30am–2:30pm (2:30–5:30pm for light fare) and 5:30pm–midnight, Sat 11:30am–2:30pm and 5:30pm–midnight, Sun 5:30–10pm. Metro: Archives–Navy Memorial. LATIN AMERICAN/CARIBBEAN.

This place rocks on weekend nights, a favorite hot spot in Washington's burgeoning downtown. The colorful, three-tiered restaurant throbs with Latin, calypso, and reggae music, and everyone is having a good time—including, it seems, the waitstaff. If the place is packed, see if you can snag a seat at the third-level bar, where you can watch the genial bartender mix the potent drinks for which Cafe Atlantico is famous, like the *caipirinha,* made of limes, sugar, and *cachacha* (sugar cane liqueur), or the *mojito,* a rum and crushed mint cocktail.

Seated at the bar or table, you get to watch the waiter make fresh guacamole right in front of you. As for the main dishes, you can't get a more elaborate meal for the price. The seviche, empanadas, and *asopao* (a Puerto Rican shrimp and crab stew) are standouts, and tropical side dishes and pungent sauces produce a burst of color on the plate. Since the menu changes about every 2 months, these items may not be available; ask your waiter for guidance.

Capitol City Brewing Company

1100 New York Ave. NW. ☎ **202/628-2222.** Also 2 Massachusetts Ave. NW. ☎ **202/842-2337.** Reservations accepted for groups of 15 or more. Main courses $8.95–$18.95. Sun–Thurs 11am–11pm, Fri–Sat 11am–midnight; the bar stays open until 1am. AE, DC, DISC, MC, V. Metro: Metro Center. AMERICAN.

These two brewpubs are popular with singles, who enjoy swilling good beer in nicer-than-normal bar surroundings. The huge pubs are each situated within historic buildings: one across from the convention center, the other in the old City Post Office Building across from Union Station (upstairs from the National Postal Museum). Daily beer specials are posted on a chalkboard. The menu consists mostly of typical bar food, though here and there you find the odd item worth trying (like the mushroom quesadilla). Custom-cooked burgers and the fried oyster sandwich are commendable. The service, however, is not. If you want to be waited on in this decade, sit at the bar. A basket of soft pretzels accompanied by a horseradish-mustard dip is complimentary.

✪ Coco Loco

810 7th St. NW (between H and I sts.). ☎ **202/289-2626.** Reservations recommended. Tapas mostly $4.95–$10.50; churrascaria with antipasti bar $20.95 at lunch, $29.95 at dinner; antipasti bar only $12.95 at lunch, $18.50 at dinner. AE, MC, V. Mon–Thurs 11:30am–2:30pm and 5:30–10pm, Fri 11:30am–2:30pm and 5:30–11pm, Sat 5:30–11pm. Metro: Gallery Place. BRAZILIAN/MEXICAN.

At 8pm on a Wednesday night, the dance floor is filled with young, well-dressed couples trying their hand at salsa. Weekends, you can't even get in the joint. Besides the music and dancing, much of the action emanates from the open kitchen and the U-shaped bar. If you want a quieter setting, head for the window-walled front room or the garden patio. The exuberantly tropical interior space centers on a daily changing buffet table where cheeses, fresh fruits, salads (ranging from roasted tomatoes with mozzarella to garbanzos with figs), cold cuts, and other antipasti are temptingly arrayed on palm fronds and banana leaves.

An extensive selection of Mexican tapas includes interesting quesadillas and pan-roasted shrimp on chewy black (squid-infused) Chinese jasmine rice. Coco Loco's most popular dish is churrascaria, the Brazilian mixed grill. Waiters serve you chunks of the sausage, chicken, beef, and pork from skewers. It comes with salsa, fried potatoes, and coconut-flavored rice and includes antipasti bar offerings. All this and tiramisu for dessert, too. The wine list is small but well chosen. French chef Yannick Cam, also of Provence, is one of Coco Loco's owners.

Jaleo

480 7th St. NW (at E St.). ☎ **202/628-7949.** Reservations accepted until 6:30pm. Main courses $7.50–$9.95 at lunch, $10.50–$28 at dinner; tapas $2.95–$7.50. AE, DC, DISC, MC, V. Mon–Sat 11:30am–2:30pm (with a limited tapas menu served 2:30–5:30pm); Mon 5:30–10pm, Tues–Thurs 5:30–11:30pm, Fri–Sat 5:30pm–midnight, Sun 11:30am–3pm and 5:30–10pm. Metro: Archives or Gallery Place. SPANISH REGIONAL/TAPAS.

In theater season, Jaleo's dining room fills and empties each evening according to the performance schedule of the Shakespeare Theater, right next door. Lunchtime always draws a crowd from nearby office buildings and the Hill. The restaurant, which opened in April 1993, may be credited for initiating the tapas craze in Washington. Among the menu items are mild but savory warm goat cheese served with toast points, a skewer of grilled chorizo sausage atop garlic mashed potatoes, and a delicious mushroom tart served with roasted red pepper sauce. Paella is among the few heartier entrées listed. Spanish wines, sangrias, and sherries are available by the glass, and fresh-baked chewy bread comes in handy for soaking up tangy sauces. Finish with a rum- and butter-soaked apple charlotte in bread pastry or a plate of Spanish cheeses. The casual-chic interior focuses on a large mural of a flamenco dancer based on John Singer Sargent's painting *Jaleo*, which inspired the restaurant's name; on Wednesday evenings at 8:30, 9:30, and 10:30, flamenco (Sevillanas) dancers perform in 15-minute rounds.

Old Ebbitt Grill

675 15th St. NW (between F and G sts.). ☎ **202/347-4801.** Reservations recommended. Main courses $4.50–$6.95 at breakfast, $5.95–$12.95 at brunch, $7.95–$12.95 at lunch, $9.95–$15.95 at dinner; burgers and sandwiches $6.25–$10.95; raw bar $8.95–$15.95. AE, DC, DISC, MC, V. Mon–Fri 7:30am–1am, Sat 8am–1am, Sun 9:30am–1am. Bar Sun–Thurs to 2am, Fri–Sat to 3am. Raw bar open to midnight daily. Metro: McPherson Square or Metro Center. Complimentary valet parking from 6pm Mon–Sat, from noon Sun. AMERICAN.

Located 2 blocks from the White House, this is the city's oldest saloon, founded in 1856. Among its artifacts are animal trophies bagged by Teddy Roosevelt, and Alexander Hamilton's wooden bears—one with a secret compartment in which it's said he hid whiskey bottles from his wife. The Old Ebbitt is an attractive place, with Persian rugs strewn on beautiful oak and marble floors, beveled mirrors, flickering gas lights, etched-glass panels, and paintings of Washington scenes. The long, dark mahogany Old Bar area gives it the feeling of a men's saloon.

You may see preferential treatment given to movers and shakers, and you'll always have a wait for a table if you don't reserve ahead. The waitstaff is friendly in a programmed sort of way; service could be faster. Menus change daily but always include certain favorites: burgers, the trout parmesan (Virginia trout dipped in egg batter and Parmesan cheese, deep-fried), crabcakes, and oysters (there's an oyster bar). The tastiest dishes are usually the seasonal ones, whose fresh ingredients make the difference.

INEXPENSIVE

Full Kee

509 H St. NW. ☎ **202/371-2233.** Reservations accepted. Main courses $4.25–$9 at lunch, $6.95–$12.95 at dinner. No credit cards. Mon–Fri 11am–3pm, Fri 11am–3am, Sat 11am–3am, Sun 11am–1am; Mon–Thurs 5pm–1am. Metro: Gallery Place/Chinatown. CHINESE.

This is probably Chinatown's best restaurant, in terms of the actual food. Forget decor: Full Kee's two rooms are brightly lit and crammed with Chinese-speaking customers sitting upon metal-legged chairs at plain rectangular tables. There's no such thing as a non-smoking section. A cook works at the small open kitchen at the front of the room, hanging roasted pig's parts on hooks and wrapping dumplings.

Chefs from some of Washington's best restaurants often congregate here after hours, and here's their advice. Order from the typed back page of the menu. Two selections are especially noteworthy: the jumbo breaded oyster casserole with ginger and scallions (I can second that) and the whole steamed fish. Check out the laminated tent card on the table and find the soups; if you love dumplings, order the Hong Kong-style shrimp dumpling broth: You get eight shrimp dumplings if you order the broth without noodles, only four if you order the broth with noodles. Bring your own wine or beer (and your own glasses in which to pour it) if you'd like to have a drink, since Full Kee does not serve any alcohol and accepts no responsibility for helping you imbibe.

Haad Thai

1100 New York Ave. NW (entrance on 11th St. NW). ☎ **202/682-1111.** Reservations recommended. Main courses $6–$8 at lunch, $7–$11 at dinner. AE, DC, MC, V. Mon–Fri 11:30am–2:30pm and 5–10:30pm, Sat noon–10:30pm, Sun 5–10:30pm. Metro: Metro Center. THAI.

The Washington area has lots of Thai restaurants, but not many are downtown. Fewer still offer food this good in such pretty quarters. Haad Thai is a short walk from the Convention Center and its surrounding hotels. Plants and a pink and black mural of the Thai beach decorate the dining room. The dishes to order are the standards: pad thai, panang gai (chicken sautéed with fresh basil leaves in curry, with peanut sauce), and satays, although all dishes are flavorful and only mildly spicy. If you happen to like your food really hot, ask for it that way.

Reeve's Restaurant & Bakery

1306 G St. NW. ☎ **202/628-6350.** Main courses $5.50–$8; sandwiches $3.50–$6; buffet breakfast $5.25 Mon–Fri, $6.25 Sat and holidays. MC, V. Mon–Sat 7am–6pm. Metro: Metro Center. AMERICAN.

There's no place like Reeve's, a Washington institution since 1886, although in a new building since 1992. J. Edgar Hoover used to send a G-man to pick up chicken sandwiches, and Lady Bird Johnson and daughter Lynda Bird worked out the latter's wedding plans over lunch here. It's fronted by a long bakery counter filled with scrumptious pies and cakes. Brass-railed counter seating on both floors uses the original 19th-century wooden stools. The ambience is cheerful, and much of the seating is in cozy booths and banquettes.

Everything is homemade with top-quality ingredients: the turkeys, chickens, salads, breads, desserts, even the mayonnaise. At breakfast, you can't beat the all-you-can-eat buffet: scrambled eggs, home fries, French toast, pancakes, doughnuts, corned-beef hash, grits, bacon, sausage, stewed and fresh fruit, biscuits with sausage gravy, and more. Hot entrées run the gamut from golden-brown Maryland crabcakes to country-fried chicken with mashed potatoes and gravy. Reeve's pies are famous: strawberry, peach, chocolate cream, you name it. No alcoholic beverages are served.

7 Downtown, 16th Street NW & West

VERY EXPENSIVE

✪ Galileo

1110 21st St. NW. ☎ **202/293-7191.** Reservations recommended. Main courses $2.95–$9.95 at breakfast, $11–$19 at lunch, $17–$30 at dinner. AE, CB, DC, DISC, MC, V. Mon–Fri 7:30–9:30am, 11:30am–2pm, and 5:30–10pm; Sat 5:30–10:30pm; Sun 5–10pm. Metro: Foggy Bottom. ITALIAN.

Food critics mention Galileo as one of the best Italian restaurants in the country and Roberto Donna as one of our best chefs. The likable Donna opened the white-walled, grottolike Galileo in 1984; since then, he has opened several other restaurants in the area, including **Il Radicchio** and **Pesce** (see Dupont Circle listings), has written a cookbook, and has established himself as an integral part of Washington culture.

Galileo features the cuisine of Donna's native Piedmont region, an area in northern Italy influenced by neighboring France and Switzerland—think truffles, hazelnuts, porcini mushrooms, and veal. A SWAT team of male waiters attend. The atmosphere is relaxed; diners are dressed in jeans and suits alike. For starters, munch on the Piedmont-style crostini—paper-thin toast dipped in pureed cannellini beans with garlic. The menu boasts more than 900 vintages of Italian wine (40% Piedmontese). Typical entrées include: Sautéed Chesapeake Bay oysters, served on a bed of leeks and porcini mushrooms; pansotti (a pasta) of truffled potatoes and crispy pancetta in a porcini mushroom sauce; and grilled rack of venison with a wild berry sauce. Finish with a traditional tiramisu or, better yet, the warm pear tart with honey vanilla ice cream and caramel sauce—spectacular.

Le Lion d'Or

1150 Connecticut Ave. NW (at M St.). ☎ **202/296-7972.** Reservations required. Main courses $24–$36. AE, CB, DC, MC, V. Mon–Sat 6–10pm. Jacket required. Metro: Farragut North. FRENCH.

This is old-guard French, where the waiters sometimes treat you like you're Americans in Paris. Owner-chef Jean-Pierre Goyenvalle has run Le Lion d'Or for decades now, and little has changed. The decor still features dark-brown tufted-leather banquettes under tented silk canopies and ecru silk walls adorned with provincial French faience platters. And the cooking is still classic French cuisine at its best. A not-to-be-missed hors d'oeuvre is the ravioli de foie gras: a large poached pasta pocket stuffed with fresh duck foie gras. A red snapper entrée "aux senteurs de Provence" (with the aroma of Provence) comes lightly roasted in extra virgin olive oil and served on a bed of fennel with a side dish of new potatoes. The soufflés are famous. Le Lion d'Or offers an extensive wine list, primarily French and Californian, and house wines are bottled with the restaurant's own label.

Lespinasse

923 16th St. NW (in the Carlton Hotel). ☎ **202/879-6900.** Reservations recommended. Main courses $8–$19 at breakfast, $22–$25 at lunch, $27–$39 at dinner; $19 for tea. AE, DISC, MC, V. Mon–Fri 7–10:30am, noon–2pm, and 6–10pm; Sat 7–11am and 6–10pm; Sun 7–11am; daily tea 3–5:30pm. Jacket required. Metro: Farragut North. FRENCH.

A $6-million renovation of Lespinasse's opulent dining room endowed it with a castlelike hand-stenciled wood beam ceiling, creamy gold-hued walls, royal blue stamped banquettes and floral carpeting, and comfortable yellow leather chairs. The china is Limoges, the crystal Riedel. You pay for the embellishments: This Washington branch of New York's Lespinasse is now the most expensive restaurant in town. St. Regis chef Gray Kunz has sent his sous-chef, Troy Dupuy, to command this kitchen. Sommelier Vincent Feraud is the best, having presided at Jean-Louis (now closed). One unexpected thing about the wine list is that it offers a nice selection of reasonably priced good wines by the glass.

Dupuy contrasts textures as he melds exotic fruit and vegetable flavors with meat and seafood dishes. A winning appetizer is the foie gras with cape gooseberries—it slides down the throat. The risotto with truffles and coriander, which comes with a precious silver saucepot of mushroom fricassee, is already established as a signature dish. The perfectly roasted squab entrée tastes amazingly rich and is served with mashed and wedged potatoes, leeks, and truffles. If desserts, like stewed quince and green apple in pastry, don't appeal, the after-dinner plate of petits fours should. A dinner at Lespinasse takes time—not because of the service, which is smooth and attentive, but because the kitchen is slow. But maybe that's for the good: the meal over which you linger becomes an event in itself

Prime Rib

2020 K St. NW. ☎ **202/466-8811.** Reservations recommended. Main courses $10–$18 at lunch, $18–$29.95 at dinner. AE, CB, DC, MC, V. Mon–Thurs 11:30am–3pm and 5–11pm, Fri 11:30am–3pm and 5–11:30pm, Sat 5–11:30pm. Jacket and tie required. Free valet parking after 5pm. Metro: Farragut West. STEAKS/CHOPS/SEAFOOD.

The Prime Rib has plenty of competition now, but it makes no difference. Beef lovers still consider this The Place. It's got a definite men's club feel about it: brass-trimmed black walls, leopard-skin carpeting, comfortable black leather chairs and banquettes. Waiters are in black tie, and a pianist at the baby grand plays show tunes.

The meat is from the best grain-fed steers and has been aged for 4 to 5 weeks. Steaks and cuts of roast beef are thick, tender, and juicy. For less carnivorous diners, there are about a dozen seafood entrées, including an excellent crab imperial. Mashed potatoes are done right, as are the fried potato skins. Bar drinks here, by the way, are made with fresh-squeezed juices and Evian water.

✪ The Restaurant at The Jefferson

1200 16th St. NW (at M St.). ☎ **202/347-2200.** Reservations recommended. Main courses $13–$22 at lunch, $22–$28 at dinner; Sun brunch $19.50–$28. AE, CB, DC, JCB, MC, V. Daily 6:30–10:30am, 11am–3pm, and 6–10:30pm. Metro: Farragut North. NATURAL AMERICAN.

Cozy, rather than intimidatingly plush, the Jefferson Hotel's restaurant is actually pretty romantic (ask to be seated in "the snug," tables 39 or 40). The emphasis on privacy and the solicitous, but not imposing, service also make it a good place to do business.

Chef James Hudock changes his menus seasonally. Appetizers we enjoyed from a late winter menu included a baby spinach salad sprinkled with goat cheese and dressed with tangerine ginger dressing, and a warm artichoke heart salad with designer lettuce and scallops, resting upon a thin potato galette. Among the entrées were a caramelized black grouper with Kalamata olives, roasted peppers, English peas, and roasted potatoes, and perfectly done lamb chops. Our meal ended with a divine coffee creme brulee. An extensive wine list includes many by-the-glass selections.

✪ Taberna del Alabardero

1776 I St. NW (entrance on 18th St. NW). ☎ **202/429-2200.** Reservations recommended. Main courses $10–$18 at lunch, $18–$28 at dinner; pre-theater $30. AE, DC, DISC, MC, V. Mon–Thurs 11:30am–2:30pm and 6–10pm, Fri 11:30am–2:30pm and 6–11pm, Sat 6–11pm. Jacket and tie required for men. Metro: Farragut West. SPANISH.

Dress up to visit this truly elegant restaurant, where you receive royal treatment from the Spanish staff who are quite used to attending to the real thing: Spain's King Juan Carlos and Queen Sofia and their children regularly dine here when in Washington.

The dining room is Old World ornate, with lace antimacassars placed upon velvety banquettes and heavy brocadelike drapes framing the large front windows. Order a plate of tapas to start: lightly fried calamari, shrimp in garlic and olive oil, thin smoky ham, and marinated mushrooms. Although the a la carte menu changes monthly, always available are four paellas (each requires a minimum of two people to order). The lobster and seafood paella served on saffron rice is rich and flavorful. (Ask to have the lobster de-shelled; otherwise, you do the cracking.) Chef Josu Zubikarai's Basque background figures prominently, especially in signature dishes such as Txangurro Gratinado (Basque-style crabmeat).

This is the only Taberna del Alabardero outside of Spain, where there are three. All are owned and operated by Father Luis de Lezama, who opened his first tavern outside the palace gates in Madrid in 1974, as a place to train delinquent boys for employment.

EXPENSIVE

✪ Bombay Club

815 Connecticut Ave. NW. ☎ **202/659-3727.** Reservations recommended. Main courses $7.50–$18.50 at lunch and dinner, Sun brunch $16.50; pre-theater $22. AE, CB, DC, DISC, MC, V. Mon–Thurs 11:30am–2:30pm and 6–10:30pm, Fri 11:30am–2:30pm and 6–11pm, Sat 6–11pm, Sun 11:30am–2:30pm and 5:30–9pm. Metro: Farragut West. INDIAN.

The Clintons have eaten here many times, and diners know it; when Secret Service types swept the restaurant recently at lunch, the place was abuzz with anticipation, only to see Prince Bandar bin Sultan, the Saudi ambassador, enter the room.

The Indian menu here ranges from fiery green chili chicken ("not for the faint-hearted," the menu warns) to the delicately prepared lobster malabar, a personal favorite. Tandoori dishes, like the chicken marinated in a yogurt, ginger, and garlic dressing, are specialties, as is the vegetarian fare—try the black lentils cooked overnight on a slow fire. Patrons are as fond of the service as the cuisine: Waitstaff seem straight out of *Jewel in the Crown*, attending to your every whim. This is one place where you can linger over a meal as long as you like. Slow-moving ceiling fans and wicker furniture accentuate the colonial British ambience.

Daily Grill

1200 18th St. NW. ☎ **202/822-5282.** Reservations recommended. Main courses $7.95–$15 at lunch, $8.95–$22 at dinner. AE, DC, DISC, MC, V. Mon–Thurs 11:30am–11pm, Fri 11:30am–midnight, Sat 5pm–midnight, Sun 10am–3pm and 5–10pm. Metro: Farragut North or Dupont Circle. AMERICAN.

Step right in and get your Cobb salad, your chicken pot pie, your fresh fruit cobbler, your meat and potatoes. Talk about retro; in the case of the Daily Grill, retro means revisiting the food favorites of decades past. The California-based restaurant itself is not that old—less than a year. It's a big space (seating up to 240), with a nice bar at the front and windows on three sides. Like its chain siblings, the DC grill is gaining a reputation for American-friendly service and large portions. It's also known for a dish invented in San Francisco before World War II, called "Joe's Special," which combines ground sirloin sautéed with onions, fresh spinach, scrambled eggs, and mushrooms. The "Grill Combo" of tiny onion rings over skinny fries is a must for table-sharing.

George

1915 K St. NW. ☎ **202/452-9898.** Reservations recommended. Main courses $11.75–$19.50 at lunch, $14.50–$23.50 at dinner. AE, DC, MC, V. Mon–Fri 11:30am–2pm; Mon–Sat 5:30–10pm. Metro: Farragut West. MEDITERRANEAN.

This place bustles at weekday lunch with a lawyerly crowd, but is quieter at dinner. Warm-yellow stuccoed walls and an oak proscenium give it the feel of a postmodern hacienda, or maybe a Mediterranean villa. Anyway, Mediterranean is the food focus, as chef George Vetsch fuses elements from Middle Eastern, North African, and Italian cuisines. A good example is the appetizer of prosciutto-wrapped sea scallops and shrimp marinated in *harissa* (a North African seasoning), both centered on a tiny new potato stuffed with mascarpone. An especially noteworthy entrée combines rigatoni with spicy lamb sausage, harissa, spinach, roasted peppers, mascarpone, and parmesan cheese. Half portions of pasta are available. Unusual combinations prove unusually good: seared duck breast with caramelized pear, sour cream dumplings, and calimyrna figs. The wine list is thin but interesting. The bread is crusty-rustic, and desserts are made in-house.

✪ Georgetown Seafood Grill on 19th St.

1200 19th St. NW. ☎ **202/530-4430.** Reservations recommended. Main courses $9.95–$17.95 at lunch, $10.95–$21.95 at dinner, salads and sandwiches $8.95–$12.95. AE, DC, DISC, MC, V. Sun–Fri 11:30am–11:30pm, Sat 5–11:30pm. Metro: Dupont Circle. SEAFOOD.

In the heart of downtown is this hint of the seashore. Two big tanks of lobsters greet you as you enter, and the decor throughout follows a nautical theme: aquariums set in walls, canoes fastened to the ceiling, models of tall ships placed here and there. Meanwhile, music from another era is heard—"Young at Heart," and the like. It's enough to make you forget what city you're in.

A bar and sets of tables sit at the front of the restaurant, an open kitchen is in the middle, and tall wooden booths on platforms lie at the rear. The lobster thermidor special is a mix of Pernod, scallions, mushrooms, and cream mixed with bits of lobster. But if you want really healthy chunks of lobster, order the lobster club, served on brioche with applewood bacon and mayo, or better yet, the fresh lobster delivered daily from Maine. As is the rule in many seafood restaurants, your best bets are the most simply prepared: Besides the lobster, you can choose from a list of at least eight "simply grilled" fish entrées. Raw bar selections list oysters from Canada, Virginia, and Oregon, and these may be the freshest in town. Service is excellent.

Legal Sea Foods

2020 K St. NW. ☎ **202/496-1111.** Reservations recommended, especially at lunch. Main courses $7.95–$15.95 at lunch (sandwiches $6.95–$8.95), $10–$25 at dinner. AE, DC, DISC, MC, V. Mon–Thurs 11am–10pm, Fri 11am–10:30pm, Sat 4–10:30pm, Sun 4–9pm. Metro: Farragut North or Farragut West. SEAFOOD.

This famous family-run, Boston-based seafood empire, whose motto is "If it's not fresh, it's not Legal," made its Washington debut in August l995. The softly lit dining room is plush, with terrazzo marble floors and rich cherrywood paneling. Sporting events, especially Boston games, are aired on a TV over the handsome marble bar/raw bar, and you can get a copy of the *Boston Globe* near the entrance. Not only is everything here fresh, but it's all from certified-safe waters.

Legal's buttery rich clam chowder is a classic. Other worthy appetizers include garlicky golden-brown farm-raised mussels au gratin and fluffy pan-fried Maryland lump crabcakes served with zesty corn relish and mayo-mustard sauce. Legal's signature dessert is a marionberry and blueberry cobbler with a brown-sugary oatmeal-crisp crust; it's topped with a scoop of homemade vanilla ice cream. An award-winning wine list is a plus. At lunch, oyster po' boys are a treat.

McCormick & Schmick's

1652 K St. NW (at corner of 17th St. NW). ☎ **202/861-2233.** Reservations suggested. Main courses $6.60–$19.95 at lunch and dinner. AE, DC, DISC, MC, V. Mon–Thurs 11am–11pm, Fri 11am–midnight, Sat 5pm–midnight, Sun 5–10pm. Metro: Farragut North and Farragut West. SEAFOOD.

In this branch of a Pacific Northwest–based restaurant, stained glass in the chandeliers and ceiling evince a patriotic theme; and shoeshiner Ego Brown, a Washington fixture for decades, has set up his station in the window. This huge place seats its patrons in booths, at a 65-foot bar, and at linen-laid tables. The vast menu offers selections of fresh fish from both nearby and Pacific waters—the more simply prepared, the better. Oyster lovers will choose happily from the half-dozen kinds stocked daily. For good value, look at the list of light entrées ranging from oyster stew to chicken picatta and costing $6.60 to $9.95. For best value, head to the bar to enjoy a giant burger, fried calamari, quesadillas, fish tacos, and more, for only $1.95, Monday through Friday 3:30 to 6:30pm, Monday through Thursday 10:30pm to midnight, and Friday and Saturday 10pm to midnight. Friendly bartenders make you feel at home as they concoct mixed drinks with juice they squeeze from fruit right at the bar.

The Palm

1225 19th St. NW. ☎ **202/293-9091.** Reservations recommended. Main courses $8–$29. AE, DC, MC, V. Mon–Fri 11:30am–11pm, Sat 6–10:30pm, Sun 5:30–9pm. Complimentary valet parking at dinner. Metro: Dupont Circle. STEAKHOUSE.

The Palm is one in a chain that started 75 years ago in New York—but here in D.C., it feels like an original. The Washington Palm is 26 years old; its walls, like all Palms, are covered with the caricatures of regulars, famous and not-so. (Look for my friend, Bob Harris.) You can't go wrong with steak, whether it's offered as a 36-ounce, dry-aged New York strip, or sliced in a steak salad. Oversize lobsters are a specialty, and certain side dishes are a must: creamed spinach, onion rings, Palm fries (something akin to deep-fried potato chips), and hash browns. Several of the longtime waiters like to kid with you a bit; service is always fast.

✪ Vidalia

1990 M St. NW. ☎ **202/659-1990.** Reservations recommended. Main courses $13–$18 at lunch, $18–$22 at dinner. AE, DISC, MC, V. Mon–Thurs 11:30am–2:30pm and 5:30–10pm,

Fri 11:30am–2:30pm and 5:30–10:30pm, Sat 5:30–10:30pm, Sun 5–9:30pm. Complimentary valet parking at dinner. Metro: Dupont Circle. PROVINCIAL AMERICAN.

Down a flight of steps from the street, the charming Vidalia turns out to be a tiered dining room, with cream stucco walls hung with gorgeous dried-flower wreaths and works by local artists.

Chef Jeff Buben's "provincial American" menus (focusing on Southern-accented regional specialties) change frequently, but recommended constants include crisp East Coast lump crabcakes, a fried grits cake with portobello mushrooms, and something that fans refer to simply as "the onion": a roasted whole Vidalia onion that's cut and opened up, like the leaves of a flower. Venture from the regular items, and you may delight in a timbale of roasted onion and foie gras.

A signature entrée is the scrumptious sautéed shrimp on a mound of creamed grits and caramelized onions in a chopped tomato and fresh thyme sauce. Try to make room for side dishes like garlic mashed potatoes and the onion casserole. Vidalia is known for its lemon chess pie, which tastes like pure sugar; I prefer the cobblers and cakes. A carefully chosen wine list highlights American vintages.

INEXPENSIVE

Oodles Noodles

1120 19th St. NW. ☎ **202/293-3138.** Reservations recommended for 5 or more at dinner. Main courses $7–$9. AE, DC, MC, V. Mon–Thurs 11:30am–3pm and 5–10pm, Fri 11:30am–3pm and 5–10:30pm, Sat 5–10:30pm. Metro: Dupont Circle, Farragut North. ASIAN.

Asian waiters, Asian background music, and calligraphy figures drawn on the walls put you in the right frame of mind for Pan-Asian noodle dishes. You can order Japanese dumplings, Szechuan dan dan noodles (egg noodles), Vietnamese vermicelli, Thai drunken noodles, and so on. Many of the items come within a soup, such as the Shanghai roast pork noodles soup and the Siam noodles soup, which is a spicy sweet and sour broth with shrimp, minced chicken, and squid.

But not everything is a noodle. Appetizers include satays, spring onions cakes, and vegetable spring rolls. Entrées include curry, teriyaki, and similar spicy non-noodle fare.

Though Washington food critics give Oodles Noodles high marks, I find it a hit or miss place. On a recent visit, my Noodles on the Boat (grilled marinated lemon chicken with rice vermicelli, bean sprouts, vegetables, peanuts, and fried onions) was bland, and my husband's Spices Chicken "wasn't spicy at all." You can't beat the prices, though, and my children, at least, were content with their Chicken Wonton Soup and Ravioli (pork dumplings).

8 Foggy Bottom/West End

VERY EXPENSIVE

✪ Aquarelle

In the Watergate Hotel, 2650 Virginia Ave. NW. ☎ **202/298-4455.** Reservations recommended. Main courses $10.75–$18 at breakfast, $15.75–$19.75 at lunch, $17–$27 at dinner; pre-theater $35. AE, CB, DC, DISC, MC, V. Daily 7–10:15am for breakfast, 11:30am–2:30pm for lunch, 5:30–10:15pm for dinner. Metro: Foggy Bottom. AMERICAN.

The Watergate has a new chef in its new restaurant in the old spot where Jean-Louis' Palladin used to be. In Aquarelle's cheery room overlooking the Potomac, Chef Robert Wiedmaier presents his own version of "Euro-American" cuisine. The menu changes seasonally and focuses on game and fish. A crab gateau appetizer is a creamy custard of crab in a swirl of buttery sauce. A duck foie gras with figs is a treat, as is anything Wiedmaier does with asparagus. Wiedmaier is German-born and Belgian-trained, but he's thoroughly American in his exuberance, which shines in dishes like the flavorful grilled meats and fish, as well as in pastas topped with rich vegetable and garlic sauces. The Aquarelle is popular as a pre-theater dinner spot for those going to the Kennedy Center, and wins the drama award for its in-kitchen dinners offered nightly.

Roof Terrace Restaurant / Hors d'Oeuvrerie

In the Kennedy Center, New Hampshire Ave. NW (at Rock Creek Pkwy.). ☎ **202/416-8555.** Reservations recommended for the Roof Terrace Restaurant, but not accepted for the Hors d'Oeuvrerie. Roof Terrace: Main courses $12–$19 at lunch, $21–$29 at dinner; Sun prix-fixe buffet brunch $25.95. Hors d'Oeuvrerie, light-fare items mostly $8–$15. AE, CB, DC, MC, V. Roof Terrace, matinee days only 11:30am–2pm; nightly 5:30–9pm, Sun 11:30am–3pm. Hors d'Oeuvrerie, daily 5pm to half an hour after the last show. Note: The Roof Terrace is occasionally closed when there are few shows; call before you go. Metro: Foggy Bottom. AMERICAN REGIONAL.

A meal at the Roof Terrace is not only convenient for theatergoers, it's a gourmet experience in a glamorous dining room, where ornate crystal candelabra chandeliers hang from a lofty ceiling and immense windows provide panoramic views of the Potomac.

Executive chef Carolyn Flinn changes the menu with the seasons, usually keeping the list to six or seven appetizers and seven to nine entrées, including one special. You might see a Chesapeake Bay seafood chowder or a pot pie of escargot among the appetizers. Entrée possibilities range from grilled filet mignon with spinach flan and three peppercorn sauce, to Maryland crabcakes with crisp confetti slaw, to grilled Pacific Northwest salmon. Many premium wines are offered by the glass. Every Sunday, the restaurant puts on its kitchen brunch buffet, a lavish spread that includes custom-made omelets, pastas, smoked meats and fish, fancy French toast, and tons of desserts; the $25.95 price entitles you to the buffet and either a glass of champagne, a mimosa, or a glass of fresh squeezed O.J.

After-theater munchies and cocktails are served in the adjoining and equally plush **Hors d'Oeuvrerie.** Stop here before or after a show for a glass of wine or champagne and a light supper—perhaps seafood strudel, grilled vegetable pizza, or jumbo shrimp cocktail. It's gourmet snack fare. Desserts and coffee are also available.

EXPENSIVE

Asia Nora

2213 M St. NW. ☎ **202/797-4860.** Reservations recommended. Main courses $18–$24. MC, V. Mon–Sat starting at 5:45pm, with last reservation at 10pm Thurs, 10:30pm Fri–Sat. Metro: Dupont Circle or Foggy Bottom. ASIAN FUSION.

Everything's set at a slant here: the tables, the bar, the banquette at the back on the first floor, and the triangular cutaway balcony on the second. Museum-quality artifacts from Asian countries—batik carvings, Japanese helmets, and Chinese puppets—decorate the gold-flecked jade walls. It's intimate and exotic, a charged combination. Try sitting at the bar first, on the most comfortable bar stools in town. If you like good bourbons and single malt scotches, you're in luck.

Waitstaff dressed in black-satin martial arts pajamas serve Asian fusion cuisine, all prepared with organic ingredients. Hence, a salad of smoked trout with field greens and Fuji apples, a "small dish" of crispy spinach and shitake spring rolls, and a main dish of banana leaf grilled sea bass. It actually sounds more far out than it tastes.

✪ Goldoni

1113 23rd St. NW. ☎ **202/293-1511.** Reservations recommended. Main courses $11–$19 at lunch, $17–$24 at dinner. AE, DC, DISC, MC, V. Mon–Thurs 11:30am–2pm and 5:30–10pm, Fri 11:30am–2pm and 5–10:30pm, Sat 5–10:30pm, Sun 5–9:30pm. Metro: Foggy Bottom. ITALIAN.

A lot of restaurants have occupied this space over the years, but with any luck, the year-old Goldoni is here to stay. It's dramatically large, high-ceilinged and skylit; white walls display modern art evoking the Venetian carnivale, and outbursts of operas play now and again during your meal.

The Fred Astaire-ish maitre' d, Julian Russell, escorts you past the bar to your table, where more drama awaits. A risotto with grapefruit, basil, and baby shrimp is cradled in a grapefruit half. Chef/owner Fabrizio Aielli's signature dish, grilled whole fish (we had rockfish, but snapper, sea bass, and others may be available), arrives on a huge platter, served with polenta and shitake mushrooms. A salad with radicchio, goat cheese, and ground walnuts is excellent. Sorbets are a specialty, as is the beautifully presented tiramisu. Bring a party of people; Goldoni is a good spot for a celebration.

✪ Kinkead's

2000 Pennsylvania Ave. NW. ☎ **202/296-7700.** Reservations recommended. Main courses $9.50–$16 at lunch, $18–$22 at dinner, $7.50–$13 at Sun brunch. AE, DC, DISC, MC, V. Daily 11:30am–11pm. Metro: Foggy Bottom. AMERICAN/SEAFOOD.

When a restaurant has been as roundly praised as Kinkead's, you start to think no place can be that good—but Kinkead's is. An appetizer, like oysters wrapped in pancetta, leaves you with a permanent longing for oysters. A taste of potato-crusted rockfish provides a nice crunch before melting in your mouth. Vegetables you may normally disdain—cabbage, for instance—taste delicious here.

The award-winning chef/owner Bob Kinkead is the star at this three-tiered, 220-seat restaurant. He wears a headset and orchestrates his kitchen staff in full view of the upstairs dining room, where booths and tables neatly fill the nooks and alcoves of the town house. At street level is a scattering of tables overlooking the restaurant's lower level, the more casual bar and cafe, where a jazz group or pianist performs in the evening and at Sunday brunch.

Kinkead's menu features primarily seafood, like the chef's signature dish of pepita-crusted salmon with crab, corn, and chilies; but the menu (which changes for lunch and again for dinner each day) also includes at least one meat and one poultry entrée. The wine list comprises more than 300 selections. You can't go wrong with the desserts, variations on homey standards like apple-pecan crisp with cinnamon ice cream.

✪ Melrose

In the Park Hyatt Hotel, 1201 24th St. NW (at M St.). ☎ **202/955-3899.** Reservations recommended. Main courses $9–$14 at breakfast, $13–$18.50 at lunch, $18.50–$24 at dinner; pre-theater $25; $31 at Sun brunch. AE, CB, DC, DISC, JCB, MC, V. Mon–Sat 6:30–11am, Sun 6:30–10:30am; daily 11am–2:30pm and 5:30–10:30pm. Complimentary valet parking all day. Metro: Foggy Bottom. AMERICAN.

Situated in an upscale hotel, this pretty restaurant offers fine cuisine presented with friendly flourishes. In nice weather, dine outdoors on the beautifully landscaped, sunken terrace whose greenery and towering fountain protect you from traffic noises. The glass-walled dining room overlooks the terrace and is decorated with more greenery and grand bouquets of fresh flowers, in accents of marble and brass.

Brian McBride is the beguiling executive chef who sometimes emerges from the kitchen to find out how you like the angel hair pasta with mascarpone and lobster, or his sautéed Dover sole with roasted peppers, forest mushrooms, and mache. McBride, like Bob Kinkead (see above), is known for his seafood, which makes up most of the entrées and nearly all of the appetizers. If you prefer to do without sauces, there's a short selection of simply grilled seafood. Desserts, like the raspberry creme brulée or the chocolate bread pudding with chocolate sorbet, are excellent. The wine list offers 30 wines by the glass.

🎎 Family-Friendly Restaurants

Baby-boomer parents (and I am one) are so insistent upon taking their children with them everywhere that sometimes it seems all restaurants are, of necessity, family-friendly (though you may wish certain ones were not). Hotel restaurants, no matter how refined, usually welcome children, since they may be guests of the hotel. The cafeterias at tourist attractions (see section 13, later in this chapter) are always a safe bet, since they cater to the multitudes. Inexpensive ethnic restaurants tend to be pretty welcoming to kids, too. Aside from those suggestions, I offer these:

Old Glory Barbecue *(see p. 135)* A loud, laid-back place where the waitstaff is friendly without being patronizing. Go early, since the restaurant becomes more of a bar as the evening progresses. There is a children's menu, but you may not need it; the barbecue, burgers, muffins, fries, and desserts are so good, everyone can order from the main menu.

Austin Grill *(see p. 137)* Another easygoing, good-service joint, with great background music. Kids will probably want to order from their own menu here, and their drinks arrive in unspillable plastic cups with tops and straws, for taking with you if need be.

Il Radicchio *(see p. 109)* A spaghetti palace to please the most finicky, at a price that should satisfy the family budget.

America *(see p. 112)* The cavernous restaurant with its voluminous menu offers many distractions for a restless brood. No children's menu, but why would you need one, when macaroni and cheese, peanut butter and jelly, pizza, and chicken tenders are among the selections offered to everyone?

Provence

2401 Pennsylvania Ave. NW. ☎ **202/296-1166.** Reservations recommended. Main courses $11.95–$19.50 at lunch, $16.50–$28 at dinner. AE, CB, DC, MC, V. Mon–Fri noon–2pm and 6–10pm, Sat 5:30–11pm, Sun 5:30–9:30pm. Complimentary valet parking evenings. Metro: Foggy Bottom. FRENCH.

With an exhibition kitchen arrayed with gleaming copper ware, Provence's interior is country French. Panels of rough-hewn stone are framed by rustic shutters, antique hutches display provincial pottery, and delicate chandeliers and shaded sconces provide a soft amber glow.

Yannick Cam's provincial cuisine *"personalisée"* refers to his unique interpretations of traditional Mediterranean recipes, which lose nothing in the way of regional integrity. An appetizer of pan-roasted young squid—stuffed with finely ground scallops and shrimp, sautéed shallots and garlic, wild mushrooms, parsley, toasted pine nuts, and lavender blossoms—was complemented by buttery pan juice. And an entrée of crisp-skinned organic roast chicken—perfumed with bay leaf, rosemary, sweet garlic, and a soupçon of anchovy—was accompanied by superb roasted potatoes and artichoke hearts in a sauce of red wine, citrus, tomato concassé, garlic, chopped olives, and rosemary-infused olive oil. For dessert, two large dollops of praline-studded white chocolate mousse were sandwiched between delicate crunchy almond waffles. The knowledgeable waitstaff can suggest appropriate wines from the 90%-French list.

9 Georgetown

VERY EXPENSIVE

Citronelle

In the Latham Hotel, 3000 M St. NW. ☎ 202/625-2150. Reservations recommended. Main courses $9.50–$18.50 at lunch/brunch, $24–$29 at dinner; 3-course pre-theater dinner $35 (until 6:30pm), 5- and 6-course prix-fixe dinners $55 and $65, respectively ($100 for the latter with wines); 6-course Chef's Table served in the kitchen $85 (add $25–$35 with wines). AE, DC, MC, V. Daily 6:30–10:30am, 11am–3pm, and 5:30–10:30pm. Complimentary valet parking at dinner. CONTEMPORARY FRENCH.

Citronelle is an East Coast branch of Los Angeles's famed Citrus, the creation of exuberant French chef Michel Richard. It's a great venue for special-occasion or romantic dinners; the bilevel atrium is charming—updated French-country, with a stone wall and a rustic pine table displaying wines and a lavish flower arrangement. Candlelit tables, some in intimate alcoves, are set amid potted palms and other greenery.

But it's the bustling exhibition kitchen that's the focal point. Signature dishes include an exquisite Chinese salmon salad and the crunchy Kataifi shrimp, which is wrapped in wheat pastry and deep-fried. Menus vary seasonally, but you can always count on the freshest ingredients combined in dazzlingly dramatic presentations—for instance, a fan of pan-seared and roasted Muscovy duck, surrounded by a feuilleté cornucopia anchored in a dollop of garlic mashed potatoes and filled with couscous and diced figs, apricots, and apples. The dessert of choice: sumptuous, velvety hot chocolate cake drizzled with orange/ginger sauce. Citronelle's extensive wine list offers 17 premium by-the-glass selections.

Morton's of Chicago

3251 Prospect St. NW. ☎ 202/342-6258. Reservations recommended. Main courses $17.95–$29.95. AE, CB, DC, MC, V. Mon–Sat 5:30–11pm, Sun 5–10pm. Free valet parking. STEAKS/CHOPS/SEAFOOD.

Arnie Morton, a flamboyant former Playboy Enterprises executive, created this empire of Morton's steakhouses, of which Washington now has three (the newest is at the corner of Connecticut Avenue and L Street NW; ☎ 202/955-5997). Politicos, media types, and regular folks come here, sitting upon comfortable cream-colored leather booths at white-linened tables lit by pewter oil lamps in the shape of donkeys or elephants.

Morton's is known for its huge—some say grotesquely large—portions of succulent USDA prime midwestern beef and scrumptious side dishes. Start off with an appetizer such as smoked Pacific salmon or a lump-crabmeat cocktail served with mustard-mayonnaise sauce. Steaks (ribeye, double filet mignon, porterhouse, or New York sirloin) are perfectly prepared to your specifications. Other entrée choices include veal or lamb chops, fresh swordfish steak in sauce béarnaise, and baked Maine lobster. Side orders of flavorfully fresh al dente asparagus served with hollandaise or hash browns are highly recommended. Consider taking home a doggie bag if you want to leave room for dessert—perhaps a soufflé Grand Marnier or fresh raspberries in sabayon sauce.

Seasons

In the Four Seasons Hotel, 2800 Pennsylvania Ave. NW. ☎ 202/944-2000. Reservations recommended. Main courses $10–$17.25 at breakfast, $12.75–$21 at lunch, $17.25–$34 at dinner. AE, DC, JCB, MC, V. Mon–Fri 7–11am, Sat–Sun 8am–noon; Mon–Fri noon–2:30pm; nightly 6–10:30pm. Metro: Foggy Bottom. Free valet parking. AMERICAN.

Although Seasons is the signature restaurant of one of Washington's most upscale hotels, and a major celebrity haunt, it takes a casual approach to formal dining: relaxed atmosphere, no dress code, friendly service. Seasons is candlelit at night, sunlit during the day, with windows overlooking the C&O Canal.

Scottish chef William Douglas McNeill's cuisine focuses on fresh market fare. Stellar entrées ranged from crisp-fried sea bass served on a bed of julienned and gingered Oriental vegetables to roast rack of lamb encrusted with Indian spices (it came with saffroned rice studded with raisins, pine nuts, morsels of dried apricot, pistachios, and slivered almonds). A basket of scrumptious fresh-baked breads might include rosemary flat bread or sun-dried tomato bread drizzled with Parmesan. For dessert, consider an ambrosial mango creme brulee garnished with mint and creme fraiche. For the 10th consecutive year, *Wine Spectator* magazine has named Seasons's vast and carefully researched wine cellar one of the 100 best worldwide.

1789

1226 36th St. NW (at Prospect St.). ☎ **202/965-1789.** Reservations recommended. Main courses $18–$32; prix-fixe pre-theater menu $25. AE, CB, DC, DISC, MC, V. Sun–Thurs 6–10pm, Fri 6–11pm, Sat 5–11pm. Jackets required. Complimentary valet parking. AMERICAN REGIONAL.

The restaurant 1789 is as cozy as a country inn. Housed in a Federal town house, its intimate dining areas are typified by the John Carroll Room, where the walls are hung with Currier and Ives prints and old city maps, a log fire blazes in the hearth, and a gorgeous flower arrangement is displayed atop a hunting-themed oak sideboard. Throughout, silk-shaded brass oil lamps provide romantic lighting. You might spot anyone from cabinet members and senators to Sharon Stone at the next table.

Noted chef Ris Lacoste varies her menus seasonally. Appetizer options might include macadamia-crusted grilled shrimp. Typical entrées range from osso buco with risotto Milanese to roast rack of lamb with creamy feta potatoes au gratin in a red pepper purée-infused merlot sauce. A memorable dessert was the delicate tuile (crisp, rounded cookie) filled with chocolate, orange, and pistachio mascarpone on a bitter orange sauce. The wine list is long and distinguished. A great bargain here: The pre-theater menu offered nightly through 6:45pm includes appetizer, entrée, dessert, and coffee for just $25!

EXPENSIVE

✪ Mendocino Grille and Wine Bar

2917 M St. NW. ☎ **202/333-2912.** Reservations recommended. Main courses $6.75–$18.75 at lunch, $15.75–$24.75 at dinner. AE, DC, DISC, MC, V. Mon–Thurs 11:30am–3pm and 5:30–10pm, Fri–Sat 11:30am–3pm and 5:30–11pm, Sun 5:30–10pm. Metro: Foggy Bottom. AMERICAN VIA CALIFORNIA.

Rough-textured slate walls alternate with painted patches of Big Sur sky to suggest a West Coast winery and California's wine-growing region. The wall sconces resemble rectangles of sea glass and the dangling light fixtures look like turned over wineglasses. The California-casual works, and so does the food.

Grilled seafood is the highlight: yellowfin tuna presented on wilted spinach and roasted pepper purée, wild rockfish accompanied by wild rice pilaf. Non-seafood choices include free-range chicken stuffed with porcini mushrooms and wild rice, and grilled tenderloin of beef. Ever in search of the perfect crabcake, I found a close call here in the form of the jumbo lump crabmeat and smoked salmon cake appetizer.

All 85 wines on the list are West Coast selections and have received high ratings from connoisseurs. California casual doesn't mean cheap: Prices hover around $50 a bottle, although you can order a Beringer White Zinfandel for $13 or a Groth Vineyards Reserve 92 Cabernet Sauvignon Napa Valley for $135.

The Sea Catch

1054 31st St. NW (just below M St.). ☎ **202/337-8855.** Reservations recommended. Main courses $10–$16 at lunch, $15–$25 at dinner. AE, CB, DC, DISC, JCB, MC, V. Mon–Sat noon–3pm and 5:30–10:30pm. Complimentary valet parking. SEAFOOD.

Before the recent onslaught of seafood restaurants in Washington, there was The Sea Catch, around since 1989. It sits on the bank of the C&O Canal and has an awning-covered wooden deck from which you can watch ducks, punters, and mule-drawn barges glide by while you dine. Inside, the innlike main dining room has a working fireplace and rough-hewn walls made of fieldstone dug from Georgetown quarries. There's also a handsome white Carrara-marble raw bar and a deluxe brasserie. Classic jazz tapes play in the background.

For openers, plump farm-raised oysters, clams, house-smoked fish, and other raw-bar offerings merit consideration. The entrée focus is on daily changing fresh fish and seafood specials, such as big, fluffy jumbo lump crabcakes served with crunchy Oriental-style napa cabbage slaw or grilled marinated squid with fennel and basil aioli. The kitchen willingly prepares fresh fish and seafood dishes to your specifications, including live lobster from the tanks. An extensive wine list highlights French, Italian, and American selections. Fresh-baked desserts usually include an excellent Key lime pie.

MODERATE

Aditi

3299 M St. NW. ☎ **202/625-6825.** Reservations recommended. Main courses $4.25–$9.95 at lunch, $5.95–$13.95 at dinner. AE, DC, DISC, MC, V. Mon–Sat 11:30am–2:30pm, Sun noon–2:30pm; Sun–Thurs 5:30–10pm, Fri–Sat 5:30–10:30pm. INDIAN.

This charming, three-level restaurant provides a serene setting in which to enjoy first-rate Indian cookery to the tune of Indian music. A must here is the platter of assorted appetizers—*bhajia* (a deep-fried vegetable fritter), deep-fried cheese-and-shrimp pakoras, and crispy vegetable samosas stuffed with spiced potatoes and peas. Favorite entrées include lamb biryani, which is a basmati rice pilaf tossed with savory pieces of lamb, cilantro, raisins, and almonds; and the skewered jumbo tandoori prawns, chicken, lamb, or beef—all fresh and fork tender—barbecued in the tandoor (clay oven). Sauces are on the mild side, so if you like your food fiery, inform your waiter. A kachumber salad, topped with yogurt and spices, is a refreshing accompaniment to entrées. For dessert, try kheer, a cooling rice pudding garnished with chopped nuts. There's a full bar.

✪ Bistrot Lepic

1736 Wisconsin Ave. NW. ☎ **202/333-0111.** Reservations required. Main courses $9–$12.25 at lunch, $14–$18 at dinner. AE, DISC, MC, V. Tues–Sun 11:30am–2:30pm; Tues–Thurs 5:30–10pm, Fri–Sat 5:30–10:30pm, Sun 5:30–9:30pm. FRENCH.

So tiny it has no waiting area for new arrivals, Bistrot Lepic is the real thing, a charming French restaurant like one you might find on a Parisian side street. The atmosphere is bustling and cheery, and you hear a lot of French spoken—not just by the waitstaff and the young proprietress Cecile Fortin (her husband Bruno is chef), but by customers.

This is traditional French cooking, updated. The seasonal menu offers such seafood and meat entrées as grilled rockfish served with green lentils du Puy and aged balsamic sauce, and roasted rack of lamb with Yukon gold mashed potatoes and garlic juice. We opted for specials: tuna prepared quite rare, as it's supposed to be, and served on fennel with a citrusy vinaigrette, and grouper with a lightly spicy lobster sauce upon a bed of spinach.

The modest sized French wine list offers a fairly good range, but the house wine, Le Pic Saint Loup, is a nice complement to most menu choices and priced at less than $20 a bottle.

Clyde's

3236 M St. NW. ☎ **202/333-9180.** Reservations recommended. Main courses mostly $6.95–$10.95 at lunch/brunch, $9.95–$16.95 at dinner (most under $12); burgers and sandwiches under $7 all day. AE, DC, DISC, MC, V. Mon–Thurs 11:30am–2am, Fri 11:30am–3am, Sat 9am–3am, Sun 9am–2am; brunch Sat–Sun 9am–4pm. AMERICAN.

Clyde's has been a favorite watering hole for an eclectic mix of Washingtonians since 1963. You'll see university students, Capitol Hill types, affluent professionals, Washington Redskins, romantic duos, and well-heeled "ladies who lunch" bogged down with shopping bags from Georgetown's posh boutiques. A 1996 renovation transformed Clyde's from a saloon to a theme park, whose dining areas include a cherry-paneled front room with oil paintings of sport scenes, and an atrium with vintage model planes dangling from the glass ceiling and a 16th-century French limestone chimneypiece in the large fireplace.

Clyde's is known for its burgers, chili, and crabcake sandwich. Appetizers are a safe bet, and the Clyde's take on the classic niçoise is also recommended: chilled grilled salmon with greens, oven-roasted Roma tomatoes, green beans, and grilled new potatoes in a tasty vinaigrette. Sunday brunch is a tradition (brunch is also served on Saturday). The menu is reassuringly familiar—steak and eggs, omelettes, waffles—with variations thrown in for good measure, like an eggs Benedict that uses a grilled portobello mushroom in place of ham and roasted red pepper hollandaise. Among bar selections are at least ten draft beers and seven microbrews.

Martin's Tavern

1264 Wisconsin Ave. NW. ☎ **202/333-7370.** Reservations accepted. Main courses $5.50–$11.95 at breakfast, $5.50–$11.95 at brunch, $6.50–$10.95 at lunch (sandwiches and salads average $5.95), $5.75–$19.95 at dinner (most items under $15). AE, CB, DC, DISC, MC, V. Sun–Thurs 8am–11pm, Fri–Sat 8am–1am. AMERICAN.

A good old-fashioned neighborhood pub—that's Martin's. Out-of-towners (especially French and Japanese) come here often, but Martin's boasts a loyal following of locals as well. I once heard a couple at the bar joking that they chose their new house on the basis of its proximity to Martin's. It has operated continuously since 1933, when it was opened by former New York Giants player William G. Martin, and his father, William S. These days, Billy Martin, great grandson of William S., is behind the bar; his wife Kelli supervises the kitchen and staff, some of whom have been here for more than a decade. Sit at the bar, and you'll hear the lore about famous regulars over the years—from the Kennedys to Art Buchwald. If you crave intimacy, just ask for the "dugout." The menu mainstays are the crabcakes, steak sandwich, the shad and shad roe, and linguine with clam sauce. Lots of paneling, old photos, and draft beers on tap.

Paolo's

1303 Wisconsin Ave. NW (at N St.). ☎ **202/333-7353.** Reservations accepted at lunch and brunch only. Pastas mostly $8.25–$11.95; pizzas $7.25–$9.25; main courses $12.95–$16.95. AE, CB, DC, DISC, MC, V. Sun–Thurs 11:30am–midnight, Fri–Sat 11:30am–12:30am. Bar open (pizza is served) Sun–Thurs till 1am, Fri–Sat till 2am; brunch Sat–Sun 11am–3pm. CALIFORNIA-STYLE ITALIAN.

Restaurateur Paul Cohn is a virtuoso when it comes to creating a scene that crackles with excitement. (See Georgia Brown's and the Georgetown Seafood Grill on 19th St., above, two of his other properties.) In warm weather, tables spill out onto the street from an open-air patio. In cold weather, diners enjoy basking in the warm glow of the front room's pizza-oven fire. The cherrywood-paneled back room also has an exhibition kitchen. Paolo's draws an "in" crowd of young and hip, older and sophisticated. Many come here just to munch on the complimentary warm, soft, seeded bread sticks and tapenade—if you don't get them, ask. And ask what to order, for the waitstaff is honest: our waiter told me the double-stuffed Italian toast offered at brunch was "really bad." The pizza frittata I ordered instead was fine, with its applesmoked bacon, goat cheese, pepper topping, though the crust was soppy. Best to get here are salads, like the Caesar and the chicken salad, which are a step above the ordinary, and pastas, such as the pasta Bolognese, interesting with its inclusion of fresh radicchio. There's live music Sundays from noon to 3pm.

Sequoia

3000 K St. NW (at Washington Harbour). ☎ **202/944-4200.** Reservations recommended (not accepted for outdoor seating). Main courses $6.95–$28.95; salads and sandwiches $6.95–$12.95. AE, DISC, MC, V. Sun–Thurs 11:30am–midnight, Fri–Sat 11:30am–1am. Paid parking available at the Harbour, discounted to restaurant patrons at dinner on weekends. AMERICAN REGIONAL.

In the Washington-restaurant-with-a-view category, no setting is more spectacular than Sequoia's terrace, where umbrella-shaded tables overlook the boat-filled Potomac between two bridges. If outside tables are taken, you can enjoy the same river vista from the window-walled interior.

The view is the main reason people frequent Sequoia, and it's especially popular as a place to come for drinks after work. The restaurant is huge and often the setting for large parties, so don't look for intimacy.

The varied and extensive menu runs the gamut from burgers, sandwiches, pastas, and pizzas to mint-marinated lamb chops with garlic smashed potatoes and napa cabbage. Save room for one of Sequoia's excellent desserts, perhaps toasted pecan/whiskey pie. Many wines are offered by the glass, and regional beers and ales are featured.

INEXPENSIVE

Music City Roadhouse

1050 30th St. NW. ☎ **202/337-4444.** Reservations recommended. Family-style meal $13, $5.95 for children 6–12, children under 6 can share with adults; late night courses $3–$7.50, brunch $13. AE, CB, DC, DISC, MC, V. Tues–Sat 4:30–10pm, Sun 3–11pm; late night Tues–Sat 10pm–1am; brunch Sun 11am–2pm. SOUTHERN/AMERICAN.

The downstairs of Music City Roadhouse is a large and raucous two-room bar with pool tables. Upstairs is the restaurant where live, mostly blues, bands play while you pig out on fried and barbecued chicken, barbecued spare ribs, fried catfish, pot roast, and country fried steak. The deal is, for $12.95 each, you may choose up to three entrées and three side dishes for your table. The sides, such as mashed regular and sweet potatoes, coleslaw, greens, and green beans with bacon, are replenishable.

The music is great, but so loud it overwhelms conversation, and the small tables are packed tightly next to each other (most seating is family style, at long tables). The food is plentiful and tastes of the true South (that is, the greens are soggy). And the roadhouse validates your parking ticket from the underground garage, a rarity for Georgetown. *Note:* If you've got kids, make sure they go to the bathroom before you get here. The only rest room is downstairs in the bar, which, at 6:30 on a Saturday night is already noisy and jammed with beer-guzzling behemoths.

Old Glory Barbecue

3139 M St. NW. ☎ **202/337-3406.** Reservations for 6 or more Sun–Thurs, reservations not accepted Fri–Sat. Main courses $6.50–$16; late night entrées $5.25–$6.75; brunch buffet

$11.95, $5.95 for kids 11 and under. AE, DC, DISC, MC, V. Sun–Thurs 11:30am–1am, Fri–Sat 11:30am–3am; Sun brunch 11am–3pm. Metro: Foggy Bottom. AMERICAN/BARBECUE.

Raised wooden booths flank one side of the restaurant; an imposing, old-fashioned dark wood bar with saddle-seat stools extends down the other. Blues, rock, and country songs play in the background. Old Glory boasts the city's "largest selection of single-barrel and boutique bourbons," a claim which two buddies at the bar appear to be confirming firsthand. In a few hours, when the two-story restaurant is packed with the young and the restless, these two may be swinging from the ceiling's tin-colander lampshade lighting fixtures.

In early evening, though, Old Glory is prime for anyone—singles, families, an older crowd. Come for the messy, tangy, delicious spare ribs, hickory smoked chicken, tender, smoked beef brisket, or marinated, wood-fried shrimp. Six sauces are on the table, the spiciest being the vinegar-based East Carolina and Lexington, the least spicy but most popular the sweet Memphis sauce. My Southern-raised husband favored the Savannah version, which reminded him of that city's famous Johnny Harris barbecue sauce. The complimentary corn muffins and biscuits, side dishes of collard greens, succotash, and potato salad, and desserts like apple crisp and coconut cherry cobbler all hit the spot.

Patisserie Café Didier

3206 Grace St. NW (off Wisconsin Ave. just below M St.). ☎ **202/342-9083.** Main courses $7.99–$9.99; breakfast pastries, muffins, croissants, and desserts $1.15–$7.99. CB, DC, DISC, MC, V. Tues–Sat 8am–7pm, Sun 8am–5pm. FRENCH/PATISSERIE.

The croissants are the butteriest, most delicious you'll find anywhere, but at $1.69 each, they are also the most expensive for their teeny tiny size. This sunny little patisserie, hidden away on a side street in Georgetown, serves hot chocolate made from scratch with chunks of Belgian chocolate; the tartelettes, eclairs, cakes, and precious, bite-size cookies are beyond compare. Available at lunch are homemade soups served with a basket of fresh-baked breads, quiches, soufflés, sandwiches, salads, and hot items such as lamb couscous or grilled trout served with fresh vegetables. Dieter Schorner, former pastry chef at New York's Le Cirque and La Côte Basque, came to D.C. in 1988, and his marvelous creations have graced many of this city's most fashionable parties.

Zed's

3318 M St. NW. ☎ **202/333-4710.** Reservations accepted for large parties only. Main courses $5.95–$10.75 at lunch, mostly $6.95–$12.95 at dinner. AE, CB, DC, DISC, MC, V. Sun–Thurs 11am–11pm, Fri–Sat 11am–1am. ETHIOPIAN.

Though Ethiopian cuisine has long been popular in Washington, few restaurants can match Zed's in Georgetown, which offers truly authentic, high-quality fare. Zed's is a trilevel, charming little place with indigenous paintings, posters, and artifacts adorning pine-paneled walls. Tables are set with fresh flowers, and Ethiopian music enhances the ambience.

Diners use a sourdough crepelike pancake called *injera* to scoop up food. Highly recommended are the *doro watt* (chicken stewed in a tangy hot red chili pepper sauce), the *infillay* (strips of tender chicken breast flavored with seasoned butter and honey wine and served with a delicious chopped spinach and rice side dish), flavorful lamb dishes and the deep-fried whole fish. Vegetables have never been tastier. Consider ordering more of the garlicky chopped collard greens, red lentil purée in spicy red pepper sauce, or a purée (served chilled) of roasted yellow split peas mixed with onions, peppers, and garlic. There's a full bar, and, should you have the inclination, there are Italian pastries for dessert.

10 Glover Park

MODERATE

Busara

2340 Wisconsin Ave. NW. ☎ **202/337-2340.** Reservations recommended. Main courses $6–$8.25 at lunch, $7.25–$15.25 at dinner. AE, DC, DISC, MC, V. Mon–Fri 11:30am–3pm, Sat–Sun 11:30am–4pm; Sun–Thurs 5–11pm, Fri–Sat 5pm–midnight. THAI.

Like many Thai restaurants, Busara gives you big portions for a pretty good price. The pad thai is an excellent, less sweet than normal version, the satays are well marinated, and an appetizer called "shrimp bikini" serves up not-at-all-greasy deep-fried shrimp in a thin springroll covering. The number of chili pepper icons next to the name of a dish on the menu indicates degree of spiciness.

Busara's dining room is large, with a picture window overlooking Wisconsin Avenue, modern art on the neon blue walls, and dimly set track lighting angled this way and that. Service is solicitous, but not pushy. If the dining room is full, you can eat at the bar (at dinner only), which is in a separate, small, and rather inviting room. In warm weather, Busara also serves diners in its oriental garden.

✪ Sushi-Ko

2309 Wisconsin Ave. NW. ☎ **202/333-4187.** Reservations recommended. Main courses $6.50–$17 at lunch, $7.50–$18 at dinner. AE, MC, V. Tues–Fri noon–2:30pm; Mon–Fri 6–10:30pm, Sat 5–10:30pm, Sun 5–10pm. JAPANESE.

This is the best place in Washington for sushi, and people know it; so even if you've reserved a table, you may have a wait. Chef Kazuhiro (Kaz) Okochi is something of a personality and fun to watch at the sushi bar, so try to sit there. At any rate, you can expect superb versions of sushi and sashimi standards, but the best items are those invented by Kaz—like a sushi napoleon of diced sea trout layered between rice crackers, or a snapper carpaccio. Even if you're not much for sushi, you might enjoy Sushi-Ko for its excellent tempuras and teriyakis.

Xing Kuba

2218 Wisconsin Ave. NW. ☎ **202/965-0665.** Reservations recommended. Main courses $6–$8 at lunch, $3.25–$5 at brunch, $12–$20 at dinner (most are $15 and under). AE, DISC, MC, V. Mon–Fri 11:30am–2:30pm; Sun–Thurs 5:30–10:15pm, Fri–Sat 5–11:15pm; brunch (dim sum/tapas) Sat–Sun 11:30am–3pm. ASIAN/SOUTHWESTERN.

This is a neighborhood-casual sort of place, never very crowded when we've been here, though the staff says it gets that way weekend nights. Fresh flowers, lantern lamps, and faux leopard-skin covered bar stools are part of the eclectic decor. The menu's eclectic, too.

As its name suggests, Xing Kuba fuses Caribbean and Asian cuisines, along with American and Southwestern touches. My special first course, a springroll that wrapped a thin flour tortilla around chunks of fresh crabmeat with chopped onion and cilantro, tasted wildly flavorful without the melted cheese that binds such ingredients in the more common Southwestern quesadilla. The thick Cuban black bean soup had an extra kick, thanks to the wasabi creme fraiche that was swirled across the top. Try the baked salmon with a light pinenut-plantain crust, cilantro cream and sautéed wild mushrooms, and sesame Japanese rice, and see whether you're not pleased.

INEXPENSIVE

✪ Austin Grill

2404 Wisconsin Ave. NW. ☎ **202/337-8080.** Reservations not accepted., Lunch, Sat–Sun brunch and dinner $6–$13. AE, DC, DISC, MC, V. Mon–Thurs 11:30am–11pm, Fri–Sat 11:30am–midnight, Sun 11am–11pm. TEX-MEX.

Come with the kids, a date, or your friends for fun and good food. Austin Grill is loud; as the night progresses, conversation eventually drowns out the sound of the taped music (everything from Ry Cooder to Natalie Merchant).

Owner Rob Wilder opened his grill in 1988 to replicate the easygoing lifestyle, Tex-Mex cuisine, and music he'd loved when he lived in Austin. The grill is known for the fresh ingredients used to create outstanding crabmeat quesadillas, "Lake Travis" nachos (tostidas slathered with chopped red onion, refried beans and cheese), a daily fish special (like rockfish fajitas), Key lime pie, and excellent versions of standard fare (chicken enchiladas, guacamole, pico de gallo, and so on).

Austin Grill's upstairs overlooks the abbreviated bar area below. An upbeat decor includes walls washed in shades of teal and clay and adorned with whimsical coyotes, cowboys, Indians, and cacti. Arrive by 6pm weekends if you don't want to wait; weekdays are less crowded. This is the original Austin Grill; suburban locations are in Old Town Alexandria and West Springfield, VA, and in Bethesda, MD.

11 U Street Corridor

INEXPENSIVE TO MODERATE

Coppi's

1414 U St. NW. ☎ **202/319-7773.** Reservations not accepted. Main courses $7–$11.50. AE, DC, DISC, MC, V. Mon–Thurs 5pm–midnight, Fri–Sat 5pm–1am, Sun 5–11pm. Metro: U Street–Cardoza. ITALIAN.

Crowded with neighborhood customers and hungry clubgoers headed for one of the nearby music houses, Coppi's is a narrow room decorated with wooden booths and bicycle memorabilia from Italian bike races. The wood-burning oven turns out a mean pizza, a stiff competitor to that of topdog Pizzeria Paradiso (see above). The crust is chewy and the toppings of good quality ham, pancetta, cheeses, and vegetables. You can count on finding an extensive Italian wine list and entrées all under $12. Another, larger, Coppi's is located in the Cleveland Park neighborhood, at 3421 Connecticut Ave. NW (☎ **202/244-6437**).

U St. Wine Bar and Tapas Bistro

1416 U St. NW. ☎ **202/588-7311.** Reservations recommended. Tapas $3.50–$7.95; main courses $9.95–$15.95. AE, MC, V. Sun–Thurs 5–11pm, Fri–Sat 5pm–midnight. Metro: U Street–Cardoza. TAPAS.

Bottles of mostly Spanish wine fill the racks that line the walls of this cozy space in Washington's newest hot neighborhood. The room has a high ceiling, with slanted panels on either side that are covered with large murals of dancers and diners and card players, platters of food, and bottles of wine. The ambience and tapas are the reasons to come here. The extensive tapas menu changes regularly but emphasizes seafood, like the smoked salmon with grilled fennel, radicchio, and sundried tomato purée. The shorter entrées list includes pastas, grilled fish, and grilled meat. Two versions of creme brulee are on the menu, the usual one and one with raspberries (both good).

12 Woodley Park

EXPENSIVE

✪ Mrs. Simpson's

2915 Connecticut Ave. NW. ☎ **202/332-8300.** Reservations recommended. Main courses $5.50–$11.95 at lunch, $6.95–$22.95 at dinner; $6.95–$13.95 at Sun brunch, $16.95 for 3-course champagne Sun brunch. AE, CB, DC, DISC, MC, V. Mon–Fri noon–4pm, Sat 10:30am–

4pm, Sun brunch 10:30am–4pm; dinner daily from 4pm until about 9:30 or 10pm. Metro: Woodley Park–Zoo. AMERICAN.

Mrs. Simpson's lies 1 block up and across Connecticut Avenue from the Sheraton Washington Hotel, whose guests often stumble delightedly upon the restaurant. More and more, though, you'll see people from the neighborhood, drawn by the gracious welcome, the popular brunch, and a menu that offers just enough variety to please small and hearty eaters, traditional and inquisitive palates.

Specials are always worth investigating. A smoky mushroom soup of puréed, grilled portabella and shitake mushrooms tastes creamy, though it is broth based. The grilled Canadian salmon al pesto is perfectly prepared and worth ordering simply for the vegetable pancake that accompanies it. Crabcakes are the traditional version—mostly crab—and a house specialty.

Your waiter will urge dessert on you, and you should succumb. Chocolate roulade cake, fresh lemon mousse, and raspberry creme brulee are tops.

○ New Heights

2317 Calvert St. NW. ☎ **202/234-4110.** Reservations recommended. Main courses $7.75–$11.50 at brunch, $16–$25 at dinner. AE, CB, DC, DISC, MC, V. Sun–Thurs 5:30–10pm, Fri–Sat 5:30–11pm, Sun 11am–2:30pm. Metro: Woodley Park–Zoo. AMERICAN/INTERNATIONAL.

This attractive second-floor dining room has a bank of windows looking out to Rock Creek Park and walls hung with the colorful works of a Florida artist. New Heights attracts a casually upscale clientele, who fill the room every night. Certain features, like the excellent black bean pâté with smoked tomato and green onion sauces, and the choice of appetizer or entrée portions, are fixtures. But Matthew Lake, the restaurant's 26-year-old chef, is responsible for innovations such as the heavenly potato-crusted Arctic char, which is prepared with ginger-braised leeks and walnuts in a porcini mushroom beurre blanc. Best to ask about menu items whose descriptions use unfamiliar though intriguing words; for example, "crispy eggplant fritters with rocket pesto and lime tahini." An almond torte dessert proves a perfect antidote.

MODERATE

Lebanese Taverna

2641 Connecticut Ave. NW. ☎ **202/265-8681.** Reservations accepted. Main courses $8–$14 at lunch, $10–$16 at dinner. AE, CB, DC, DISC, MC, V. Mon–Fri 11:30am–2:30pm, Sat 11:30am–3pm; Mon–Thurs 5:30–10:30pm, Fri–Sat 5:30–11pm, Sun 5–10pm. Metro: Woodley Park–Zoo. LEBANESE.

This family-owned restaurant gives you a taste of Lebanese culture, not just through the cuisine, but in decor and music as well. It's so popular on weekends that sometimes you'll see people standing in line to get in, even though the restaurant does take reservations. Diners, once seated in the courtyardlike dining room, where music plays and prayer rugs hang on walls, hate to leave. The wood-burning oven at back bakes the pita breads and several appetizers. Order a demi mezze, with pita for dipping, and you get 12 sampling dishes, including hommos, tabbouleh, baba ghannouge, and pastry-wrapped spinach pies (*fatayer b'sbanigh*), enough for dinner for two, or hors d'oeuvres for four. The wealth of meatless dishes will delight vegetarians, while rotisserie items, especially the chicken and the chargrilled kebabs of chicken and shrimp, will please all others.

Petitto's

2653 Connecticut Ave. NW. ☎ **202/667-5350.** Reservations recommended. Main courses $11–$17.75. AE, CB, DC, DISC, MC, V. Mon–Sat 6–10:30pm, Sun 6–9:30pm. Dolce Finale, Mon–Thurs 5pm–12:30am, Fri–Sat 5pm–1:30am. Metro: Woodley Park–Zoo. NORTHERN ITALIAN.

⭐ Favorite Restaurants Outside Washington

Ask a Washingtonian to name his or her favorite local restaurant, and the answer you get may surprise you: Washingtonians consistently put at the top of their list four restaurants that lie outside Washington. It's not that the city lacks for superb cuisine—this chapter attests to the range and excellence of capital dining. It's just that these four restaurants, in particular, have endeared themselves to locals, and to outsiders who have discovered them. Each location involves a pretty drive. So if you have the time, book a table (if it's not too late), and head out of the city.

The Inn at Little Washington, Middle and Main streets, Washington, VA (☎ 540/675-3800), is the most famous, its exquisite American regional food prepared by chef Patrick O'Connell; the food gains accolades from the world's best chefs. The English-style inn is a Relais et Chateaux property and lies in Washington, VA, about 50 miles south of Washington.

L'Auberge Chez François, 332 Springvale Rd., Great Falls, VA (☎ 703/759-3800), is the oldest and most beloved, having opened in downtown Washington in 1954. Francois Haeringer moved his Auberge in 1976 to this picturesque setting at a bend in a country road. The 77-year-old Francois continues to rule the kitchen, with help from his family and staff, producing Alsatian-influenced French food with great celebration.

Ashby Inn, 692 Federal St., Paris, VA (☎ 540/592-3900), lies about 60 miles outside D.C., just past the quaint town of Middleburg. This small country inn boasts a magnificent view of the Blue Ridge Mountains; it's run by John and Roma Sherman, who present seasonally influenced American cuisine.

Old Angler's Inn, 10801 MacArthur Blvd., Potomac, MD (☎ 301/365-2425), is across from the C&O Canal. The inn features outdoor dining on the patio in warm weather, cozy dining by the fireplace in cold weather, and fine American food prepared by chef Jeffrey Tomchek.

This is an old-fashioned neighborhood restaurant whose three dining rooms, each with a working fireplace, occupy the first floor of a turn-of-the-century town house. Operatic arias (sometimes live) provide the appropriate background music. In nice weather, you can dine alfresco at umbrella tables on the street.

A "symphony of pasta" sampler platter (three varieties) offers the best value. Choices include a falasche alla Petitto (homemade spinach and egg noodles tossed with mushrooms, prosciutto, and peas in a cream sauce) and penne tossed with chunks of bacon and hot peppers in red sauce. Aside from the sampler, the linguini with lump crabmeat and peppers is notable for its fresh chunks of crab in a light cream sauce. Nonpasta entrées change weekly, but always list veal and fresh seafood dishes; for example, cacciucco, an array of lobster, scallops, mussels, clams, and squid. A moderately priced and well-chosen list of Italian wines is augmented by costlier vintages (including French and California selections).

Dolce Finale, in Petitto's candlelit, brick-walled wine cellar, features a variety of cappuccinos, wines, grappas, liqueurs, fruits and cheeses, and an array of sumptuous desserts. It can be visited separately from the restaurant.

13 Dining at Sightseeing Attractions

With so many great places to eat in Washington, I have a hard time recommending those at sightseeing attractions. Most of these are overpriced and too crowded, even if they are convenient. A few, however, are worth mentioning—for their admirable cuisine, noteworthy setting, or both.

Head for the Capitol's numerous restaurants for a chance to rub elbows with your senators and representatives. But keep in mind these spots are usually open only for lunch and can get *very* crowded; to lessen the chances of a long wait, try going about 30 minutes before the posted closing time. You'll find the **House of Representatives Restaurant** (also called the "Members' Dining Room") in Room H118, at the South end of the Capitol (☎ 202/225-6300). This fancy, chandelier-and-gilt-framed eatery is open to the public but doesn't take reservations (it's also open for breakfast). Senators frequent the **Senate Dining Room,** but you'll need a letter from your senator to eat here (jacket and tie required for men, no jeans for men or women). More accommodating is the **Refectory,** first floor, Senate side of the Capitol (☎ 202/224-4870), which serves sandwiches and other light luncheon fare.

Most Hill staffers eat at places like the **Longworth Building Cafeteria,** Independence Avenue and South Capitol Street SE (☎ 202/225-4410), where they can just grab a bite and go. But by far the best deal for visitors is the **Dirksen Senate Office Building South Buffet Room,** First and C sts. NE (☎ 202/224-4249). For just $8.75 (including a nonalcoholic drink and dessert), you can choose from a buffet that includes a carving station and eight other hot entrées. It's often crowded, but they will take reservations for parties of more than six.

In the same neighborhood, two institutions offering great deals and views (of famous sites or people) are the Library of Congress's **Cafeteria** (☎ 202/707-8300), and its more formal **Montpelier Room** (☎ 202/707-8300), where the prix-fixe lunch is only $8.50; and the Supreme Court's **Cafeteria** (☎ 202/479-3246), where you'll likely spy a justice or two enjoying the midday meal.

Among museum restaurants, the ones that shine are The Corcoran Gallery of Art's **Café des Artistes** (☎ 202/639-1786); the National Air & Space Museum's two spots, **Flight Line** (☎ 202/371-8750) and **The Wright Place** (☎ 202/371-8777); the National Gallery Of Art's **Terrace Café** and **Garden Café** (☎ 202/347-9401); the National Portrait Gallery's and the National Museum of American Art's restaurant, **Patent Pending** (☎ 202/357-2700), situated in a corridor connecting the two museums; and the Phillips Collection's snug **Café** (☎ 202/387-2151).

7

What to See & Do in Washington, D.C.

If you are one of the 21 million people planning a visit to Washington, D.C., this year, you already may have mapped out your agenda. You'll want to see the Capitol, you're thinking, and the monuments, and the White House, and the Smithsonian museums, and. . . so much more.

You won't be able to do it all. My advice is to consider the whole picture, and then decide what it is that really interests you. Don't assume that you need to follow the crowd. The National Air and Space Museum, Union Station, and the National Museum of Natural History are the three most visited attractions in Washington, each marvelous in its own way (and almost always swarming with sightseers); but if these sights don't appeal, don't go. There's plenty else to do.

Here's what I mean. While you are in the neighborhood of the "big name" sights, you may want to pop in to a lesser known attraction for a different kind of experience. For example, the Capitol, the Supreme Court, and the Library of Congress all dovetail nicely at the intersection of 1st Street and East Capitol Street. But if you crave a fix of something unrelated to government, walk a block past the Library of Congress on East Capitol to the Folger Shakespeare Library, where you can admire Tudor architecture and exhibits from the collection of Renaissance books, paintings, and musical instruments, and later have a picnic in the Elizabethan garden.

Finally, be sure not to miss what's new in the city. This past year saw the opening of the 7-acre Franklin Delano Roosevelt Memorial in West Potomac Park and the Military Women's Memorial in Arlington Memorial Cemetery. The nation's theater, the John F. Kennedy Center for the Performing Arts, has begun to host free concerts every night in its Grand Foyer. A consortium of museums and other organizations now operate a Museum Bus, which provides inexpensive and convenient transportation to about 22 museums all over the city (see "Motor Around Town with the Museum Bus" in chapter 4). And all of the museums offer new exhibits all the time—look for the box of information in this chapter about 1998 shows at the various museums.

So go at your own pace, see what you want to see, and if you don't get to everything, come back for another visit.

SUGGESTED ITINERARIES

If You Have 1 Day

Make the Mall your destination, visiting whichever museums appeal to you the most. Take a breather: If you have young children, let them ride the carousel across from the Smithsonian's Arts and Industries Building. With or without kids, stroll through the Enid A. Haupt Garden, outside the Smithsonian "Castle" (the Information Center) in the same area. Rest up, dine in the Dupont Circle neighborhood, stroll Connecticut Ave., then visit the Lincoln Memorial at night.

If You Have 2 Days

On your first day, take a narrated tour of the city (see list of options at end of this chapter) for an overview of the city's attractions, hopping off at the Jefferson, FDR, Lincoln, and Vietnam Veterans memorials, and at the Washington Monument. Use the tour to determine your choices of mall museums to visit. After taking in the Washington Monument, walk up 15th Street to the Old Ebbitt Grill for lunch (expect a wait unless you made a reservation). Following lunch, visit your top-pick museums on the Mall. Start your second day by visiting the Capitol, followed by a tour of the Supreme Court. Walk to Massachusetts Avenue for lunch at Cafe Berlin, then spend the afternoon visiting the Library of Congress, the Folger Shakespeare Library, and, if you have time, Union Station and the National Postal Museum.

Have dinner in Georgetown and browse the shops.

If You Have 3 Days

Spend your first 2 days as described above. On the morning of your third day, tour the White House and the National Archives. In the afternoon, ride the Museum Bus (in operation June through October) to visit the Washington National Cathedral or some of the non-Mall art museums, for example, the Phillips Collection, the National Portrait Gallery, the Museum of American Art, or the Corcoran. Enjoy a pre-theater dinner at one of the many restaurants that offer these good deals, then head to the Kennedy Center for a performance.

If You Have 5 Days or M ore

Spend your first 3 days as suggested above.

On the fourth day, get an early start on the FBI tour, and spend the rest of the morning at Ford's Theatre. Use the afternoon for outdoor activities—go to the zoo or for a hike along the C&O Canal. Alternatively, you might visit the U.S. Holocaust Memorial Museum (not recommended for children under 12); this will require most of a day to see. Have dinner downtown at one of the 7th Street district restaurants, then go on to see Shakespeare performed at the Lansburgh, or head to Coco Loco to practice your samba.

On the fifth day, consider a day trip to Alexandria, Virginia. Or spend the morning touring Mount Vernon and the afternoon seeing the sights you've missed. Have dinner in Adams-Morgan, then, if it's the right night, enjoy the blues at Madam's Organ. (Or try jazz at one of the clubs; see chapter 10 for suggestions.)

1 The Three Major Houses of Government

Three of the most visited sights in Washington are the buildings housing the executive, legislative, and judicial branches of the U.S. government. All are stunning and offer considerable insight into the workings of America.

✪ The White House

1600 Pennsylvania Ave. NW (visitor entrance gate on E. Executive Ave.). ☎ **202/456-7041** or 202/208-1631. Free admission. Tues–Sat 10am–noon. Closed some days for official functions; check before leaving your hotel by calling the 24-hour number. Metro: McPherson Square (if you are going straight to the White House), Federal Triangle (if you are getting tour tickets from the White House Visitor Center).

"I never forget," said Franklin Delano Roosevelt in one of his fireside chats, "that I live in a house owned by all the American people." Not only do Americans own the White House, but they're welcome to visit, making it almost unique among world residences of heads of state. The White House has been the scene of many great moments in American history. It is the central theater of government, where decisions on national and international policies are made. And, of course, it's also the private home of the president and his family, where their personal lives are as much of national interest as political happenings. Inside is a repository of art and furnishings, reflecting the tastes of our chief executives and first ladies from the earliest years of the American Republic to the present. Highlights of the tour include the following rooms:

The gold-and-white **East Room,** scene of presidential receptions, weddings of presidents' daughters (Lynda Bird Johnson, for one), and other dazzling events. This is where the president entertains visiting heads of state and the place where seven of the eight presidents who died in office (all but Garfield) laid in state. It was also the scene of Nixon's resignation speech. The room is decorated in the early–20th-century style of the Theodore Roosevelt renovation; it has parquet Fontainebleau oak floors and white-painted wood walls with fluted pilasters and classical relief inserts. Note the famous Gilbert Stuart portrait of George Washington that Dolley Madison saved from the British torch during the War of 1812.

The **Green Room,** today used as a sitting room, was Thomas Jefferson's dining room. He designed a revolving door with trays on one side, so servants could leave dishes on the kitchen side. Then he would twirl the door and allow guests to help themselves, thus retaining his privacy. In the room, green watered-silk fabric covers walls with notable paintings by Gilbert Stuart and John Singer Sargent, which look

White House Touring Tips

More than 1.2 million people line up annually to see the Executive Mansion. Your best bet is to obtain tickets in advance from your congressperson or senator for the VIP tours at 8:15, 8:30, and 8:45am (see chapter 2 for details). This will ensure your entrance, even during the tourist season when more than 6,000 people try to squeeze in during the 2 hours each day the White House is open. It will also entitle you to a more extensive, and guided, tour; during the regular visiting hours, there are guides on hand to answer questions, but no actual tour is given. A good idea, before you take any tour, is to pick up a book called *The White House: An Historic Guide,* available at the White House Visitor Center and at many of the top sights. Then you'll know what to look for in each room. You can order it in advance (as well as another book, *The Living White House,* which gives more biographical information about the presidents and their families) from the **White House Historical Association,** 740 Jackson Place NW, Washington, DC 20503 (☎ **202/737-8292**). Send $8 for a paperback or $9.50 for a hardcover edition of either book (prices include costs for shipping and handling).

The White House Visitor Center

The White House Visitor Center, 1450 Pennsylvania Ave., in the Department of Commerce Building, between 14th and 15th streets NW (☎ **202/208-1631,** or 202/456-7041 for recorded information), opened in 1995 to provide extensive interpretive data about the White House (as well as other Washington tourist attractions) and serve as a ticket-distribution center. It is run under the auspices of the National Park Service. Here visitors can view a 26-minute video about the White House called *Within These Walls,* which provides interior views of the presidential precincts and features footage with both the president and Hillary Clinton. On-premises exhibits include:

Architectural History of the White House (including the grounds and extensive renovations to its structure and interior that have taken place since its cornerstone was laid in 1792).

Symbol and Image, showing how the White House has been portrayed by photographers, artists, journalists, political cartoonists, and others.

First Families, with displays about the people who have lived here (such as prankster Tad Lincoln who once stood in a window above his father and waved a Confederate flag at a military review).

The Working White House, focusing on the vast staff of servants, chefs, gardeners, Secret Service people, and others who maintain this institution.

Ceremony and Celebration, depicting notable White House events from a Wright Brothers' aviation demonstration in 1911 to a ballet performance by Baryshnikov during the Carter administration.

White House Interiors, Past and Present, including photographs of the ever-changing Oval Office as decorated by administrations from Taft through Clinton.

The center is open daily from 7:30am to 4pm. It is closed Thanksgiving, Christmas, and New Year's Day.

down upon a number of early–19th-century furnishings attributed to the famous cabinetmaker Duncan Phyfe.

The oval **Blue Room,** where presidents and first ladies have officially received guests since the Jefferson administration, is today decorated in the French Empire style chosen by James Monroe in 1817. It was, however, Van Buren's decor that began the "blue room" tradition. The walls, on which hang portraits of five presidents (including Rembrandt Peale's portrait of Thomas Jefferson and G. P. A. Healy's of Tyler), are covered in reproductions of early–19th-century French and American wallpaper. Grover Cleveland, the only president ever to wed in the White House, was married in the Blue Room; the Reagans, Nancy wearing symbolic yellow, here greeted the 53 Americans liberated after being held hostage in Iran for 444 days; and every year it's the setting for the White House Christmas tree.

Several portraits of past presidents—plus Albert Bierstadt's *View of the Rocky Mountains* and a Gilbert Stuart portrait of Dolley Madison—hang in the **Red Room.** It's used as a reception room, usually for afternoon teas. The satin-covered walls and most of the Empire furnishings are red.

Modeled after late–18th-century neoclassical English houses, the **State Dining Room** is a superb setting for state dinners and luncheons. Theodore Roosevelt, a big-game hunter, had a large moose head over the fireplace and other trophies on the walls. Below G. P. A. Healy's portrait of Lincoln is an inscription written by John

Adams on his second night in the White House (FDR had it carved into the mantel): "I Pray Heaven to Bestow The Best of Blessings on THIS HOUSE and on All that shall here-after Inhabit it. May none but Honest and Wise Men ever rule under This Roof."

A Brief History of the White House: Since its cornerstone was laid in 1792, the White House has gone through numerous changes. It was designed by Irishman James Hoban, so it isn't surprising that it resembles the house of the duke of Leinster in Dublin. The South Portico was added in 1824, the North Portico in 1829. Electricity was first installed during Benjamin Harrison's presidency in 1891.

In 1902, repairs and refurnishings of the White House cost nearly $500,000. No other great change took place until Harry Truman added his controversial "balcony" inside the columns of the South Portico. Also in 1948, after the leg of Margaret Truman's piano cut through the dining room ceiling, nearly $6 million was allotted to reconstruct the building. The Trumans lived at Blair House across the street for close to 4 years while the White House interior was shored up with steel girders and concrete. It's as solid as Gibraltar now.

In 1961, Jacqueline Kennedy formed a Fine Arts Committee to help restore the famous rooms to their original grandeur.

The White House is open mornings only, Tuesday through Saturday. Tickets are required year-round. If you don't have VIP tour tickets, you can pick up your free tickets at the **White House Visitor Center** (see box above for details). Tickets are timed for tours between 10am and noon, and are issued on the day of the tour on a first-come, first-served basis starting at 7am. One person may obtain up to four tickets. The number of tickets for each day is limited (approximately 4,500 are distributed), and the ticket counter closes when the supply for that day is gone. Hence, it is essential that you arrive early (even before 7am, to ensure admission). Tickets are valid only for the day and time issued. After obtaining your tickets, you'll probably have quite a bit of time to spare before your tour time; consider enjoying a leisurely breakfast at Reeve's or the Old Ebbitt Grill, both close by (see chapter 6 for details).

Note: All visitors, even those with VIP congressional tour passes, should call ☎ 202/456-7041 before setting out in the morning; occasionally the White House is closed to tourists on short notice because of unforeseen events.

✪ The Capitol
At the east end of the Mall, entrance on E. Capitol St. and 1st St. NW. ☎ **202/225-6827.** Free admission. Mar–Sept daily 9:30am–8pm; guided tours Mon–Fri 9:30am–8pm and Sat 9:30am–3:45pm, with guides posted to assist but not guide you on Sun from 1–4:30pm. Sept–Feb daily 9am–4:30pm; guided tours Mon–Sat 9am–3:45pm. Closed Jan 1, Thanksgiving Day, and Dec 25. Parking at Union Station. Metro: Union Station or Capitol South.

As America's most tangible national symbol since its first wing was completed in 1800, and the place where the country's laws are debated and passed, the Capitol is perhaps the most important edifice in the United States. For 135 years it sheltered not only both houses of Congress but the Supreme Court, and for 97 years the

---

Impressions

It has a damp, wheezy, Dickensian sort of winter hardly equalled by London, and a steaming tropical summer not surpassed by the basin of the Nile.

—Alistair Cooke

Take an umbrella, an overcoat, and a fan, and go forth.

—Mark Twain

Impressions

It is our national center. It belongs to us, and whether it is mean or majestic, whether arrayed in glory or covered with shame, we cannot but share its character and its destiny.

—Frederick Douglass

I went to Washington as everybody goes there prepared to see everything done with some furtive intention, but I was disappointed—pleasantly disappointed.

—Walt Whitman

Library of Congress as well. As you tour the Capitol, you'll learn about America's history as you admire the place in which it unfolded. Classic architecture, interior embellishments, and hundreds of paintings, sculptures, and other artworks are all integral elements of the Capitol.

On the massive bronze doors leading to the **Rotunda** are portrayals of events in the life of Columbus. The Rotunda—a huge, 96-foot-wide, circular hall that is capped by a 180-foot-high dome—is the hub of the Capitol. Nine presidents have lain in state here; when Kennedy's casket was displayed, the line of mourners stretched 40 blocks. On the circular walls are eight immense oil paintings of events in American history, such as the presentation of the Declaration of Independence and the surrender of Cornwallis at Yorktown. In the dome is an allegorical fresco masterpiece by Constantino Brumidi, *Apotheosis of Washington,* a symbolic portrayal of George Washington surrounded by Roman gods and goddesses watching over the progress of the nation. Brumidi was known as the "Michelangelo of the Capitol," for the many works he created throughout the building. Take another look at the dome and find the woman poised directly below Washington; the triumphant *Armed Freedom* figure is said to be modeled after Lola Germon, a young and beautiful actress with whom the 60-year-old Brumidi had a child. Beneath the dome is a trompe l'oeil frieze that depicts events in American history from Columbus through the Wright brothers' flight at Kitty Hawk.

Newly added to the Rotunda is the sculpture of suffragists Elizabeth Cady Stanton, Susan B. Anthony, and Lucretia Mott. Until recently, the ponderous monument had been relegated to the Crypt, one level directly below the Rotunda. Women's groups organized to place the statue in its more prominent position in the Rotunda. Meanwhile, a black women's political congress is mounting a campaign to add a statue of black abolitionist and 19th-century feminist Sojourner Truth to the Rotunda—by the time you read this, she may be there.

National Statuary Hall was originally the chamber of the House of Representatives. In 1864 it became Statuary Hall, and the states were invited to send two statues each of native sons and daughters to the hall. As the room filled up, statues spilled over into the Hall of Columns, corridors, and anywhere that might accommodate the bronze and marble artifacts. Many of the statues honor individuals who played important roles in American history, such as Henry Clay, Ethan Allen, and Daniel Webster.

The south and north wings are occupied by the House and Senate chambers, respectively. The House of Representatives chamber is the largest legislative chamber in the world. The president delivers his annual State of the Union address there.

✪ Supreme Court

East of the Capitol on 1st St. NE (between E. Capitol St. and Maryland Ave.). ☎ **202/479-3000.** Free admission. Mon–Fri 9am–4:30pm. Closed weekends and all federal holidays. Metro: Capitol South or Union Station.

Capitol Touring Tips

If you have fewer than 15 people in your party, you may tour the Capitol on your own, and I recommend this. (See "An Art-Full Tour of the Capitol," below.) You enter on the ground floor, where you can pick up a brochure that will help you as you go. In spring and summer, especially in the morning, you will have a long wait for a guided tour. Guided tours are free, last 20-to-30 minutes, and leave from the Rotunda at least every 15 minutes, more frequently in peak season. If a guided tour is what you want, try to arrange in advance for **VIP tour tickets** from a representative or senator for the morning tours (departing at intervals between 8 and 8:45am); see chapter 2 for details. Also request **visitor passes** for each member of your party to view a session of the House and/or Senate. If you don't get advance tickets, and if you don't receive visitor passes in the mail (not every senator or representative sends them), they're obtainable at your senator's office on the Constitution Avenue side of the building or your representative's office on the Independence Avenue side (noncitizens can present a passport at the first-floor appointment desk on the Senate side or at the third-floor House gallery and ask for a pass). You'll know when the House or Senate is in session when you see flags flying over their respective wings of the Capitol. Or you can check the weekday "Today in Congress" column in the *Washington Post* for details on times of House and Senate committee meetings. This column also tells you which sessions are open to the public, allowing you to pick one that interests you.

The highest tribunal in the nation, the Supreme Court is charged with deciding whether actions of Congress, the president, the states, and lower courts are in accord with the Constitution, and with applying the Constitution's enduring principles to novel situations and a changing country. It has the power of "judicial review"— authority to invalidate legislation or executive action that conflicts with the Constitution. Out of the 6,500 cases submitted to it each year, the Supreme Court hears only about 100 cases, many of which deal with issues vital to the nation. The Court's rulings are final, reversible only by another Supreme Court decision, or in some cases, an Act of Congress or a Constitutional amendment.

Until 1935 the Supreme Court met in the Capitol. Architect Cass Gilbert designed the stately Corinthian marble palace that houses the Court today. The building was considered rather grandiose by early residents: One justice remarked that he and his colleagues ought to enter such pompous precincts on elephants.

If you're in town when the Court is in session, try to see a case being argued (call ☎ **202/479-3211** for details). The Court meets Monday through Wednesday from 10am to noon and, on occasion, from 1 to 2pm, starting the first Monday in October through late April, alternating, in approximately 2-week intervals, between "sittings," to hear cases and deliver opinions, and "recesses," for consideration of business before the Court. Mid-May to late June, you can attend brief sessions (about 15 minutes) at 10am on Monday, when the justices release orders and opinions. You can find out what cases are on the docket by checking the *Washington Post*'s "Supreme Court Calendar." Arrive at least an hour early—even earlier for highly publicized cases—to line up for seats, about 150 of which are allotted to the general public.

At 10am the entrance of the justices is announced by the marshal, and all present rise and remain standing while the justices are seated following the chant: "The Honorable, the Chief Justice and Associate Justices of the Supreme Court of the United States. *Oyez! Oyez! Oyez!* [French for "Hear ye!"] All persons having business before the Honorable, the Supreme Court of the United States, are admonished to draw near and give their attention, for the Court is now sitting. God save the United States and

Capitol Hill

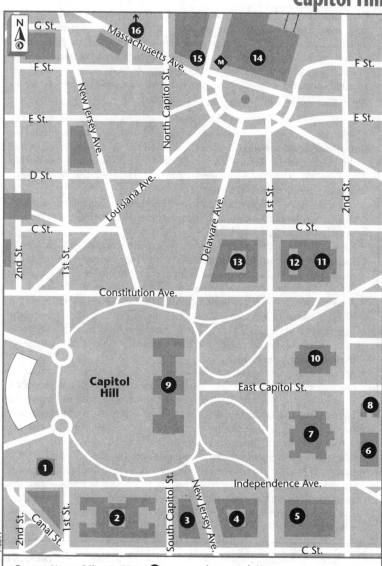

An Art-Full Tour of the Capitol

One glance at the Capitol's grand architecture is enough to tell you that the building is about more than history and politics. The place is also about art. Within a superb design, the Capitol contains more than 800 artworks, from gilded 19th-century frames and the grand paintings they encase, to frescoes, ornamental bronze stair railings, and stained glass windows. Take a guided tour of the Capitol, if you like, and sit in on a session of Congress, but try to save some time to explore on your own. Here are some special things to look for:

- There's a lot to admire in the Rotunda, but don't miss the life-size marble statue of Lincoln, sculpted by Vinnie Ream—a woman!—which was quite unusual for the times; Ream was only 19 when she received the commission and 23 when she completed it. Ream sketched Lincoln in half-hour sessions during what proved to be the final 5 months of his life. This is a solemn rendering of a pensive president in deep thought.
- If you like Ream's work, seek out two other statues she sculpted, one of politician Samuel Jordan Kirkwood of Iowa, the other of Cherokee leader Sequoya of Oklahoma, in Statuary Hall.
- For more of Brumidi's art, find the first floor of the Senate wing. Covering the vaulted ceilings and the crescent-shaped spaces over doorways are Brumidi's decorative paintings of 40 different kinds of birds, plus flowers, fruits, and animals, and portraits of famous Americans and Revolutionary War leaders.
- An immense 20-by-30-foot painting in the east staircase of the Senate wing is William Powell's 1873 *Battle of Lake Erie,* depicting the moment during the War of 1812 when Oliver Hazard Perry (known for his victorious pronouncement "We have met the enemy and they are ours.") transfers the colors of his flagship to one in better shape.
- Another huge painting is the 20-by-30-foot fresco by Emanuel Leutze, better known for his *Washington Crossing the Delaware,* than for this *Westward the Course of Empire Takes Its Way,* covering the wall over the west stairway of the House wing. The 1862 painting is a tumultuous display of covered wagons and hopeful immigrants making their way over Rocky Mountains to the west. It's as colorful as the artist, who was known to drink with his subjects as he worked.
- Albert Bierstadt's works hang in illustrious places, like the White House, the Corcoran Gallery of Art . . . and here, on a private stairway landing in the House wing. It's hard to find it, and when you do, you'll need to peer up from the steps, but it's worth it. Bierstadt was one of the country's best 19th-century landscape painters: *Entrance Into Monterey, 1770* is the name of this superb painting.

this Honorable Court!" There are many rituals here. Unseen by the gallery is the "conference handshake"; following a 19th-century tradition symbolizing a "harmony of aims if not views," each justice shakes hands with each of the other eight when they assemble to go to the bench. The Court has a record before it of prior proceedings and relevant briefs, so each side is allowed only a 30-minute argument.

The Supreme Court is cloaked in mystery, purposefully. You can't take cameras or recording devices into the courtroom. The justices never give speeches or press conferences. The media reports that Justice Thomas is famously silent, Justice Scalia argumentative, and Ginsburg talkative; all of the justices tend to be intimidating. See for yourself.

If the Court is not in session during your visit, you can attend a free **lecture** in the courtroom about Court procedure and the building's architecture. Lectures are given every hour on the half hour from 9:30am to 3:30pm.

After the talk, explore the Great Hall and go down a flight of steps to see the 20-minute film on the workings of the Court. The ground floor is a good vantage point to view one of two grand spiral staircases here similar to those at the Vatican and the Paris Opéra. There are also interesting exhibits and a gift shop on this level, and good meals are served in the adjoining cafeteria.

2 The Presidential Memorials

Few American presidents have been singled out for recognition with great monuments in Washington, D.C. Until recently, there were only three; the last, to Thomas Jefferson, was dedicated in 1943 during cherry-blossom time. Three years later, the idea for a memorial to Franklin Delano Roosevelt was conceived. Though the site was selected in 1959, ground wasn't broken until 1991. Finally, on May 2, 1997, our fourth presidential memorial was dedicated.

For the time being, that's it for presidential memorials. Plans for other memorials on or near the Mall are in the works, though. In the coming years, you should see monuments to World War II soldiers, Thomas Paine, George Mason, and Black Revolutionary War Patriots.

✪ Washington Monument

Directly south of the White House (at 15th St. and Constitution Ave. NW). ☎ **202/426-6841.** Free admission. Early Apr–Sept, daily 8am–midnight; the rest of the year, daily 9am–5pm. Last elevators depart 15 minutes before closing (arrive earlier). Closed Dec 25, open till noon July 4. Metro: Smithsonian; then a 10-minute walk.

The 555-foot stark marble obelisk that shimmers in the sun and glows under floodlights at night is the city's most visible landmark. It is, like the Eiffel Tower in Paris or London's Big Ben, a symbol of the city.

The idea of a tribute to George Washington first arose 16 years before his death at the Continental Congress of 1783. An equestrian statue was planned, and Washington himself approved the site for it, on the Mall, west of the future Capitol and south of the "President's Palace." However, more than a century elapsed before a very different monument was completed. The new nation had more pressing problems, and funds were not readily available. It wasn't until the early 1830s, with the 100th anniversary of Washington's birth approaching, that any action was taken. Then there were several fiascoes. A mausoleum was provided for Washington's remains under the Capitol Rotunda, but a grand-nephew, citing Washington's will, refused to

Washington Monument Touring Tips

Tickets are required for admission to the Washington Monument in winter, from 9am to 3pm, and the rest of the year, from 8am to 8pm. If you come before or after these set times, you simply go to the Washington Monument and stand in line—always check first with a ranger or at the ticket booth to be sure, though. The ticket booth is located at the bottom of the hill from the monument, on 15th Street NW between Independence and Constitution avenues. The tickets grant admission at half-hour intervals between the stated hours. You can obtain these tickets on the day of the tour; if you want to save yourself the trouble and get them in advance (up to six tickets per person), call Ticketmaster (☎ **800/505-5040**), but you'll pay $1.50 per ticket plus a 50¢ service charge per transaction.

allow the body to be moved from Mount Vernon. In 1830 Horatio Greenough was commissioned to create a memorial statue for the Rotunda. He came up with a bare-chested Washington, draped in classical Greek garb; a shocked public claimed he looked as if he were "entering or leaving a bath," and so the statue was relegated to the Smithsonian. Finally, in 1833 prominent citizens organized the Washington National Monument Society. Treasury Building architect Robert Mills's design (originally with a circular colonnaded Greek temple base, but later discarded for lack of funds) was accepted. The cornerstone was laid on July 4, 1848; for the next 37 years, watching the monument grow, or not grow, was a local pastime. Declining contributions and the Civil War brought construction to a halt at an awkward 150 feet. The unsightly stump remained until 1876 when President Grant approved federal monies to complete the project. Rejecting plans for ornate embellishment that ranged from English Gothic to Hindu pagoda designs, authorities put the U.S. Army Corps of Engineers to work on the obelisk. Dedicated in 1885, it was opened to the public in 1888.

The 360° views are spectacular. To the east are the Capitol and Smithsonian buildings; to the north, the White House; to the west, the Lincoln and Vietnam Memorials, and Arlington National Cemetery beyond; and to the south, the gleaming-white shrine to Thomas Jefferson, and the Potomac River. It's a marvelous orientation to the city.

Rangers give 30-minute talks year-round, as time allows throughout the day. Climbing the 897 steps is verboten, but a large elevator whisks visitors to the top in just 70 seconds. If, however, you're avid to see more of the interior, **"Down the Steps" tours** are given, subject to staff availability, weekends at 10am and 2pm. For details, call before you go or ask a ranger on duty. On this tour you'll learn more about the building of the monument and get to see the 192 carved stones inserted into the interior walls. The stones are from all 50 states and from countries and organizations.

Light snacks are sold at a snack bar on the grounds, where you'll also find a few picnic tables. There's limited, free 2-hour parking at the 16th Street Oval.

✪ Lincoln Memorial

Directly west of the Mall in Potomac Park (at 23rd St. NW, between Constitution and Independence aves.). ☎ **202/426-6842.** Free admission. Daily 8am–midnight, except Dec 25. Metro: Foggy Bottom; then about a 20-minute walk.

The Lincoln Memorial attracts some 6 million visitors annually. It's a beautiful and moving testament to a great American, its marble walls seeming to embody not only the spirit and integrity of Lincoln, but all that has ever been good about America. Visitors are silently awed in its presence.

The monument was a long time in the making. Although it was planned as early as 1867, 2 years after Lincoln's death, it was not until 1912 that Henry Bacon's design was completed, and the memorial itself was dedicated in 1922.

A beautiful neoclassical templelike structure, similar in architectural design to the Parthenon in Greece, the memorial has 36 fluted Doric columns representing the states of the Union at the time of Lincoln's death, plus two at the entrance.

Impressions

May the spirit which animated the great founder of this city descend to future generations.

—John Adams

On the attic parapet are 48 festoons symbolic of the number of states in 1922 when the monument was erected. Hawaii and Alaska are noted in an inscription on the terrace. To the west, the Arlington Memorial Bridge crossing the Potomac recalls the reunion of North and South. To the east is the beautiful Reflecting Pool, lined with American elms and stretching 2,000 feet toward the Washington Monument and the Capitol beyond.

The memorial chamber, under 60-foot ceilings, has limestone walls inscribed with the Gettysburg Address and Lincoln's Second Inaugural Address. Two 60-foot murals by Jules Guerin on the north and south walls depict, allegorically, Lincoln's principles and achievements. On the south wall, an Angel of Truth freeing a slave is flanked by groups of figures representing Justice and Immortality. The north-wall mural depicts the unity of North and South and is flanked by groups of figures symbolizing Fraternity and Charity. Most powerful, however, is Daniel Chester French's 19-foot-high seated statue of Lincoln in deep contemplation in the central chamber. Its effect is best evoked by these words of Walt Whitman: "He was a mountain in grandeur of soul, he was a sea in deep undervoice of mystic loneliness, he was star in steadfast purity of purpose and service and he abides." It is appropriate to the heritage of Lincoln that on several occasions those who have been oppressed have expressed their plight to America and the world at the steps of his shrine. Most notable was a peaceful demonstration of 200,000 people on August 28, 1963, at which another freedom-loving American, Dr. Martin Luther King, Jr., proclaimed "I have a dream."

An information booth and bookstore are on the premises. Rangers present 20- to 30-minute programs as time permits throughout the day, year-round. Limited free parking is available along Constitution Avenue and south along Ohio Drive.

✪ Jefferson Memorial

South of the Washington Monument on Ohio Dr. (at the south shore of the Tidal Basin). ☎ **202/426-6841.** Free admission. Daily 8am–midnight, except Dec 25. Transportation: Tourmobile.

Pres. John F. Kennedy, at a 1962 dinner honoring 29 Nobel Prize winners, told his guests they were "the most extraordinary collection of talent, of human knowledge, that has ever been gathered together at the White House, with the possible exception of when Thomas Jefferson dined alone." A fascinating and enigmatic man, Jefferson penned the Declaration of Independence, and served in America's government as George Washington's secretary of state, John Adams's vice president, and our third president. He spoke out against slavery but kept slaves himself, and fathered several children by one of them. In addition, he established the University of Virginia and pursued wide-ranging interests including architecture, astronomy, anthropology, music, and farming.

The site for the Jefferson Memorial, in relation to the Washington and Lincoln Memorials, was of extraordinary importance. The Capitol, the White House, and the Mall were already located in accordance with L'Enfant's plan, and there was no spot for such a project if the symmetry that guided L'Enfant was to be maintained. So the memorial was built on land reclaimed from the Potomac River, now known as the Tidal Basin. Franklin Delano Roosevelt had all the trees between the Jefferson Memorial and the White House cut down, so that he could see it every morning and draw inspiration from it.

It's a beautiful memorial, a columned rotunda in the style of the Pantheon in Rome, which Jefferson so admired. On the Tidal Basin side, the sculptural group above the entrance depicts Jefferson with Benjamin Franklin, John Adams, Roger Sherman, and Robert Livingston, who worked on drafting the Declaration of

Independence. The domed interior of the memorial contains the 19-foot bronze statue of Jefferson standing on a 6-foot pedestal of black Minnesota granite. The sculpture is the work of Rudolph Evans, who was chosen from more than 100 artists in a nationwide competition. Jefferson is depicted wearing a fur-collared coat given to him by his close friend, the Polish general, Tadeusz Kosciuszko. Inscriptions from Jefferson's writing engraved on the interior walls expand on Jefferson's philosophy, which is best expressed in the circular frieze quotation: "I have sworn upon the altar of God eternal hostility against every form of tyranny over the mind of man."

Rangers present 20- to 30-minute programs throughout the day as time permits, year-round. Spring through fall, a refreshment kiosk at the Tourmobile stop offers snack fare. A bookshop is on the premises. There's free 1-hour parking.

✪ Franklin Delano Roosevelt Memorial

In West Potomac Park about midway between the Lincoln and Jefferson Memorials, on the west shore of the Tidal Basin. ☎ **202/426-6841.** Free admission. Ranger staff on duty 8am–midnight daily, except Dec 25. Transportation: Tourmobile, Washington Water Bus (see "Organized Tours," near the end of this chapter).

Conceived in 1946, the FDR Memorial has been in the works for 50 years. Part of the delay in its construction can be attributed to the president himself. FDR had told his friend, Supreme Court Justice Felix Frankfurter, "If they are to put up any memorial to me, I should like it to be placed in the center of that green plot in front of the Archives building. I should like it to consist of a block about the size of this," he said, as he pointed to his desk. In fact, there is such a plaque in front of the National Archives building. Friends and relatives have struggled to honor Roosevelt's request to leave it at that, but finally, Congress and national sentiment have overridden them.

On May 2, 1997, President Clinton officiated at the dedication ceremony of the 7½-acre site. The memorial lies directly across the Tidal Basin from the Washington Monument, on a sight line between the Jefferson and Lincoln memorials, in a spot that the McMillan Commission had reserved in 1901 for a presidential memorial, not knowing whose it would be. Designed by architect Lawrence Halprin, the memorial features a park of granite walls, waterfalls, and bronze sculptures that depict Roosevelt's presidency from 1933 to 1945.

Visitors enter a sequence of four "outdoor rooms," each devoted to one of Roosevelt's four terms in office during the Depression and World War II. Ten bronze sculptures (by Leonard Baskin, John Benson, Neil Estern, Robert Graham, Thomas Hardy, and George Segal) honor Franklin and Eleanor Roosevelt, and memorialize the institution of the presidency, the struggles of the Great Depression, and America's rise to world leadership.

Roosevelt's inspirational words are carved into red Dakota granite amid waterfalls and quiet pools. Designers of the memorial had many to choose from—among FDR's notable quotations are these: from the Depression ("The only thing we have to fear is fear itself") through World War II ("I have seen war. I have seen war on land and sea. I have seen blood running from the wounded . . . I have seen the dead in the mud. I have seen cities destroyed . . . I have seen children starving. I have seen the agony of mothers and wives. I hate war.").

As with other presidential memorials, this one opened to some controversy. Advocates for people with disabilities were incensed that the memorial sculptures did not show the president in a wheelchair, which he used from the age of 39 after contracting polio. President Clinton asked Congress to allocate funding for an

❓ Did You Know?

- Architect Pierre L'Enfant's bill for designing Washington came to $95,000; years later he settled for Congress's offer of $2,500.
- In 1835, Andrew Jackson paid off the national debt; it was the first and last time in U.S. history that the federal books have been balanced.
- When the *Washington Post* sponsored a public music competition, John Philip Sousa was asked to compose a march for the awards ceremony; the result was *The Washington Post March,* for which Sousa earned the grand sum of $35.
- The only presidential inauguration ceremony to be held in the White House was that of Franklin D. Roosevelt, in 1941.
- Ambassadors to Washington in the early days were given "hardship pay" for having to endure the inconveniences of living there.
- A famous beverage was concocted for a Missouri lobbyist, Col. J. K. Rickey; originally rye whiskey was used, but later some "barbarous New Yorkers" substituted gin—hence, "Gin Rickey."

additional statue portraying a wheelchair-bound FDR; at this writing, that statue was not in place. The monument does display a replica of Roosevelt's wheelchair, as well as one of the rare photographs taken of the president sitting in a wheelchair.

The other source of dissatisfaction comes from the lack of good public access to the site. The closest Metro stations are at least a mile away, the closest bus route is across the Mall, and parking is minimal. Your choice is to walk to it from one of the other memorials, to take the Tourmobile, or to use the Washington Water Bus, which drops you close to the FDR Memorial. (See "Organized Tours," below.)

3 The Smithsonian Museums

The Smithsonian's collection of more than 140 million objects encompasses the entire world and its history, as well as its peoples and animals (past and present) and our attempts to probe into the future. The sprawling institution comprises 14 museums (nine of them on the Mall) as well as the National Zoological Park in Washington, D.C., plus two additional museums in New York City.

It all began with a $500,000 bequest from James Smithson, an English scientist who had never visited this country. When he died in 1829, he willed his entire fortune to his nephew, stipulating that should the nephew die without heirs (which he did in 1835), the estate should go to the United States to found "at Washington . . . an establishment for the increase and diffusion of knowledge. . . ." In 1846 Congress created a corporate entity to carry out Smithson's will, and the federal government agreed to pay 6% interest on the bequeathed funds in perpetuity. Since then, other munificent private donations have swelled Smithson's original legacy many times over. Major gallery and museum construction through the years stands as testament to thoughtful donors.

In 1987, the **Sackler Gallery** (Asian and Near Eastern art) and the **National Museum of African Art** were added to the Smithsonian's Mall attractions. The **National Postal Museum** opened in 1993. And future plans call for moving the **National Museum of the American Indian** (currently in New York) here in 2001.

Smithsonian Information Center

1000 Jefferson Dr. SW. ☎ **202/357-2700,** or TTY 202/357-1729. Daily 9am–5:30pm; info desk 9am–4pm. Closed Dec 25. Metro: Smithsonian.

Make your first stop the impressively high-tech and very comprehensive Smithsonian Information Center, located in the institution's original Norman-style red sandstone building, popularly known as the "Castle."

The main information area here is the Great Hall, where a 20-minute video overview of the institution runs throughout the day in two theaters. There are two large schematic models of the Mall (as well as a third in Braille), and two large electronic maps of Washington allow visitors to locate 69 popular attractions and Metro and Tourmobile stops. Interactive videos, some at children's heights, offer extensive information about the Smithsonian and other capital attractions and transportation (the menus seem infinite).

The entire facility is accessible to persons with disabilities, and information is available in a number of foreign languages. Daily Smithsonian events appear on monitors; in addition, the information desk's volunteer staff (some of whom speak foreign languages) can answer questions and help you plan a Smithsonian sightseeing itinerary. Most of the museums are within easy walking distance of the facility. While you're here, notice the charming vestibule, which has been restored to its turn-of-the-century appearance, with a gold-trimmed ceiling representing a grape arbor with brightly plumed birds and sky peeking through a trellis. Designed at the turn of the century for exhibits displayed at a child's eye level, it has a gold-trimmed ceiling decorated to represent a grape arbor with brightly plumed birds and blue sky peeking through the trellis. Furnishings are peacock themed, and large Chinese paintings adorn the walls. And be sure to stroll through the stunning Enid A. Haupt Garden behind the south entrance when you leave.

✪ National Museum of American History

On the north side of the Mall (between 12th and 14th sts. NW), with entrances on Constitution Ave. and Madison Dr. ☎ **202/357-2700.** Free admission. Daily 10am–5:30pm. Summer hours, sometimes extended, are determined annually. Closed Dec 25. Metro: Smithsonian or Federal Triangle.

The National Museum of American History deals with "everyday life in the American past" and the external forces that have helped to shape our national character. Its massive contents range from General George Washington's Revolutionary War tent to Archie Bunker's chair.

Exhibits on the **first floor** (enter on Constitution Avenue) explore the development of farm machinery, power machinery, transportation, timekeeping, phonographs, and typewriters. The Palm Court on this level includes the interior of Georgetown's Stohlman's Confectionery Shop as it appeared around 1900 and part of an actual 1902 Horn and Hardart Automat, where you can stop and have an ice cream. You can have your mail stamped "Smithsonian Station" at a post office that had been located in Headsville, West Virginia, from 1861 to 1971, when it was brought lock, stock, and barrel to the museum. An important first-floor exhibit, "A

Information, Please

If you want to know what's happening at any of the Smithsonian museums, just get on the phone; **Dial-a-Museum** (☎ **202/357-2020,** or 202/633-9126 for Spanish), a recorded information line, will bring you news of daily activities and special events. For other information call ☎ 202/357-2700.

Material World," deals with the changing composition of artifacts—from predominantly natural materials such as wood and stone to the vast range of synthetics we have today. "Information Age" considers the ways information technology has changed society during the past 150 years. And "Science in American Life" analyzes the impact of science on society from the 1870s to the present.

If you enter from the Mall, you'll find yourself on the **second floor** facing the original Star-Spangled Banner, 30 by 42 feet, that inspired Francis Scott Key to write the U.S. national anthem in 1814. "After the Revolution," a major exhibition, focuses on the everyday activities of ordinary 18th-century Americans, and "Field to Factory" tells the story of African-American migration, south to north, 1915–40.

Also on this level is the Foucault Pendulum, a copy of the original model that was exhibited in Paris in 1851 with the accompanying teaser, "You are invited to witness the earth revolve." (The pendulum vibrates in a single plane, tracing in sand what seems to be a scattered series of lines, but what is actually the proof of the Earth's rotation.) Don't miss it! One of the most popular exhibits on the second floor is "First Ladies: Political Role and Public Image," which displays the first ladies' gowns as it tells you a bit about each of these women. Infinitely more interesting, I think, is the neighboring exhibit, "From Parlor to Politics: Women and Reform in America, 1890–1925," which chronicles the changing roles of women as they've moved from domestic to political and professional pursuits.

A vast collection of ship models, uniforms, weapons, and other military artifacts is located on the **third floor,** where major exhibits focus on the experiences of GIs in World War II (and the postwar world) as well as the wartime internment of Japanese Americans. Other areas include Money and Medals, Textiles, Printing and Graphic Arts, and Ceramics. Here, too, is the first American flag to be called Old Glory (1824).

Inquire at the information desk about highlight tours, films, lectures, and concerts, and hands-on activities for children and adults. The gift shop is vast—it's the largest of the Smithsonian shops.

○ National Museum of Natural History

On the north side of the Mall, at 10th St. and Constitution Ave. NW, with entrances on Madison Dr. and Constitution Ave. ☎ **202/357-2700.** Free admission. Daily 10am–5:30pm, with extended hours in summer. Closed Dec 25. Metro: Smithsonian or Federal Triangle.

Children refer to this Smithsonian showcase as the dinosaur museum (there's a great dinosaur hall), or sometimes the elephant museum (a huge African bush elephant is the first amazing thing you see if you enter the museum from the Mall). Whatever you call it, the National Museum of Natural History is the largest of its kind in the world, and one of the most visited of all of Washington's museums. It contains more than 120 million artifacts and specimens, everything from Ice Age mammoths to the legendary Hope Diamond.

Free highlight **tours** are given every Monday through Thursday at 10:30am and 1:30pm, and on Friday at 10:30am. A **Discovery Room,** filled with creative hands-on exhibits "for children of all ages" is on the first floor. Call ahead or inquire at the information desk about hours.

On the **Mall Level,** off the Rotunda, is the fossil collection, which traces evolution back billions of years with exhibits of a 3.5-billion-year-old stromatolite (blue-green algae clump) fossil—one of the earliest signs of life on earth—and a 70-million-year-old dinosaur egg. "Life in the Ancient Seas" features a 100-foot-long mural depicting primitive whales, a life-size walk-around diorama of a 230-million-year-old coral reef, and more than 2,000 fossils that chronicle the evolution of marine life. The Dinosaur Hall displays giant skeletons of creatures that dominated the earth for 140 million years before their extinction about 65 million years ago. Suspended from the ceiling over Dinosaur Hall are replicas of ancient birds, including a life-size model of the pterosaur, which had a 40-foot wingspan. Also residing above this hall is an ancient shark—or at least the jaw of one, the *Carcharodon megalodon,* that lived in our oceans 5 million years ago. A monstrous 40-foot-long predator, its teeth were 5 to 6 inches long, and it could have consumed a Volkswagen "bug" in one gulp! Here, too, you'll find a spectacular living coral reef in a 3,000-gallon tank, a second 1,800-gallon tank housing a subarctic sea environment typical of the Maine coast, and a giant squid exhibit focusing on the world's largest invertebrates.

Upstairs is the popular O. Orkin Insect Zoo, where kids will enjoy looking at tarantulas, centipedes, and the like, and crawling through a model of an African termite mound. The Ocean Planet exhibit gives you a video tour of what lies beneath the ocean surface, and teaches you about ocean conservation. The Hope Diamond is also on display on the second floor, where a renovation of the Gems and Minerals Hall has ended after years of work. The new hall has a new name: the Janet Annenberg Hooker Hall of Geology, Gems, and Minerals, and includes all you want to know about earth science, from volcanology to the importance of mining in our daily lives. Interactive computers, animated graphics, and a multimedia presentation of the "big picture" story of the earth are some of the things that have brought the exhibit and museum up to date. Additional exhibits include "South America: Continent and Culture," with objects from the Inca civilization, among others, and "Origin of Western Culture," from about 10,000 years ago to A.D. 500.

The museum opened a new gift shop in 1997; its cafeteria is closed because of renovations.

✪ National Air & Space Museum

On the south side of the Mall (between 4th and 7th sts. SW), with entrances on Jefferson Dr. or Independence Ave. ☎ **202/357-2700,** or 202/357-1686 for IMAX ticket information. Free admission. Daily 10am–5:30pm with extended hours in summer. Closed Dec 25. Metro: L'Enfant Plaza (Smithsonian Museums/Maryland Ave. exit).

The National Air and Space Museum is the most visited museum in the world. The Museum chronicles the story of our mastery of flight, from Kitty Hawk to outer space, in 23 galleries filled with exciting exhibits. Plan to devote at least 3 or 4 hours exploring these exhibits and, especially during the tourist season and on holidays, arrive before 10am to make a rush for the film-ticket line when the doors open. The not-to be-missed **IMAX films** shown in the Samuel P. Langley Theater here, on a screen five stories high and seven stories wide, are immensely popular; tickets tend to sell out quickly (although the first show seldom sells out). Five or more films play each day, most with aeronautical or space-exploration themes: To Fly, Cosmic Voyage, and Magic of Flight are the names of three. Tickets cost $4.50 for adults, $3.25 for ages 2 to 21 and seniors 55 and older; they're free for children under 2. You can also see IMAX films most evenings after closing (call for details and ticket

Smithsonian Touring Tips

The Information Center opens 1 hour earlier than the museums. The Castle's 19th century dining room, known as The Commons, is the site each Sunday for brunch, 11am to 3pm, featuring everything from omelets to baked ham, for $18.95 per person (less for children and senior citizens). Call ☎ 202/357-2957 before 10am or after 3pm to make a reservation.

Did You Know?

Alexander Graham Bell was the regent charged with bringing Smithson's remains to the United States from Italy in 1904. The remains were reinterred in a chapel-like room of the Smithsonian Castle.

prices). At the same time, purchase tickets (same prices) for a show at the **Albert Einstein Planetarium.**

In between shows, you can view the exhibits; free 1¹/₂-hour highlight **tours** are given daily at 10:15am and 1pm. Audio tours are also available for rental. Interactive computers and slide and video shows enhance the exhibits throughout.

Highlights of the **first floor** include famous airplanes (such as the *Spirit of St. Louis*) and spacecraft (the *Apollo 11* Command Module); the world's only touchable moon rock; numerous exhibits on the history of aviation and air transportation; galleries in which you can design your own jet plane and study astronomy; and rockets, lunar-exploration vehicles, manned spacecraft, and guided missiles. An exhibit on the *Enola Gay,* the plane that dropped the atomic bomb on Hiroshima, includes parts of the vehicle and videotaped interviews with crew members. And "How Things Fly," a gallery that opened in 1996 to celebrate the museum's 20th anniversary, includes wind and smoke tunnels, a boardable Cessna 150 airplane, and dozens of interactive exhibits that demonstrate principles of flight, aerodynamics, and propulsion. All the aircraft, by the way, are originals.

Kids love the "walk-through" Skylab orbital workshop on the **second floor.** Other galleries here highlight the solar system, U.S. manned space flights, sea-air operations, aviation during both world wars, and artists' perceptions of flight. An important exhibit is "Beyond the Limits: Flight Enters the Computer Age," illustrating the primary applications of computer technology to aerospace.

A very attractive cafeteria and a rather elegant restaurant, **Flight Line** and the **Wright Place,** respectively, are on the premises.

National Museum of American Art

8th and G sts. NW. ☎ **202/357-2700.** Free admission. Daily 10am–5:30pm. Closed Dec 25. Metro: Gallery Place–Chinatown.

Don't wait to see the National Museum of American Art and the National Portrait Gallery: The two museums will close by the year 2000 for a 2-year overhaul. The National Museum of American Art owns more than 37,500 works representing 2 centuries of our national art history. About 1,000 of these works are on display at any given time, along with special exhibitions highlighting various aspects of American art. The museum is the largest of the Smithsonian's art museums and the country's oldest federal art collection—it was founded in 1829, predating the Smithsonian. The collection, along with the National Portrait Gallery (described below), is housed in the palatial quarters of the 19th-century Greek Revival Old Patent Office Building, partially designed by Washington Monument architect Robert Mills and Capitol dome architect Thomas U. Walter. Fronted by a columned portico evocative of the Parthenon, it was originally a multipurpose facility housing a jumble of items ranging from the original Declaration of Independence to a collection of shrunken heads.

Twentieth-century art occupies the most exalted setting, the third-floor Lincoln Gallery, with vaulted ceilings and marble columns. In this room, 4,000 revelers celebrated Lincoln's second inaugural in 1865. On view are works of post–World War II artists (de Kooning, Kline, Noguchi, and others). Other 20th-century works on this floor include paintings commissioned during the New Deal era.

Washington, D.C., Attractions

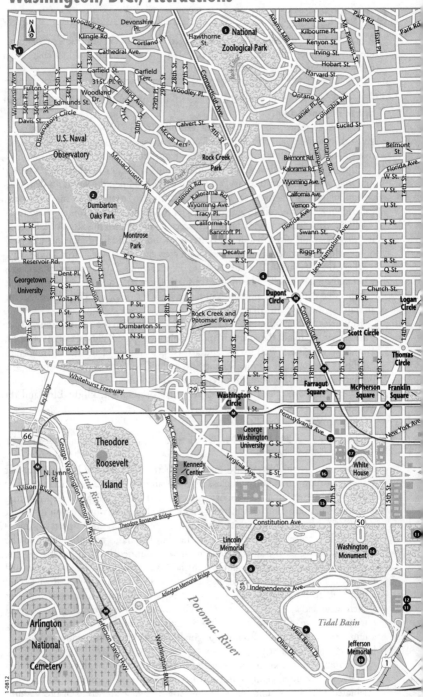

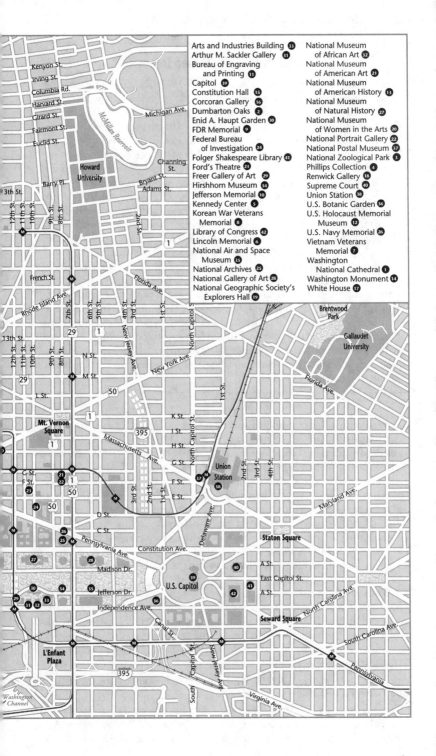

Arts and Industries Building ㉝
Arthur M. Sackler Gallery ㉛
Bureau of Engraving
  and Printing ⑪
Capitol ㊴
Constitution Hall ⑮
Corcoran Gallery ⑯
Dumbarton Oaks ②
Enid A. Haupt Garden ㉚
FDR Memorial ⑨
Federal Bureau
  of Investigation ㉔
Folger Shakespeare Library ㊶
Ford's Theatre ㉓
Freer Gallery of Art ㉙
Hirshhorn Museum ㉞
Jefferson Memorial ⑩
Kennedy Center ⑤
Korean War Veterans
  Memorial ⑧
Library of Congress ㊷
Lincoln Memorial ⑥
National Air and Space
  Museum ㉟
National Archives ㉕
National Gallery of Art ㉘
National Geographic Society's
  Explorers Hall ⑲

National Museum
  of African Art ㉜
National Museum
  of American Art ㉑
National Museum
  of American History ⑬
National Museum
  of Natural History ㉗
National Museum
  of Women in the Arts ⑳
National Portrait Gallery ㉒
National Postal Museum ⑰
National Zoological Park ③
Phillips Collection ④
Renwick Gallery ⑱
Supreme Court ㊵
Union Station ㊳
U.S. Botanic Garden ㊱
U.S. Holocaust Memorial
  Museum ⑫
U.S. Navy Memorial ㉖
Vietnam Veterans
  Memorial ⑦
Washington
  National Cathedral ①
Washington Monument ⑭
White House ⑰

A Liberal & Enlightened Donor

Wealthy English scientist James Smithson (1765–1829), the illegitimate son of the Duke of Northumberland, never explained why he willed his vast fortune to the United States, a country he had never visited. Speculation is that he felt a new nation, lacking established cultural institutions, stood in greatest need of his bequest. Smithson died in Genoa, Italy, in 1829. Congress accepted his gift in 1836; 2 years later, a shipment of 105 bags of gold sovereigns (about half a million dollars' worth— a considerable sum in the 19th century) arrived at the U.S. Mint in Philadelphia. For the next 8 years, Congress debated the best possible use for these funds. Finally, in 1846, James Polk signed an act into law establishing the Smithsonian Institution and providing "for the faithful execution of said trust, according to the will of the liberal and enlightened donor." It authorized a board to receive "all objects of art and of foreign and curious research, and all objects of natural history, plants, and geological and mineralogical specimens . . . for research and museum purposes."

In addition to the original Smithson bequest—which has been augmented by many subsequent endowments—the Smithsonian is also supported by annual congressional appropriations. Today it comprises a complex of 16 museums in Washington, D.C., and New York, plus the National Zoological Park. Its holdings, in every area of human interest, range from a 3.5-billion-year-old fossil to part of a 1902 Horn and Hardart Automat. Thousands of scientific expeditions sponsored by the Smithsonian have pushed into remote frontiers in the deserts, mountains, polar regions, and jungles. And its traveling exhibits are sent to other museums, schools, and libraries.

Mid–to late–19th-century artists such as Winslow Homer, Mary Cassatt, Albert Pinkham Ryder, and John Singer Sargent are on the second floor, as is a suite of galleries devoted to the Gilded Age. Here, too, are works by such early American masters as Charles Willson Peale, Benjamin West, and Samuel F. B. Morse.

A unique work of folk art on the first floor is James Hampton's visionary religious piece (completely covered in aluminum and gold foil), *Throne of the Third Heaven of the Nation's Millennium General Assembly.* Other first floor displays include the $1.4 million Herbert Waide Hemphill, Jr. Folk Art Collection (19th and 20th centuries) and an Art of the West Gallery featuring paintings by John Mix Stanley and Charles Bird King, along with George Catlin's Native American portraits from the collection he showed in Paris in the 1840s (the museum owns 445 of them).

When you enter, pick up a map and calendar of events and ask about current temporary exhibits at the information desk. Free walk-in tours are given at noon weekdays and at 2pm Saturday and Sunday. The Patent Pending cafe lies in a hall connecting the museum to the National Portrait Gallery; in good weather, you can dine in the lovely courtyard that's enclosed within the walls of the museums.

National Portrait Gallery

8th and F sts. NW. ☎ **202/357-2700.** Free admission. Daily 10am–5:30pm. Closed Dec 25. Metro: Gallery Place–Chinatown.

If the prospect of a gallery of "heroes and villains, thinkers and doers, conservatives and radicals" fascinates you, don't delay seeing the National Portrait Gallery: Along with the National Museum of American Art, this museum will close for a 2-year overhaul by the year 2000. The gallery enshrines those who have made "significant contributions to the history, development, and culture of the United States" in paintings, sculpture, photography, and other forms of portraiture. Although the museum didn't open until 1968, the concept of a national portrait gallery first arose in the mid–19th century when Congress commissioned G. P. A. Healy to paint a series of presidential portraits for the White House. And American portraiture dates back even further, as evidenced by those predating the Revolution (of Pocahontas, among others), and of those by Rembrandt Peale. In May 1998, Peale's portraits of George and Martha Washington return to the gallery after a 3-year stint at the Boston Museum of Fine Arts. It's great fun to wander these corridors, putting faces to famous names for the first time. And it's enlightening to discover portraits of accomplished Americans whose names you've never heard.

In addition to the Hall of Presidents (on the second floor), notable exhibits include Gilbert Stuart's famed "Lansdowne" portrait of George Washington, a portrait of Mary Cassatt by Degas, 19th-century silhouettes by French-born artist Auguste Edouart, Jo Davidson's sculpture portraits (including a Buddhalike Gertrude Stein), and photographs by Mathew Brady. On the mezzanine, the Civil War is documented in portraiture, including one of the last photographs ever taken of Abraham Lincoln. Take a look at the magnificent Great Hall on the third floor. Originally designed as a showcase for patent models, it later became a Civil War hospital, where Walt Whitman came frequently to "soothe and relieve wounded troops."

Pick up a calendar of events at the information desk to find out about the museum's comprehensive schedule of temporary exhibits, lunchtime lectures, concerts, films, and dramatic presentations. Walk-in tours are given at varying hours; inquire at the information desk.

Renwick Gallery of the National Museum of American Art

Pennsylvania Ave. and 17th St. NW. ☎ **202/357-2700.** Free admission. Daily 10am–5:30pm. Closed Dec 25. Metro: Farragut West or Farragut North.

A department of the National Museum of American Art (though nowhere near it), the Renwick, a showcase for American creativity in crafts, is housed in a historic mid-1800s landmark building of the French Second Empire style. The original home of the Corcoran Gallery, it was saved from demolition by First Lady Jacqueline Kennedy in 1963, when she recommended that it be renovated as part of the Lafayette Square restoration. In 1965 it became part of the Smithsonian and was renamed for its architect, James W. Renwick, who also designed the Smithsonian Castle. Although the setting—especially the magnificent Victorian Grand Salon with its wainscoted plum walls and 38-foot skylight ceiling—evokes another era, the museum's contents are mostly contemporary. The rich and diverse display of objects here includes both changing crafts exhibitions and contemporary works from the museum's permanent collection. Typical exhibits range from "Uncommon Beauty: The Legacy of African-American Craft Art" to "Calico and Chintz: Antique Quilts from the Patricia Smith Collection." The above-mentioned Grand Salon on the second floor, furnished in opulent 19th-century style, displays paintings by 18th- and 19th-century artists. (The great thing about this room, besides its fine art and grand design, is its cushiony, velvety banquettes, perfect resting places for the weary sightseer.)

The Renwick offers a comprehensive schedule of crafts demonstrations, lectures, and films. Inquire at the information desk. And check out the museum shop near the entrance for books on crafts, design, and decorative arts, as well as craft items, many of them for children.

Hirshhorn Museum & Sculpture Garden

On the south side of the Mall (at Independence Ave. and 7th St. SW). ☎ **202/357-2700.** Free admission. Daily 10am–5:30pm, Sculpture Garden 7:30am–dusk. Closed Dec 25. Metro: L'Enfant Plaza (Smithsonian Museums/Maryland Ave. exit).

This museum of modern and contemporary art is named after Latvian-born Joseph H. Hirshhorn, who, in 1966, donated his vast art collection—more than 4,000 drawings and paintings and some 2,000 pieces of sculpture—to the United States "as a small repayment for what this nation has done for me and others like me who arrived here as immigrants." At his death in 1981, Hirshhorn bequeathed an additional 5,500 artworks to the museum, and numerous other donors have since greatly expanded his legacy.

Constructed 14 feet above the ground on sculptured supports, the museum's contemporary cylindrical concrete-and-granite building shelters a verdant plaza courtyard where sculpture is displayed. The light and airy interior follows a simple circular route that makes it easy to see every exhibit without getting lost in a honeycomb of galleries. Natural light from floor-to-ceiling windows makes the inner galleries the perfect venue for viewing sculpture, second only, perhaps, to the magnificently beautiful tree-shaded sunken Sculpture Garden across the street (don't miss it). Paintings and drawings are installed in the outer galleries, along with intermittent sculpture groupings.

A rotating show of about 600 pieces is on view at all times. The collection features just about every well-known 20th-century artist and touches on most of the major trends in Western art since the late 19th century, with particular emphasis on our contemporary period. Among the best-known pieces are Rodin's *The Burghers of Calais* (in the Sculpture Garden), Hopper's *First Row Orchestra,* de Kooning's *Two Women in the Country,* and Warhol's *Marilyn Monroe's Lips.*

Pick up a free calendar when you come in to find out about free films, lectures, concerts, and temporary exhibits. An outdoor cafe is open during the summer. Free **tours** of the collection are given daily at noon, with an additional 2pm tour on weekends. Tours of the Sculpture Garden are given at 12:15pm Monday through Saturday during the months of May and October.

Arthur M. Sackler Gallery

1050 Independence Ave. SW. ☎ **202/357-2700.** Free admission. Daily 10am–5:30pm, with extended hours on summer Thursdays. Closed Dec 25. Metro: Smithsonian.

Opened in 1987, the Sackler, a national museum of Asian art, presents traveling exhibitions from major cultural institutions in Asia, Europe, and the United States. In the recent past, these have focused on such wide-ranging areas as 15th-century Persian art and culture, contemporary Japanese woodblock prints and ceramics, photographs of Asia, and art highlighting personal devotion in India. Art from the permanent collection supplements the traveling shows: It includes Khmer ceramics, ancient Chinese jades, bronzes, paintings, and lacquerware; 20th-century Japanese ceramics and works on paper; ancient Near Eastern works in silver, gold, bronze, and clay; and stone and bronze sculptures from South and Southeast Asia. Since the museum's opening, 11th- to 19th-century Persian and Indian paintings, manuscripts, calligraphies, miniatures, and bookbindings from the collection of Henri Vever have enhanced Sackler's original gift.

The Sackler is part of a museum complex that also houses the National Museum of African Art. And it shares its staff and research facilities with the adjacent Freer Gallery, to which it is connected via an underground exhibition space.

For information about museum programs (including many wonderful experiences for children and families), free highlight tours given daily (highly recommended), films, events, and temporary exhibits, inquire at the information desk or call ☎ **202/ 357-2700.**

National Museum of African Art

950 Independence Ave. SW. ☎ **202/357-2700.** Free admission. Daily 10am–5:30pm. Closed Dec 25. Metro: Smithsonian.

Founded in 1964, and part of the Smithsonian since 1979, the National Museum of African Art moved to the Mall in 1987 to share a subterranean space with the Sackler Gallery (see above) and the Ripley Center. Its above-ground domed pavilions reflect the arch motif of the neighboring Freer.

Although the museum collects and exhibits ancient and contemporary art from the entire African continent, its permanent collection of more than 7,000 objects (shown in rotating exhibits) highlights the traditional arts of the vast sub-Saharan region. Most of the collection dates from the 19th and 20th centuries. Also among the museum's holdings are the Eliot Elisofon Photographic Archives, comprising 300,000 photographic prints and transparencies and 120,000 feet of film on African arts and culture. Permanent exhibits include "The Ancient West African City of Benin, A.D. 1300–1897"; "The Ancient Nubian City of Kerma, 2500–1500 B.C." (ceramics, jewelry, and ivory animals); "The Art of the Personal Object" (everyday items such as chairs, headrests, snuff boxes, bowls, and baskets); and "Images of Power and Identity."

Inquire at the desk about special exhibits, workshops (including excellent children's programs), storytelling, lectures, docent-led tours, films, and demonstrations. A comprehensive events schedule here (together with exhibitions) provides a unique opportunity to learn about the diverse cultures and visual traditions of Africa.

✪ National Postal Museum

2 Massachusetts Ave. NE (at 1st St.). ☎ **202/357-2700.** Free admission. Daily 10am–5:30pm. Closed Dec 25. Metro: Union Station.

Opened in 1993, this most recent addition to the Smithsonian complex occupies the lower level of the palatial beaux-arts quarters of the City Post Office Building designed by architect Daniel Burnham. Created to house and display the Smithsonian's national philatelic and postal history collection of more than 16 million objects, it is, somewhat surprisingly, a great deal of fun to visit for everyone in the family.

Here's why: The museum is not overwhelming; it occupies a single floor. Many of its exhibits are interactive and easy to understand, ranging from nickelodeon films about train wrecks and robberies to postal-themed video games. And, despite our increasing use of e-mail, fax machines, and cellular phones for communicating, the act of writing and receiving letters still holds a special appeal for us—and that appeal is a lot of what this museum is about.

The museum documents America's postal history from 1673 (about 170 years before the advent of stamps, envelopes, and mailboxes) to the present. In the central gallery, titled "Moving the Mail," three planes that carried mail in the early decades of the 20th century are suspended from a 90-foot atrium ceiling. Here, too, are a railway mail car, an 1851 mail/passenger coach, a Ford Model A mail truck, and a replica of an airmail beacon tower. In "Binding the Nation," historic correspondence illustrates how mail kept families together in the developing nation. Several exhibits deal with the famed Pony Express, a service that lasted less than 2 years but was romanticized to legendary proportions by Buffalo Bill and others. In the Civil War section you'll learn about Henry "Box" Brown, a slave who had himself "mailed" from Richmond to a Pennsylvania abolitionist in 1856. "The Art of Cards and Letters" gallery displays personal correspondence from World War I through

Operation Desert Storm, as well as greeting cards and postcards. And an 800-square-foot gallery called "Artistic License: The Duck Stamp Story," focuses on federal duck stamps (first issued in 1934 to license waterfowl hunters), with displays on the hobby of duck hunting and the ecology of American water birds. In addition, the museum houses a vast research library for philatelic researchers and scholars, a stamp store, and a museum shop. Inquire about free walk-in tours at the information desk.

Freer Gallery of Art

On the south side of the Mall (at Jefferson Dr. and 12th St. SW). ☎ **202/357-2700.** Free admission. Daily 10am–5:30pm. Closed Dec 25. Metro: Smithsonian (Mall or Independence Ave. exit).

Charles Lang Freer, a collector of Asian art and American art from the 19th and early 20th centuries, gave the nation 9,000 of these works for the Freer Gallery's opening in 1923. Freer's original interest was, in fact, American art, but his good friend James McNeill Whistler encouraged him to collect Asian works as well. Eventually the latter became predominant. Freer's gift included funds to construct a museum and an endowment to add objects of the highest quality to the Asian collection only, which now numbers over 28,000 objects. It includes Chinese and Japanese sculpture, lacquer, metalwork, and ceramics; early Christian illuminated manuscripts; Iranian manuscripts, metalwork, and miniatures; ancient Near Eastern metalware; and South Asian sculpture and paintings.

Among the American works are more than 1,200 pieces (the world's largest collection) by Whistler, including the famous Peacock Room. Originally a dining room designed by an architect named Thomas Jeckyll for the London mansion of F. R. Leyland, the Peacock Room displayed a Whistler painting called *The Princess from the Land of Porcelain*. But after his painting was installed, Whistler was dissatisfied with the room as a setting for his work. When Leyland was away from home, Whistler painted over the very expensive leather interior, and embellished it with paintings of golden peacock feathers. Not surprisingly, a rift ensued between Whistler and Leyland. After Leyland's death, Freer purchased the room, painting and all, and had it shipped to his home in Detroit. It is now permanently installed here. Other American painters represented in the collections are Thomas Wilmer Dewing, Dwight William Tryon, Abbott Henderson Thayer, John Singer Sargent, and Childe Hassam.

Housed in a recently renovated granite-and-marble building that evokes the Italian Renaissance, the Freer has lovely skylit galleries. The main exhibit floor centers on a garden court open to the sky. An underground exhibit space connects the Freer to the neighboring Sackler Gallery, and both museums share The Meyer Auditorium, which is used for free chamber music concerts, dance performances, Asian feature films, and other programs. Inquire about these, as well as children's activities and free tours given daily, at the information desk, or call ☎ **202/357-2700.**

Arts & Industries Building

900 Jefferson Dr. SW (on the south side of the Mall). ☎ **202/357-2700.** Free admission. Daily 10am–5:30pm. Closed Dec 25. Metro: Smithsonian.

Completed in 1881 as the first U.S. National Museum, this redbrick and sandstone structure was the scene of President Garfield's Inaugural Ball. From 1976 through the mid-1990s, it housed exhibits from the 1876 United States International Exposition in Philadelphia—a celebration of America's 100th birthday that featured the latest advances in technology. Some of these are still on display, but, at this writing, the museum is in transition and offering changing exhibitions. You can find out what's happening here at the Smithsonian Information Center.

Singers, dancers, puppeteers, and mimes perform in the **Discovery Theater** (open all year except in August, with performances Monday through Friday and on selected Saturdays—call ☎ **202/357-1500** for show times and ticket information; admission of about $5 is charged). Don't miss the charming Victorian-motif shop on the first floor. Weather permitting, a 19th-century carousel operates across the street.

National Zoological Park

Adjacent to Rock Creek Park, main entrance in the 3000 block of Connecticut Ave. NW. ☎ **202/673-4800** (recording), or 202/673-4717. Free admission. Daily May to mid-Sept (weather permitting): grounds, 6am–8pm; animal buildings, 10am–6pm. Daily mid-Sept to May: grounds, 6am–6pm; animal buildings, 10am–4:30pm. Closed Dec 25. Metro: Cleveland Park or Woodley Park–Zoo.

Established in 1889, the National Zoo is home to several thousand animals of some 500 species, many of them rare and/or endangered. A leader in the care, breeding, and exhibition of animals, it occupies 163 beautifully landscaped and wooded acres and is one of the country's most delightful zoos. Star resident is Hsing-Hsing, a rare giant panda donated by the People's Republic of China. He's best observed at feeding times, 11am and 2:30pm, and is generally livelier at the morning feeding.

Enter the zoo at the Connecticut Avenue entrance; you will be right by the Education Building, where you can pick up a map and find out about feeding times and special activities taking place during your visit.

Zoo animals live in large, open enclosures—simulations of their natural habitats—along two easy-to-follow numbered paths, **Olmsted Walk** and the **Valley Trail.** You can't get lost, and you won't unintentionally miss anything. Signs indicate the presence of baby animals born on the premises. One thing you'll want to keep in mind, especially if you have young children, is that the zoo is situated on a hill. From the zoo's main entrance, you're headed downhill; the return walk can prove trying on a hot day with little ones. As noted below, the zoo does rent strollers and offers plenty of refreshment stands.

If you follow the Olmsted Walk, you'll find cheetahs and zebras to the left of the path, on your way to the camels, elephants, and panda. If you follow the Valley Trail, you'll come upon tapirs and antelope (grass grazers), and the **Wetlands Exhibit,** where, from a boardwalk path, you can view brown pelicans, herons, and other waterfowl amid water lilies and cattails. Proceed to Hsing-Hsing via the **Australia Pavilion,** which is bracketed with kangaroos, camels, and antelopes at the center of the park. Just across the way are four of the largest land mammals: hippos, rhinos, giraffes, and elephants. Continue north on Olmsted Walk to the **Great Ape House;** it adjoins, via an overhead Orangutan Transport System, the **Think Tank,** an intriguing facility focusing on the biology of animal thought. Up ahead is the **Reptile Discovery Center,** home to Indonesian Komodo dragons, the world's largest lizards. In the same area, the **Invertebrate Exhibit** is the only one in the country to house both terrestrial and aquatic species; on display are starfish, sponges, giant crabs, anemones, insects, and other spineless creatures. Lions and tigers live nearby in a moated circular habitat surrounding a water-filled moat. Down a flight of stairs is the **Bat Cave.** Continuing south on the U-shaped Olmsted Walk, you can stop for awhile to watch the always amusing antics of prairie dogs in a small earth mound. Across the way, back on the Valley Trail, is **Amazonia,** a lush rain forest habitat that includes a cascading tropical "Amazon River" and a Science Gallery that re-creates a tropical biology field station. Occupying a futuristic building under a 50-foot dome, it is

---

Alert

The Anacostia Museum was closed for renovations most of 1997; call ahead to make sure the museum has reopened.

---

home to 358 species of plants, dozens of animals and tropical birds, and immense naturalistic aquariums that simulate deep river pools. Continue uphill past the "spectacled" bears (rare South American black bears with light-colored lines around their eyes) to see seals and sea lions cavorting in their pool.

Zoo facilities include stroller-rental stations, a number of gift shops, a bookstore, and several paid-parking lots. The lots fill up quickly, especially on weekends, so arrive early or take the Metro. Snack bars and ice-cream kiosks are scattered throughout the park.

Anacostia Museum

1901 Fort Place SE (off Martin Luther King Jr. Ave.). ☎ **202/287-3382** or 202/357-2700. Free admission. Daily 10am–5pm. Closed Dec 25. Metro: Anacostia; then take a W1 or W2 bus directly to the museum.

This unique Smithsonian establishment was created in 1967 as a neighborhood museum. Expanding its horizons over the years, the museum is today a national resource devoted to the identification, documentation, protection, and interpretation of the African-American experience, focusing on Washington, D.C., and the Upper South. The permanent collection includes about 5,000 items, ranging from videotapes of African-American church services to art, sheet music, and historic documents. In addition, the Anacostia produces a varying number of shows each year and offers a comprehensive schedule of free educational programs and activities in conjunction with exhibit themes. For instance, to complement an exhibition called "The African-American Presence in American Quilts," the museum featured a video about artist/quilt maker Faith Ringgold, quilting workshops for adults and children, talks by local quilting societies, and storytelling involving quilts.

Call for an events calendar (which always includes children's activities) or pick one up when you visit.

4 Elsewhere on the Mall

✪ National Archives

Constitution Ave. NW (between 7th and 9th sts.). ☎ **202/501-5000** for information on exhibits and films, or 202/501-5400 for research information. Free admission. Exhibition Hall, Apr–Aug, daily 10am–9pm; Sept–Mar, daily 10am–5:30pm. Call for research hours. Closed Dec 25. Metro: Archives.

Keeper of America's documentary heritage, the National Archives displays our most cherished treasures in appropriately awe-inspiring surroundings. Housed in the Rotunda of the Exhibition Hall are the nation's three charter documents—the Declaration of Independence, the Constitution of the United States, and its Bill of Rights, as well as the 1297 version of the Magna Carta—each on permanent display to the public.

High above and flanking the documents are two larger-than-life murals painted by Barry Faulkner. One, entitled *The Declaration of Independence,* shows Thomas Jefferson presenting a draft of the Declaration to John Hancock, the presiding officer of the Continental Congress; the other, entitled *The Constitution,* shows James Madison submitting the Constitution to George Washington and the Constitutional Convention. In the display cases on either side of the Declaration of Independence are exhibits that rotate over a 3-year period, for instance, "American Originals," 26 compelling American historical documents ranging from George Washington's Revolutionary War expense account to the Louisiana Purchase Treaty signed by Napoléon. There are also temporary exhibits in the Circular Gallery.

The Archives serves as much more than a museum of cherished documents. Famous as a center for genealogical research—Alex Haley began his work on *Roots* here—it is sometimes called "the nation's memory." This federal institution is charged with sifting through the accumulated papers of a nation's official life—billions of pieces a year—and determining what to save and what to destroy. The Archives' vast accumulation of census figures, military records, naturalization papers, immigrant passenger lists, federal documents, passport applications, ship manifests, maps, charts, photographs, and motion picture film (and that's not the half of it) spans 2 centuries. And it's all available for the perusal of anyone age 16 or over (call for details). If you're casually thinking about tracing your roots, stop by Room 400 where a staff member can advise you about the time and effort that will be involved, and, if you decide to pursue it, exactly how to proceed.

Even if you have no research project in mind, the National Archives merits a visit. The neoclassical building itself, designed by John Russell Pope in the 1930s (also architect of the National Gallery of Art and the Jefferson Memorial) is an impressive example of the beaux-arts style. Seventy-two columns create a Corinthian colonnade on each of the four facades. Great bronze doors herald the Constitution Avenue entrance, and allegorical sculpture centered on *The Recorder of the Archives* adorns the pediment. On either side of the steps are male and female figures symbolizing guardianship and heritage, respectively. Guardians of the Portals at the Pennsylvania Avenue entrance represent the past and the future, and the theme of the pediment is destiny.

Free **tours** are given weekdays at 10:15am and 1:15pm by appointment only; call ☎ **202/501-5205** for details. Pick up a schedule of events (lectures, films, genealogy workshops) when you visit.

✪ National Gallery of Art

On the north side of the Mall, on Constitution Ave. NW, between 3rd and 7th sts. NW. ☎ **202/737-4215.** Free admission. Mon–Sat 10am–5pm, Sun 11am–6pm. Closed Jan 1 and Dec 25. Metro: Archives, Judiciary Square, or Smithsonian.

Most people don't realize it, but the National Gallery of Art is not really part of the Smithsonian complex; hence its listing here apart from the other Mall museums.

Housing one of the world's foremost collections of Western painting, sculpture, and graphic arts from the Middle Ages through the 20th century, the National Gallery has a dual personality. The original West Building, designed by John Russell Pope (architect of the Jefferson Memorial and the National Archives), is a neoclassic marble masterpiece with a domed rotunda over a colonnaded fountain and high-ceilinged corridors leading to delightful garden courts. It was a gift to the nation from Andrew W. Mellon, who also contributed the nucleus of the collection, including 21 masterpieces from the Hermitage, two Raphaels among them. The ultramodern East Building, designed by I. M. Pei and opened in 1978, is composed of two adjoining triangles with glass walls and lofty tetrahedron skylights. The pink Tennessee marble from which both buildings were constructed was taken from the same quarry; it forms an architectural link between the two structures.

The West Building: On the main floor of the West Building, about 1,000 paintings are always on display. To the left (as you enter off the Mall) is the Art Information Room, housing the Micro Gallery, where those so inclined can design their own tours of the permanent collection and enhance their knowledge of art via user-friendly computers. Continuing to the left of the rotunda are galleries of 13th- through 18th-century Italian paintings and sculpture, including what is generally considered the finest Renaissance collection outside Italy; here you'll see the only painting by Leonardo da Vinci housed outside Europe, *Ginevra de' Benci.* Paintings by El Greco, Ribera, and Velázquez highlight the Spanish galleries; Grünewald, Dürer, Holbein, and Cranach can be seen in the German; Van Eyck, Bosch, and rubens in the Flemish; and Vermeer, Steen, and Rembrandt in the Dutch. To the right of the rotunda, galleries display 18th- to 19th-century French paintings (including one of the world's greatest impressionist collections), paintings by Goya, works of late–18th- and 19th-century Americans—such as Cole, Stuart, Copley, Homer, Whistler, and Sargent—and of somewhat earlier British artists, such as Constable, Turner, and Gainsborough. Room decor reflects the period and country of the art shown: Travertine marble heralds the Italian gallery, and somber oak panels define the Dutch galleries. Down a flight of stairs are prints and drawings, 15th- through 20th-century sculpture (with many pieces by Daumier, Degas, and Rodin), American naive 18th- and 19th-century paintings, Chinese porcelains, small Renaissance bronzes, 16th-century Flemish tapestries, and 18th-century decorative arts.

The East Building: The scene of major changing exhibits, the East Building contains an important collection of 20th-century art, including a massive aluminum Calder mobile under a seven-story skylight and, outside the front entrance, an immense bronze sculpture by Henry Moore.

In addition to its permanent collection, the National Gallery hosts a wide range of important temporary exhibits. Recent shows have ranged from "Splendors of Imperial China" to "Picasso: The Early Years."

Pick up a floor plan and calendar of events at an information desk to find out about exhibits, films, tours, lectures, and concerts. Highly recommended are the free highlight **tours** (call for exact times) and audio tours. There are several dining options here.

✪ United States Holocaust Memorial Museum

100 Raoul Wallenberg Place (formerly 15th St. SW; near Independence Ave., just off the Mall). ☎ **202/488-0400.** Free admission. Daily 10am–5:30pm. Closed Yom Kippur and Dec 25. Metro: Smithsonian.

The United States Holocaust Museum is America's national institution for the documentation, study, and interpretation of Holocaust history, and serves as the nation's memorial to the 6 million Jews and millions of others who were murdered during the Holocaust. Chartered by a unanimous act of Congress in 1980 and located adjacent to the Mall, the museum strives to broaden public understanding of Holocaust history. Within its walls are permanent and temporary exhibitions, an interactive computer learning center, a registry of Holocaust survivors, a library, archives, and permanent collections. Since its opening in April 1993, the museum has drawn 2 million visitors each year.

The permanent exhibit is where you will spend most of your time—anywhere from 1 to 5 hours—and it is for this main section of the museum that you need a pass. The exhibit takes up three floors, presenting the information chronologically.

When you enter, you will be issued an identity card of an actual victim of the Holocaust. By 1945, 66% of those whose lives are documented on these cards were dead. The tour begins on the fourth floor, where exhibits portray the events of 1933 to 1939, the years of the Nazi uprising. On the third floor (documenting 1940 to 1944), exhibits illustrate the narrowing choices of people caught up in the Nazi machine. You board a Polish freight car of the type used to transport Jews from the

Holocaust Museum Touring Tips

Because so many people want to visit the museum, tickets specifying a visit time (in 15-minute intervals) are required. Reserve them via Protix (☎ **800/400-9373**). There's a small service charge. You can also get them at the museum beginning at 10am daily (lines form earlier).

Warsaw ghetto to Treblinka and hear recordings of survivors telling what life in the camps was like. This part of the museum documents the details of the Nazis' "Final Solution" for the Jews.

The second floor tells a more heartening story: It tells of how non-Jews throughout Europe, by exercising individual action and responsibility, saved Jews at great personal risk. Denmark—led by a king who swore that if any of his subjects wore a yellow star, so would he—managed to hide and save 90% of its Jews. Exhibits follow on the liberation of the camps, life in Displaced Persons camps, emigration to Israel and America, and the Nuremberg trials. A highlight at the end of the permanent exhibition is a 30-minute film called "Testimony," in which Holocaust survivors tell their own stories. The tour ends in the hexagonal Hall of Remembrance, where you can meditate on what you've experienced and light a candle for the victims.

Dozens of educational interactive videos further enhance understanding, as do films, lectures, cultural events, and temporary exhibits. The displays are designed so you can shield children (or yourself) from the most graphic material.

The museum recommends not bringing children under 11; for older children, it's advisable to prepare them for what they'll see. There's a cafeteria and museum shop on the premises. Other resources include the **Resource Center for Educators,** which provides materials and services to Holocaust educators and students. Researchers may use the library, Holocaust survivor registry, and archival collections to retrieve historic documents, photographs, oral histories, films, and videos. The museum has a Web site at **http://www.ushmm.org**.

You can see some parts of the museum without tickets. These include two special exhibit areas on the first floor and concourse, *Daniel's Story: Remember the Children,* and *Hidden History of the Kovno Ghetto;* the **Wall of Remembrance** (Children's Tile Wall), which commemorates the 1.5 million children killed in the Holocaust; and the second floor **Wexner Learning Center,** a multimedia computer center that allows self-directed visitors to learn about the Holocaust.

5 Other Government Agencies

Bureau of Engraving & Printing

14th and C sts. SW. ☎ **202/874-3188** or 202/874-2330. Free admission. Mon–Fri 9am–1:50pm; June–Aug additional evening tours 5–7:30pm. Closed Dec 25–Jan 1 and federal holidays. Metro: Smithsonian (Independence Ave. exit).

This is where the cash is. A staff of 2,600 works around the clock churning it out at the rate of about 22.5 million notes a day. Everyone's eyes pop as they walk past rooms overflowing with fresh green bills. But although the money draws everyone in, it's not the whole story. The bureau prints many other products, including 25 billion postage stamps per year, presidential portraits, and White House invitations.

As many as 5,000 people line up each day to get a peek at all that moola, so arriving early, especially during the peak tourist season, is essential (unless you have secured VIP tickets from your senator or congressperson; details in chapter 2). April through September, you must obtain a ticket that specifies a tour time, including tours taken in the evening; the ticket booth on Raoul Wallenberg Place (formerly 15th Street) opens at 8am. The rest of the year no ticket is needed; you just have to line up on 14th Street.

The 40-minute **guided tour** begins with a short introductory film. Then you'll see, through large windows, the processes that go into the making of paper money: the inking, stacking of bills, cutting, and examination for defects. Most printing here is done from engraved steel plates in a process known as "intaglio," the hardest to counterfeit, because the slightest alteration will cause a noticeable change in the portrait in use. Additional exhibits include bills no longer in use, counterfeit money, and a $100,000 bill designed for official transactions (since 1969, the largest denomination printed for the general public is $100).

After you finish the tour, allow time to explore the **Visitor Center,** where exhibits include informative videos, money-related electronic games, and a display of $1 million. Here, too, you can buy gifts ranging from bags of shredded money—no, you can't tape it back together—to copies of documents such as the Gettysburg Address.

Federal Bureau of Investigation

J. Edgar Hoover FBI Building, E St. NW (between 9th and 10th sts.). ☎ **202/324-3447.** Free admission. Mon–Fri 8:45am–4:15pm. Closed Jan 1, Dec 25, and other federal holidays. Metro: Metro Center or Federal Triangle.

In these headquarters, more than half a million visitors annually (many of whom are kids) learn why crime doesn't pay. Tours begin with a short videotape presentation about the priorities of the bureau: organized crime, white-collar crime, terrorism, foreign counterintelligence, illicit drugs, and violent crimes. En route, you'll learn about this organization's history (it was established in 1908) and its activities over the years. You'll see some of the weapons used by big-time gangsters such as Al Capone, Dillinger, Bonnie and Clyde, and "Pretty Boy" Floyd; and an exhibit on counterintelligence operations. There are photos of the 10 most-wanted fugitives (2 were recognized at this exhibit by people on the tour, and 10 have been located via the FBI-assisted TV show *America's Most Wanted*).

Other exhibits deal with white-collar crime, organized crime, terrorism, drugs, and agent training. On display are more than 5,000 weapons, most confiscated from criminals; they're used for reference purposes.

You'll also visit the DNA lab, the Firearms Unit (where it's determined whether a bullet was fired from a given weapon), the Material Analysis Unit (where the FBI can determine the approximate make and model of a car from a tiny piece of paint), the unit where hairs and fibers are examined, and a Forfeiture and Seizure Exhibit—a display of jewelry, furs, and other proceeds from illegal narcotics operations. The tour ends with a bang, lots of them in fact, when an agent

FBI Touring Tips

To beat the crowds, arrive before 8:45am or write to a senator or congressperson for a scheduled reservation as far in advance as possible (details in chapter 2). **Tours** last 1 hour and are conducted every 20 to 30 minutes, depending upon staff availability. The building closes at 4:15pm, so you must arrive at least 1 hour before closing if you want to make the last tour (arrive even earlier in high season). Once inside, you'll undergo a security check.

gives a sharpshooting demonstration and discusses the FBI's firearms policy and gun safety.

⊙ Library of Congress

1st St. SE (between Independence Ave. and E. Capitol St.). ☎ **202/707-8000.** Free admission. Madison Building Mon–Fri 8:30am–9:30pm, Sat 8:30am–6pm. Jefferson Building Mon–Sat 10am–5:30pm. Closed Sun and all federal holidays. Metro: Capitol South.

This is the nation's library, established in 1800 "for the purchase of such books as may be necessary for the use of Congress." Over the years, it has expanded to serve all Americans, from the blind, for whom books are recorded on cassette and/or translated into braille, to research scholars and college students. Its first collection of books was destroyed in 1814 when the British burned the Capitol (where the library was then housed) during the War of 1812. Thomas Jefferson then sold the institution his personal library of 6,487 books as a replacement, and this became the foundation of what would grow to become the world's largest library. Today the collection contains a mind-boggling 110 million items. Its three buildings house, among many other things, more than 17 million catalogued books, nearly 48 million manuscripts, the letters of George Washington, almost 13 million prints and photographs, over 2 million audio holdings (discs, tapes, talking books, and so on), more than 700,000 movies and videotapes, musical instruments from the 1700s, and the papers of everyone from Freud to Groucho Marx. The library offers a year-round program of concerts, lectures, and poetry readings, and houses the Copyright Office.

As impressive as the scope of the library's effects and activities is its original home, the ornate Italian Renaissance–style **Thomas Jefferson Building,** which reopened to the public May 1, 1997, after an $81.5 million, 10-year overhaul of the entire library. The Jefferson Building was erected between 1888 and 1897 to hold the burgeoning collection and establish America as a cultured nation with magnificent institutions equal to anything in Europe. Fifty-two painters and sculptors worked for 8 years on its interior. There are floor mosaics of Italian marble, allegorical paintings on the overhead vaults, more than 100 murals, and numerous ornamental cornucopias, ribbons, vines and garlands within, as well as 42 granite sculptures and yards of bas-reliefs on the outside. Especially impressive are the exquisite marble Great Hall and the Main Reading Room, the latter under a 160-foot dome. Originally intended to hold the fruits of at least 150 years of collecting, the Jefferson was, in fact, filled up in 13. It is now supplemented by the **James Madison Memorial Building** and the **John Adams Building.** On permanent display in the Jefferson Building's Great Hall is an exhibit called "Treasures of the Library of Congress," which rotates a selection of more than 200 of the rarest and most interesting items from the Library's collection—like Thomas Jefferson's rough draft of the Declaration of Independence with notations by Benjamin Franklin and John Adams in the margins, and the contents of Lincoln's pockets when he was assassinated.

Stop at the information desk inside the Jefferson Building's west entrance on First Street to obtain same-day, free tickets to tour the Library; tours of the Great Hall take place Monday through Saturday at 11:30am, 1pm, 2:30pm and 4pm. If you have a wait ahead of you, take in the 15-minute orientation film in the Jefferson's new visitors' theater or browse in its new gift shop.

Pick up a calendar of events when you visit. The Madison Building offers interesting exhibits and features classic, rare, and unusual films in its Mary Pickford Theater. It also houses a cafeteria and the more formal Montpelier Room restaurant, both of which are open for lunch Monday through Friday.

6 War Memorials & Cemeteries

Arlington National Cemetery

Just across the Memorial Bridge from the base of the Lincoln Memorial. ☎ **703/607-8052.**
Free admission. Apr–Sept   8am–7pm, Oct–Mar 8am–5pm. Metro: Arlington National
Cemetery. If you come by car, parking is $1.25 an hour for the first 3 hours, $2 an hour there-
after. The cemetery is also accessible via Tourmobile.

Upon arrival, head over to the **Visitor Center,** where you can view exhibits, pick up
a detailed map, use the rest rooms (there are no others until you get to Arlington
House), and purchase a Tourmobile ticket allowing you to stop at all major sights
and then reboard whenever you like. Service is continuous, and the narrated commentary is informative. (See "Getting Around" in chapter 4 for details.) If you've got
plenty of stamina, consider doing part or all of the tour on foot. Remember as you
go that this is a memorial frequented not just by tourists but by those visiting the
graves of beloved relatives and friends who are buried here.

This shrine occupies approximately 612 acres on the high hills overlooking the
capital from the west side of the Memorial Bridge. It honors many national heroes
and more than 240,000 war dead, veterans, and dependents. Many graves of the famous at Arlington bear nothing more than simple markers. Five-star General John
J. Pershing's is one of those. Secretary of State John Foster Dulles is buried here. So
are President William Howard Taft and Supreme Court Justice Thurgood Marshall.
Cemetery highlights include:

The **Tomb of the Unknowns,** containing the unidentified remains of service
members from both world wars, the Korean War, and the Vietnam War. It's an
unembellished massive white-marble block, moving in its simplicity. Inscribed are the
words: "Here rests in honored glory an American Soldier known but to God." The
changing of the guard takes place every half-hour April to September and every hour
on the hour October to March.

Arlington House (☎ **703/557-0613**) was for 30 years (1831–61) the legal residence of Robert E. Lee, where he and his family lived off and on until the Civil War.
Lee married the great-granddaughter of Martha Washington, Mary Anna Randolph
Custis, who inherited the estate upon the death of her father. It was at Arlington
House that Lee, having received the news of Virginia's secession from the Union,
decided to resign his commission in the U.S. Army. During the Civil War, the estate was taken over by Union forces, and troops were buried there. A year before the
defeat of the Confederate forces at Gettysburg, the U.S. government bought the estate. A fine melding of the styles of the Greek Revival and the grand plantation houses
of the early 1800s, it has been administered by the National Park Service since 1933.

You tour the house on your own; park rangers are on-site to answer your questions.
About 30% of the furnishings are original. Slave quarters and a small museum ad-
join. Admission is free. It's open daily 9:30am to 4:30pm but is closed January 1 and
December 25.

Pierre Charles L'Enfant's Grave was placed near Arlington House at a spot that
is believed to offer the best view of Washington, the city he designed.

Below Arlington House is the **Gravesite of John Fitzgerald Kennedy.** Simplicity is the key to grandeur here, too. John Carl Warnecke designed a low crescent wall
embracing a marble terrace, inscribed with memorable words of the 35th U.S. president, including his famous utterance, "And so my fellow Americans, ask not what
your country can do for you, ask what you can do for your country." Jacqueline
Kennedy Onassis rests next to her husband, and Senator Robert Kennedy is buried
close by. The Kennedy graves attract streams of visitors. Arrive close to 8am to

contemplate the site quietly; otherwise, it's mobbed. Looking north, there's a spectacular view of Washington.

About 1¹/₂ miles from the Kennedy Graves, the **Marine Corps Memorial,** the famous statue of the marines raising the flag on Iwo Jima, stands near the north (or Orde & Weitzel Gate) entrance to the cemetery as a tribute to marines who died in all wars. On Tuesday evenings in summer, there are military parades on the grounds at 7pm.

Close to the Iwo Jima statue is the **Netherlands Carillon,** a gift from the people of the Netherlands, with 50 bells. Every spring thousands of tulip bulbs bloom on the surrounding grounds. Carillon concerts take place from 2 to 4pm on Saturday during April, May, and September; and from 6 to 8pm on Saturday from June to August. (Sometimes the hours change; call ☎ **703/285-2598** before you go.) Visitors are permitted to enter the tower to watch the carillonneur perform and enjoy panoramic views of Washington.

In October 1997, **The Women's Memorial** was added to Arlington Cemetery, to honor the more than 1.8 million women who have served in the armed forces from the American Revolution to the present. The new memorial lies just beyond the gated entrance to the cemetery. An upper terrace features views of Arlington National Cemetery and the monuments of Washington; an arc of large glass panels contains etched quotations from servicewomen. A lower terrace places a reflecting pool and plaza before a hemicycle wall. Behind the wall and completely underground is the Education Center, housing a Hall of Honor, a theater, and a computer register of servicewomen, which visitors may access for information about individual women, past and present, in the military. Hours are October through March 8am to 5pm and April through September 8am to 7pm. The memorial is open every day but Christmas.

The Korean War Veterans Memorial

Just across from the Lincoln Memorial (east of French Dr., between 21st and 23rd sts. NW). ☎ **202/426-6841.** Free admission. Rangers on duty 8am–midnight daily except Dec 25. Ranger-led interpretive programs are given throughout the day. Metro: Foggy Bottom.

This privately funded new memorial, focusing on an American flag, honors those who served in Korea, a 3-year conflict (1950–53) that produced almost as many casualties as Vietnam. It consists of a circular "Pool of Remembrance" in a grove of trees and a triangular "Field of Service." The latter is highlighted by statues of 19 infantrymen, with several emerging from the woods creating the impression there are legions to follow. In addition, a 164-foot-long black granite wall depicts the array of combat and combat support troops that served in Korea (nurses, chaplains, airmen, gunners, mechanics, cooks, and others); a raised granite curb lists the 22 nations that contributed to the UN's effort there; and a commemorative area honors KIAs, MIAs, and POWs. Limited parking is available along Ohio Drive.

United States Navy Memorial and Naval Heritage Center

701 Pennsylvania Ave. NW. ☎ **800/723-3557** or 202/737-2300. Free admission. Mon–Sat 9:30am–5pm, Sun noon–5pm. Closed Thanksgiving, New Year's Day, and Dec 25. Metro: Archives–Navy Memorial.

Authorized by Congress in 1980 to honor the men and women of the U.S. Navy, this memorial is comprised of a 100-foot-diameter circular plaza bearing a granite world map flanked by fountains and waterfalls salted with waters from the seven seas. A statue of *The Lone Sailor* watching over the map represents all who have served in the navy. And two sculpture walls adorned with bronze bas-reliefs commemorate navy history and related maritime services.

The building adjoining the memorial houses a naval heritage center in which museum highlights include interactive video kiosks proffering a wealth of information

Arlington National Cemetery

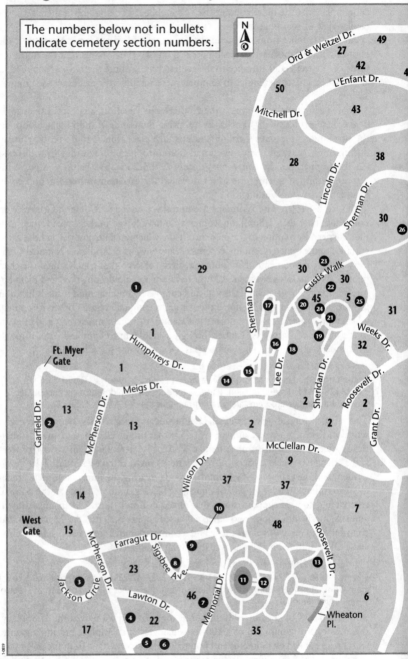

The numbers below not in bullets indicate cemetery section numbers.

N

Ord & Weitzel Dr.

L'Enfant Dr.

Mitchell Dr.

Lincoln Dr.

Sherman Dr.

Custis Walk

Sherman Dr.

Humphreys Dr.

Ft. Myer Gate

Meigs Dr.

Garfield Dr.

McPherson Dr.

Lee Dr.

Sheridan Dr.

Weeks Dr.

Roosevelt Dr.

Grant Dr.

McClellan Dr.

Wilson Dr.

West Gate

McPherson Dr.

Farragut Dr.

Sigsbee Ave.

Memorial Dr.

Roosevelt Dr.

Roosevelt Dr.

Jackson Circle

Lawton Dr.

Wheaton Pl.

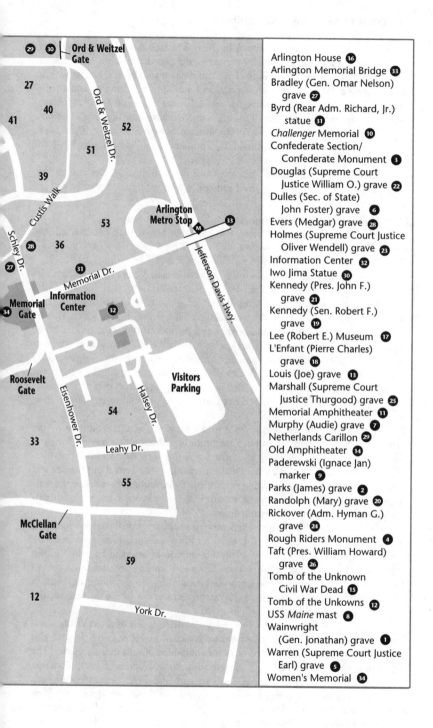

Arlington House ⓰
Arlington Memorial Bridge ㉝
Bradley (Gen. Omar Nelson)
    grave ㉗
Byrd (Rear Adm. Richard, Jr.)
    statue ㉛
Challenger Memorial ⑩
Confederate Section/
    Confederate Monument ③
Douglas (Supreme Court
    Justice William O.) grave ㉒
Dulles (Sec. of State)
    John Foster) grave ⑥
Evers (Medgar) grave ㉘
Holmes (Supreme Court Justice
    Oliver Wendell) grave ㉓
Information Center ㉜
Iwo Jima Statue ㉚
Kennedy (Pres. John F.)
    grave ㉑
Kennedy (Sen. Robert F.)
    grave ⑲
Lee (Robert E.) Museum ⓱
L'Enfant (Pierre Charles)
    grave ⑱
Louis (Joe) grave ⑬
Marshall (Supreme Court
    Justice Thurgood) grave ㉕
Memorial Amphitheater ⑪
Murphy (Audie) grave ⑦
Netherlands Carillon ㉙
Old Amphitheater ⑭
Paderewski (Ignace Jan)
    marker ⑨
Parks (James) grave ②
Randolph (Mary) grave ⑳
Rickover (Adm. Hyman G.)
    grave ㉔
Rough Riders Monument ④
Taft (Pres. William Howard)
    grave ㉖
Tomb of the Unknown
    Civil War Dead ⑮
Tomb of the Unkowns ⑫
USS *Maine* mast ⑧
Wainwright
    (Gen. Jonathan) grave ①
Warren (Supreme Court Justice
    Earl) grave ⑤
Women's Memorial ㉞

about navy ships, aircraft, and history; the Navy Memorial Log Room, a computerized record of past and present navy personnel; the Presidents Room, honoring the six U.S. presidents who served in the navy and the two who became secretary of the navy; the Ship's Store, filled with nautical and maritime merchandise; and a wide-screen 70mm Surroundsound film called *At Sea* (by the makers of *To Fly*), which lets viewers experience the grandeur of the ocean and the adventure of going to sea on a navy ship. The 35-minute film plays every Monday through Saturday at 10am, noon, 2pm, and 4pm, and on Sunday at 11am, 1pm, and 3pm; admission is $3.75 for adults, $3 for seniors and students 18 and under.

Guided **tours** are available from the front desk, subject to staff availability. The plaza is the scene of many free band concerts in spring and summer; call for details.

✪ The Vietnam Veterans Memorial

Just across from the Lincoln Memorial (east of Henry Bacon Dr. between 21st and 22nd sts. NW). ☎ **202/426-6841.** Free admission. Rangers on duty 8am–midnight daily except Dec 25. Ranger-led programs are given throughout the day. Metro: Foggy Bottom.

A most poignant sight in Washington is the Vietnam Veterans Memorial: two long, black granite walls inscribed with the names of the men and women who gave their lives, or remain missing, in the longest war in our nation's history. Even if no one close to you died in Vietnam, it's wrenching to watch visitors grimly studying the directories at either end to find out where their husbands, sons, and loved ones are listed. The slow walk along the 492-foot wall of names—it names close to 60,000 people, many of whom died very young—powerfully evokes the tragedy of all wars. It's also affecting to see how much the monument means to Vietnam vets who visit it. Because of the raging conflict over U.S. involvement in the war, its veterans had received virtually no previous recognition of their service.

The memorial was conceived by Vietnam veteran Jan Scruggs and built by the Vietnam Veterans Memorial Fund, a nonprofit organization that raised $7 million for the project. The VVMF was granted a 2-acre site in tranquil Constitution Gardens to erect a memorial that would make no political statement about the war and would harmonize with neighboring memorials. By separating the issue of the wartime service of individuals from the issue of U.S. policy in Vietnam, VVMF hoped to begin a process of national reconciliation.

Yale senior Maya Ying Lin's design was chosen in a national competition open to all citizens over 18 years of age. It consists of two walls in a quiet, protected park setting, angled at 125° to point to the Washington Monument and the Lincoln Memorial. The wall's mirrorlike surface reflects surrounding trees, lawns, an monuments. The names are inscribed in chronological order, documenting an epoch in American history as a series of individual sacrifices from the date of the first casualty in 1959 to the date of the last death in 1975.

The wall was erected in 1982. In 1984 a life-size sculpture of three Vietnam soldiers by Frederick Hart was installed at the entrance plaza. He describes his work this way: "They wear the uniform and carry the equipment of war; they are young. The contrast between the innocence of their youth and the weapons of war underscores the poignancy of their sacrifice. . . . Their strength and their vulnerability are both evident." Near the statue a flag flies from a 60-foot staff. Another sculpture, the Vietnam Veterans Women's Memorial, depicting three servicewomen tending a wounded soldier was installed on Veterans Day 1993. Limited parking is available along Constitution Avenue.

7 More Museums

☉ Corcoran Gallery of Art

500 17th St. NW (between E St. and New York Ave.). ☎ **202/639-1700** or 202/638-1439. Free admission. Wed and Fri–Mon 10am–5pm, Thurs 10am–9pm. Suggested contribution $3 adults, $1 students and senior citizens, $5 for families; children 12 and under are free. Closed Tues, Jan 1, and Dec 25. Metro: Farragut West or Farragut North.

The first art museum in Washington (and one of the first in the nation), the Corcoran Gallery was housed from 1874 to 1896 in the redbrick and brownstone building that is now the Renwick. The collection outgrew its quarters and was transferred in 1897 to its present beaux-arts building, designed by Ernest Flagg.

The collection itself, shown in rotating exhibits, focuses chiefly on American art. A prominent Washington banker, William Wilson Corcoran was among the first wealthy American collectors to realize the importance of encouraging and supporting this country's artists. Enhanced by further gifts and bequests, the collection comprehensively spans American art from 18th-century portraiture to 20th-century moderns like Nevelson, Warhol, and Rothko. Nineteenth-century works include Bierstadt's and Remington's imagery of the American West; Hudson River School artists like Cole, Church, and Durand; genre paintings; expatriates like Whistler, Sargent, and Mary Cassatt; and two giants of the late 19th century, Homer and Eakins.

The Corcoran is not, however, an exclusively American art museum. On the first floor is the collection from the estate of Sen. William Andrews Clark, an eclectic grouping of Dutch and Flemish masters, European painters, French impressionists, Barbizon landscapes, Delft porcelains, a Louis XVI salon dore transported in toto from Paris, and more. Clark's will stated that his diverse collection, which any curator would undoubtedly want to disperse among various museum departments, must be shown as a unit. He left money for a wing to house it, which opened in 1928. Don't miss the small, walnut-paneled room known as "Clark Landing," which showcases 19th-century French impressionist and American art, a room of exquisite Corot landscapes, another of medieval Renaissance tapestries, and numerous Daumier lithographs donated by Dr. Armand Hammer.

Free 45-minute **tours** are given at noon (and on Thursday also at 7:30pm). Pick up a schedule of events—temporary exhibits, gallery talks, concerts, art auctions, and more. Families should inquire about the Corcoran's series of Saturday Family Days and Sunday Traditions. (Family Days are especially fun for everyone and always feature great live music.) Both programs are free, but you need to reserve a slot for the Sunday events. The charming Cafe at the Corcoran is open for lunch 11am–3pm, Monday through Saturday, for afternoon tea and dinner on Thursday, and for Sunday brunch (reservations are not accepted for brunch; call ☎ **202/639-1786** for more information).

Dumbarton Oaks

1703 32nd St. NW (entrance to the collections on 32nd St., between R and S sts.; garden entrance at 31st and R sts.). ☎ **202/339-6401.** Garden, $3 adults, $2 children under 12

Fun Fact

Displayed on the second floor of the Corcoran is the white-marble female nude, *The Greek Slave,* by Hiram Powers, considered so daring in its day that it was shown on alternate days to men and women.

and senior citizens; collections, free. Garden (weather permitting), Nov–Mar, daily 2–5pm; Apr–Oct, daily 2–6pm. Collections, Tues–Sun 2–5pm. Gardens are closed federal holidays and Dec 24.

Many people associate Dumbarton Oaks, a 19th-century Georgetown mansion named for a Scottish castle, with the 1944 international conference that led to the formation of the United Nations. Today the 16-acre estate is a research center or studies in Byzantine and pre-Columbian art and history, as well as landscape architecture. Its yards, which wind gently down to Rock Creek Ravine, are magical, modeled after European gardens. The pre-Columbian museum, designed by Philip Johnson, is a small gem, and the Byzantine collection is a rich one.

This unusual collection originated with Robert Woods Bliss and his wife, Mildred. In 1940 they turned over the estate, their extensive Byzantine collection, a library of works on Byzantine civilization, and 16 acres (including 10 acres of exquisite formal gardens) to Mr. Bliss's alma mater, Harvard, and provided endowment funds for continuing research in Byzantine studies. In the early 1960s they also donated their pre-Columbian collection and financed the building of a wing to house it, as well as a second wing for Mrs. Bliss's collection of rare books on landscape gardening. The Byzantine collection includes illuminated manuscripts, a 13th-century icon of St. Peter, mosaics, ivory carvings, a 4th-century sarcophagus, jewelry, and more. The pre-Columbian works, displayed chronologically in eight marble- and oak-floored glass pavilions, feature Olmec jade and serpentine figures, Mayan relief panels, textiles from 900 B.C. to the Spanish Conquest, funerary pottery, gold necklaces made by the lost-wax process, and sculptures of Aztec gods and goddesses.

The historic music room, furnished in French, Italian, and Spanish antiques, was the setting for the 1944 Dumbarton Oaks Conversations about the United Nations. It has a beamed, painted 16th-century French-style ceiling and an immense 16th-century stone fireplace. Among its notable artworks is El Greco's *The Visitation*.

Don't miss the formal gardens, which include an Orangery, a Rose Garden (final resting place of the Blisses amid 1,000 rose bushes), wisteria-covered arbors, herbaceous borders, groves of cherry trees, and magnolias. You can picnic nearby in Montrose Park.

The Folger Shakespeare Library

201 E. Capitol St. SE. ☎ **202/544-7077**. Free admission. Mon–Sat 10am–4pm. Closed federal holidays. Metro: Capitol South.

"Shakespeare taught us that the little world of the heart is vaster, deeper, and richer than the spaces of astronomy," wrote Ralph Waldo Emerson in 1864. A decade later, Amherst student Henry Clay Folger was profoundly affected upon hearing a lecture by Emerson similarly extolling the bard. Folger purchased an inexpensive set of Shakespeare's plays and went on to amass a prodigious mass—by far the world's largest—of his printed works, today housed in the Folger Shakespeare Library. By 1930, when Folger and his wife, Emily (whose literary enthusiasms matched his own), laid the cornerstone of a building to house the collection, it comprised 93,000 books, 50,000 prints and engravings, and thousands of manuscripts. The Folgers gave it all as a gift to the American people.

The building itself has a marble facade decorated with nine bas-relief scenes from Shakespeare's plays; it's a striking example of art-deco classicism. A statue of Puck stands in the west garden, and quotations from the bard and from contemporaries such as Ben Jonson adorn the exterior walls. An Elizabethan garden on the east side of the building is planted with flowers and herbs of the period, many of them mentioned in the plays. Docent-led tours identifying these plants, and placing them within the plays, are given at 10am and 11am on the third Saturday of the month, April to October.

The facility, which houses some 250,000 books, 100,000 of which are rare, is an important research center not only for Shakespearean scholars, but for those studying any aspect of the English and continental Renaissance. And the oak-paneled Great Hall, reminiscent of a Tudor long gallery, is a popular attraction for the general public. It has an intricate plaster ceiling decorated with Shakespeare's coat of arms, fleurs-de-lis, and other motifs. On display are rotating exhibits from the permanent collection: books, paintings, playbills, Renaissance musical instruments, and more.

At the end of the Great Hall is a theater designed to suggest an Elizabethan inn-yard where plays, concerts, readings, and Shakespeare-related events take place (see chapter 10 for details).

Free walk-in **tours** are given daily at 11am, with an additional 1pm tour on Saturday.

Ford's Theatre & Lincoln Museum

517 10th St. NW (between E and F sts.). ☎ **202/426-6925.** Free admission. Daily 9am–5pm. Closed Dec 25. Metro: Metro Center.

On April 14, 1865, President Lincoln was in the audience of Ford's Theatre, one of the most popular playhouses in Washington. Everyone was laughing at a funny line from Tom Taylor's celebrated comedy, *Our American Cousin,* when John Wilkes Booth crept into the president's box, shot the president, and leapt to the stage, shouting "Sic semper tyrannis" (Thus ever to tyrants). With his left leg broken from the vault, Booth mounted his horse in the back alley and galloped off. Doctors carried Lincoln across the street to the house of William Petersen, where the president died the next morning.

After Lincoln's assassination, the theater was closed by order of Secretary of War Edwin M. Stanton. For many years afterward it was used as an office by the War Department. In 1893, 22 clerks were killed when three floors of the building collapsed. It remained in disuse until the 1960s, when it was remodeled and restored to its appearance on the night of the tragedy. Except when rehearsals or matinees are in progress (call before you go), visitors can see the theater and trace Booth's movements on that fateful night. Free 15-minute talks on the history of the theater and the story of the assassination are given throughout the day. Be sure to visit the **Lincoln Museum** in the basement, where exhibits—including the Derringer pistol used by Booth and a diary in which he outlines his rationalization for the deed—focus on events surrounding Lincoln's assassination and the trial of the conspirators. The theater stages productions most of the year—see chapter 10 for information.

The House Where Lincoln Died (The Petersen House)

516 10th St. NW. ☎ **202/426-6924.** Free admission. Daily 9am–5pm. Closed Dec 25. Metro: Metro Center.

After the shooting, Lincoln was carried across the street to the home of William Petersen, a tailor. Now furnished with period pieces, it looks much as it did on that fateful April night. You'll see the front parlor where an anguished Mary Todd Lincoln spent the night with her son, Robert. Her emotional state was such that she was banned from the bedroom because she was creating havoc. In the back parlor, Secretary of War Edwin M. Stanton held a Cabinet meeting and began questioning witnesses. From this room, Stanton announced at 7:22am on April 15, 1865, "Now he belongs to the ages."

Twelve years after Lincoln's death, the house was sold to Louis Schade, who published a newspaper called the *Washington Sentinel* in its basement for many years. In 1896 the government bought the house for $30,000, and it is now maintained by the National Park Service.

National Geographic Society's Explorers Hall

17th and M sts. NW. ☎ **202/857-7588.** Free admission. Mon–Sat 9am–5pm, Sun 10am–5pm. Closed Dec 25. Metro: Farragut North (Connecticut Ave. and L St. exit) or Farragut West.

The National Geographic Society was founded in 1888 for "the increase and diffusion of geographic knowledge." At Explorers Hall, dozens of fascinating displays, most of them using interactive videos, put that knowledge literally at your fingertips. In Geographica, on the north side of the hall, you can touch a tornado, find out what it's like inside the earth, explore the vast Martian landscape, and study the origin of humankind. The major exhibit here is Earth Station One, an interactive amphitheater (centered on an immense free-floating globe) that simulates an orbital flight. You can also peer into a video microscope that zooms in clearly on slides showing such specimens as a hydra (a simple multicellular animal) or mosquito larva.

Also on display are a scale model of Jacques Cousteau's diving saucer in which he descended to 25,000 feet; the flag and dog sled, among other equipment, of Admiral Robert E. Peary, the first man to reach the North Pole; an *Aepyornis maximus* egg, from Madagascar's extinct 1,000-pound flightless "elephant bird"; and the world's largest freestanding globe. Also on view are a full-size replica of a giant Olmec stone head dating from 32 B.C. from La Venta, Mexico and a 3.9 billion-year-old moon rock. Video excerpts from the society's TV specials are shown in the National Geographic Television Room. The Hall offers an ongoing series of lectures and temporary exhibits.

This is a great place to take the kids (especially those 8 and older) after visiting the White House, which is within walking distance.

National Museum of Women in the Arts

1250 New York Ave. NW (at 13th St.). ☎ **202/783-5000.** Suggested contribution, $3 adults, $2 children. Mon–Sat 10am–5pm, Sun noon–5pm; open Thursdays June through Aug until 9pm. Closed Jan 1, Thanksgiving Day, and Dec 25. Metro: Metro Center.

Celebrating "the contribution of women to the history of art," this relatively new museum (opened 1987) is Washington's 72nd but a national first. Its 10th anniversary in 1997 saw the opening of the Elizabeth A. Kasser Wing, which adds 5,300 square feet and two new galleries to the museum. Founders Wilhelmina and Wallace Holladay, who donated the core of the permanent collection—more than 200 works by women spanning the 16th through the 20th century—became interested in women's art in the 1960s. After discovering that no women were included in H. W. Janson's *History of Art*, a standard text (this, by the way, did not change until 1986!), the Holladays began collecting art by women, and the concept of a women's art museum (to begin correcting the inequities of under-representation) soon evolved.

Since its opening, the collection has grown to more than 2,000 works by artists including Rosa Bonheur, Frida Kahlo, Helen Frankenthaler, Barbara Hepworth, Georgia O'Keeffe, Camille Claudel, Lila Cabot Perry, Mary Cassatt, Elaine de Kooning, and Käthe Kollwitz, along with many other lesser known but notable artists from earlier centuries. You will discover here, for instance, that the famed Peale family of 19th-century portrait painters included a very talented sister, Sarah Miriam Peale. The collection is complemented by an ongoing series of changing exhibits.

The museum is housed in a magnificent Renaissance Revival landmark building designed in 1907 as a Masonic temple by noted architect Waddy Wood. The charming and sunny Mezzanine Cafe serves light lunches Monday through Saturday—soups, salads, and sandwiches.

✪ Phillips Collection

1600 21st St. NW (at Q St.). ☎ **202/387-2151.** Admission Sat–Sun, $6.50 adults, $3.25 seniors and students, free for children 18 and under; contribution suggested Tues–Fri. Sept to May Tues–Wed and Fri–Sat 10am–5pm, Thurs 10am–8:30pm, Sun noon–5pm June to Aug, noon–7pm. Closed Jan 1, July 4, Thanksgiving Day, and Dec 25. Metro: Dupont Circle (Q St. exit).

Conceived as "a museum of modern art and its sources," this intimate establishment, occupying an elegant 1890s Georgian Revival mansion and a more youthful wing, houses the exquisite collection of Duncan and Marjorie Phillips, avid collectors and proselytizers of modernism. Carpeted rooms, with leaded- and stained-glass windows, oak paneling, plush chairs and sofas, and frequently, fireplaces establish a comfortable, homelike setting for the viewing of their art. Today the collection includes more than 2,500 works. Among the highlights are superb examples of Daumier, Dove, and Bonnard paintings; some splendid small Vuillards; five van Goghs; Renoir's *Luncheon of the Boating Party,* the inspiration for the popular "Impressionists on the Seine" exhibit held in late 1996 into the winter of 1997; seven Cézannes; and six works by Georgia O'Keeffe. Ingres, Delacroix, Manet, El Greco, Goya, Corot, Constable, Courbet, Giorgione, and Chardin are among the "sources" or forerunners of modernism represented. Modern notables include Rothko, Hopper, Kandinsky, Matisse, Klee, Degas, Rouault, Picasso, and many others. It's a collection no art lover should miss. The museum presents an ongoing series of temporary shows, supplementing works from the Phillips with loans from other museums and private collections.

Free **tours** are given on Wednesday and Saturday at 2pm, and a full schedule of events includes gallery talks, lectures, and free concerts in the ornate music room. (Concerts take place every Sunday at 5pm, September through May; arrive early to get a seat. Though the concert is free, admission to the museum on weekends costs $6.50.) Thursdays the museum stays open until 8:30pm for **Artful Evenings** with music, gallery talks, and a cash bar; admission is $5.

On the lower level, a charming little restaurant serves light fare.

8 Other Attractions

John F. Kennedy Center for the Performing Arts

New Hampshire Ave. NW (at Rock Creek Pkwy.). ☎ **800/444-1324,** or 202/416-8341 for information or tickets. Free admission. Daily 10am–midnight. Metro: Foggy Bottom (there's a free shuttle service from the station). Bus: 80 from Metro Center.

Opened in 1971, the Kennedy Center is both our national performing arts center and a memorial to John F. Kennedy. Carved into the center's river facade are several Kennedy quotations, including, "the New Frontier for which I campaign in public life can also be a New Frontier for American art." Set on 17 acres overlooking the Potomac, the striking $73 million facility, designed by noted architect Edward Durell Stone, encompasses an opera house, a concert hall, two stage theaters, a theater lab, and a film theater. The best way to see the Kennedy Center, including restricted areas, is to take a free 50-minute guided **tour,** given daily between 10am and 1pm. Once again, you can beat the crowds by writing in advance to a senator or congressperson for tickets for a 9:30 or 9:45am VIP tour (details in chapter 2).

The tour begins in the Hall of Nations, which displays the flags of all nations diplomatically recognized by the United States. Throughout the center you'll see gifts from more than 40 nations, including all the marble used in the building (3,700 tons), which Italy donated. First stop is the Grand Foyer, scene of many

Exhibits Scheduled at Museums in 1998

The following listing, though not comprehensive, is enough to give you an idea about upcoming or current exhibits at major Washington museums. Because schedules sometimes change, it's always a good idea to call ahead. See individual entries in this chapter for phone numbers and addresses.

Corcoran Gallery of Art   "Nothing Personal: Ida Applebroog, 1987-1997," provides an overview of paintings by this septuagenarian narrative artist (Mar 14–June 1); "Rhapsodies in Black: Art of the Harlem Renaissance" (Apr 1–June 15) brings together an international exhibit of photography, films, vintage posters, paintings, sculpture, and works on paper in a rare look at the rich Harlem culture of the early 20th century.

Freer Gallery of Art   "Chinese Gardens in the Painter's Imagination" (Feb 1997–Feb 1998) shows 25 paintings of real and imaginary gardens, from the 12th to the 19th century; "Japanese Art in the Meiji Period (1868–1912)" is the first exhibition to highlight the Freer's holdings of paintings, ceramics, cloisonne, and other art from this period in Japan, when many painters were becoming interested in Western artistic traditions—it opened Sept 20, 1997 and continues into 1998.

Hirshhorn Museum and Sculpture Garden   "An English Vision: The Paintings of Stanley Spencer" (Oct 9, 1997–Jan 11, 1998) introduces the English artist Spencer (1891–1959), well known in his country, but not overseas, for his landscapes, portraits, and paintings with religious themes or social narratives; "George Segal" (Feb 12–May 17) presents a retrospective of this contemporary American sculptor's works spanning 4 decades.

National Air and Space Museum   "Star Wars: The Magic of Myth" (opens late 1997, continuing into 1998) celebrates the Star Wars movie trilogy with this exhibit of props, artwork, costumes, and other original items used in the films.

National Gallery of Art   "Lorenzo Lotto" (Nov 2, 1997–Mar 1, 1998) was a Venetian Renaissance painter and this is the first comprehensive U.S. exhibit of his works; "Manet and the Impressionists at the Gare Saint-Lazare" (1872) (June 14–Sept 20) focuses on Manet's most famous painting, *Gare Saint-Lazare,* and how he came to paint it.

National Museum of African Art   "The Poetics of Line: Seven Artists of the Nsukka Group" (Oct 22, 1997–Apr 26, 1998) looks at the works of seven artists affiliated with the University of Nigeria, Nsukka. The exhibit inaugurates the re-modeled skylight gallery, renamed the Sylvia H. Williams Gallery, honoring the museum's late director.

free concerts and programs and the reception area for all three theaters on the main level; the 18 crystal chandeliers are a gift from Sweden. You'll also visit the Israeli Lounge (where 40 painted and gilded panels depict scenes from the Old Testament); the Concert Hall, home of the National Symphony Orchestra; the Opera House;the African Room (decorated with beautiful tapestries from African nations); the Eisenhower Theater; the Hall of States, where flags of the 50 states and four territories are hung in the order they joined the Union; the Performing Arts Library; and the Terrace Theater, a Bicentennial gift from Japan. Your guide will point out

National Museum of American Art   "Colonial Art from Puerto Rico: Selections from the Gift of Teodoro Vidal" (Oct 3, 1997–Mar 8, 1998) is a selection of colonial Puerto Rican paintings, miniatures, and sculpture, including the oldest American painting and wood sculpture in the museum's collection; "Ansel Adams, A Legacy" (Nov 14, 1997–Mar 29, 1998) celebrates the photographer by displaying 115 works from the latter parts of his career.

National Museum of American History   "Audubon at the Smithsonian" (Apr 25, 1997–May 1, 1998) sketches the life and work of the naturalist artist. At a date to be announced, the museum opens "Rock 'n' Soul: Social Crossroads" highlighting Memphis music, history, and culture. After its stint here, the exhibit moves in 1999 to a permanent location in Memphis.

National Museum of Natural History   "Forces of Change" (dates to be announced) is a new exhibit hall that shows how the Earth changes and how humans participate in (and are affected by) these changes.

National Museum of Women in the Arts   "Artists on the Road: Travel as Source of Inspiration" (Oct 27, 1997–May 23, 1998) features drawings, prints, paintings, and artist's books of world famous artist-travelers such as Sonia Delaunay and Renee Stout; "Lavinia Fontana and Her Contemporaries" (Feb 5–June 7) exhibits the paintings of the early 17th-century Italian artist who supported her husband and 11 children by working as a portraitist.

National Portrait Gallery   "George Marshall" (Nov 7, 1997–Sept 20, 1998) commemorates the 50th anniversary of the Marshall Plan by documenting the life and career of Gen. George C. Marshall (1880-1959).

National Zoological Park   A new grasslands exhibit will be opened in 1998, dates to be announced.

The Phillips Collection   "Consuelo Kanaga: An American Photographer" (Jan 24, 1997–Apr 5, 1998) is a major retrospective of the still lifes, urban and rural views, and portraits of Kanaga (1894–1978), who famously focused his lens upon African Americans; "Richard Diebenkorn: A Retrospective" (May 9–Aug 16) is a major exhibition representing different periods in the career of this abstract painter.

Renwick Gallery   "The Arts and Crafts in Boston" (Mar 6–July 5); "The Stoneware of Charles Fergus Binns" (Sept 11, 1998–Jan 3, 1999); and "Daniel Brush: Objects of Virtue" (Sept 11, 1998–Jan 19, 1999) are all on the books for the coming year.

Arthur M. Sackler Gallery   "Twelve Centuries of Japanese Art from the Imperial Collections" (Dec 14, 1997–Mar 8, 1998) offers for view more than 50 paintings and 20 works of calligraphy from the 9th to the early 20th century.

many notable works of art along the way. If rehearsals are being held, visits to the theaters are omitted.

If you'd like to attend performances during your visit, call the toll-free number above and request the current issue of *Kennedy Center News Magazine,* a free publication that describes all Kennedy Center happenings and prices.

After the tour, walk around the building's terrace for a panoramic 360° view of Washington and plan a meal in one of the Kennedy Center restaurants (see chapter 6). See chapter 10 for specifics on theater, concert, and film offerings. There is limited parking below the Kennedy Center during the day at $3 for the first hour, $6 for 2 hours, $8 for 3 hours or longer; nighttime parking (after 5pm) is a flat $8.

✪ Union Station

50 Massachusetts Ave. NE. ☎ **202/371-9441.** Free admission. Daily 24 hours. Shops, Mon–Sat 10am–9pm, Sun 10am–6pm. Metro: Union Station.

In Washington, D.C., the very train station where you arrive is itself a noteworthy sightseeing attraction. Union Station, built between 1903 and 1907 in the great age of rail travel, was painstakingly restored in the 1980s at a cost of $160 million. The station was designed by noted architect Daniel H. Burnham, an enthusiast of French beaux-arts neoclassicism and a member of the McMillan Commission, a task force assembled in 1900 to beautify the Mall and make the city an appropriately imposing world capital. The committee's philosophy was summed up by Burnham, who counseled, "Make no little plans. They have no magic to stir men's blood, and probably themselves will not be realized." The committee's "big plans" included Union Station, modeled after the Baths of Diocletian and Arch of Constantine in Rome.

When it opened in 1907, this was the largest train station in the world. The Ionic colonnades outside were fashioned from white granite, and there are 100 eagles contained in the facade. Out front a replica of the Liberty Bell and a monumental statue of Columbus hold sway. Six carved fixtures over the entranceway represent Fire, Electricity, Freedom, Imagination, Agriculture, and Mechanics. The station's interior, entered through graceful 50-foot Constantinian arches, is finished with acres of white marble flooring with red "Champlain dots," bronze grilles, elaborate coffered ceilings (embellished with a half million dollars' worth of 22-karat gold leaf!), and rich Honduran mahogany. The Main Hall is a massive rectangular room with a 96-foot barrel-vault ceiling, and a balcony adorned with 36 Augustus Saint-Gaudens sculptures of Roman legionnaires. Off the Main Hall is the East Hall, shimmering with scagliola marble walls and columns, a gorgeous hand-stenciled skylight ceiling, and stunning murals of classical scenes inspired by ancient Pompeian art. Today it's the station's plushest shopping venue.

In its heyday, this "temple of transport" witnessed many important events. President Wilson welcomed General Pershing here in 1918 on his return from France. South Pole explorer Rear Admiral Richard Byrd was also feted at Union Station on his homecoming. And Franklin D. Roosevelt's funeral train, bearing his casket, was met here in 1945 by thousands of mourners.

But after the 1960s, with the decline of rail travel, the station fell on hard times. Rain damage caused parts of the roof to cave in, and the entire building—with floors buckling, rats running about, and mushrooms sprouting in damp rooms—was sealed in 1981. That same year, Congress enacted legislation to preserve and faithfully restore this national treasure.

Today, Union Station is once again a vibrant entity patronized by locals and visitors alike. Every square inch of the facility has been cleaned, repaired, and/or replaced according to the original design. An elliptical mahogany kiosk (inspired by a Renaissance baldachin) has been erected in the center of the Main Hall to accommodate a bilevel cafe and a visitor information center. About 100 retail and food shops on three levels offer a wide array of merchandise. The skylit Main Concourse, extending the entire length of the station, has become the primary shopping area as well as a ticketing and baggage facility. And a nine-screen cinema complex and beautiful food court have been installed on the lower level. The remarkable restoration, which involved hundreds of European and American artisans using historical research, bygone craft techniques, and modern technology, is meticulous in every detail. Burnham's 1907 declaration foretells the spirit of the renovation "a noble, logical diagram once recorded will never die, but long after we are gone will be a living thing, asserting itself with ever-growing insistency. . . . Let your watchword be order and your beacon beauty."

See chapter 6 for information on Union Station restaurants and chapter 9 for information about shops.

Washington National Cathedral

Massachusetts and Wisconsin aves. NW (entrance on Wisconsin Ave.). ☎ **202/537-6200.** Admission $2 for adults, $1 for children under 12. May–Aug Mon–Fri 10am–9pm, Sat 10am–4:30pm; Sept–Apr Mon–Sat 10am–4:30pm. Sun touring hours 12:45–3:30pm year-round. No tours Thanksgiving, Christmas, Palm Sunday, and Easter. Metro: Tenleytown; then about a 20-minute walk. Bus: Any N bus up Massachusetts Ave. from Dupont Circle or any 30 series bus along Wisconsin Ave.

Pierre L'Enfant's 1791 plan for the capital city included "a great church for national purposes," but possibly because of early America's fear of mingling church and state, more than a century elapsed before the foundation for Washington National Cathedral was laid. Its actual name is the Cathedral Church of St. Peter and St. Paul. Though the church is Episcopal, it has no local congregation and seeks to serve the entire nation as a house of prayer for all people. It has been the setting for every kind of religious observance from Jewish to Serbian Orthodox.

A church of this magnitude—it's the sixth-largest cathedral in the world—took a long time to build. Its principal (but not original) architect, Philip Hubert Frohman, worked on the project from 1921 until his death in 1972. The foundation stone was laid in 1907 using the mallet with which George Washington set the Capitol cornerstone. Construction was interrupted by both world wars and periods of financial difficulty. It was completed with the placement of the final stone atop a pinnacle on the west front towers on September 29, 1990, 83 years to the day it was begun.

English Gothic in style (with several distinctly 20th-century innovations, such as a stained-glass window commemorating the flight of *Apollo 11* and containing a piece of moon rock), the cathedral is built in the shape of a cross, complete with flying buttresses and gargoyles. It is, along with the Capitol and the Washington Monument, one of the most dominant structures on the Washington skyline. Its 57-acre landscaped grounds have two lovely gardens; four schools, including the College of Preachers; an herb garden; a greenhouse; and a shop called The Herb Cottage.

Over the years the cathedral has seen much history. Services to celebrate the end of World Wars I and II were held here. It was the scene of President Wilson's funeral (he and his wife are buried here), as well as President Eisenhower's. Helen Keller and her companion, Anne Sullivan, were buried in the cathedral at her request. And during the Iranian crisis, a round-the-clock prayer vigil was held in the Holy Spirit Chapel throughout the hostages' captivity. When they were released, the hostages came to a service here, and tears flowed at Col. Thomas Shaefer's poignant greeting, "Good morning, my fellow Americans. You don't know how long I've been waiting to say those words."

The best way to explore the cathedral and see its abundance of art, architectural carvings, and statuary is to take a 45-minute **tour.** They leave continually, from the west end of the nave, Monday to Saturday 10am to 3:15pm and Sunday 12:45 to 3:30pm.

Allow additional time to tour the grounds or "close," and to visit the Observation Gallery where 70 windows provide panoramic views. Tuesday and Wednesday afternoon tours are followed by a high tea in the Observation Gallery; reservations are required and a fee is charged. And you can, of course, attend **services** at the cathedral (Monday to Saturday at 7:30am, noon, 2:30pm, and 4pm; Sunday at 8, 9, and

11am and 4 and 6:30pm). September to June there's a folk guitar mass on Sunday at 10am.

The cathedral hosts numerous events: organ recitals; choir performances; an annual flower mart; calligraphy workshops; and jazz, folk, and classical concerts. The 53-bell carillon is played on Saturday at 12:30pm. Recitals are usually given on the great organ following Sunday evening services at 5pm. Call for additional events.

A large gift shop on the premises sells replicas of cathedral statuary, religious books and art, Christmas cards, and more.

9 Further Afield: Arlington

The land that today comprises Arlington County was originally carved out of Virginia as part of the territory ceded to form the nation's new capital district. In 1847 the land was returned to the state of Virginia, although it was known as Alexandria County until 1920, when the name was changed to avoid confusion with the city of Alexandria.

The county was named to honor Arlington House, built by George Washington Parke Custis (see above), whose daughter married Robert E. Lee. The Lees lived in Arlington House on and off until the onset of the Civil War in 1861. After the first Battle of Bull Run, at Manassas, several Union soldiers were buried here; the beginnings of the national cemetery date from that time. The Arlington Memorial Bridge leads directly from the Lincoln Memorial to the Robert E. Lee Memorial at Arlington House and symbolizes the joining of forces behind the two figures of Lincoln, representing the North, and Lee, representing the South, into one Union, following the Civil War.

The Newseum & Freedom Park
1101 Wilson Blvd. (at N. Kent St.). ☎ **888-NEWSEUM** or 703/284-3544. Wed–Sun 10am–5pm. Free admission by timed entry passes; distribution of same-day tickets begins at 9:45am. Metro: Rosslyn.

The Washington area's newest museum opened on April 18, 1997, and is the world's first museum dedicated exclusively to news. The Newseum's 72,000 square feet of space occupy an existing office building, reconfigured into exhibit halls and a 220-seat theater topped by an immense dome. Using state-of-the-art multimedia presentations and interactive exhibits, the museum explores the history of news dissemination and the influence of the First Amendment, granting Americans the freedom of speech and of the press. Highlights include a geodesic globe constructed of stainless steel plates bearing the names of every existing American daily newspaper and many from around the world; a two-story-high, block-long Video Newswall displaying, via satellite and fiberoptics, more up-to-the-minute news feeds than any other site in the world; a theater featuring a signature presentation about news; a news forum/TV studio where visitors can view broadcast productions in progress and discuss news events and issues; broadcast booths where you can pretend to be a famous broadcaster (you can purchase the videotaped performance for $10); and

Pentagon Touring Tips

Tourists under 16 must be accompanied by an adult. Those 16 and older must bring a current photo ID that includes a signature and expiration date (driver's license, passport, college ID, international student ID, and so on) to be admitted. You'll have to go through a metal detector and have your bags X-rayed before the tour.

a walk-through history of news gathering from the ancient preprint oral traditions to the latest electronic developments. In the news history gallery, look for intriguing artifacts, such as a 1455 Gutenberg Bible, or a pen that belonged to Charles Dickens. The News Byte Cafe offers snack fare; the gift shop sells T-shirts, hats, and other souvenir items.

Adjoining the museum, **Freedom Park,** which opened the summer of 1996 and sits atop a never-used elevated highway, celebrates the spirit of freedom and the struggle to preserve it. Here, too, are many intriguing exhibits, among them segments of the Berlin Wall, stones from the Warsaw Ghetto, a bronze casting of a South African ballot box, a headless statue of Lenin (one of many that were pushed over and beheaded when the Soviet Union collapsed in 1991), and a bronze casting of Dr. Martin Luther King, Jr.'s Birmingham, Alabama, jail-cell door. The glass-and-steel Freedom Forum Journalists Memorial (honoring more than 900 journalists killed while on assignment) rises above the Potomac, offering views of the Washington Monument, the Lincoln and Jefferson Memorials, and the National Cathedral.

The Pentagon

Off I-395. ☎ **703/695-1776.** Free admission. Guided tours are given Mon–Fri, leaving every 30 minutes, from 9:30am to 3:30pm. Closed federal holidays and weekends. Metro: Pentagon.

This immense five-sided headquarters of the American military establishment was built during the early years of World War II. It's the world's largest office building, housing approximately 24,000 employees. For their convenience, it houses a complete indoor shopping mall, including two banks, a post office, Amtrak ticket office, beauty salon, dry cleaner, and more. It's a self-contained world. There are many mind-boggling statistics to underscore the vastness of the Pentagon—for example, the building contains enough phone cable to gird the globe three times!

You can take a free 75-minute **tour** of certain corridors, covering the distance of a mile. Departure is from the registration booth in the Concourse area at the Pentagon Metro entrance. During the tourist season, you can avoid a long wait in line by arriving by 9am, when the booth opens. Groups of 10 or more must make reservations.

The tour begins with an explanation of the Department of Defense hierarchy and a short introductory film about the development of the Pentagon. Then a military guide takes you around. You'll visit:

The **Air Force Art Collection,** which commemorates historical events involving the U.S. Air Force, including cartoons drawn by Walt Disney when he was an ambulance driver during World War I.

The **Air Force Executive Corridor,** where, as you might have guessed, air force heads have their offices.

The **POW Alcove,** hung with artists' conceptions of life in POW camps such as the "Hanoi Hilton."

The **Marine Corps Corridor,** with a small display, because the marines are actually headquartered in the Navy Annex a quarter of a mile away. Did you know the reason the marines are called "leathernecks" is that they used to wear leather collars to protect their necks from fatal sword blows?

The **Navy Executive Corridor,** lined with portraits of former secretaries and under secretaries of the Navy; glass cases display models of ships and submarines in the Navy's current fleet; the solid oak doors in this corridor are modeled after old ship captain's doors.

The **Army Executive Corridor,** or Marshall Corridor, named for Gen. George C. Marshall, the first military man to receive a Nobel Peace Prize (for the Marshall Plan that helped Europe recover after World War II). Displayed here are army command and divisional flags and 172 army campaign streamers dating from 1775 through the Gulf War.

The **Time-Life Art Collection Corridor.** During World War II *Time-Life* hired civilian artists to paint battle scenes at the front line. Most affecting is *Two-Thousand Yard Stare,* showing a soldier suffering from battle fatigue due to lack of food, sleep, and water.

Gen. Douglas MacArthur is honored in the **MacArthur Corridor;** his career spanned 52 years, during which he served in three wars under nine presidents.

The **Hall of Heroes** is where Medal of Honor recipients (3,408 to date) are commemorated. The medal is given out only during wartime and usually posthumously.

The role of women throughout U.S. armed services history is documented in **The Military Women's Corridor.**

The **Navaho Code Talkers Corridor** tells the story of the code language developed for military communications after the Japanese bombed Pearl Harbor during World War II. The U.S. military recruited the help of 400 Navahos, all Marines, to create a non-decipherable means of communication taken from the Navaho language.

State and territorial flags, from the first Union Jack to the 50-star flag of today, are displayed in the **Flag Corridor** where the tour concludes.

The best way to get to the Pentagon is via Metro's Blue or Yellow lines. If you must drive, call for directions.

10 Parks & Gardens

Like most cities, Washington intersperses manicured pockets of green between office buildings and traffic-laden streets. Unlike most cities, it's also extensively endowed with vast natural areas all centrally located within the District: thousands of parkland acres; two rivers; a 185-mile-long, tree-lined canalside trail; an untamed wilderness area; and a few thousand cherry trees. And there's much more just a stone's throw away.

GARDENS

Enid A. Haupt Garden

10th St. and Independence Ave. SW. ☎ **202/357-2700.** Free admission. Late May–Aug daily 7am–8pm; the rest of the year, daily 7am–5:45pm. Closed Dec 25. Metro: Smithsonian.

Named for its donor, a noted supporter of horticultural projects, this stunning garden presents elaborate flower beds and borders, plant-filled turn-of-the-century urns, 1870s cast-iron furnishings, and lush baskets hung from 19th-century–style lampposts. Although on ground level, it's really a rooftop garden above the subterranean Sackler and African Art Museums. A magnolia-lined parterre, framed by four floral swags, centers on a floral bed patterned after the rose window in the Commons of the Castle; it is composed of 30,000 green and yellow Alternanthera, supplemented by seasonal displays of spring pansies, begonias, or cabbage and kale. An "Island Garden" near the Sackler Gallery, entered via a 9-foot moongate, has benches backed by English boxwoods under the shade of weeping cherry trees; half-round pieces of granite in its still pool are meant to suggest ripples. A "Fountain Garden" outside the African Art Museum provides granite seating walls shaded by hawthorn trees, with tiny water channels fed by fountains and a waterfall or "chadar" inspired by the gardens of Shalimar. Three small terraces, shaded by black sour gum trees, are located near the Arts and Industries Building. And five majestic linden trees shade a seating area around the Downing Urn, a memorial to American landscapist Andrew Jackson Downing. Additional features include wisteria-covered dome-shaped trellises, clusters of trees (Zumi crabapples, ginkgoes, and American hollies), a weeping European beech, and rose gardens. Elaborate cast-iron carriage gates made according to a 19th-century design by James Renwick, flanked by four red sandstone pillars, have been installed at the Independence Avenue entrance to the garden.

✪ United States Botanic Garden

100 Maryland Ave. at First St., SW (at the east end of the Mall). ☎ **202/225-8333.** Free admission. Daily 9am–5pm. Metro: Federal Center SW.

Originally conceived by Washington, Jefferson, and Madison, and opened in 1820, the Botanic Garden is a lovely oasis. It's comprised of a series of connected glass-and-stone buildings and greenhouses (they call it a "living museum under glass") filled with pots of brightly colored flowers, rock beds of ferns, Spanish moss, palms, and shrubs. Tropical, subtropical, and desert plants highlight the collection. The Conservatory, inspired by 17th-century French orangeries, is entered via a room with two reflecting pool fountains under a skylight. Poinsettias bloom at Christmas, chrysanthemums in fall; spring is heralded by lilies, tulips, hyacinths, and daffodils; and a large collection of orchids is on display year-round. Of topical interest is the Dinosaur Garden of cycads (primitive conifers that resemble palms), ferns, mosses, and liverworts that existed in the Jurassic era, an age that predated flowering plants. The Summer Terrace, with umbrella tables amid plants and flower beds overlooking the Capitol's reflecting pool, is a lovely spot for a picnic lunch. The complex also includes the adjacent Bartholdi Park, about the size of a city block, with a stunning cast-iron classical fountain created by Frédéric Auguste Bartholdi, designer of the Statue of Liberty. Charming flower gardens bloom amid tall ornamental grasses here, benches are sheltered by vine-covered bowers, and a touch and fragrance garden contains such herbs as pineapple-scented sage. For information on special shows, tours, lectures, and classes call the above number.

United States National Arboretum

3501 New York Ave. NE. ☎ **202/245-2726.** Free admission. Daily 8am–5pm; bonsai collection 10am–3:30pm. Closed Dec 25. Metro: Stadium Armory, then take bus B2 to Bladensburg Rd. and R St. NE (or hop in a taxi; it's only a few dollars). Free parking.

A research and educational center focusing on a vast variety of landscape plants, the U.S. National Arboretum is a must-see for the horticulturally inclined. Its $9^1/2$ miles of paved roads meander through 444 hilly acres of azaleas (the most extensive plantings in the nation), magnolias, hollies, dwarf confers, and boxwoods. The highlight for me is the **National Bonsai and Penjing Museum,** which includes a Bicentennial gift from Japan of 53 beautiful miniature trees, some of them more than 3 centuries old. Each one is an exquisite work of art. The exhibit was augmented by a gift of 35 Chinese Penjing trees in 1986, and again in 1990 by the American Bonsai Collection of 56 North American plants; in 1993 a conservatory for tropical bonsai was erected. This area also includes a **Japanese Garden** and a garden of plants of American origin. The **Herbarium** contains 600,000 dried plants for reference purposes. The **Herb Garden,** another highlight, includes a historic rose garden (150 old-fashioned fragrant varieties), a contemporary interpretation of a 16th-century English-style "knot" garden, and 10 specialty gardens: a dye garden, a medicinal garden, and a culinary garden among them. Along Fern Valley Trail is the Franklin Tree, a species now extinct in the wild, discovered in 1765 by a botanist friend of Benjamin Franklin. And a magnificent sight is the arboretum's **acropolis,** 22 of the original U.S. Capitol columns designed by Benjamin Latrobe in a setting created by the noted English landscape artist Russell Page. The **American Friendship Garden** is a collection of ornamental grasses, reminiscent of prairie landscapes, and perennials, with brick walkways, terraces, and a statue of Demeter, the Greek goddess of agriculture; its colorful spring bulb plants comprise a wide variety of narcissi and irises enhanced by small flowering and fruiting trees and interesting shrubs. Carefully placed teak benches provide a place for quiet contemplation. This garden also features an extensive collection of perennials and bulb plants. And the **Asian Collections** in a landscaped valley include rare plants from China and Korea.

Magnolias and early bulbs bloom in late March or early April; azaleas, daffodils, and flowering cherry trees in mid-April; rhododendrons and peonies in May; day lilies and crape myrtles in summer. In autumn the arboretum is ablaze in reds and oranges as the leaves change color.

The arboretum offers frequent tours, lectures, and workshops (including bonsai classes), and a comprehensive guidebook is available in the gift shop.

PARKS
POTOMAC PARK

West and East Potomac Parks, their 720 riverside acres divided by the Tidal Basin, are most famous for their spring display of **cherry blossoms** and all the hoopla that goes with it.

West Potomac Park has 1,300 trees bordering the Tidal Basin, 10% of them Akebonos with delicate pink blossoms, the rest Yoshinos with white cloudlike flower clusters. It's the focal point of many of the week-long celebrations, which include the lighting of the 300-year-old **Japanese Stone Lantern** near Kutz Bridge, presented to the city by the governor of Tokyo in 1954. The trees bloom for a little less than 2 weeks beginning somewhere between March 20 and April 17; April 5 is the average date. See the calendar of events in chapter 2 for further details on cherry blossom events.

Though West Potomac Park gets more cherry blossom publicity, East Potomac Park has more trees (1,800 of them) and more varieties (11). It also has **picnic grounds, tennis courts,** three **golf courses,** a large **swimming pool,** and **biking** and **hiking** paths by the water, all of which are described in "Outdoor Activities," below.

West Potomac Park encompasses Constitution Gardens; the Vietnam, Korean, Lincoln, Jefferson, and FDR Memorials; a small island where ducks live; and the Reflecting Pool.

ROCK CREEK PARK

Created in 1890, **Rock Creek Park** was purchased by Congress for its "pleasant valleys and ravines, primeval forests and open fields, its running waters, its rocks clothed with rich ferns and mosses, its repose and tranquillity, its light and shade, its ever-varying shrubbery, its beautiful and extensive views." A 1,750-acre valley within the District of Columbia, extending 12 miles from the Potomac River to the Maryland border (another 2,700 acres), it's one of the biggest and finest city parks in the nation. Parts of it are still wild; it's not unusual to see a deer scurrying through the woods in more remote sections.

The park's offerings include the Carter Barron Amphitheater (see chapter 10), playgrounds, an extensive system of beautiful wooded hiking trails, and sports facilities, for which there are detailed listings in "Outdoor Activities," below. See also our entry in "More Museums," above, on the nearby formal gardens at Dumbarton Oaks, which include an Orangery, a 1000-bush Rose Garden, wisteria-covered arbors, herbaceous borders, groves of cherry trees, and magnolias.

For full information on the wide range of park programs and activities, visit the **Rock Creek Nature Center,** 5200 Glover Rd. NW (☎ **202/426-6829**), Wednesday to Sunday 9am to 5pm; or **Park Headquarters,** 3545 Williamsburg Rd. NW (☎ **202/282-1063**), Monday to Friday 7:45am to 4:15pm. The Nature Center itself is the scene of numerous activities, including weekend planetarium shows for kids (minimum age 4) and adults; nature films; crafts demonstrations; live animal demonstrations; and guided nature walks, plus a daily mix of lectures, films, and other events. A calendar is available on request. Self-guided nature trails begin here. All activities are free, but for planetarium shows you need to pick up tickets a half hour in advance. There are also nature exhibits on the premises. The Nature Center is closed on federal holidays.

At Tilden Street and Beach Drive, you can see a water-powered 19th-century gristmill grinding corn and wheat into flour (☎ **202/426-6908**). It's called **Pierce Mill** (a man named Isaac Pierce built it), and it's open to visitors Wednesday to Sunday 9am to 5pm. Pierce's old carriage house is today the **Art Barn** (☎ **202/244-2482**), where works of local artists are exhibited; it's open Thursday to Sunday 11am to 4:30pm (closed federal holidays and the month of August).

Call ☎ **202/673-7646** or 202/673-7647 for details, locations, and group reservations at any of the park's 30 **picnic areas,** some with fireplaces. A brochure available at Park Headquarters or the Nature Center also provides details on picnic locations.

Poetry readings and workshops are held during the summer at Miller's cabin, the one-time residence of High Sierra poet Joaquin Miller, Beach Drive north of Military Road. Call ☎ **202/426-6829** for information.

There's convenient **free parking** throughout the park. To get to the Nature Center by public transport, take the Metro to Friendship Heights and transfer to an E2 or E3 bus to Military Road and Oregon Avenue/Glover Road.

THEODORE ROOSEVELT ISLAND

A serene 88-acre wilderness preserve, Theodore Roosevelt Island is a memorial to our 26th president, in recognition of his contributions to conservation. An outdoor enthusiast and expert field naturalist, Roosevelt once threw away a prepared speech and roared, "I hate a man who would skin the land!" During his administration, 150 million acres of forest land were reserved, and five national parks, 51 bird refuges, and four game refuges were created.

Theodore Roosevelt Island was inhabited by Native American tribes for centuries before the arrival of English explorers in the 1600s. Over the years, it passed through many owners before becoming what it is today, an island preserve of swamp, marsh, and upland forest that's a haven for rabbits, chipmunks, great owls, fox, muskrat, turtles, and groundhogs. It's a complex ecosystem in which cattails, arrow arum, and pickerelweed growing in the marshes create a hospitable habitat for abundant bird life. And willow, ash, and maple trees rooted on the mudflats create the swamp environment favored by the raccoon in its search for crayfish. You can observe these flora and fauna in their natural environs on 2$\frac{1}{2}$ miles of foot trails.

In the northern center of the island, overlooking an oval terrace encircled by a water-filled moat, stands a 17-foot bronze statue of Roosevelt. From the terrace rise four 21-foot granite tablets inscribed with these tenets of his philosophy: "There are no words that can tell the hidden spirit of the wilderness, that can reveal its mystery, its melancholy, and its charm" and "The Nation behaves well if it treats the natural resources as assets which it must turn over to the next generation increased and not impaired in value."

To get to the island, take the George Washington Memorial Parkway exit north from the Theodore Roosevelt Bridge. The **parking** area is accessible only from the northbound lane; from there, a pedestrian bridge connects the island with the Virginia shore. You can also rent a canoe at **Thompson's Boat Center** (see "Outdoor Activities," below) and paddle over, walk across the pedestrian bridge at Rosslyn Circle, 2 blocks from the Rosslyn Metro station, or take the Washington Water Bus to and from the island (see "Organized Tours," below). **Picnicking** is permitted on the grounds near the memorial.

For further information, contact the **District Ranger,** Theodore Roosevelt Island, George Washington Memorial Parkway, c/o Turkey Run Park, McLean, VA 22101 (☎ **703/285-2598;** fax 703/285-2398).

CANAL ACTIVITIES

One of the great joys of living in Washington is the **C&O Canal** and its unspoiled 184¹/₂-mile towpath. One leaves urban cares and stresses behind while hiking, strolling, jogging, cycling, or boating in this lush, natural setting of ancient oaks and red maples, giant sycamores, willows, and wildflowers. However, it wasn't always just a leisure spot for city people. It was built in the 1800s, when water routes were considered vital to transportation. Even before it was completed, the B&O Railroad, which was constructed at about the same time and along the same route, had begun to render it obsolete. Today, perhaps, it serves an even more important purpose as a cherished urban refuge.

Headquarters for canal activities is the **Office of the Superintendent,** C&O Canal National Historical Park, P.O. Box 4, Sharpsburg, MD 21782 (☎ **301/739-4200**). Another good source of information is the National Park Service office at **Great Falls Tavern Visitor Center,** 11710 MacArthur Blvd., Potomac, MD 20854 (☎ **301/299-3613**). At this 1831 tavern, you can see museum exhibits and a film about the canal; there's also a bookstore on the premises. And April to November, Wednesday to Sunday, the **Georgetown Information Center,** 1057 Thomas Jefferson St. NW (☎ **202/653-5844**), can also provide maps and information. Call ahead for hours at all the above.

Hiking any section of the flat dirt towpath or its more rugged side paths is a pleasure. There are **picnic tables,** some with fire grills, about every 5 miles beginning at Fletcher's Boat House (about 3.2 miles out of Georgetown) on the way to Cumberland. Enter the towpath in Georgetown below M Street via Thomas Jefferson Street. If you hike 14 miles, you'll reach **Great Falls,** a point where the Potomac becomes a stunning waterfall plunging 76 feet. Or drive to Great Falls Park on the Virginia side of the Potomac.

Stop at **Fletcher's Boat House,** described below in "Outdoor Activities," to rent **bikes** or **boats** or purchase bait and tackle (or a license) for **fishing.** A snack bar and picnic area are on the premises.

Much less strenuous than hiking is a **mule-drawn 19th-century canal boat trip** led by Park Service rangers in period dress. They regale passengers with canal legend and lore and sing period songs. These boats depart Wednesday through Sunday from mid-April to early November; departure times and tickets are available at the **Georgetown Information Center** (☎ **202/653-5844**) or the **Great Falls Tavern** (☎ **301/299-3613**). The fare is $4 for adults, $3.50 for children aged 3 to 13 and seniors over 62.

Call any of the above information numbers for details on riding, rock climbing, fishing, bird-watching, concerts, ranger-guided tours, ice skating, camping, and other canal activities, or consult "Outdoor Activities," below.

11 Especially for Kids

Visiting the capital with parents or classmates is an intrinsic part of American childhood. Washington is a great place for family vacations, but how much fun you have depends on your approach and planning. Let the kids help develop daily itineraries—it builds anticipation and enthusiasm.

The Friday "Weekend" section of the *Washington Post* lists numerous activities (mostly free) for kids: special museum events, children's theater, storytelling programs, puppet shows, video-game competitions, and so forth. Call the **Kennedy Center,** the **Lisner,** and **National Theatre** to find out about children's shows; see chapter 10 for details.

We've checked out hotels built with families in mind in chapter 5's "Family-Friendly Hotels"; that hotel pool may rescue your sanity for an hour or two.

Also consult the "Outdoor Activities" and "Organized Tours" sections below, which allow you to structure an afternoon outdoors or go on a special tour with your kids.

FAVORITE CHILDREN'S ATTRACTIONS

Check for special children's events at museum information desks when you enter. As noted within the listings for individual museums, some children's programs are also great fun for adults. I recommend the programs at the Corcoran Gallery of Art, the Folger Shakespeare Library, and the Sackler Gallery in particular. (The gift shops in most of these museums have wonderful toys and children's books.) Call ahead to find out which programs are running. Here's a run-down of the biggest kid-pleasers in town (for details, see the full entries earlier in this chapter):

National Air and Space Museum. Spectacular IMAX films (don't miss), planetarium shows, missiles, rockets, and a walk-through orbital workshop.

National Museum of Natural History. A Discovery Room just for youngsters, an insect zoo, shrunken heads, and dinosaurs.

National Museum of American History. The Foucault Pendulum, locomotives, Archie Bunker's chair, and an old-fashioned ice-cream parlor.

Federal Bureau of Investigation. Gangster memorabilia, crime-solving methods, espionage devices, and a sharpshooting demonstration.

Bureau of Engraving and Printing. Kids enjoy looking at immense piles of money as much as you do.

National Zoological Park. Kids always love a zoo, and this is an especially good one.

Ford's Theatre and Lincoln Museum and the **House Where Lincoln Died.** Booth's gun and diary, the clothes Lincoln was wearing the night he was assassinated, and other such grisly artifacts. Kids adore the whole business.

National Geographic Society's Explorers Hall. A moon rock, the egg of an extinct "elephant bird" (if hatched, it would weigh 1,000 pounds), numerous interactive videos. The magazine comes alive.

Washington Monument. Easy to get them up there, hard to get them down. If only they could use the steps, they'd be in heaven.

Lincoln Memorial. Kids know a lot about Lincoln and enjoy visiting his memorial. A special treat is visiting it after dark (the same goes for the Washington Monument and Jefferson Memorial).

National Archives. See the original Declaration of Independence, Constitution, and Bill of Rights.

White House, Capitol, and **Supreme Court.** Kids enjoy learning how our government works.

National Postal Museum. The interactive exhibits and the manageable size of the museum make this one easy on everyone. Plus, it's in the same building as a restaurant and across the street from Union Station, with its shops, eateries, and Metro station.

12　Organized Tours

If you have the time and the inclination, start your sightseeing with an organized tour.

BY BUS

The **Gray Line** (☎ **202/289-1995**) offers a variety of tours, among them: "Washington After Dark" (3 hours; $24 per adult, $12 per child), focusing on night-lit national monuments and federal buildings; the "Washington, D.C., All-Day Combination Tour" ($42 per adult, $21 per child), which includes major Washington sights plus Arlington National Cemetery, Mount Vernon, and Alexandria; and the full-day "Interiors of Public Buildings" ($36 per adult, $18 per child), which covers Ford's Theatre, the Jefferson Memorial, the Museum of American History, the Capitol, the Supreme Court, the National Air and Space Museum, and the National Archives. There are also trips as far afield as Colonial Williamsburg ($64 per adult, $54 per child), Harper's Ferry ($45 per adult, $30 per child), Gettysburg ($45 per adult, $30 per child), and Charlottesville ($64 per adult, $54 per child). Tours depart from Gray Line's Union Station terminal, with pickups at most major hotels. Headsets and tour tapes in foreign languages are available for certain afternoon tours. Gray Line also offers multilingual tours, at $30 per adult, $15 per child.

A local company, **All About Town,** 519 6th St. NW (☎ **202/393-3696;** fax 202/393-2006), offers a similar range of tours at rates ranging from $22 to $66 per adult. Pickup is offered at major hotels.

Consider, too, **Tourmobile** and **Old Town Trolley** tours (see "Getting Around" in chapter 4 for details).

BY BOAT

Since Washington is a river city, why not see it by boat? Potomac cruises allow sweeping vistas of the monuments and memorials, Georgetown, the Kennedy Center, and other Washington sights. Read the information carefully, since not all boat cruises offer guided tours. For instance, *The Dandy,* the *Spirit of Washington,* and *Odyssey III* are restaurants that glide past the sites without informing you about them and the **Water Bus** simply transports you to different locations.

Here's a listing of boats, some of which leave from the Washington waterfront and some from Old Town Alexandria:

Spirit of Washington Cruises, Pier 4 at 6th and Water streets SW (☎ **202/554-8000**), offers a variety of trips daily from early March through October, including evening dinner, lunch and brunch, and moonlight dance cruises, as well as a half-day excursion to Mount Vernon and back. Lunch and dinner cruises include a 20-minute high-energy musical revue. Prices range from $23.50 for a sightseeing (no meals) excursion to Mount Vernon, which takes $5^{1}/_{2}$ hours in all, including a 2-hour tour break, to $65.30 for a Friday or Saturday dinner cruise, drinks not included. Call to make reservations in advance.

The *Spirit of Washington* is a luxury harbor cruise ship with climate-controlled, carpeted decks and huge panoramic windows designed for sightseeing. There are three well-stocked bars on board. Mount Vernon cruises are aboard an equally luxurious sister ship, the *Potomac Spirit.* You board both ships at the Washington waterfront, pier 4, at 6th and Water streets SW.

Potomac Party Cruises (☎ 703/683-6076) has been operating for about 20 years. Its boat, *The Dandy,* is a climate-controlled, all-weather, glassed-in, floating restaurant that operates year-round. Lunch, evening dinner/dance, and special charter cruises are available daily. You board *The Dandy* in Old Town Alexandria, the Prince Street pier, between Duke and King streets. Trips range from $31.75 for a $2^{1}/_{2}$-hour weekday lunch cruise to $70.82 for a 3-hour Saturday dinner cruise, drinks not included.

Odyssey III (☎ 202/488-6010) is Washington's newest boat and was designed specifically to glide under the bridges that cross the Potomac. The boat looks like a glass bullet, with its snub-nosed port and streamlined, 240-foot-long glass body. The wraparound see-through walls and ceiling allow for great views. Like *The Dandy,* the *Odyssey* operates all year. You board the *Odyssey* at the Gangplank Marina, on Washington's waterfront, at 6th and Water streets SW. Cruises available include lunch, Sunday brunch, and dinner excursions with live entertainment provided during each cruise. It costs $38.40 for a 2-hour weekday lunch cruise and $99.84 for a 3-hour Saturday dinner cruise, drinks excluded.

The **Potomac Riverboat Company** (☎ 703/548-9000) offers two narrated sightseeing tours April through October: aboard *The Matthew Hayes* on a 90-minute tour past Washington monuments and memorials, and aboard *The Admiral Tilp* on a 40-minute trip to Mount Vernon, where you hop off and re-board after you've toured the estate. You board the riverboats at the pier behind the Torpedo Factory in Old Town Alexandria, at the foot of King Street. *Matthew Hayes* tickets are $14 for adults, $12 for senior citizens, and $6 for children ages 2 to 12; *Admiral Tilp* tickets are $7 for adults, $6 for senior citizens, and $4 for children ages 2 to 12. A concession stand selling light refreshments and beverages is open during the cruises.

The **Capitol River Cruise's** *Nightingale II* (☎ 800/405-5511 or 301/460-7447) is a historic 65-foot steel riverboat that can accommodate up to 90 people. The *Nightingale II*'s narrated jaunts depart Georgetown's Washington Harbour every hour on the hour, from noon until 8pm weekdays and 9pm weekends, April through October. This is a 50-minute narrated tour past the monuments and memorials as you head to National Airport and back. A snack bar on board sells light refreshments, beer, wine, and sodas; you're welcome to bring your own picnic aboard. The price is $10 per adult, $5 per child ages 3 to 12.

Finally, there's **Washington Water Bus** (☎ 800/288-7925 or 202/554-2052), not an organized tour vessel, really, but a form of transportation to different parts of the city and some of the monuments. The water buses are electric boats on the Potomac that pick up and discharge passengers at points near the FDR and Jefferson Memorials, at Georgetown's Washington Harbour, and at Theodore Roosevelt Island. The season runs from about May through October, from 11am to 6pm daily, weather permitting. You purchase your tickets when you board: a $12 all-day pass, $7 roundtrip pass, or a $5 one-way pass; children's tickets are half-price.

A BOAT ON WHEELS

A company called **DC Ducks** (☎ **202/966-3825**) features unique land and water tours of Washington aboard the red, white, and blue DUKW, an amphibious army vehicle (boat with wheels) from World War II that accommodates 30 passengers. Ninety-minute guided tours aboard the open-air canopied craft include a land portion taking in major sights—the Capitol, Lincoln Memorial, Washington Monument, the White House, and Smithsonian museums—and a 30-minute Potomac cruise. Tickets can be purchased inside Union Station, at the information desk; you board the vehicle just outside the main entrance to Union Station. There are departures daily during tour season (April to November); call for hours. Tickets cost $20 for adults, $10 for children 5 to 12, under 5 free.

BIKE TOURS

Bike the Sites, Inc. (☎ **202/966-8662**) offers a more active way to see Washington. The company has designed four different biking tours of the city, including an Early Bird Fun Ride, which is a 1-hour, moderately paced ride and costs $25 per person, and the Capital Sites Ride, which takes 3 hours, covers many sites along a 10-mile stretch, and costs $35 per person. Bike the Sites provides you with a 21-speed Trek Hybrid bicycle fitted to your size, bike helmet, handlebar bag, water bottle, light snack, and two guides to lead the ride. Guides impart historical and anecdotal information as you go. The company will customize bike rides to suit your tour specifications.

13 Outdoor Activities

BICYCLING   Both **Fletcher's Boat House** and **Thompson's Boat Center** (see "Boating," below) rent bikes, as does **Big Wheel Bikes,** 1034 33rd St. NW, right near the C&O Canal just below M Street (☎ **202/337-0254**). The rate is $5 per hour, with a 3-hour minimum, or $25 for the day. Hours are 10am to 6pm daily, and till 7pm weekdays from April to September. There's another Big Wheel shop on Capitol Hill at 315 7th St. SE (☎ **202/543-1600**); call for hours. Photo ID and a major credit card are required to rent bicycles.

On Fridays, the *Washington Post* "Weekend" section lists cycling trips. **Rock Creek Park** has an 11-mile paved bike route from the Lincoln Memorial through the park into Maryland. On weekends and holidays, a large part of it is closed to vehicular traffic. The C&O Canal and the Potomac Parks, described earlier in "Parks & Gardens," also have extended bike paths. A new 7-mile path, the Capital Crescent Trail, takes you from Georgetown to the suburb of Bethesda, MD, following a former railroad track that parallels the Potomac River part of the way and passes by old trestle bridges and pleasant residential neighborhoods.

BOATING   **Thompson's Boat Center,** 2900 Virginia Ave. at Rock Creek Parkway NW (☎ **202/333-4861** or 202/333-9543), rents canoes, kayaks, and rowing shells (recreational and racing). They also offer sculling and sweep-rowing lessons. Photo ID and a $20 deposit are required for rentals. They're open daily 6am to 8pm for boat rentals usually from early May to the end of September, but boats cannot be rented after 6pm. For **bike** rentals ($4 to $6 per hour, $15 to $22 for the day; $20 deposit required), the shop is open daily from 6am to 6pm March 1 through April 30 and October and November, 6am to 7pm May 1 through September 30.

Late March to mid-September, you can rent paddleboats on the north end of the Tidal Basin off Independence Avenue (☎ **202/479-2426**). You have the choice of renting a four-seater for $14 an hour or a two-seater for $7 an hour. Hours are 10am to about an hour before sunset daily.

Fletcher's Boat House, Reservoir and Canal roads (☎ 202/244-0461), is right on the C&O Canal, about a 3.2-mile wonderfully scenic walk from Georgetown. The same family has owned it since 1850! Open March to mid-November, daily 7:30am to dusk, Fletcher's rents canoes, rowboats, and bikes ($4 per hour, with a 2-hour minimum, or $12 for the day; you aren't allowed to leave the area of the canal), and sells fishing licenses, bait, and tackle. ID is required (a driver's license or major credit card). A snack bar and rest rooms here are welcome facilities. And there are picnic tables (with barbecue grills) overlooking the Potomac. You don't have to walk to Fletcher's; it's accessible by car (west on M Street to Canal Road) and has plenty of free parking.

CAMPING   There are numerous camping areas on the C&O Canal starting at Swain's Lock, 16 miles from Georgetown. Use of campsites is on a first-come, first-served basis.

FISHING   The Potomac River around Washington holds an abundant variety of fish, some 40 species, all perfectly safe to eat. Good fishing is possible from late February to November, but mid-March to June (spawning season) is peak. Perch and catfish are the most common catch, but during bass season a haul of 20 to 40 is not unusual. The Washington Channel offers good bass and carp fishing year-round.

To make sure you stay the within legal limit of local restrictions, pick up a free regulations book on fishing, available at **Fletcher's Boat House** (☎ 202/244-0461; details above). You can also obtain the **required fishing license** here. Cost for non-residents is $7.50 a year, $3 for a 14-day permit. Residents pay $5.

GOLF   There are dozens of public courses within easy driving distance of the D.C. area, but within the District itself East Potomac Park and Rock Creek Park have the only public courses. Fees run from $9 weekdays for 9 holes to $25 weekends for 18 holes. The 18-hole **Rock Creek Golf Course** and clubhouse, at 16th and Rittenhouse streets NW (☎ 202/882-7332), are open to the public daily year-round from dawn to dusk. You will find a snack bar on the premises, and you can rent clubs and carts.

East Potomac Park has one 18-hole, par-72 layout, and two 9-hole courses. For details, call ☎ 202/554-7660.

HIKING   Check the *Washington Post* Friday "Weekend" section for listings of hiking clubs; almost all are open to the public for a small fee. Be sure to inquire about the difficulty of any hike you plan to join and the speed with which the group proceeds; some hikes are fast-paced, allowing no time to smell the flowers.

There are numerous hiking paths. The **C&O Canal** offers 184 1/2 miles alone; it would be hard to find a more scenic setting than the 9 1/2 miles of road at the **arboretum** (see "Parks & Gardens," earlier in this chapter); **Theodore Roosevelt Island** has more than 88 wilderness acres to explore, including a 2 1/2-mile nature trail (short but rugged); and in **Rock Creek Park** there are 20 miles of hiking trails for which maps are available at the Visitor Information Center or Park Headquarters.

HORSEBACK RIDING   There are stables at the **Rock Creek Park Horse Center,** near the Nature Center on Glover Road NW (☎ 202/362-0117). One-hour guided **trail rides** are offered Tuesday through Thursday at 3pm, Saturday at noon and 1:30pm, Sunday at noon, 1:30pm, and 3pm; they cost $21. Call for reservations or information on riding instruction.

ICE SKATING If you have your own skates, you can skate on the **C&O Canal.** Call ☎ **301/299-3613** for information on ice conditions. Guest Services operates the **National Sculpture Garden Ice Rink** on the Mall at 7th Street and Constitution Avenue NW (☎ **202/371-5341**), the **Pershing Park** outdoor rink at 14th Street and Pennsylvania Avenue NW (☎ **202/737-6938**), and a huge hockey-size indoor facility, the **Fort Dupont Ice Arena,** at 3779 Ely Place SE, at Minnesota Avenue in Fort Dupont Park (☎ **202/581-0199**). All three offer skate rentals. The Sculpture Garden rink is open from late October to mid-March; the Pershing Park rink from about December (some years earlier) to February, weather permitting; Fort Dupont, from Labor Day to the end of April. Call for hours and admission prices.

JOGGING A **parcourse jogging path,** a gift from Perrier, opened in Rock Creek Park in 1978. Its 1¹/₂-mile oval route, beginning near the intersection of Calvert Street NW and Rock Creek Parkway (directly behind the Omni Shoreham Hotel), includes 18 calisthenics stations with instructions on prescribed exercises. There's another Perrier parcourse, with only four stations, at 16th and Kennedy streets NW. Other popular jogging areas are the **C&O Canal** and the **Mall.**

SWIMMING There are 44 swimming pools in the District run by the **D.C. Department of Recreation Aquatic Program** (☎ **202/576-6436**). They include the Capitol East Natatorium, an indoor/outdoor pool with sundeck and adjoining baby pool at 635 North Carolina Ave. SE (☎ **202/724-4495** or 202/724-4496); the outdoor pool in East Potomac Park (☎ **202/863-1309**); a large outdoor pool at 25th and N streets NW (☎ **202/727-3285**); and the Georgetown outdoor pool at 34th Street and Volta Place NW (☎ **202/282-2366**). Indoor pools are open year-round; outdoor pools, from mid-June to Labor Day. Thirty-nine of the District pools are free; the remaining five charge about $3 per adult, $1 per child. Call for hours and details on other locations.

TENNIS The **D.C. Department of Recreation and Parks,** 3149 16th St. NW, Washington, DC 20010 (☎ **202/673-7660** or 202/673-7665), maintains 55 outdoor tennis courts throughout the District (25 of them lit for night play). Court use is on a first-come, first-served basis. Call or write for a list of locations. Most courts are open year-round, weather permitting. At **Rock Creek,** there are 15 soft-surface (clay) and 10 hard-surface **tennis courts** (five enclosed for indoor play October to May 1) at 16th and Kennedy streets NW (☎ **202/722-5949**). April to mid-November you must make a reservation in person at Guest Services on the premises to use them. Six additional clay courts are located off Park Road just east of Pierce Mill. **East Potomac Park** has 24 tennis courts, including five indoors and three lit for night play (☎ **202/554-5962**). Fees vary with court surface and time of play; call for details.

14 Spectator Sports

For tickets to most events, call ☎ **800/551-SEAT** or 202/432-SEAT.

BASEBALL Lovely 48,000-seat **Camden Yards,** 333 W. Camden St. (between Howard and Conway streets), Baltimore (☎ **410/685-9800**), is home to the American League's **Baltimore Orioles.** Unlike recent ultramodern sports stadiums and ugly domes, Camden Yards is an old-fashioned ballpark, unafraid to incorporate features of its urban environment, such as the old B&O Railroad yards. A renovated brick warehouse serves as a striking visual backdrop beyond the right-field fence.

It was here on September 6, 1995, that Cal Ripken broke Lou Gehrig's legendary consecutive-game record; he took a lap around the field and was acclaimed with a 22-minute standing ovation and a citywide celebration.

Tickets (which range from $3 to $25) were once impossible to get; now it's possible but still tough, so call ☎ **800/551-SEAT** or 410/481-SEAT well in advance of your visit if you want to catch a game. There are usually scalpers outside the stadium before a game; use your judgment if you try this option. And there's a D.C. ticket office as well, at 914 17th St. NW (☎ **202/296-2473**). From Union Station in Washington, take a MARC train to Baltimore, which lets you off right at the ballpark. If you're driving, take I-95 north to Exit 53.

BASKETBALL   The **Washington Wizards** (née Bullets) and the **Georgetown Hoyas** play home games at the newly opened MCI Center (☎ **301/499-6300**), at 7th and F streets NW, adjacent to the Gallery Place Metro station in downtown Washington. Tickets cost $19 to $65 for the Wizards and $5 to $16 for the Hoyas.

FOOTBALL   The **Washington Redskins** played their last home game at RFK Stadium in 1997 and now play at the new Jack Kent Cooke Stadium, 1600 Raljohn Rd., Raljohn, MD 20785 (☎ **301/772-8800**); Metro: Addison Road, with bus shuttle to stadium. Tickets for Redskins games have been sold out since Lyndon Johnson was in the White House, so forget about getting your hands on one, unless you are a childhood FOB (Friend of Bill) or a major Republican Party donor.

The **Baltimore Ravens** (formerly the Cleveland Browns, until Art Modell moved the team and broke the city's heart) will play their home season in Baltimore's Memorial Stadium until a new facility is built for them. Tickets cost $17 to $75; for more information, call ☎ **410/261-3267.**

HOCKEY   Home ice for the NHL's **Washington Capitals** is now the MCI Center (☎ **301/499-6300**), at 7th and F streets NW, adjacent to the Gallery Place Metro station. Tickets cost $19 to $50.

SOCCER   **D.C. United,** the champions of Major League Soccer in 1996, play at RFK Stadium (☎ **202/547-9077**); Metro: Stadium-Armory. Tickets to their games range from $12 to $32. The **Washington Warthogs** indoor soccer team plays its games at the US Airways Arena (☎ **301/350-3400**) in Landover, MD, and charges $12.50 to $15.50.

8 In and Out of Washington's Historic Houses: Three Walking Tours

As you make your way to Washington's most popular tourist attractions, you may be strolling right by or near the city's historic houses, many of which are open to the public. Though lesser known, these houses offer intriguing and more personal perspectives on the past, by revealing the stories of those who lived there decades, even centuries ago. If you'd like a break from the crowds or a different way to view Washington, try one of the following walking tours.

Washington has scores of historic dwellings; this chapter covers those that are open for tours and are within walking distance of each other in neighborhoods that are pleasant to roam. The Dupont Circle and Georgetown circuits take you along some of the city's quainter, less-traveled streets.

All three neighborhoods border each other; you can follow a tour as outlined or contrive your own to encompass, say, all three sites in my White House area tour followed by two Dupont Circle houses.

Whether you follow my jaunts or design one of your own, you need to keep certain things in mind. Historic houses keep their own time and schedules—some have posted, docent-guided tour times and keep to them; some allow walk-in, self-guided tours; and some conduct tours as people arrive. Docents at historic houses have been known to get so carried away in their narration (staff are often volunteers who work there out of love for history) that they lose track of time. If you really want to visit all of the places on a particular tour, keep your watch handy.

WALKING TOUR 1
Dupont Circle's Historic Homes

Start: 1307 New Hampshire Ave. NW (Dupont Circle Metro station).

Finish: 2320 S St. NW (Dupont Circle Metro station).

Time: Approximately 4 to 5 hours, including tours and breaks.

Best Times: If you want to see all the houses, you should start mid-morning, Wednesday through Saturday.

Worst Times: Before 10am, in late afternoon, and Sunday through Tuesday, when the houses are closed or getting ready to close.

The neighborhood you traverse in this tour gives you a good look at cosmopolitan Washington. At its center is Massachusetts Avenue, the main thoroughfare known as "Embassy Row" because of the number of embassies located along the avenue and on side streets. Many of the embassies are in magnificent mansions built in the early part of the 20th century for the city's wealthy, so it is a treat to stroll here. The historic houses you visit were built generally around the same time. As you walk around this neighborhood, you will see people from all over the world, dressed in the clothes of their countries and speaking scores of languages.

From the Dupont Circle Metro station, 19th Street exit, cross 19th Street, continue around the circle to New Hampshire Avenue, and turn left. Follow New Hampshire Avenue to its juncture with 20th Street. Here is the:

1. **Heurich House Museum,** 1307 New Hampshire Ave. NW (☎ **202/785-2068**). This four-story, brownstone and brick, turreted Victorian castle was built as a residence in 1892 for wealthy German businessman and brewer Christian Heurich and his family. (Heurich's grandson, Gary, revived the business in 1986; you may notice his Foggy Bottom Ale delivery trucks around Washington). Old Heurich was a character, as you'll learn by touring the first and third floors of the mansion. He was cautious; he constructed the house of poured concrete, making it the city's first fireproof dwelling. He incorporated his favorite drinking mottoes into the murals painted on the walls of his basement Bierstube (tavern room): "He who has never been drunk is not a brave man." and, "There is room in the smallest chamber for the biggest hangover."

But it is his heavyhanded decorating, reflective of Victorian times and his own indomitable personality, that causes the jaw to drop. Elaborate embellishments adorn every conceivable space throughout the 31 principal rooms. Allegorical paintings cover the ceilings, decorative brass grilles hide the radiators, intricately carved wood panels encase the fireplaces, gilding gelds the bathroom tiles. The foyer recalls a medieval castle, with its standing coat of armor, mosaic floor and silvered plaster medallions on the stucco walls. A Victorian garden (open to picnickers) and brick patio lie off the back of the house. The mansion serves as headquarters for the Historical Society of Washington, D.C., whose offices and library are on the second and third floors.

Tours are walk-in, self-guided, Wednesday through Saturday, 10am to 4pm. Call in advance if you'd like a guided tour. The gift shop features Victorian and turn-of-the-century items, as well as jewelry and decorative arts crafted by local artisans. Admission is $3 for adults, $1.50 for seniors and students, free for children under 6. Closed federal holidays.

Is it too soon for lunch? Cross New Hampshire Avenue at the corner to reach 20th Street, then cross 20th Street. Walk up 20th Street to P Street NW and turn left. Walk 1 block down P Street, cross 21st Street and enter the restaurant at the corner of P and 21st streets.

☕ **TAKE A BREAK**   **BeDuCi,** 2100 P St. NW (☎ **202/223-3824**), serves Mediterranean cuisine (a range of French, Spanish, Moroccan, and Italian dishes) in a sunporch-fronted dining room that opens to the outdoors in warm weather. See chapter 6 for a full listing.

Back outside, return to the corner of 21st and P streets, cross P Street and walk up 21st Street to Massachusetts Avenue NW. Turn left at the Luxury Collection Hotel, Washington, D.C., dodging the limousines pulling into the driveway, and proceed to the "house" next door.

Walking Tour 1—Dupont Circle's Historic Homes

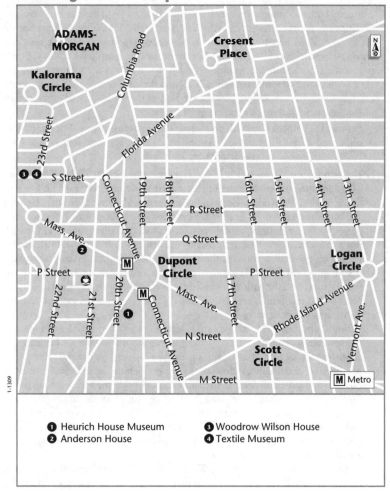

- **1** Heurich House Museum
- **2** Anderson House
- **3** Woodrow Wilson House
- **4** Textile Museum

2. Anderson House, 2118 Massachusetts Ave. NW (☎ **202/785-2040**). It took 3 years, from 1902 to 1905, to build this palatial beaux-arts mansion, which, mind you, was only the *winter* residence of Larz Anderson and his heiress wife, Isabel. Isabel's $17 million inheritance from her grandfather, shipping magnate William Fletcher Weld, helped pay for Anderson House. Anderson was a career diplomat who served as ambassador to Japan in 1912 and 1913. In 1937, following her husband's death, Isabel gave the house and much of its original art and furnishings to the Society of the Cincinnati, to which Larz had belonged. Anderson was descended from an original member of this society founded in 1783 by Continental officers who had served in the American Revolution. (George Washington was its president-general from 1783 until 1799.) The mansion's 50 rooms stagger the imagination, varying from an immense ballroom with a 30-foot-high coffered ceiling to ornate, Louis XV–style French and English parlors embellished in 23-karat gold leaf. Anderson belongings are on display throughout, including Belgian and Flemish tapestries, 17th-century wood choir stalls from Naples, Asian and European paintings and antiquities—and more. A solarium (with gilt-accented door frames and ceilings) leads through French doors to a lovely courtyard-garden. Open by appointment is the Society of the Cincinnati Library, which houses more than 40,000 works focused on the American Revolution and the "art of war" in the 18th century.

Tours are walk-in, self-guided, Tuesday through Saturday, 1 to 4pm. Admission is free. Closed on national holidays. Call about its free concert series.

From Anderson House, turn left on Massachusetts Avenue NW, away from Dupont Circle, crossing Q Street, proceeding further down Massachusetts Avenue, where you cross Florida Avenue and then cross Massachusetts Avenue to the other side. Walk up Massachusetts Avenue and around Sheridan Circle to 24th Street and turn right. Go half a block to S Street NW, turn right, and walk a few yards to the:

3. Woodrow Wilson House, 2340 S St. NW (☎ 202/387-4062). Woodrow Wilson wasn't just our 28th president, he was a besotted bean who married his second wife, Edith Galt, after a whirlwind courtship. He was also a prolific writer, whose 19 books include a popular biography of George Washington. You learn about the personal as well as the political sides of Wilson's life during a tour of this house.

Wilson served two terms in the White House, then retired to this Georgian Revival home in 1921 with Edith, whom he had courted and married while in the White House, following the death of his first wife. During 45-minute tours given continuously during the day, docents describe Wilson's career and character: He had been a mediocre lawyer, but successful president of Princeton University, then governor of New Jersey, before becoming president. You are reminded that this is the president best remembered for his international outlook, and that his efforts to promote the League of Nations contributed to a stroke and declining health until his death in 1924.

The house is preserved much as it was when the Wilsons lived here in the 1920s. The drawing room is furnished with wedding presents, including a Gobelin tapestry given to the couple by the French ambassador; it was at the drawing room window where Wilson stood to acknowledge the crowd that had gathered in the street below to honor him on Armistice Day in 1923. Among the items you see in the family room/library are Wilson's desk chair from the White House and the screen that the Wilsons pulled down to watch silent movies by Charlie Chaplin (their favorite) and other stars. As you stand in the dining room, the docent tells you that Wilson insisted that guests at dinner "wear black tie and refrain from discussing religion and politics."

Edith died in 1961, bequeathing the house and its belongings to the National Trust for Historic Preservation. The Woodrow Wilson House is the only presidential museum in the capital. The house is open Tuesday to Sunday, 10am to 4pm, and charges admission of $5 for adults, $4 for seniors, $2.50 for students, free for children age 7 and under. Gift shop. Closed on federal holidays. Call about special events and exhibits.

Now turn right from the entrance and go right next door to:

4. The Textile Museum, 2320 S St. NW (☎ **202/667-0441**). The Textile Museum occupies two buildings, the first designed by John Russell Pope, architect of the Jefferson Memorial and the West Wing of the National Gallery, and the adjoining structure designed by Waddy B. Wood, architect for the Woodrow Wilson House.

A man named George Hewitt Myers founded The Textile Museum in 1925, in what was then his home (one of several). Myers was a wealthy man, the founder of Merganthaler Linotype and of the investment firm, Y.E. Booker & Co., still in operation in Baltimore. His interest in textiles had begun in 1896, when Myers purchased an Oriental rug for his Yale dormitory room. By 1925, his collection had grown to include 275 rugs and 60 related textiles. When he died in 1957, Myers's collection encompassed not only Oriental carpets, but textiles from Africa, Asia, and Latin America.

Today, The Textile Museum holds more than 15,500 textiles and carpets, dating as far back as 3,000 B.C. They include Turkish rugs and Peruvian tunics, Suzani embroideries from central Asia, and tapestries from Egypt. Not all are on display, of course. The museum rotates exhibits from its permanent collection in high-ceilinged rooms that are dimly lit to preserve the fabrics. One of the exhibit areas holds a computer loaded with design software that visitors, especially kids, are invited to use. Friendly interns assist.

Introductory tours take place Wednesday, Saturday, and Sunday at 2pm, September through May. Or you can call 2 weeks in advance to reserve a spot on a docent-led tour. You may also walk in and tour the place on your own: The museum is open year-round Monday through Saturday, 10am to 5pm, Sunday 1 to 5pm. Closed on federal holidays and Christmas Eve. Donation suggested of $5. Call about special lectures and workshops. Poke around the garden and the intriguing giftshop.

To get back to the Metro, return to Massachusetts Avenue, turn left, and follow the avenue back around Sheridan Circle, keeping to the odd-numbered side of the street until it meets 20th Street, where you'll find the entrance to the Dupont Circle Metro station.

WALKING TOUR 2
Historic Homes Near the White House

Start: 748 Jackson Place NW (corner of H Street NW on Lafayette Square; Farragut West Metro station).
Finish: 2017 I St. NW (Foggy Bottom Metro station).
Time: Approximately 2¹/₂ hours.
Best Times: If you want to see all the houses, you should start mid-morning, Tuesday through Sunday.
Worst Times: Before 10am or in late afternoon, or Monday, when the houses are closed or getting ready to close.

This walking tour centers on another main thoroughfare, Pennsylvania Avenue, best known as the street on which the president lives. You'll walk by the White House on this tour, but not go in. (See chapter 7 for information about touring the White House.) Each of the houses on this tour lies in close proximity to it, so it makes sense that their individual histories intertwine with particular presidencies. As you make your way to these historic landmarks, you'll be mingling with the many office workers, college students, and administrators who make this part of town bustle during the day.

From the Farragut West Metro station, 17th Street exit, cross I Street and walk down 17th Street, passing H Street and turning left, continuing until you reach the gift shop entrance at 748 Jackson Place NW, where you purchase your ticket and begin your tour.

1. **Decatur House,** 748 Jackson Place NW, on Lafayette Square (☎ **202/842-0920**). Noted architect Benjamin Latrobe (the Capitol, the White House) designed this Federal-style brick town house in 1817 for Commodore Stephen Decatur, famous War of 1812 naval hero. Decatur and his wife Susan established themselves as gracious hosts in the 14 short months they lived here. Two days after hosting a ball for President James Monroe's daughter, Marie, in March 1820, Decatur was killed in a "gentleman's duel" by his former mentor, James Barron, who blamed Decatur for his 5-year suspension from the Navy following a court-martial in which Decatur had played an active role. Susan moved to Georgetown.

Other distinguished occupants have been Henry Clay (while secretary of state), Martin Van Buren, and George M. Dallas (vice president from 1845 to 1849). Since 1956, the National Trust for Historic Preservation has owned and maintained Decatur House, converting the house into a museum and bookstore.

Thirty-minute tours given every hour and half-hour inform you about the house's history, architecture, and interior design. Ground floor rooms reflect Federal period decorating and lifestyles. For example, a room on the first floor appears as it might have in Decatur's day, as an office, with naval war scenes on the wall, books from the period on the shelves, and maps showing Decatur's investments around the city; the desk and chair you see were Decatur's. Upstairs decor reflects the life of the last occupant, Marie Oge Beale (Mrs. Truxton Beale) during the year of 1944, telling her story as a world traveler, early preservationist, well-known hostess, and writer. Mr. Beale came from a prominent California family, which may explain the California state seal inlaid in the north drawing room's parquet floor.

Decatur House is open for guided tours only, Tuesday through Friday, 10am to 3pm; Saturday and Sunday, noon to 4pm. Admission of $4 for adults, $2.50 for students and senior citizens. Closed Thanksgiving, Christmas, and New Year's. Annual special events include a Mother's Day Open House in May and a Nineteenth Century Christmas for 3 weeks in December.

Your tour puts you back on H Street, where you want to turn right, walk to the corner, and turn right again. You are walking past Decatur House now, facing the White House. Your next stop will be The Octagon, but on your way, you pass:

2. **Lafayette Square,** a small public park, known best today as a gathering spot for protestors and as a favorite resting place for homeless people. Originally an open-air market and military encampment, the square takes its name from the day in 1824 when Lafayette visited Washington and crowds swarmed the park for a sight of him. But it's General Andrew Jackson whose statue centers the park—his was America's first equestrian statue when erected in 1853. Elsewhere in the square are memorials to those from other countries who helped the colonists fight in the War for Independence, the Marquis de Lafayette, Steuben (the Prussian drillmaster of Valley Forge), and Kosciuszko (Polish soldier and statesman) among them.

When you reach the corner, you've arrived at:

3. **Pennsylvania Avenue,** the 2-block section that's been closed to traffic since 1995 in an effort to thwart terrorists and crazies from getting near the president. The closing of the street has been controversial, but one good result (aside from ensuring the safety of the president, that is) is that the street has turned into a festive promenade area, especially in warm weather, a place where in-line skaters and bicyclists whiz around and Frisbee games erupt impromptu. Hovering over Pennsylvania Avenue is:

4. **The White House,** which we cover fully in chapter 7. Now turn right down Pennsylvania Avenue and pass:

Walking Tour 2—Historic Homes Near the White House

1. Decatur House
2. Lafayette Square
3. Pennnsylvania Ave.
4. The White House
5. Renwick Gallery
6. Old Executive Office Building
7. Octagon
8. Arts Club of Washington

5. The Renwick Gallery of the National Museum of American Art, where it meets 17th Street NW. See chapter 7 for details about this museum, which specializes in American crafts. Turn left on 17th Street, where you walk right by the:

6. Old Executive Office Building (as opposed to the New Executive Office Building, located behind the Renwick Gallery). Known as the "OEB" by insiders who work in or with the Executive Office of the President, this huge, ornately styled building originally was called the State, War and Navy Building. It was constructed between 1872 and 1888; on completion, it was the largest office building in the world. During the Iran-Contra scandal of the Reagan presidency, the OEB became famous as the site of document shredding by Colonel Oliver North and his secretary Fawn Hall.

Cross 17th Street, walk a couple of blocks to New York Avenue, and turn right. Follow New York Avenue to 18th Street and you have found:

7. The Octagon, 1799 New York Ave. NW (☎ 202/638-3221). One of the oldest houses in Washington, The Octagon is also one of the most interesting. The 1801 building served as a temporary president's home for James and Dolley Madison after the British burned the White House in 1814. President Madison sat at the circular table in the upstairs circular room and signed the Treaty of Ghent, ending the War of 1812. The Octagon, which has only six sides, was designed by Dr. William Thornton, first architect of the U.S. Capitol (and Tudor Place, see below), and completed in 1801. Built for the wealthy Tayloe family, it is an

Pennsylvania Avenue: A Street with a Past

Pennsylvania Avenue is neither the city's oldest street (that honor goes to the creatively named Water Street SW, a fixture on the waterfront before the American Revolution), nor is it the city's longest (Massachusetts Avenue is, intersecting the Northwest, Southeast, and Northeast quadrants). Pennsylvania Avenue *is*, undoubtedly, the capital's, not to say the country's, best known thoroughfare. This is the street on which the president of the United States lives, the grand boulevard that connects the White House with the Capitol.

For all its renown, there's a lot even the natives don't know about Pennsylvania Avenue. Ask a Washingtonian how one of the most important streets in the world came to be named for the state of Pennsylvania, and you're likely to receive a blank look.

In 1790, Congress designated land on the Maryland side of the Potomac River as the permanent site of the nation's capital, previously located in Philadelphia. The naming of Washington's main street "Pennsylvania" was supposed to make up for the transfer of the capital, albeit this illustrious roadway was really nothing more than a muddy morass at the time.

Some other facts about Pennsylvania Avenue:

- The first president to stage an inaugural parade down the avenue was Thomas Jefferson.
- The only president to defy Jefferson's tradition was Franklin D. Roosevelt, whose parades streamed along Constitution Avenue.
- The longest parade on Pennsylvania Avenue began May 23, 1865, and continued for 2 full days and nights, celebrating the end of the Civil War. To the tune of fife and drums, more than 200,000 troops marched down the avenue.
- Pennsylvania Avenue grew grandly for decades but began a decline in the 20th century occasioned by the uptown exodus of hotels and restaurants. By 1961, the street had so deteriorated that President Kennedy was moved to recommend plans to revitalize this artery and neighborhood, following his inaugural ride down Pennsylvania Avenue. These proposals eventually led Congress in 1972 to institute the Pennsylvania Avenue Redevelopment Corporation, to oversee the preservation and development of the area. The PARC was abolished in April 1996 because it had fulfilled its purpose.

exquisite example of Federal-period architecture, with unusual features: round rooms, an oval shaped staircase that curves gracefully up three floors, hidden doors, and triangular chambers.

Tours are guided and last about 30 minutes, during which you learn more about the house and about the Tayloes, their slaves, and life in the 1800s. The museum hosts changing exhibits, usually on an architectural theme, in two upstairs rooms and has a permanent exhibit in the English basement, where you learn about the "downstairs" side of life in the 1800s—these were the servants' quarters and work rooms. The American Architectural Foundation administers The Octagon, which is open Tuesday through Sunday, 10am to 4pm. Admission is $3 for adults, $1.50 for students and senior citizens.

From The Octagon, head up 18th Street to Pennsylvania Avenue and turn left. Cross Pennsylvania Avenue at 20th Street, proceed 1 block to I Street, and turn left again. In the middle of the block is the:

8. Arts Club of Washington, 2017 I St. NW (☎ **202/331-7282**). You will have to ring the buzzer here for entry, and then you'll find you're on your own to wander. Chances are, too, that a luncheon or some other soiree will be in full swing in the first floor rooms. The Arts Club, founded in 1916 to promote the arts in greater Washington, occupies this town house duplex and allows members and others to rent its facilities for special events.

But the reason the site is historic is because this is where James Monroe lived for the first 6 months of his presidency, while the White House was being rebuilt after being torched by the British in the War of 1812. Monroe's inaugural ball was held here. The rear wing of the structure dates from 1802, the front portion from 1805.

It's a little bit funky now, as you'll see if you explore a bit: Flights of stairs take you into little alcoves and hidden wings. Art by local artists hangs on the walls throughout the adjoining buildings.

The Arts Club is free and open to the public Tuesday and Thursday 10am to 5pm, Wednesday and Friday 2 to 5pm, Saturday 10am to 2pm, and Sunday 1 to 5pm. Call in advance if you'd like a guided tour of the club.

☕ **WINDING DOWN   Kinkead's,** 2000 Pennsylvania Ave. NW (☎ **202/ 296-7700**). There are plenty of sandwich shops in this part of town, but if you want to eat at one of Washington's best restaurants, try Kinkead's. Its attractive, multileveled dining room serves wondrous seafood dishes. Because the restaurant is so popular, consider playing it safe and reserving in advance. See chapter 6 for details.

From Kinkead's, turn left outside the restaurant and walk to the end of the block to reach 21st Street. Turn left and walk the few steps to I Street. Cross 21st Street and follow I Street to the Foggy Bottom Metro station and 23rd and I streets NW.

WALKING TOUR 3
Georgetown's Historic Homes

Start: 3051 M St. NW (Foggy Bottom Metro station).
Finish: 1703 32nd St. NW (Dupont Circle Metro station).
Time: Approximately 5 hours, including tours and breaks.
Best Times: If you want to see all the houses, you should start first thing in the morning, Wednesday through Saturday, because two of the houses close after the early part of the afternoon.
Worst Times: In August, when Dumbarton House is closed, and in late afternoon, when two of the houses are closed.

The Georgetown famous for its shops, restaurants, and bars is not the Georgetown you'll see on this walking tour. Instead, the circuit will take you along quiet streets lined with charming houses and stately trees that remind you of the town's age and history. The town of George, comprising 60 acres and named for the king of England, was officially established in 1751. It assumed new importance in 1790 when George Washington specified a nearby site on the Potomac River for America's new capital city. It was incorporated into the District of Columbia in 1871.

From the Foggy Bottom Metro station, walk up 23rd Street NW to Washington Circle, and go left around the circle to Pennsylvania Avenue. Continue on Pennsylvania Avenue until you reach M Street NW.

TAKE A BREAK **Seasons,** Four Seasons Hotel, 2800 Pennsylvania Ave. NW (☎ **202/342-0810**). Before you get walking, give yourself something to walk off. Breakfast here is sumptuous but pricey: $7.75 for blueberry pancakes, $11.50 for continental breakfast, and so on. For a quicker, cheaper fix, stop at the Starbucks at 3122 M St. NW.

Once satiated, head to the:

1. **Old Stone House,** 3051 M St. NW (☎ **202/426-6851**). Located on one of the busiest streets in Washington, the unobtrusive Old Stone House offers a quiet look back at pre-Revolutionary times, when its first owner, a carpenter, used the ground floor as a workshop. The house dates from 1765, making it the only surviving pre-Revolutionary building in the city. Acquired by the National Park Service in 1926, the Old Stone House today shows its four small rooms furnished as they would have been in the late 18th century, during the period when Georgetown was a significant tobacco and shipping port. Park rangers provide information and sometimes demonstrate cooking on an open fireplace, spinning and making pomander balls. Beyond the house is a pretty, terraced lawn and 18th-century English flower garden, a spot long frequented by Georgetown shop and office workers seeking a respite.

The Old Stone House is open to the public 9am to 5pm daily Memorial Day to Labor Day, and 9am to 5pm Wednesday to Sunday the rest of the year. Admission is free. Closed federal holidays.

From the Old Stone House, walk down M Street to 28th Street and turn left. Follow 28th Street to Q Street and turn right, where you'll have no trouble finding:

2. **Dumbarton House,** 2715 Q St. NW (☎ **202/337-2288**). This stately mansion lies behind a long brick wall and dominates the block. Begun in 1799, completed in 1805, the house is exemplary of Federal period architecture, meaning its rooms are exactly symmetrical, below and above stairs, and are centered by a large hall. Federal period furnishings fill the house, too, like the dining room's late–18th-century sideboard, over which hangs a painting by Charles Willson Peale.

On guided, 40-minute tours, you learn a bit of the history of the house. For example, one of its first owners was Joseph Nourse, first Register of the U.S. Treasury, who lived here with his family from 1805–13. Recent research has confirmed that Dolley Madison stopped here for a cup of tea, on her escape route from the burning White House in 1812, before crossing by ferry into Virginia.

Dumbarton House serves as headquarters for The Colonial Dames of America, who restored the house. It is open for guided tours only, Tuesday through Saturday, starting at 10am, with the last tour at 12:15pm. A $3 donation is requested; students are free. Dumbarton House is closed in August and December 25 through January 1.

Turn right when you exit the house and follow Q Street as far as 31st Street. This is a quiet and pleasant stroll, along wide, brick-laid sidewalks, past old town houses with turrets and other examples of Georgetown's fine architecture. For some reason, many of these streets bear no street signs. Fortunately, 31st Street is not only marked, it also tells you to turn right on 31st Street to reach Tudor Place. So, turn right and walk to the grand gates at mid-block and press the buzzer to gain entry.

3. **Tudor Place,** 1644 31st St. NW (☎ **202/965-0400**). Commanding an entire city block, Tudor Place is a 5.5-acre estate of sloping green lawn and exquisite gardens. At its summit is the magnificent, Palladian-style manor house designed by

Walking Tour 3—Georgetown's Historic Homes

EMBASSY ROW   **Rock Creek Park**

Whitehaven St.

Wisconsin Ave.

Rock Creek

Belmont Rd.

Kalorama Rd.

Whitehaven Park

Dumbarton Oaks Park

California St.

24th St.

36th St.

35th St.

34th St.

R St.

S St.

Montrose Park

❹

❺

❻

Reservoir Rd.

Dent Pl.

32nd St.

Wisconsin Ave.

Q St.

❸

Q St.

❷

→ **To Dupont Circle Metro**

P St.

P St.

O St.

P St.

GEORGETOWN

36th St.

O St.

33rd St.

Potomac St.

N St.

N St.

Dumbarton St.

31st St.

30th St.

29th St.

O St.

Prospect St.

❶

M St.

N

1-1311

❶ Old Stone House   ❹ Dumbarton Oaks
❷ Dumbarton House   ❺ Oak Hill Cemetery
❸ Tudor Place   ❻ Evermay

Dr. William Thornton, the first architect of the U.S. Capitol. Martha Custis Peter, Martha Washington's granddaughter, purchased Tudor Place in 1805 with an $8,000 legacy left her by her step-grandfather, George Washington. Martha Custis Peter was married to Georgetown mayor Thomas Peter; their descendants lived here until 1984.

The house has an exceptional architecture—note the clever pullup windows to the domed portico overlooking the south lawn, a feature found in another Thornton creation, The Octagon. Many of the furnishings were inherited or were purchased at auction from Mount Vernon. On your tour, you'll have the chance to scan a loving letter written by George Washington to Martha on June 18, 1775, upon receiving command of the Revolutionary Army: ". . . I should enjoy more real happiness and felicity in 1 month with you, at home, than I have the most distant prospect of reaping abroad . . ."

Henry Clay, Daniel Webster, and John Calhoun visited Tudor Place. The Marquis de Lafayette attended a reception held here in his honor in 1824. Robert E. Lee was a close friend of the family, who were Confederate sympathizers.

If you have arrived between the normal tour times of Tuesday to Friday at 10am, 11:30am, 1pm, and 2:30pm, and Saturday on the hour, 10am to 3pm, take the opportunity to visit the delightful 5-acre Federal-period garden, which includes centuries-old boxwoods, a lily pond, a bowling green garden, pear trees, ivy-covered arbors, and intimate seating alcoves. You tour the Tudor Place mansion by guide only, in 45-minute sessions. Donations of $6 per adult, $5 for seniors, $3 for students are requested. The gardens are open Monday through Saturday, 10am to 4pm, for self-guided tours; a $2 per person donation is requested. You receive a map to guide you through the gardens. Tudor Place is closed for major holidays.

From Tudor Place, turn left on 31st Street, away from the direction you came, and follow 31st Street to R Street and turn left again. Walk along R Street for about 2 blocks, and you reach Wisconsin Avenue. Cross Wisconsin Avenue and walk the few steps to:

☕ **TAKE A BREAK** **Bistrot Lepic,** 1736 Wisconsin Ave. NW (☎ **202/ 333-0111**). Very French, Bistrot Lepic is a small place with a large following. Because of the restaurant's small size and great popularity, it's best to reserve a table in advance if you want to sample its traditional (onion tart) and nouvelle (grape leaves stuffed with crab) cuisine. See chapter 6 for details.

Now retrace your steps, crossing Wisconsin Avenue again to return to R Street. Turn right and walk a block to 32nd Street, turning left. Go to the imposing double doors and enter at:

4. Dumbarton Oaks, 1703 32nd St. NW (☎ **202/339-6401**). The oldest part of this grand mansion dates from 1800. Since then, the house has undergone considerable change, most notably at the hands of a couple named Robert and Mildred Bliss.

The wealthy Blisses retired here in 1933, ending Robert's 33-year career in the Foreign Service. Over the years, the Blisses had amassed collections of Byzantine and Pre-Columbian art, and books relating to those studies, as well as to the history of landscape architecture. Their move into Dumbarton Oaks began a remodeling of the mansion to accommodate the collections and the library, which now occupy the entire building. When the Blisses relocated in 1940, they conveyed the house, gardens, and Byzantine art collection to Harvard University, Robert's alma mater. In 1963, the house/museum completed two new wings, one to house the Pre-Columbian works, the other to hold Mrs. Bliss's gardening books.

You may guide yourself through the exhibit rooms to view these unique artworks, from Byzantine illuminated manuscripts, jewelry, and mosaic icons to Pre-Columbian Olmec jade figures (the Olmec is the earliest known civilization in Mexico) and Mayan pottery. Pre-Columbian works are displayed chronologically in an octet of glass pavilions.

Dumbarton Oaks is famous as the site, in 1944, of two international conferences, which cemented the principles later incorporated into the United Nations charter. The conferences took place in the Music Room, which you should visit to admire the immense, 16th-century stone chimney piece, 18th-century parquet floor, and antique French, Italian, and Spanish furniture, as well as the El Greco painting, *The Visitation.*

Today, Dumbarton Oaks is a research center for studies in Byzantine and pre-Columbian art and history, and in landscape architecture. Most Washingtonians know Dumbarton Oaks for its magnificent 10-acre garden of terraced design and including an orangery, wisteria-covered arbors, groves of cherry trees, magnolias, and herbaceous borders. You can't picnic here, though; for that, you must go down the block to Montrose Park.

Dumbarton Oaks collections are open year-round, for a $1 donation, Tuesday through Sunday, 2 to 5pm; the gardens (entrance on R Street) are open daily, free of charge, 2 to 5pm. Both gardens and collections are closed on national holidays; the gardens may also close during inclement weather.

You can wind down your tour by walking away from Wisconsin Avenue on R Street, passing Montrose Park and:

5. **Oak Hill Cemetery,** the 25-acre Victorian landscaped burial place founded in 1850 and whose graves include those of William Wilson Corcoran (of the Corcoran Gallery of Art), Edwin Stanton (Lincoln's secretary of war), and Dean Acheson (secretary of state under Truman). If you want to stroll, purchase a map of the graves at the gatehouse, 3001 R St. NW, itself a beautiful brick and sandstone Italianate structure built in 1850. The cemetery is open Monday through Friday, 10am to 4pm.

As you leave, note the beautiful house across the street at 2920 R St.: It's the home of *Washington Post* publisher Katherine Graham.

Follow the brick sidewalk and iron fence as it curves down 28th Street to:

6. **Evermay,** 1623 28th St. NW, which you can't visit, since it's a private residence, but which you can gape at from the gate. You also can't see much of it, the brick ramparts and foliage hide it so well, but what's on view is impressive. As the plaque on the estate wall tells you, Evermay was built in 1792–94 by Scotsman Samuel Davidson, with the proceeds Davidson made from the sale of lands he owned around the city, including part of the present day White House and Lafayette Square property.

Note: From here, believe it or not, you are only about a 15- or 20-minute walk from the Dupont Circle part of town—and the Metro. Walk down to Q Street NW, turn left, and follow Q Street across the Dumbarton Bridge to Massachusetts Avenue NW. Walk along Massachusetts Avenue to 20th Street NW and turn left. Continue another block, and you're at the Dupont Circle Metro station.

Shopping the District

I f Washington isn't known for great shopping, that's only because there are so many other things to do here. The city has its share of stores, let me tell you, from the tony Tiffany's to the bargain hunter's Filene's Basement. The shopping scene is getting grander and more diverse all the time, the better to suit a clientele that ranges from ambassadors to aging baby boomers, college students, and suburbanites. But stores are spread out—instead of a single shopping district, the city has many.

If you're on Capitol Hill, **Union Station** is the best place—really the only place—to go. This turn-of-the-century beaux-arts railway station has been magnificently restored to house stores selling everything from political memorabilia to museum-quality, hand-crafted jewelry. Its arcade bustles with travelers wending their way trainward, lobbyists and hill staffers heading to the Metro or to lunch (Union Station has several good restaurants, as well as a food court), and throngs of shoppers and tourists.

If you want a business-day rush, mix with the suits from K Street to Dupont Circle on **Connecticut Avenue NW.** On weekends, the avenue is fairly tame, but during the week, shoppers and office workers jostle for sidewalk space past a stretch of stores that include Burberry's and Victoria's Secret. Some of the best shopping—upscale and beyond—is found in Friendship Heights along upper Wisconsin Avenue where D.C. meets Maryland.

1 The Shopping Scene

SHOPPING AREAS

Adams-Morgan   This is a lively part of town that spills over with the sounds, sights, and smells of different cultures. Defined by 18th Street and Columbia Road, NW, Adams-Morgan is a neighborhood of ethnic eateries interspersed with the odd second-hand bookshop and eclectic collectibles store. Though Adams-Morgan has more nightclubs and bistros than actual stores, it's still a fun area for walking and shopping. Parking is impossible. Closest Metro: Dupont Circle; exit at Q Street NW and walk up Connecticut Avenue NW to Columbia Road NW.

Connecticut Avenue/Dupont Circle   Running from the mini-Wall Street that is K Street north to S Street, Connecticut Avenue

NW is a main thoroughfare, where you'll find traditional clothing at Brooks Brothers, Talbots and Burberry's, casual duds at the Gap and Liz Claiborne, discount items at Filene's Basement and Hit or Miss, and haute couture at Rizik's. The closer you get to Dupont Circle, the fewer business-types you see. People are younger, mellower, and sport more pierced body parts. This pedestrian-friendly section of the avenue is studded with coffee bars and neighborhood restaurants, as well as art galleries, book and record shops, vintage clothing stores, and gay and lesbian boutiques. Metro: Farragut North, at one end, Dupont Circle at the other.

Downtown   Between 12th and 14th streets NW lies an interesting stretch of Pennsylvania Avenue. On the White House side, within the Willard Inter-Continental Hotel's courtyard, are three tony shops: Chanel, Harriet Kassman, Jackie Chalkley. Down 1 block are the Shops at National Place, a four-level mall whose 80-odd stores include Curious Kids and Sharper Image. This is where beloved, family-owned department stores like Garfinckel's, Raleigh's, and Woodward & Lothrop used to be located. Now, Hecht's, at 12th and G streets, is the sole carrier of the department store flag downtown. Metro: Metro Center.

Meanwhile, back on Pennsylvania Avenue at 11th Street, the Pavilion at the Old Post Office is worth a visit, if only to admire the architecture or travel to the top of the 315-foot-high clocktower to view the city. The pavilion's three lower levels contain 30 or so touristy shops and kiosks selling mostly souvenirs, novelty items, and food. Metro: Federal Triangle.

Georgetown   Georgetown used to be more fun, when Hare Krishnas hung out on its corners and the streets were less, well, tourist-ridden. These days, Georgetown is a great place to shop, but you may come away with a headache from its crowded streets, sidewalks, and shops. Weekends, especially, bring out all kinds of yahoos, who are mainly there to drink. Visit Georgetown on a weekday morning, if you can. The heart of the shopping district is at the intersection of Wisconsin Avenue and M Street NW, where shops fan out broadly. Weeknights are another good time to visit, for dinner and strolling afterwards. On afternoons, early evenings, and weekends, traffic is heavy, and parking can be tough. Consider taking a bus or taxi—the closest Metro stop is at Foggy Bottom, a good 20- to 30-minute walk away. If you drive, you'll find parking lots expensive and tickets even more so, so be careful where you plant your car.

Old Town Alexandria   If you've done Georgetown, or even if you haven't, Old Town is a nice place to visit. The drive alone is worth the trip. From Memorial Bridge, near the Lincoln Memorial, you follow the George Washington Parkway alongside the Potomac River (the same route that takes you to National Airport) about 14 miles, where the parkway becomes Washington Street. Look for a parking spot on King Street and then walk. Shops run the length of King Street, from the waterfront up to Washington Street, and from Washington Street west to the Masonic Temple. You can also take the Metro to King St. See chapter 11, which includes Alexandria as one of its "Side Trips from Washington."

Upper Wisconsin Avenue Northwest   In a residential section of town known as Friendship Heights on the DC side and Chevy Chase on the Maryland side, is a quarter-mile shopping district that extends from Saks Fifth Avenue at one end to Roche Bobois at the other. In between lie the Lord & Taylor, Nieman-Marcus, and Hecht Company department stores; a bevy of top shops, such as Tiffany's and Gianni Versace; two malls, the Mazza Gallerie and its younger, more chi-chi sister, the Chevy Chase Pavilion, whose offerings range from Country Road Australia to Hold Everything; and several stand-alone staples, such as Banana Republic. The street is too wide and traffic always too snarled to make this a strolling kind of district. People head for particular stores and leave. Drive here if you want; the malls offer 2 hours of free parking. Or Metro it; the strip is right on the Red Line of the subway, with the "Friendship Heights" exits leading directly into each of the malls and into Hecht's.

2 Shopping A to Z

ANTIQUES

While you won't find many bargains in Washington area antique stores, you will see beautiful and rare decorative furniture, silver, jewelry, art, and fabrics, from Amish quilts to Chinese silks. Antique shops dot the greater Washington landscape, with the richest concentrations found in Old Town Alexandria; Capitol Hill; Georgetown; Adams-Morgan; and Kensington, Maryland.

Antique Row

Howard and Connecticut aves., Kensington, Maryland.

A few miles north of the city is not far to go for the good deal or true bonanza you're likely to discover among these 40-odd antiques and collectibles shops. The stores are situated all in a row along Howard Avenue and offer every sort of item in a mix of styles, periods, and prices.

✪ Antiques-on-the-Hill

701 North Carolina Ave. SE. ☎ **202/543-1819.** Metro: Eastern Market.

A Capitol Hill institution since the 1960s, this place sells silver, furniture, glassware, jewelry, porcelain, and lamps.

✪ The Brass Knob Architectural Antiques

2311 18th St. NW. ☎ **202/332-3370.** Metro: Dupont Circle.

When early homes and office buildings are demolished in the name of progress, these savvy salvage merchants spirit away saleable treasures, from chandeliers to wrought-iron fencing.

Cherishables

1608 20th St. NW. ☎ **202/785-4087.** Metro: Dupont Circle.

An adorable shop specializing in 18th- and 19th-century American furniture, folk art, quilts, and decorative accessories. Shows furniture in roomlike settings. The store is known for a world-renowned line of Christmas ornaments designed each year around a new theme: the garden, architecture, and breeds of dogs are some from years past.

The Iron Gate

1007 King St., Alexandria. ☎ **703/549-7429.** Metro: King Street, with a short walk.

A little less expensive than some of its neighbors, this shop sells country pieces that seem to fit with any style of decorating. The nice owner is happy to find "the special item" you're desperately seeking.

Millenium

1528 U St. NW. ☎ **202/483-1218.** Metro: U Street/Cardozo.

Antique shopping for the TV generation, where anything before 1990 is considered collectible. Funky wares run from Heywood-Wakefield blond-wood beauties to used drinking glasses.

Old Print Gallery

1220 31st St. NW. ☎ **202/965-1818.** Metro: Foggy Bottom, with a 20-minute walk.

This gallery carries original American and European prints from the 18th and 19th centuries, including British political cartoons, maps and historical documents.

Retrospective

2324 18th St. NW. ☎ **202/483-8112.** Metro: Woodley Park–Zoo.

This is a chic boutique full of well-designed relics of the prehistoric pre-1960s.

Susquehanna Antiques

3216 O St. NW. ☎ **202/333-1511.** Metro: Foggy Bottom, with a 25-minute walk.

This store specializes in Americana, with pre-1840 American and European furniture and paintings.

ART GALLERIES

Art galleries abound in Washington, but are especially prolific in two sections of the city: Dupont Circle and the downtown area of D and Seventh streets NW. Here's a selection from these two neighborhoods.

DUPONT CIRCLE

For all galleries listed below, the closest Metro stop is Dupont Circle.

✪ Addison/Ripley Gallery, Ltd.

9 Hillyer Court NW. ☎ **202/328-2332.**

This gallery displays contemporary works by Americans, some but not all by locals. Edith Kuhnle, Richard Hunt, and Wols Kahn are a few of the artists represented here.

Anton Gallery

2108 R St. NW. ☎ **202/328-0828.**

Expect to find contemporary American paintings, photography, ceramics, prints, wood sculpture, metal sculpture, everything. All of the artists shown live locally but hail from around the world, from Japan to Chile, New Zealand to California.

Fonda del Sol Visual Arts and Media Center

2112 R St. NW. ☎ **202/483-2777.**

This is a lively gallery in a picturesque town house, showcasing the art and cultures of Latin American, Native American, Caribbean, and African-American artists.

H. H. Leonards' Mansion on O Street

2020 O St. NW. ☎ **202/659-8787.**

Not an art gallery in the usual sense. H. H. Leonards' consists of three Victorian five-story town houses joined together, decorated throughout with more than 5,000 antiques and artworks, in styles ranging from art deco to avant garde. Everything's for sale, even the beds on which owner H. and son Z. sleep. This is the Leonards' home, a special events spot, and a luxurious B&B to boot. (Christie Brinkley, Alec Baldwin, and Kim Bassinger are among her clients.) H. tells you to help yourself to champagne or coffee in the English kitchen and then wander around on your own, which you could do for hours. Parking is such a problem that neighbors are trying to shut her down.

Osuna

1914 16th St. NW. ☎ **202/296-1963.**

Around since 1979, this gallery features Old Masters, Italian (early–17th-century artist Guido Reni is one example), and Baroque paintings in particular.

Very Special Arts Gallery

1300 Connecticut Ave. NW. ☎ **202/628-0800.**

This one-of-a-kind gallery represents about 800 American artists with disabilities who have created astounding works that include folk art, paintings, and sculptures.

SEVENTH STREET ARTS CORRIDOR

406 Group

406 7th St. NW, between D and E sts. Metro: Archives/Navy Memorial.

Several first-rate art galleries, some interlopers from Dupont Circle, occupy this historic building, with its 13-foot-high ceilings and spacious rooms. They include: **David Adamson Gallery** (☎ **202/628-0257**), which is probably the largest gallery space in D.C., with two levels featuring the works of contemporary artists, including those of locals Kevin MacDonald and rising star Renee Stout, and prints and drawings by David Hockney; **Baumgartner Gallery** (☎ **202/232-6320**), showing national and international artists, including painters Ross Bleckner and Peter Halley. Though this gallery gets a lot of good press, other galleries have works every bit as impressive, or more so; **Touchstone Gallery** (☎ **202/347-2787**), which is a self-run co-op of 15 artists who take turns exhibiting their work.

Mickelson Gallery

709 G St. NW. ☎ **202/628-1734.** Metro: Gallery Place.

Around the corner from the Seventh Street gang, this is one of the oldest D.C. galleries, approaching 40 years, with a framing business going back 80 years. The gallery shows contemporary artists and has one of the largest collections for sale in the United States for M.C. Escher's works (you must make an appointment to view them), as well as a large selection of works by George Bellows.

✪ Zenith Gallery

413 7th St. NW. ☎ **202/783-2963.**

Across the street from the 406 Group, this 18-year-old gallery shows diverse works of contemporary artists, most American, about half of whom are local. You can get a good deal here, paying anywhere from $50 to $50,000 for a piece. Among other things you'll find here are annual humor shows, annual neon exhibits, realism, abstract expressionism, and landscapes.

BEAUTY

With a few exceptions, the best salons are in Georgetown and cater to both men and women. If you don't want to take a chance, these are the places to go. Expect to spend a little money.

Bogart

1063 Wisconsin Ave. NW. ☎ **202/333-6550.** Metro: Foggy Bottom, with a 20-minute walk, or take one of the 30-series buses (30, 32, 34, 36, 38B) from downtown into Georgetown.

Favored by certain local TV news anchors. Facials cost $50; haircuts average $45 for women, $35 for men.

Elizabeth Arden

5225 Wisconsin Ave. NW. ☎ **202/362-9890.** Metro: Friendship Heights.

Does it all. Facials cost $65; haircuts average $65 for women, $30 for men.

✪ Ilo Day Spa

1637 Wisconsin Ave. NW. ☎ **202/342-0350.** Metro: Foggy Bottom, with a 30-minute walk, or take one of the 30-series buses (30, 32, 34, 36, 38B) from downtown into Georgetown.

A large and trendy operation, Ilo's may not be as gracious as other top salons, but neither is it as intimidating. Facials cost $70; haircuts start at $60 for women, $40 for men.

IPSA for Hair

1629 Wisconsin Ave. NW. ☎ **202/338-4100.** Metro: Foggy Bottom, with a 30-minute walk, or take one of the 30-series buses (30, 32, 34, 36, 38B) from downtown into Georgetown.

This salon won the most votes for favorite hair styling salon in a local count, but it only does hair. It provides valet parking for $2. Haircuts average $55 for women, $35 for men.

✪ Okyo

2903 M St. NW. ☎ **202/342-2675.** Metro: Foggy Bottom, with a 10-minute walk, or take one of the 30-series buses (30, 32, 34, 36, 38B) from downtown into Georgetown.

Owner Bernard Portelli used to color Catherine Deneuve's hair in France, which means he's so booked that he isn't taking any new clients. They only do hair here, at surprisingly reasonable rates: cuts start at $40 for women, $25 for men.

Saks Fifth Avenue

5555 Wisconsin Ave., Chevy Chase, MD. ☎ **301/657-9000.** Metro: Friendship Heights, Red.

Saks caters to an older clientele. Facials cost $50; haircuts average $30 for women and men, without a blowdry.

3303 Inc

3303 M St. NW. ☎ **202/965-4000.** Metro: Foggy Bottom, with a 20-minute walk, or take one of the 30-series buses (30, 32, 34, 36, 38B) from downtown into Georgetown.

Facials cost $75; haircuts start at $55 for women, $40 for men. You have to know what you want, but these stylists can do it.

Ury & Associates

3109 M St. NW. ☎ **202/342-0944.** Metro: Foggy Bottom, with a 20-minute walk, or take one of the 30-series buses (30, 32, 34, 36, 38B) from downtown into Georgetown.

Lots of model types come here, where they get rapt attention from Ury. Non-model types come here, too, for expert styling by other hairdressers. Facials cost $55; haircuts start at $55 for women, $35 for men.

BOOKS

Washingtonians are readers, so bookstores pop up throughout the city. An increasingly competitive market means that stores besides Crown Books offer discounts. Here are favorite bookstores in general, used, and special interest categories.

GENERAL

Barnes & Noble

See entry in Georgetown walking tour, below.

B. Dalton

Union Station. ☎ **202/289-1750.** Metro: Union Station.

Your average all-round bookstore, heavy on the bestsellers. They sell magazines, too.

Borders Books & Music

1800 L St. NW. ☎ **202/466-4999.** Metro: Farragut North.

With its overwhelming array of books, records, videos, and magazines, this outpost of the rapidly expanding chain has taken over the town. Most hardcovers are 10% off; *NYT* and the *Washington Post* hardcover bestsellers are 30% off. People hang out here, hovering over the magazines or sipping espresso in the cafe as they read their books. The store often hosts performances by local musicians.

Bridge Street Books

2814 Pennsylvania Ave. NW. ☎ **202/965-5200.** Metro: Foggy Bottom.

A small, serious shop with a good selection of current fiction, literary criticism, and publications you won't find elsewhere. Bestsellers and discounted books are not its raison d'etre.

Chapters Literary Bookshop

1512 K St. NW. ☎ **202/347-5495.** Metro: McPherson Square or Farragut North.

Chapters is strong in new and backlisted fiction, and is always hosting author readings. No discounts. Tea is always available, and on Friday afternoons they break out the sherry and cookies.

Crown Books

2020 K St. NW. ☎ **202/659-2030.** Metro: Foggy Bottom.

Crown has the best discounts but not the best selection: 10% off all paperbacks, 20% off all hardcovers, 40% off hardcover bestsellers, and 25% off paperback bestsellers.

SuperCrown Books

11 Dupont Circle. ☎ **202/319-1374.** Metro: Dupont Circle.

Same discounts as the main Crown bookstore, but a wider selection.

Kramer Books & Afterwords

1517 Connecticut Ave. NW. ☎ **202/387-1400.** Metro: Dupont Circle.

The first bookstore/cafe in the Dupont Circle area, this place has launched countless romances. It's jammed and often noisy, stages live music Wednesday through Saturday evenings, and is open all night weekends. Paperback fiction takes up most of its inventory, but the store carries a little of everything. No discounts.

✪ Olsson's Books and Records

See entry in Georgetown walking tour.

✪ Politics and Prose Bookstore

5015 Connecticut Ave. NW. ☎ **202/364-1919.** Metro: the closest is Van Ness–UDC, but you'll have to walk about a half-mile from there.

This is a two-story shop in a residential part of town. A devoted neighborhood clientele helped move this shop, book by book, across the street to larger quarters in 1990 (it's expanded again since then). It has vast offerings in fiction and nonfiction alike, with the largest psychology section in the city (possibly on the East Coast). A warm, knowledgeable staff will help you find what you need. Downstairs is a cozy coffeehouse frequented by booklovers of all description: professorial types to moms treating themselves to a cappuccino. No discounts.

Trover Shop

227 Pennsylvania Ave. SE. ☎ **202/543-8006.** Metro: Capitol South.

The only general bookstore on Capitol Hill, Trover's strengths are its political selections and its magazines. The store discounts 20% on *Washington Post* hardcover fiction and nonfiction bestsellers, computer books and cookbooks, and non-reference books costing more than $25.

Waldenbooks

Georgetown Park Mall. ☎ **202/333-8033.** Metro: Foggy Bottom, with a 20-minute walk.

Another of your chain, general-selection bookstores.

OLD & USED BOOKS

Booked Up

1204 31st St. NW. ☎ **202/965-3244.** Metro: Foggy Bottom, with a 20-minute walk, or take one of the 30-series buses (30, 32, 34, 36, 38B) from downtown into Georgetown.

An antiquarian bookstore in Georgetown where you can stumble upon some true collectors' items.

Idle Time Books

2410 18th St. NW. ☎ **202/232-4774.** Metro: Woodley Park–Zoo.

A dusty two-story treasure trove of used books in Adams-Morgan.

Second Story Books

2000 P St. NW. ☎ **202/659-8884.** Metro: Dupont Circle.

If it's old, out of print, custom-bound, or a small-press publication, this is where to find it. The store also specializes in used CDs and vinyl, and has an amazing collection of antique French and American advertising posters.

SPECIAL-INTEREST BOOKS

American History Museum Bookstore

National Museum of American History Giftshop, Constitution Ave. between 12th and 14th sts. NW. ☎ **202/357-1784.** Metro: Federal Triangle or Smithsonian.

You'll find a wonderful selection of books on American history and culture here, including some for children.

American Institute of Architects Bookstore

1735 New York Ave. NW. ☎ **202/626-7475.** Metro: Farragut West.

This store carries books and gifts related to architecture.

Backstage

2101 P St. NW. ☎ **202/775-1488.** Metro: Dupont Circle.

This is the headquarters for Washington's theatrical community, which buys its books, scripts, trades and sheet music here.

Franz Bader Bookstore

1911 I St. NW. ☎ **202/337-5440.** Metro: Farragut West.

This store stocks books on art, art history, architecture, and photography.

Cheshire Cat Children's Bookstore

5512 Connecticut Ave. NW. ☎ **202/244-3956.** On the L2 bus line.

The owners are extremely knowledgeable about children's literature, from the classics to the current market. They are also big promoters of local talent and host frequent author visits. The store's way out on Connecticut Avenue.

Lambda Rising

1625 Connecticut Ave. NW. ☎ **202/462-6969.** Metro: Dupont Circle.

It was a big deal when this gay and lesbian bookstore opened with a plate glass window revealing its interior to passersby. Now it's an unofficial headquarters for the gay/lesbian/bi community.

Mystery Books

1715 Connecticut Ave. NW. ☎ **202/483-1600.** Metro: Dupont Circle.

The name of the store should give you a clue. Here's where to find out whodunit. It has more paperbacks than hardcovers.

Travel Books & Language Center

4931 Cordell Ave., Bethesda, MD. ☎ **301/951-8533.** Metro: Bethesda.

A 20-minute ride on the Metro from downtown takes you to the heart of Bethesda and this bookstore, which has the best-in-the-area assortment of guidebooks and maps covering the entire world, as well as language dictionaries and learning tapes, travel diaries, memoirs, and novels famous for their evocation of particular places.

Yes! Bookshop
See entry in Georgetown walking tour, below.

CAMERAS & PHOTOGRAPHIC EQUIPMENT

Photography is a big business in this image-conscious tourist town. A wide range of services and supplies, from inexpensive point-and-shoot cameras to deluxe German and Japanese equipment, is available at competitive prices. Some shops offer repair services and have multilingual staff.

Baker's Photo Supply
4433 Wisconsin Ave. NW. ☎ **202/362-9100.** Metro: Tenleytown.

This store carries Hasselblad, Nikon, Graflex, Beseler, and other less expensive equipment, and also has a repair service.

Congressional Photo
209 Pennsylvania Ave. SE. ☎ **202/543-3206.** Metro: Capitol South.

This is the professional's choice for custom finishing. Full camera repair service and budget processing are available.

✪ Penn Camera Exchange
915 E St. NW. ☎ **202/347-5777** or 800/347-5770. Metro: Gallery Place or Metro Center.

Across the street from the FBI Building, Penn Camera does a brisk trade with professionals and concerned amateurs. The store offers big discounts on major brand-name equipment, such as Olympus and Canon. Penn has been owned and operated by the Zweig family since 1953; its staff is quite knowledgeable, its inventory wide-ranging. Their specialty is quality equipment and processing—not cheap, but worth it.

Ritz Camera Centers
1740 Pennsylvania Ave. NW. ☎ **202/466-3470.** Metro: Farragut West.

This place sells camera equipment and develops film with 1-hour processing for the average photographer. Call for other locations—there are many throughout the area.

CRAFTS

American Hand Plus
See entry in Georgetown walking tour, below.

Appalachian Spring
See entry in Georgetown walking tour, below.

Indian Craft Shop
Department of the Interior, 1800 C St. NW. ☎ **202/208-4056.** Weekday hours only. Metro: Farragut West or Foggy Bottom.

The Indian Craft Shop has represented authentic Native American artisans since 1938, selling their handwoven rugs and handcrafted baskets, jewelry, figurines, paintings, pottery, and other items. You need a photo ID to enter the building.

✪ The Phoenix
1514 Wisconsin Ave. NW. ☎ **202/338-4404.** Metro: Foggy Bottom, with a 30-minute walk, or take one of the 30-series buses (30, 32, 34, 36, 38B) from downtown into Georgetown.

Around since 1955, The Phoenix still sells those embroidered Mexican peasant blouses popular in hippie days, as well as Mexican folk and fine art, handcrafted, sterling silver jewelry from Mexico and all over the world, clothing in natural fibers from Mexican and American designers, collectors' quality masks, and decorative doodads in tin, brass, copper, and wood.

✪ Torpedo Factory Art Center

105 North Union St. ☎ **703/838-4565.** Metro: King Street, then take the DASH bus (AT2 or AT5), eastbound to the waterfront.

This three-story, converted munitions factory houses more than 83 working studios and the works of about 160 artists, who tend to their crafts before your very eyes, pausing to explain their techniques or to sell their pieces, if you so desire. Artworks include paintings, sculpture, ceramics, glasswork, and textiles.

CRYSTAL/SILVER/CHINA

Neiman-Marcus (see "Department Stores," below) and Tiffany's (see "Jewelry," below) sell many of these items, so you may want to visit them. First, though, consider visiting two Georgetown landmarks, **Little Caledonia** and **Martin's.** For more information, see the Georgetown walking tour, below.

DEPARTMENT STORES

Bloomingdale's

White Flint Mall, Kensington, MD. ☎ **301/984-4600.** Metro: White Flint.

This outpost of the famous New York–based chain features trendsetting fashions for men, women and children, as well as shoes, accessories, household goods, furnishings, and cosmetics. Don't look for the same variety and selection found in New York, however: The Washington versions seem restrained by comparison.

Hecht's

Metro Center, 1201 G St. NW. ☎ **202/628-6661.** Metro: Metro Center.

Everything from mattresses to electronics, children's underwear to luggage, can be bought in this mid-priced emporium.

Lord & Taylor

5255 Western Ave. NW. ☎ **202/362-9600.** Metro: Friendship Heights.

This is another lesser version of a New York chain. Its women's clothing and accessories department are probably its strong suit; go elsewhere for gadgets and gifts.

Macy's

Fashion Center at Pentagon City, 1000 S. Hayes St., Arlington, VA. ☎ **703/418-4488.** Metro: Pentagon City.

A household name for many East Coasters, this Macy's (though nowhere near the size of its Manhattan counterpart), hopes to fulfill the same role for Washington customers. Expect mid- to upscale merchandise and prices.

Neiman-Marcus

Mazza Gallerie, 5300 Wisconsin Ave. NW. ☎ **202/966-9700.** Metro: Friendship Heights.

The legendary Texas institution's catalogs and "his-and-hers" Christmas gifts are exercises in conspicuous consumption. Look for remarkably good bargains at their "Last Call" half-yearly sales; otherwise, this store is pretty pricey. It sells no furniture or home furnishings, except for exquisite china and crystal.

✪ Nordstrom

Fashion Center at Pentagon City. 1400 S. Hayes St., Arlington, VA. ☎ **703/415-1121.** Metro: Pentagon City.

This Seattle-based retailer's reputation for exceptional service is well deserved—a call to the main information number confirms this. In keeping with the store's beginnings as a shoe store, this location has three entire departments devoted to women's shoes (designer, dressy, and just plain fun); if you can't find your size or color, they'll order it.

Saks Fifth Avenue

5555 Wisconsin Ave., Chevy Chase, MD. ☎ **301/657-9000.** Metro: Friendship Heights.

If you can make it past the cosmetics counters without getting spritzed by the makeup-masked young women aiming perfume bottles at you, you've accomplished something special. On other levels, you'll find designer and tailored men's and women's clothing, and some for children.

FARMERS & FLEA MARKETS

Alexandria Farmers' Market

301 King St., at Market Sq. in front of the city hall, in Alexandria. Metro: King Street, then take the DASH bus (AT2 or AT5) eastbound to Market Square.

The oldest continually operating farmers' market in the country (since 1752), this market offers the usual assortment of locally grown fruits and vegetables, along with delectable baked goods, cut flowers, and plants. Saturday mornings, 5am to 10am, year-round.

D.C. Open Air Farmers' Market

Oklahoma Ave. and Benning Rd. NE (at RFK Stadium parking lot #6). Metro: Stadium/Armory.

This market features fresh vegetables, seafood, hams, and arts and crafts. Thursday and Saturday, 7am to 5pm, year-round; Tuesday, 7am to 5pm, June to September.

✪ Eastern Market

7th St. SE, between North Carolina Ave. and C St. Metro: Eastern Market.

This is the one everyone knows about, even if they've never been here. Located on Capitol Hill, Eastern Market is an inside/outside bazaar of stalls, where greengrocers, butchers, bakers, farmers, artists, crafts people, florists and other merchants vend their wares daily (except Monday), but especially on weekends. Saturday morning is the best time to go. On Sundays, the food stalls become a flea market.

✪ Georgetown Flea Market

In a parking lot bordering Wisconsin Ave., between S and T sts. NW. Metro: Foggy Bottom, with a 30- to 40-minute walk, or take one of the 30-series buses (30, 32, 34, 36, 38B) from downtown into Georgetown.

Grab a coffee at Starbucks across the lane and get ready to barter. The Georgetown Flea Market is an institution frequented by all types of Washingtonians looking for a good deal—they often get it—on antiques, painted furniture, vintage clothing, and decorative garden urns. Nearly 100 vendors sell their wares here. Open Sundays from 9am to 5pm March through December.

Montgomery County Farm Woman's Cooperative Market

7155 Wisconsin Ave., in Bethesda. Metro: Bethesda.

Vendors set up inside every Saturday, year-round from 7am to about 3:30pm, to sell preserves, homegrown veggies, cut flowers, slabs of bacon and sausages, and mouthwatering pies, cookies, and breads. Outside, on Saturdays and Wednesdays, are flea market vendors selling rugs, tablecloths, furniture, sunglasses, everything.

GOOD FOOD TO GO

Demanding jobs and hectic schedules leave Washingtonians less and less time to prepare their own meals. Or so they say. At any rate, a number of fine-food shops and bakeries are happy to come to the rescue. Even the busiest bureaucrat can find the time to pop into one of these gourmet grocers for a moveable feast.

Dean & Deluca
3276 M St. NW. ☎ **202/342-2500.** Metro: Foggy Bottom.

This famed New York store has set down roots in Washington, in a historic Georgetown building that was once an open-air market. Though it is now closed in, it still feels airy because of the scale of the room, its high ceiling, and the presence of windows on all sides. You'll pay top prices, but maybe it's worth it, for the charcuterie, produce, prepared sandwiches and cold pasta salads, and the hot-ticket desserts, like creme brulée and tiramisu. Also on sale are housewares; on site is an espresso bar/cafe. In addition, the chain has two other cafe locations, where you can sit and eat, or take out: 1299 Pennsylvania Ave. NW (☎ **202/628-8155**); 19th and I sts. NW (☎ **202/296-4327**).

Lawson's Gourmet
1350 Connecticut Ave. NW. ☎ **202/775-0400.** Metro: Dupont Circle.

At this subway-situated Lawson's, with its cluster of outside tables and chairs, you're at a real Washington crossroads, watching the comings and goings of sharply dressed lawyers, bohemian artistes and panhandlers. You can buy elaborate sandwiches made to order and very nice desserts, wines, breads, and salads. Other locations include 1350 I St. (☎ **202/789-0800**) and Metro Center, 601 G St. NW (☎ **202/393-5500**).

Marvelous Market
1514 Connecticut Ave. NW. ☎ **202/986-2222.** Metro: Dupont Circle.

First there were the breads: sourdough, baguettes, olive, rosemary, croissants, scones. Now, there are things to spread on the bread, like smoked salmon mousse and tapenade; pastries to die for, from gingerbread to flourless chocolate cake; and prepared foods, such as empanadas and pasta salads. The breakfast spread on Sunday mornings is sinful, and individual items, like the croissants, are tastier and less expensive here than at other bakeries. Another location is at 5035 Connecticut Ave. NW (☎ **202/686-4040**).

Reeves Bakery
1305 G St. NW. ☎ **202/628-6350.** Metro: Metro Center.

Razed to the ground in 1988 to make way for yet another office building, this dieter's nightmare took more than 3 years to find a new home 2 blocks away. Meanwhile, fans pined for the famous strawberry pie, the pineapple dream cake, the blueberry doughnuts, and chicken salad sandwiches at the counter. The offerings here are 1950s-style, tasty but not elegant. See chapter 6 for further information.

Sutton Place Gourmet
3201 New Mexico Ave. NW. ☎ **202/363-5800.**

In 1980, Sutton Place was the first full-scale, one-stop fancy food store to open in the Washington area, and residents took to it immediately. Now there are nine. Shoppers can be obnoxious—everyone who comes here is "somebody," or thinks he is. It's an expensive store, but reliable: you'll always find the best meats, raspberries when no one else has them, a zillion types of cheeses, and ingredients for recipes in *Gourmet* magazine. Their Sutton on the Run branch is at 1647 20th St. NW, at Connecticut Ave. NW (☎ **202/588-9876**).

Uptown Bakers
3313 Connecticut Ave. NW. ☎ **202/362-6262.** Metro: Cleveland Park.

If you're visiting the zoo and need a sweets fix, walk down the street to this bakery for a muffin, sweet tart or a delicious "Vicki" bun, a cinnamon roll named for the long-gone worker who invented it. Coffee, sandwiches, and a wide range of breads also available.

JEWELRY

Beadazzled
1522 Connecticut Ave. NW. ☎ 202/265-BEAD. Metro: Dupont Circle.

The friendly staff helps you assemble your own affordable jewelry from an eye-boggling array of beads and artifacts.

C de Carat
Mayflower Hotel, 1127 Connecticut Ave. NW. ☎ 202/887-5888. Metro: Farragut North.

The District's only authorized Cartier dealer, this boutique is also known for its Italian designer jewelry: Antonini, Cassis; Lagos sterling silver and 18-karat gold jewelry; and Breitling watches. Amiable staff.

Charles Schwartz & Son
Willard Hotel, 1401 Pennsylvania Ave. NW. ☎ 202/737-4757. Metro: Metro Center.

In business since 1888, Charles Schwartz specializes in diamonds and sapphires, rubies and emeralds, and is one of the few distributors of Baccarat jewelry. The professional staff also repairs watches and jewelry. There's another branch at the Mazza Gallerie (☎ 202/363-5432; Metro: Friendship Heights).

✪ Galt & Brothers
607 15th St. NW. ☎ 202/347-1034. Metro: Metro Center.

In existence since 1802, Galt's is the capital's oldest business and America's oldest jewelry store. The shop sells and repairs high-quality jewelry, diamonds, and all manner of colored gems. Gifts of crystal, silver, and china are also sold.

✪ Tiffany and Company
5500 Wisconsin Ave., Chevy Chase, MD. ☎ 301/657-8777. Metro: Friendship Heights.

Tiffany's is known for exquisite diamonds and other jewelry that can cost hundreds of thousands of dollars, but what you may not know is that the store carries less expensive items, as well: $35 candlesticks, for example. And if you've ever seen the movie, "Breakfast at Tiffany's," you know Tiffany's will engrave, too. Other items include tabletop gifts and fancy glitz: china, crystal, flatware, and bridal registry service.

✪ Tiny Jewel Box
1147 Connecticut Ave. NW. ☎ 202/393-2747. Metro: Farragut North.

The first place Washingtonians go for estate and antique jewelry.

MALLS

Chevy Chase Pavilion
5345 Wisconsin Ave. NW. ☎ 202/686-5335. Metro: Friendship Heights.

This is a manageably sized mall with about 50 stores and restaurants, anchored by an Embassy Suites Hotel. The inside is unusually pretty, with three levels winding around a skylit atrium. Giant palm trees, arrangements of fresh flowers, and seasonal events, such as a ballet performance by a visiting Russian troop at Christmastime, add panache. Stores include the outrageously priced Oilily for children's and women's clothing, Laura Ashley, a shop selling National Cathedral knickknacks, and a Joan and David shoe store. A small food court, the Cheesecake Factory, and the California Pizza Kitchen are among the eating options.

Fashion Center at Pentagon City

1400 S. Hayes St., Arlington, VA. ☎ **703/415-2400.** Metro: Pentagon City.

Nordstrom's and Macy's are the biggest attractions in this block-long, five-story, elegant shoppers' paradise that also houses a Ritz-Carlton Hotel, office suites, multiplex theaters, and a sprawling food court. Villeroy and Boch, Crate & Barrel, and Eddie Bauer are among the nearly 150 shops.

The Shops at Georgetown Park

3222 M St. NW. ☎ **202/342-8180.** Metro: Foggy Bottom, then a 20-minute walk.

This is a deluxe mall, where you'll see beautiful people shopping for beautiful things, paying stunning prices at stores with European names: Christian Bernard, Arpelli's (leather goods), and Tartine et Chocolat (children's clothes from Paris). The diplomatic set and well-heeled foreign travelers favor these stores, so you're bound to hear a number of languages, especially French and Italian. For more information, see the description in Georgetown walking tour, below. Wander here, then set off for the streets of Georgetown for more shopping.

Mazza Gallerie

5100 Wisconsin Ave. NW. ☎ **202/966-6114.** Metro: Friendship Heights.

Despite the presence of Neiman-Marcus, this mall is less luxurious than it used to be, thanks to the additions of discount/low-priced stores Filene's Basement and Paul Harris—and maybe because McDonald's is its main restaurant at the moment. But the Mazza remains an attractive shopping center, with its skylit atrium and stores like Ann Taylor and Benetton's. There are theaters on the lower level, and there is access to Chevy Chase Pavilion, the subway, and to the Hecht's department store via the Metro tunnel.

The Pavilion at the Old Post Office

1100 Pennsylvania Ave. NW. ☎ **202/289-4224.** Metro: Federal Triangle.

This is mainly a tourist trap holding souvenir shops and a food court. Noontime concerts are a draw, as is the view of the city from the building's clock tower, 315 feet up.

Potomac Mills

30 miles south on I-95, accessible by car only. ☎ **703/490-5948.**

When you are stuck in the traffic that always clogs this section of I-95, you may wonder if a trip to Potomac Mills is worth it. Believe it or not, this place attracts more visitors than any other in the Washington area, and twice as many as the next top draw, the Smithsonian's National Air and Space Museum. It's the largest indoor outlet mall around, with shops such as New York's Barney's, DKNY, Nordstrom's, and IKEA.

The Shops at National Place

1331 Pennsylvania Ave. NW. ☎ **202/783-9090.** Metro: Metro Center.

You enter through the J.W. Marriott Hotel or at F Street, between 13th and 14th streets. National Place has more than 80 specialty shops, including Papillon and Leather Man, for men, and Casual Corner, The Limited, and Victoria's Secret, for women.

Tyson's Corner/Tyson's I

9160 Chain Bridge Rd., McLean, VA. ☎ **703/893-9400.** Tyson's Corner II, The Galleria, 2001 International Dr., McLean, VA. ☎ 703/827-7700. Metro: West Falls Church, take shuttle.

Facing each other across Chain Bridge Road, these two gigantic malls could lead to shopper's overload. Tyson's Corner I, the first and less expensive, has Nordstrom's, Bloomingdale's, and JCPenney, and specialty stores, such as Abercrombie & Fitch and Crabtree & Evelyn. The Galleria has Macy's, Saks Fifth Avenue, and more than 100 upscale boutiques.

✪ Union Station

50 Massachusetts Ave. NE. ☎ **202/371-9441.** Metro: Union Station.

After the National Air & Space Museum, this is the next most popular stop within Washington itself. The architecture is magnificent. Its more than 120 shops include The Nature Company, Brookstone, and Appalachian Spring; among the places to eat are America, B. Smith, and an international food court. There's also a nine-screen movie theater complex.

White Flint Mall

11301 Rockville Pike, Kensington, MD. ☎ **301/468-5777.** Metro: White Flint, then take the free "White Flint" shuttle, which runs every 12 to 15 minutes.

Another Bloomingdale's, another long trip in the car or on the Metro, but once you're there, you can shop, take in a movie, or dine cheaply or well. Notable stores include Lord & Taylor, a huge Borders Books & Music, Ann Taylor, and The Coach Store.

MEN'S CLOTHES & SHOES

Banana Republic

Wisconsin and M sts. ☎ **202/333-2554.** Metro: Foggy Bottom, with a 20-minute walk.

All Banana Republic labels–casual to dressy: wool gabardine and wool crepe pants, khakis, shorts, vests, and jackets. Mid to high prices. Another location is at F and 13th streets NW (☎ **202/638-2724**).

Beau Monde

International Sq., 1814 K St. NW. ☎ **202/466-7070.** Metro: Farragut West.

This boutique sells all Italian-made clothes, some double-breasted traditional suits, but mostly avant-garde.

Britches of Georgetown

See entry in Georgetown walking tour, below.

Brooks Brothers

1840 L St. NW. ☎ **202/659-4650.** Metro: Farragut West or Farragut North.

This is where to go for the K Street/Capitol Hill pinstriped power look. Brooks sells the fine line of Peal's English shoes.

Burberry's

1155 Connecticut Ave. NW. ☎ **202/463-3000.** Metro: Farragut North.

Here you'll find those plaid-lined trenchcoats, of course, along with well-tailored but conservative English clothing for men and women.

Gianfranco Ferre

5301 Wisconsin Ave. NW. ☎ **202/244-6633.** Metro: Friendship Heights.

Shop here for the sleek and sexy European look: this store features interesting suits and some casual wear.

Giotto

Georgetown Park. ☎ **202/338-6223.** Metro: Foggy Bottom, with a 20-minute walk.

You'll find Italian designer sports and dress wear here.

Urban Outfitters

3111 M St. NW. ☎ **202/342-1012.** Metro: Foggy Bottom, with a 20-minute walk.

For the unisex, ugly-is-in look. The salespeople wear suitably disgusted expressions.

MISCELLANEOUS

Al's Magic Shop

1012 Vermont Ave. NW. ☎ **202/789-2800.** Metro: McPherson Square.

This first-rate novelty shop is presided over by prestidigitator and local character Al Cohen, who is only too happy to demonstrate his latest magic trick or practical joke.

Animation Sensations

See entry in Georgetown walking tour, below.

Chocolate Moose

1800 M St. NW. ☎ **202/463-0992.** Metro: Farragut North.

Here's where to go when you need a surprising and unexpected gift—they stock wacky cards; a range of useful, funny and lovely presents; candies; eccentric clothing; and jewelry.

Ginza

1721 Connecticut Ave. NW. ☎ **202/331-7991.** Metro: Dupont Circle.

Everything Japanese, from incense and kimonos, to futons, to Zen rock gardens.

Map Store

1636 I St. NW. ☎ **202/628-2608.** Metro: Farragut West.

Going somewhere? Or just daydreaming about leaving? This fascinating boutique is always packed with map and globe fetishists. It's a good spot for D.C. souvenirs.

MUSEUM SHOPS

The gift stores in the Smithsonian's 14 Washington museums are terrific places to shop, with wares related to the focus of the individual museums. The largest Smithsonian store is in the **National Museum of American History.** The mart in the Smithsonian's **Arts and Industries Building** is nearly as extensive, since it sells all of the items offered in the museum catalogs. Smithsonian's museum shop buyers travel the world for unusual items, many of which are made exclusively for the shops.

The Smithsonian doesn't corner the market on museum merchandise, however. Here's a sample of smaller museum gift shops and some of the unique gifts that make them worth a stop. (See chapter 7 for museum locations and hours.)

The National Gallery of Art gift shop is not so small, actually. Its wares include printed reproductions, stationery, and jewelry, whose designs are all based on works in the gallery's permanent collections, as well as those from special exhibitions. The shop also has one of the largest selections of books on art history and architecture in the country, and a generous offering of children's products (books, art kits, games, and so on), too.

The gift shop at the Textile Museum offers an extensive selection of books on carpets and textiles, as well as Indian silk scarves, kilim pillows, Tibetan prayer rugs, and other out-of-the-ordinary items.

Washington National Cathedral's main shop, in the crypt of the Gothic cathedral, sells books, stained glass, and tapes. The Herb Cottage is a delightful oasis, selling dried herbs and garden gifts. The Greenhouse shop is one of the best and certainly most charming places in town to buy flowering plants and live herbs.

POLITICAL MEMORABILIA

Capitol Coin and Stamp Co. Inc.

1701 L St. NW. ☎ **202/296-0400.** Metro: Farragut North.

A museum of political memorabilia—pins, posters, banners—and all of it is for sale. This is also a fine resource for the endangered species of coin and stamp collectors.

✪ Political Americana

Union Station. ☎ **202/547-1685.** Metro: Union Station.

This is another great place to pick up souvenirs from a visit to D.C. The store sells political novelty items, books, bumper stickers, old campaign buttons, and historical memorabilia. Other locations include Georgetown Park, 3222 M St. NW (☎ **202/543-7300**) and 685 15th St. NW (☎ **202/547-1817**).

RECORDS, TAPES & CDS

Borders Books & Music

1800 L St. NW. ☎ **202/466-4999.** Metro: Farragut North.

Besides being a fab bookstore, Borders offers the best prices in town for CDs and tapes, and a wide range of music.

HMV

1229 Wisconsin Ave. NW. ☎ **202/333-9292.** Metro: Foggy Bottom, with a 20-minute walk.

This London-based record and tape store is fun to visit, with its cunning clientele, party atmosphere, and headphones at the ready for easy listening. But you can get a better deal almost anywhere else.

Melody Record Shop

1623 Connecticut Ave. NW. ☎ **202/232-4002.** Metro: Dupont Circle.

CDs, cassettes, and tapes are discounted 10% to 20% here, new releases 20% to 30%. Melody offers a wide variety of rock, classical, jazz, pop, show, and folk music, as well as a vast number of international selections. This is also a good place to shop for discounted electronic equipment, blank tapes, and cassettes. Its knowledgeable staff is a plus.

Olsson's Books & Records

See entry in Georgetown walking tour, below.

Tower Records

2000 Pennsylvania Ave. NW. ☎ **202/331-2400.** Metro: Foggy Bottom.

When you need a record at midnight on Christmas Eve, you go to Tower. The large, funky store, across the street from George Washington University, has a wide choice of records, cassettes, and compact discs in every category—but the prices are high.

12" Dance Records

2010 P St. NW, 2nd floor. ☎ **202/659-2010.** Metro: Dupont Circle.

Disco lives. If you ever moved to it on a dance floor, Wresch Dawidjian and his staff of DJs have got it, or they can get it. There's always a DJ mixing it up live in the store, and they pump the beats out into the street.

SPORTS & CAMPING

Eddie Bauer

See entry in Georgetown walking tour, below.

Fleet Feet

1840 Columbia Rd. NW. ☎ **202/387-3888.** Metro: Woodley Park–Zoo, with a 15-minute walk.

Everything for the runner, and the running-savvy staff knows where the trails are. A city-wide running group meets here on Saturday mornings.

Hudson Trail Outfitters

4530 Wisconsin Ave. NW. ☎ **202/363-9810.** Metro: Tenleytown.

This shop specializes in outdoor recreational equipment for backpackers, flyfishermen and women, kayakers, canoeists, and mountain bikers.

WINE & SPIRITS

The following liquor stores are among the best in the city for choice and value.

Calvert Woodley Liquors

4339 Connecticut Ave. NW. ☎ **202/966-4400.** Metro: Van Ness–UDC.

This is a large store with a friendly staff, nice selections, and good cheeses and other foods to go along with your drinks.

✪ Central Liquor

726 9th St. NW. ☎ **202/737-2800.** Metro: Metro Center or Gallery Place.

This is like a clearinghouse for liquor: Its great volume allows the store to offer the best prices in town on wines and liquor.

Eagle Wine & Liquor

3345 M St. NW. ☎ **202/333-5500.**

Georgetown residents come to this longtime establishment for its discounts and for assistance from a well-informed staff.

MacArthur Liquor

4877 MacArthur Blvd. NW. ☎ **202/338-1433.**

It's always busy, because the staff is so knowledgeable and enthusiastic, and because the shop has such an extensive and reasonably priced selection of excellent wines, both imported and domestic.

WOMEN'S CLOTHES & SHOES

If Washington women don't dress well, it isn't for lack of stores. The following boutiques range in styles from baggy grunge to the crisply tailored, from Laura Ashley to black leather.

Ann Taylor

Union Station. ☎ **202/371-8010.** Metro: Union Station.

Specializes in American-look, chic clothing, Joan and David and other footwear, and accessories. Other locations include 1720 K St. NW (☎ **202/466-3544**) and Georgetown Park, 3222 M St. NW (☎ **202/338-5290**).

Betsy Fisher

1224 Connecticut Ave. NW. ☎ **202/785-1975.** Metro: Dupont Circle.

A walk past the store is all it takes to know that this shop is a tad different. Its windowfront and racks show off whimsically feminine fashions, including hats, of new American designers.

Chanel Boutique

1455 Pennsylvania Ave. NW, in the courtyard of the Willard Inter-Continental Hotel. ☎ **202/638-5055.** Metro: Metro Center.

A modest selection of Chanel's signature designs, accessories, and jewelry, at immodest prices.

✪ Commander Salamander

1420 Wisconsin Ave. NW. ☎ **202/337-2265.** Metro: Foggy Bottom, with a 20-minute walk.

Too cool. Commander Salamander has a little bit of everything: Jean Paul Gaultier and Oldham creations; Betsey Johnson dresses for no more than $130; $1 ties and handmade jackets with Axl jewelry sewn on, for over $1000. Loud music, young crowd, funky.

Hit or Miss

The Shops at National Place. ☎ **202/347-0280.** Metro: Metro Center.

Here you'll find a mixture of professional and casual clothes for women at bargain prices. Other locations include 1140 Connecticut Ave. NW (☎ **202/223-8231**) and 900 19th St. (☎ **202/785-2226**).

Pirjo

1044 Wisconsin Ave. NW. ☎ **202/337-1390.** Metro: Foggy Bottom, with a 20-minute walk.

The funky, baggy, and pretty creations of designers like the Finnish Marimekko and others: Bettina, Flax, VIP. Styles range from casual to dressy; Pirjo sells elegant jewelry to boot.

Rizik's

1100 Connecticut Ave. NW. ☎ **202/223-4050.** Metro: Farragut North.

This is downtown high fashion, closer to art than clothing. Designs are by Caroline Herrara, Armani, Oscar de la Renta, and their ilk.

Saks-Jandel

5510 Wisconsin Ave., Chevy Chase, MD. ☎ **301/652-2250.** Metro: Friendship Heights.

This store displays elegant afternoon and evening wear by major European and American designers—Chanel, Valentino, Christian Dior, Yves Saint-Laurent rive gauche, Isaac Mizrahi (this was the site of the designer's promo for his movie, "Unzipped"), John Galliano, Prada, and many others. Saks-Jandel has an international clientele.

Secondhand Rose

See entry in Georgetown walking tour, below.

Talbots

1227 Connecticut Ave. NW. ☎ **202/887-6973.** Metro: Farragut North.

Talbots sells career and casual clothes with a decidedly conservative bent, and accessories to go with them. Another branch is at Georgetown Park, 3222 M St. NW (☎ **202/338-3510**).

Toast & Strawberries

1608 Connecticut Ave. NW. ☎ **202/234-2424.** Metro: Dupont Circle.

You'll see clothes from around the world and from local designers, too. Many in the collection are one-of-a-kind; some are casual and some ethnic, but all are fun to wear. The shop also sells some accessories.

Victoria's Secret

The Shops at National Place. ☎ **202/347-3535.** Metro: Metro Center.

Washington women really like the chain's feminine, sexy array of lingerie, so you'll find you're never too far from one of the shops.

WALKING TOUR
Georgetown Shopping

Start: M and 29th streets NW.

Directions: To get to Georgetown by public transportation, you can ride the Metro to Foggy Bottom and walk for 10 or 15 minutes, or take one of the 30-series buses (30, 32, 34, 36, 38B), all of which travel from downtown into Georgetown. Call **Metro** (☎ 202/637-7000) for exact information.

Finish: Wisconsin Avenue and Q Street NW.

Time: Allow 1 to 3 hours, depending on how much time you spend browsing or actually shopping.

Best Times: During store hours.

In Georgetown you can combine shopping and browsing (there are hundreds of stores) with a meal at a good restaurant, crowd-watching over cappuccino at a cafe, even a little sightseeing. The hub is at Wisconsin Avenue and M Street, and most of the stores are on those two arteries. In addition to shops, you'll encounter street vendors hawking T-shirts and handmade jewelry.

If you drive into Georgetown—this is definitely not advised because parking is almost impossible—check out the side streets off Wisconsin Avenue above M Street for spots. The Shops at Georgetown Park (see below) offers validated parking with purchases of $10 or more.

    Along M Street NW   For the first part of this shopping tour, we'll stroll along M Street, with a few diversions, from 29th to 33rd streets. Start at the:

1. **Spectrum Gallery,** 1132 29th St. NW (just below M Street) (☎ 202/333-0954), a cooperative venture since 1968, in which 32 professional Washington area artists, including painters, potters, sculptors, photographers, collagists, and printmakers, share in shaping gallery policy, maintenance, and operation. The art is reasonably priced. Open Tuesday to Saturday noon to 6pm, Sunday noon to 5pm, and by appointment.

    Walk around the corner onto M Street to:

2. **Grafix,** 2904 M St. NW (☎ 202/342-0610), which carries a noteworthy collection of vintage posters (from 1895 on), 16th- to 20th-century maps, 19th-century prints, vintage magazines from the turn of the century through the 1930s, and other collectibles. Open Tuesday, Wednesday, and Friday 11am to 6pm, Thursday 11am to 9pm, and Saturday 11am to 5pm.

3. ✪ **American Hand Plus,** 2906 M St. NW (☎ 202/965-3273), features exquisite contemporary handcrafted American ceramics and jewelry, plus international objets d'art. Open Monday to Saturday 11am to 6pm, Sunday 1 to 5pm.

4. **Animation Sensations,** 2914 M St. NW (☎ 202/337-5024). It's fun to peruse this collection of original animation cels and drawings, comic book/strip art, vintage movie posters, movie star autographs, Disney/Warner Brothers/Hanna-Barbera character figurines, and movie memorabilia. Open Monday to Saturday 11am to 7pm, Sunday noon to 5pm.

5. **Georgetown Antiques Center,** 2918 M St. NW, houses the **Cherub Antiques Gallery** (☎ 202/337-2224) specializes in art nouveau and art deco, art glass (signed Tiffany, Steuben, Lalique, and Gallé), Liberty arts and crafts, and Louis Icart etchings. Sharing the premises is **Michael Getz Antiques** (☎ 202/338-3811), which sells American, English, and continental silver; porcelain lamps; and many fireplace accessories. Open Monday to Saturday 11am to 6pm, Sunday noon to 5pm; closed Sunday July and August.

☕ **TAKE A BREAK** At Washington Harbour (30th Street, a block south of M Street) is a riverside development with an esplanade leading to a fountain and a group of restaurants with indoor windowed and outdoor umbrella-table seating overlooking the Potomac. The best of these is **Sequoia,** which features American fare (details in chapter 6).

Backtrack to M Street and turn left, walking until you see:

6. **Barnes & Noble,** 3040 M St. NW (☎ **202/965-9880**), a wonderful three-story shop that discounts all hardcovers 10%, *New York Times* hardcover bestsellers 30%, and *New York Times* paperback bestsellers 20%. It has sizable software, travel book, and children's title sections. A cafe on the second level hosts concerts. Open daily 9am to 11pm.

7. **Eddie Bauer** (☎ **202/342-2121**), which shares the same address, is a handsome two-level emporium specializing in outdoorsy sportswear for men and women. Come here for fly-fishing equipment (and books about fishing), backpacks, English Barbour jackets, hunter's caps, Stetson hats, luggage, flashlights, binoculars, hiking boots, Swiss Army knives, and other accoutrements of the adventurous lifestyle.

Turn left on 31st Street NW and continue past the canal; on your left is the:

8. **Yes! Bookshop,** 1035 31st St. NW (☎ **800/YES-1516,** or 202/338-7874 for a free catalog). A wealth of literature (both books and books on tape) on personal growth and personal transformation subjects can be found on the shelves of this rather unique store, along with books on health, natural medicine, men's and women's studies, mythology, creative writing, Jungian psychology, how to save the planet, ancient history, and Native American traditions. CDs and cassettes include non-Western music, instrumental music, New Age music, and instruction in everything from quitting smoking to astral projection and hypnosis. They also sell a large number of instructional videocassettes here. Open Monday to Thursday 10am to 7pm, Friday and Saturday 10am to 8pm, Sunday noon to 6pm.

Now turn onto South Street and walk 1 block further to Wisconsin Avenue, turning right and stopping just before the C&O Canal, where you can:

☕ **TAKE A BREAK** Stop in for croissants and cappuccino, a Camembert sandwich on baguette, or afternoon tea with sumptuous desserts at **Patisserie Café Didier,** 3206 Grace St. NW.

Now continue along Wisconsin Avenue, crossing the canal and walking until you reach:

9. ✪ **The Shops at Georgetown Park,** 3222 M St. NW (at Wisconsin Avenue) (☎ **202/298-5577**). This four-story complex of about 100 shops belongs, architecturally, to two worlds: outside, quietly Federal, in keeping with the character of the neighborhood; inside, flamboyantly Victorian, with a huge skylight, fountains, and ornate chandeliers. You could spend hours here exploring branches of the nation's most exclusive specialty stores. Represented are Ann Taylor, bebe (upscale women's clothing), Caché, J. Crew, Polo/Ralph Lauren (for men and women), and Abercrombie and Fitch (for upscale casual wear). Men will find *GQ*-caliber Italian designer sportswear at Giotto and Italian-designer evening wear at Nicolo. Also featured are many gift/lifestyle boutiques such as Circuit City Express, Sharper Image, Crabtree & Evelyn, and the fascinating Gallery of History (framed collector historical documents). If you have kids, take them to F.A.O. Schwarz and Learning-smith (billing itself as "the general store for the

Walking Tour—Georgetown Shopping

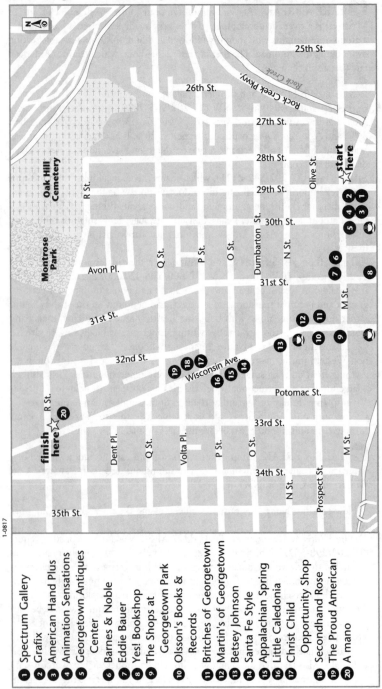

1. Spectrum Gallery
2. Grafix
3. American Hand Plus
4. Animation Sensations
5. Georgetown Antiques Center
6. Barnes & Noble
7. Eddie Bauer
8. Yes! Bookshop
9. The Shops at Georgetown Park
10. Olsson's Books & Records
11. Britches of Georgetown
12. Martin's of Georgetown
13. Betsey Johnson
14. Santa Fe Style
15. Appalachian Spring
16. Little Caledonia
17. Christ Child Opportunity Shop
18. Secondhand Rose
19. The Proud American
20. A mano

1-0817

curious mind," it has many interactive facilities for children). An Old Town Trolley ticket booth (see chapter 4) is on the premises. There are several restaurants, including Clyde's (see chapter 6 for details), gourmet emporium/cafe Dean and Deluca, and the parklike Canal Walk Café Food Court with a painted sky overhead, and many plants and garden furnishings. An archaeological exhibit of artifacts found during the complex's excavation can be viewed on Level 2. Georgetown Park maintains a full-service Concierge Center offering gift wrapping, worldwide shipping, postal/fax/photocopy services, gift certificates, even sightseeing information. Validated parking in the underground garage is available with minimum $10 purchase. Open Monday to Saturday 10am to 9pm, Sunday noon to 6pm.

Along Wisconsin Avenue NW   Walk back up Wisconsin Avenue crossing M Street en route to:

10. ✪ **Olsson's Books and Records,** 1239 Wisconsin Ave. NW, between M and N streets (☎ **202/338-9544**). This 20-year-old, independent quality bookstore chain has about 60,000 to 70,000 books on its shelves. Members of its helpful staff know what they're talking about and will order books they don't have in stock. Competition has forced them to offer discounts: 25% off *Washington Post* bestsellers, 20% off certain hardcover books, and 10% off certain paperbacks that are promoted as "good reads" by store staff. Similar discounts exist for tapes and CDs. Regular prices are pretty good. Open Monday to Thursday 10am to 11pm, Friday and Saturday 10am to midnight, Sunday 11am to 10pm.

11. Britches of Georgetown, 1247 Wisconsin Ave. NW (☎ **202/338-3330**), is much patronized by well-dressed Washington men. It sells moderately priced to expensive dress apparel, both designer wear and from its own label. You'll find Hugo Boss, St. Andrews, Southwick, and Nick Hilton here. Hours are Monday through Wednesday, Friday and Saturday 11am to 6pm, Thursday 11am to 9pm, and Sunday noon to 6pm. Also check out the casual/sportswear division, **Britches Great Outdoors,** at 1225 Wisconsin Ave. NW (☎ **202/333-3666**).

12. Martin's of Georgetown, 1304 Wisconsin Ave. NW (☎ **202/338-6144**). This shop has been proffering exquisite wares since 1929. Come in and feast your eyes on Martin's selection of Lalique vases, Christofle silver, hand-painted Herend china, and Limoges boxes, along with other fine lines of china, silver, crystal, flatware, and dinnerware. Martin's is a prestigious bridal registry (both the Nixon and Johnson daughters were registered here). You'll find stuffed animals, baby gifts, picture frames, and other quality gift items here, too. Open Tuesday to Saturday 10am to 6pm.

☕ **TAKE A BREAK**   **Paolo's,** for California-style Italian cuisine in a simpatico setting, is just down the street at 1303 Wisconsin Ave. NW, at N Street. See chapter 6 for details.

13. Betsey Johnson, 1319 Wisconsin Ave. NW (☎ **202/338-4090**). New York's flamboyant flower-child designer has a Georgetown shop. She personally decorated the bubble-gum pink walls. Her sexy, offbeat play-dress-up styles are great party and club clothes for the young and the still-skinny young at heart. Open Monday to Friday 11am to 7pm, Saturday 11am to 8pm, Sunday noon to 6pm.

14. Santa Fe Style, 1413 Wisconsin Ave. NW (☎ **202/333-3747**). Here you'll find high-quality Southwest merchandise, mostly handmade items from New Mexico and Arizona. The inventory includes silver jewelry, picture frames, oxidized-iron animal decorations, barbed-wire art, furniture, pottery, colorful painted sculptures made from barn-roof tin, birdhouses, Southwest cookbooks, and more. Open Monday to Saturday 10am to 6pm, Sunday noon to 5pm.

15. Appalachian Spring, 1415 Wisconsin Ave. NW, at P Street (☎ **202/337-5780**), brings country crafts to citified Georgetown. They sell pottery, jewelry, newly made pieced and appliqué quilts, stuffed dolls and animals, candles, rag rugs, hand-blown glassware, an incredible collection of kaleidoscopes, glorious weavings, and wooden kitchen ware. Everything in the store is made by hand in the USA There's another branch in Union Station. Open Monday to Saturday 10am to 6pm, Sunday noon to 6pm, with extended hours in the spring and fall.

16. ✪ Little Caledonia, 1419 Wisconsin Ave. NW (☎ **202/333-4700**), is a delightful rabbit warren of tiny rooms filled with indoor and outdoor furnishings (18th- and 19th-century mahogany reproductions are featured), ceramic figures, exquisite upholstery and drapery fabrics, candles, tablecloths, wallpapers, lamps, and much, much more. It's been here for 60 years. Open Monday to Saturday 10am to 6pm, and Thanksgiving to Christmas Sunday noon to 5pm.

17. Christ Child Opportunity Shop, 1427 Wisconsin Ave. NW (☎ **202/333-6635**). Proceeds from merchandise bought here go to children's charities. Among the first-floor items (all donations), I saw a wicker trunk for $5 and the usual thrift shop jumble of jewelry, clothes, shoes, hats, and odds and ends. Upstairs, higher quality merchandise is left on consignment; it's more expensive, but if you know antiques, you might find bargains in jewelry, silver, china, quilts, and other items. Open Tuesday to Saturday 10am to 3:45pm; closed in August.

18. Secondhand Rose, 1516 Wisconsin Ave. NW, between P and Q streets (☎ **202/337-3378**). This upscale second-floor consignment shop specializes in designer merchandise. Creations by Chanel, Armani, Donna Karan, Calvin Klein, Yves Saint-Laurent, Ungaro, Ralph Lauren, and others are sold at about a third of the original price, like a gorgeous Scaasi black velvet and yellow satin ball gown for $400 (it was $1,200 new) and Yves Saint-Laurent pumps in perfect condition for $45. Everything is in style, in season, and in excellent condition. Secondhand Rose is also a great place to shop for gorgeous furs, designer shoes and bags, and costume jewelry. Open Monday to Friday 11am to 6pm, Saturday 10am to 6pm.

19. The Proud American, 1529 Wisconsin Ave. NW (☎ **202/625-1776**) is somewhat of a misnomer. Though its offerings include some American pieces, the store specializes in 18th- and 19th-century European furnishings, decorative accessories, paintings, prints, and porcelains. Open Tuesday to Saturday 10am to 6pm.

20. ✪ A mano, 1677 Wisconsin Ave. NW (☎ **202/298-7200**) sells unique handmade imported French and Italian ceramics that owner Adam Mahr brings back from his frequent forages to Europe. Open Monday to Saturday 10am to 6pm, Sunday noon to 5pm.

Washington by day is a city so full of things to do that you'll never get to them all. Washington by night is no different. The venues for every kind of theater, dance, and musical entertainment are here, with new ones opening every day. The Kennedy Center alone offers six theaters under one roof. The downtown area between 15th and 7th streets NW is becoming again what it was in the mid–19th to mid–20th centuries, Washington's theater district: This is where you'll find the National, Warner, Ford's, and Shakespeare Theaters; the MCI Center; and, coming in about 5 years, the Washington Opera House.

Just north of this area is the up-and-coming U Street corridor, known mainly for its nightclubs. Further north and west of U Street is the neighborhood of Adams-Morgan, another center of bars and nightclubs. A pocket of excellent repertory theaters—the Studio, Woolly Mammoth, and Source Theaters—overlap both the U Street and Adams-Morgan neighborhoods. My own favorite Washington theater, Arena, is off on its own on the waterfront, in southeast Washington.

Even if you're on a limited budget, you'll find lots to do at night in Washington. For one thing, many of the museums and other attractions you visit during the day often stage free or inexpensive cultural performances in the evening. Secondly, you should know about the Kennedy Center's "Performing Arts for Everyone" program. Launched in the spring of 1997, the program offers free concerts by mostly local performers each evening at 6pm in its Grand Foyer, as well as "pay what you can" tickets, good on certain days for selected performances on the center's stages. Read on for details.

In addition to the listings below, check the Friday "Weekend" section of the *Washington Post*, which will inform you about children's theater, sports events, flower shows, and all else. *The City Paper*, available free at restaurants, bookstores, and other places around town, is another good source.

TICKETS

TICKETplace now has two locations: in George Washington University's Lisner Auditorium, 1730 21st St. NW (at H Street; Metro: Foggy Bottom) and in the Old Post Office Pavilion, 1100 Pennsylvania Ave. NW (Metro: Federal Triangle). Call ☎ **202/ TICKETS** for information. **TICKETplace** is a service of the

Cultural Alliance of Greater Washington; the Old Post Office Pavilion kiosk is a co-operative venture between the Cultural Alliance and the Kennedy Center. On the day of performance only (except Sunday and Monday, see below), you can buy half-price tickets (for cash only) to performances at most major Washington area theaters and concert halls, not only for dramatic productions, but for opera, ballet, and other events as well. The Lisner Auditorium booth also serves as a **Ticketmaster** outlet. TICKETplace is open Tuesday to Friday from noon to 6pm and Saturday from 11am to 5pm; half-price tickets for Sunday and Monday shows are sold on Saturday.

Full-price tickets for most performances in town can also be bought through **Ticketmaster** (☎ 202/432-SEAT) at **Hecht's Department Store,** 12th and G streets NW. You can purchase tickets to Washington theatrical, musical, and other events before you leave home by calling ☎ 800/551-SEAT. Another similar ticket outlet is **Protix** (☎ **800/955-5566** or 703/218-6500).

1　Theater

D.C.'s theatrical productions are first-rate and varied. Almost anything on Broadway has either been previewed here or will eventually come here. Washington, D.C., also has several nationally acclaimed repertory companies and a theater specializing in Shakespearean productions. Additional theater offerings, including those at the **Kennedy Center,** are listed under "Other Performing Arts" later in this chapter.

Arena Stage

6th St. and Maine Ave. SW. ☎ **202/488-3300.** Tickets $23–$42; discounts available for students, people with disabilities, groups, and senior citizens. A limited number of half-price tickets, called HOTTIX, are available 90 minutes before most performances (call for details). Metro: Waterfront.

Founded by the brilliant Zelda Fichandler, the Arena Stage, now in its fifth decade, is home to one of the oldest acting ensembles in the nation. Several works nurtured here have moved to Broadway, and many graduates have gone on to commercial stardom, among them Ned Beatty, James Earl Jones, Robert Prosky, Jane Alexander, and George Grizzard.

Arena presents eight subscription-season productions annually on two stages: the **Fichandler** (a theater-in-the-round) and the smaller, fan-shaped **Kreeger.** In addition, the Arena houses the **Old Vat,** a space used for new play readings and special productions.

A recent September-to-June season (sometimes shows are extended into summer) included productions of Molière's *The Miser,* Tom Stoppard's *Arcadia,* Brian Freel's *Molly Sweeney,* the Stephen Sondheim/James Lapine musical *Sunday in the Park with George,* Eugene O'Neill's *Anna Christie,* and Pearl Cleage's *Blues for an Alabama Sky* (starring Phylicia Rashad). Arena's lineup for 1998 includes Chekhov's *Uncle Vanya; Lovers and Executioners* by Montfleury, adapted by John Strand; and Moss Hart and George Kaufman's *You Can't Take It With You.* The theater has always championed new plays and playwrights and is committed to producing the works of playwrights from diverse cultures. Douglas C. Wager is the Arena Stage's artistic director.

Ford's Theatre

511 10th St. NW (between E and F sts.). ☎ **202/347-4833,** TDD 202/426-1749 for listings, 800/955-5566 or 703/218-6500 to charge tickets. Tickets $27–$40; discounts available for families, also for senior citizens at matinee performances and any time on the "day of" for evening shows; both seniors and students with ID can get "rush" tickets an hour before performances if tickets are available. Metro: Metro Center or Gallery Place.

This is the actual theater where, on the evening of April 14, 1865, actor John Wilkes Booth shot President Lincoln. The assassination marked the end of what had been John T. Ford's very popular theater; it remained closed for more than a century. In 1968 Ford's reopened, completely restored to its 1865 appearance, based on photographs, sketches, newspaper articles, and samples of wallpaper and curtain material from museum collections. The presidential box is decorated and furnished as it was on that fateful night, including the original crimson damask sofa and framed engraving of George Washington.

Ford's season is more or less year-round (it's closed for awhile in the summer). Several of its productions have gone on to Broadway and off-Broadway. Recent shows have included *Paper Moon, Twilight in Los Angeles,* and *The Fantasticks.*

A big event here is the nationally televised "A Festival at Ford's," which is a celebrity-studded bash usually held in the fall, and attended by the president and first lady. A Washington tradition is the holiday performance of Dickens' *A Christmas Carol.*

National Theatre

1321 Pennsylvania Ave. NW. ☎ **202/628-6161.** Tickets $20–$70; discounts available for students, senior citizens, military personnel, and people with disabilities. Metro: Metro Center.

The luxurious, Federal-style National Theatre, elegantly renovated to the tune of $6.5 million in 1983, is the oldest continuously operating theater in Washington (since 1835) and the third-oldest in the nation. It's exciting just to see this stage on which Sarah Bernhardt, John Barrymore, Helen Hayes, and so many other notables have performed. The National is the closest thing Washington has to a Broadway-style playhouse. Managed by New York's Shubert Organization, it presents star-studded hits, often pre- or post-Broadway, most of the year. A recent season included productions of *Chicago* and *Rent.* The National seats 1,672.

The National also offers free public-service programs: Saturday-morning children's theater (puppets, clowns, magicians, dancers, and singers), free summer films, and Monday-night showcases of local groups and performers. Call ☎ **202/783-3370** for details.

Shakespeare Theatre

450 7th St. NW (between D and E sts.). ☎ **202/393-2700.** Tickets $13.50–$49.50, $10 for standing-room tickets sold 2 hours before sold-out performances; discounts available for students, groups, and senior citizens. Metro: Archives–Navy Memorial or Gallery Place.

This internationally renowned classical ensemble company, which for 2 decades performed at the Folger Shakespeare Library, moved to larger quarters at the above address in 1992. Under the direction of Michael Kahn, it offers three Shakespearean productions plus two other modern classics each September-to-June season. The 1997–98 season includes *The Tempest, Othello* (starring 1997 William Shakespeare Award winner Patrick Stewart in an otherwise all African-American cast), *The Merry Wives of Windsor,* Ibsen's *Peer Gynt,* and Tennessee Williams's *Sweet Bird of Youth* (starring Elizabeth Ashley). Other well-known actors such as Jean Stapleton, Tom Hulce, Kelly McGillis, and Richard Thomas have joined the company for specific productions. This is top-level theater. Furthermore, the company offers admission-free summer Shakespearean productions at the Carter Barron Amphitheatre in Rock Creek Park (see listing for Carter Barron below, under "Outdoor Pavilions and Stadiums").

Source Theatre Company

1835 14th St. NW (between S and T sts.). ☎ **202/462-1073** for information, 800/955-5566 or 703/218-6500 to charge tickets. Tickets $20–$25, OFF HOURS shows $15, Washington Theatre Festival shows $8–$15.

Washington's major producer of new plays, the Source also mounts works of established playwrights—for example, David Mamet's *The Cherry Orchard,* Arthur Miller's *A View from the Bridge,* and A. R. Gurney's *A Cheever Evening.* It presents top local artists in a year-round schedule of dramatic and comedy plays, both at the above address and, during the summer, at various spaces around town. The theater is also used for an OFF HOURS series of productions geared to a contemporary urban audience. Annual events here include the Washington Theatre Festival each July, a 4-week showcase of about 50 new plays. The Source, which produces many African-American works, welcomes original scripts from unknowns.

Studio Theatre

1333 P St. NW. ☎ **202/332-3300.** Tickets $19.50–$29.50, Secondstage shows $15. Discounts available for students and senior citizens. Metro: Dupont Circle or McPherson Square.

Under artistic director Joy Zinoman, the Studio has consistently produced interesting contemporary plays, nurtured Washington acting talent, and garnered numerous Helen Hayes Awards for outstanding achievement. Many plays come here from off-Broadway. Recent productions have included Thomas W. Jones II's *The Birth of the Boom,* David Mamet's *The Cryptogram,* John Osborne's *Look Back in Anger,* and Terrence McNally's *Love! Valour! Compassion!* The Studio also houses Secondstage, a 50-seat space on the third floor where emerging artists, directors, and actors can showcase their work. The season runs year-round. A $4.5 million renovation completed in 1997 remodeled the main theater and added a wonderful new one, the Milton. Street parking is easy to find, and there's a pay lot at P Street between 14th and 15th streets.

Woolly Mammoth Theatre Company

1401 Church St. NW (between P and Q sts.). For tickets, call Protix ☎ **703/218-6500.** Tickets $13–$28. They offer a range of ticket discounts, including reduced prices for seniors and students, and pay-what-you-can nights; inquire at the box office. Free parking across the street. Metro: Dupont Circle, about 5 blocks away. You might prefer to take a cab from there, since the neighborhood is often rather deserted at night; on request, they'll call a cab for you after the show.

Established in 1980, the Woolly Mammoth offers as many as six productions each year-long season, specializing, according to a publicist, in "new, offbeat, and quirky plays." "I'm not interested in theater where people sit back and say, 'That was nice. I enjoyed that,'" says artistic director Howard Shalwitz. "I only look for plays that directly challenge the audience in some important way." The 1997–98 lineup includes *Brimstone and Treacle* by Dennis Potter, *The Gene Pool* by Christi Stuart-Brown, *Man, Woman, Dinosaur* by Regina Porter, and *Dead Funny* by Terry Johnson. This company has garnered 14 Helen Hayes Awards, among other accolades, and is consistently reviewed by *The New York Times.*

2 Other Performing Arts

The following listings are a potpourri of places offering a mixed bag of theater, opera, classical music, headliners, jazz, rock, dance, and comedy. Here you'll find some of the top entertainment choices in the District.

MULTICULTURAL FACILITIES

DAR Constitution Hall

18th and D sts. NW. ☎ **202/638-2661** or 202/628-4780, 800/551-SEAT or 202/432-SEAT to charge tickets. Tickets $15–$50. Metro: Farragut West.

Housed within a beautiful, turn-of-the-century beaux-arts–style building is this fine, 3,746-seat auditorium. Its excellent acoustics make it a prime venue for hearing the eclectic music that plays here—the Boston Symphony, John Hiatt, Count Basie Orchestra, Los Angeles Philharmonic, Lee Greenwood, Diana Ross, Jay Leno, Ray Charles, Buddy Guy, The Temptations, Trisha Yearwood, Roy Clark, Kathleen Battle, and Marilyn Horne.

The Folger Shakespeare Library

201 E. Capitol St. SE. ☎ **202/544-7077.** Students and seniors receive discounts with proof of ID. Call for information about ticket prices, which can range from $5 to $40, depending upon the event. Metro: Capitol South.

The Folger Shakespeare Library is open year-round, featuring exhibits and tours of its Tudor-style great rooms (see chapter 7 for details). Its theatrical programs and special events generally coincide with the academic year, from October through May. Among the offerings are the **Folger Consort,** an early music ensemble, which performs medieval, Renaissance, and baroque music, troubadour songs, madrigals, and court ensembles; between October and May, they give 30 concerts over the course of 7 weekends.

The Folger presents theatrical and musical performances, lectures, readings, and other events in its Elizabethan Theatre, which is styled after the innyard theatre from Shakespeare's time.

In addition, an **evening lecture series** called "Places in the Mind" features writers, artists, actors, and performers (such as playwright Wendy Wasserstein and writer Roger Angell) speaking on cities around the globe. On selected evenings, **readings** feature such poets as Jorie Graham, Seamus Heany, Gwendolyn Brooks, Michael Ondaatje, and John Ashbery. Another exciting program is the Friday-night **PEN/Faulkner series** of fiction readings by noted authors Joyce Carol Oates, Ann Beattie, Susan Power, Albert Murray, Joan Didion, and Richard Ford. And the Folger offers Saturday **programs for children** ranging from medieval treasure hunts to preparing an Elizabethan feast.

John F. Kennedy Center for the Performing Arts

At the southern end of New Hampshire Ave. NW and Rock Creek Pkwy. ☎ **800/444-1324** or 202/467-4600. Discounts of 50% are offered (for most attractions) to students, seniors 65 and over, people with permanent disabilities, and enlisted military personnel with a valid ID. Metro: Foggy Bottom (though it's a fairly short walk, there's a free shuttle between the station and the Kennedy Center, departing every 15 minutes from 7pm to midnight). Bus: 80 from Metro Center.

Our national performing arts center, the hub of Washington's cultural and entertainment scene, is actually made up of six different theaters. You can find out what is scheduled during your stay (and charge tickets) before leaving home by calling the above toll-free number. Half-price tickets are available for full-time students, senior citizens, enlisted military personnel, people with disabilities, and persons with fixed, low income (call ☎ **202/416-8340** for details).

As mentioned in the introduction to this chapter, the Kennedy Center began in 1997 a series of free concerts by area musicians, staged each evening at 6pm in the center's Grand Foyer. The Friday "Weekend" section of the *Washington Post* lists the free performances scheduled for the coming week. Also call about "pay what you can" performances, scheduled throughout the year on certain days, for certain shows.

The 26-year-old center is in the process of a $50 million overhaul scheduled to continue until the year 2007. The Concert Hall was the first to be renovated; following ten months of work, the hall reopened in October 1997 with improvements that include wheelchair accessibility for 4% of the seats and enhanced acoustics.

Opera House   This plush red-and-gilt 2,300-seat theater is designed for ballet, modern dance, and musical comedy, as well as opera, and it's also the setting for occasional gala events such as the Kennedy Center Honors, which you've probably seen on TV (Neil Simon, B. B. King, and Sidney Poitier have been honorees). Other offerings have included performances by the Joffrey Ballet, the Bolshoi Ballet, the Kirov Ballet, the Royal Ballet, and the American Ballet Theatre. In 1998, the Washington Opera, under the artistic direction of Placido Domingo, will bring Puccini's *La Rondine*, Mozart's *Don Giovanni*, and Conrad Susa and Philip Littell's *The Dangerous Liaisons* to the Opera House. Recent theater productions here have included Rodgers and Hammerstein's *The King and I* (starring Hayley Mills) and *Phantom of the Opera.*

Concert Hall   This is the home of The National Symphony Orchestra, which presents concerts from September to June. Tickets are available by subscription and for individual performances. Guest artists have included Itzhak Perlman, Vladimir Ashkenazy, Zubin Mehta, Pinchas Zukerman, André Previn, Jean-Pierre Rampal, and Isaac Stern. Headliner entertainers such as Ray Charles, Patti LuPone, Bill Cosby, and Harry Belafonte also appear here. Among the 1998 performances planned are the National Symphony Orchestra's Russian Festival, under the artistic direction of Mstislav Rostropovich; a Caribbean Festival; and the fourth annual Mozart Festival.

Terrace Theater   Small chamber works, choral recitals, musicals, comedy revues, cabarets, and theatrical and modern-dance performances are among the varied provinces of the 500-seat Terrace Theater, a Bicentennial gift from Japan. It's been the setting for solo performances by violinist Eugene Fodor, pianists Santiago Rodriguez and Peter Serkin, soprano Dawn Upshaw, and jazz singer Barbara Cook. Performance artists Laurie Anderson and Michael Moschen have performed here, and jazz evenings have included tributes to Count Basie, Louis Armstrong, and Duke Ellington. Every spring the Terrace (along with the Theater Lab) hosts productions of six finalists in the American College Theatre Festival competition.

Eisenhower Theater   A wide range of dramatic productions can be seen here. Some recent examples: *Angels in America, Master Class* starring Zoe Caldwell as the legendary diva Maria Callas, Athol Fugard's *Valley Song,* the Royal Shakespeare Company's *A Midsummer Night's Dream,* and in late 1997, Neil Simon's new play, *Proposals,* among other things. The Eisenhower is also the setting for smaller productions of the **Washington Opera** from December to February, solo performances by the likes of Harry Belafonte, dance presentations by the Paul Taylor Dance Company, and others. Tickets for most theatrical productions are in the $25 to $55 range. Prices for opera seats tend to soar higher.

Theater Lab and More   By day, the Theater Lab is Washington's premier stage for children's theater. Evenings it becomes a cabaret, now in a long run of *Shear Madness,* a comedy whodunit (tickets are $25 to $29). Elsewhere at the center, there are family concerts by the National Symphony Orchestra several times each year, not to mention clowns, jugglers, dance troupes, improvisational theater, storytellers, and films. Many events are scheduled around the Christmas and Easter holidays.

See also "Cinema," below, for details on the **AFI** (American Film Institute), yet another Kennedy Center facility.

Limited underground parking at the Kennedy Center is $8 for the entire evening after 5pm; if that lot is full, go to the Columbia Plaza Garage at 2400 Virginia Ave. NW, which runs a free shuttle back to the facility.

Lincoln Theater

1215 U St. NW. ☎ **202/328-6000.** Tickets range in price from $10 to $25 and are available at the theater box office and through Ticketmaster outlets or by calling 800/551-SEAT or 202/432-SEAT to charge tickets. Metro: U Street/Cardozo.

In the heart of happening U Street, the Lincoln was once a movie theater, vaudeville house, and nightclub featuring black stars like Louis Armstrong and Cab Calloway. The theater closed in the 1970s and reopened in 1994 after a renovation returned the theater to its former elegance. Today the theater books jazz, R&B, gospel, and comedy acts, and events like the D.C. Film Festival.

Lisner Auditorium

On the campus of George Washington University, 21st and H sts. NW. ☎ **202/994-1500.** Tickets average $15–$50 depending upon event. Tickets are available through Protix (703/218-6500), Ticketmaster (800/551-SEAT or 202/432-SEAT), and TICKETplace (202/TICKETS). Discounts may be available for students and others, depending upon promoter. Metro: Foggy Bottom.

One of my favorite places to hear good music, Lisner is small, only 1,500 seats, and you always feel close to the stage. Bookings include musical groups like Los Lobos and Siouxsie and the Banshees, comedians like "Weird Al" Yankovic, and children's entertainers like Raffi, but mostly cultural shows, everything from a Pakistani rock group to the Washington Revels' annual romp at Christmas.

Warner Theatre

1299 Pennsylvania Ave. NW (entrance on 13th St., between E and F sts.). ☎ **800/551-SEAT,** 202/783-4000, or 202/432-SEAT to charge tickets. Play tickets $20–$60. Metro: Metro Center. Parking is available in the Warner Building PMI lot on 12th St. NW, for $6.

Opened in 1924 as the Earle Theatre (a movie/vaudeville palace) and restored to its original appearance in 1992 at a cost of $10 million, this stunning neoclassical-style theater features a gold-leafed grand lobby and auditorium. Everything is plush and magnificent, from the glittering crystal chandeliers to the gold-tasseled swagged-velvet draperies. It's worth coming by just to see its ornately detailed interior. The 2,000-seat auditorium offers year-round entertainment, alternating dance performances (from Baryshnikov to the Washington Ballet's Christmas performance of *The Nutcracker*) and Broadway/off-Broadway shows (the fabulous *Stomp* and *Jelly's Last Jam*) with headliner entertainment (Sheryl Crow, k. d. lang, Natalie Merchant, Chris Isaak, Wynton Marsalis). Call ahead for a schedule of events taking place during your visit.

HUGE ARENAS

Baltimore Arena

201 W. Baltimore St., Baltimore, MD. ☎ **410/347-2020,** 800/551-SEAT or 410/481-SEAT for tickets.

This 13,500-seat arena, a few blocks from Baltimore's Inner Harbor and around the corner from Camden Yards, is home to several local sports teams. When they're not playing, the arena hosts big-name concerts and family entertainment shows. The Beatles appeared here back in the 1960s. More recently, they've presented *Sesame Street Live,* Ringling Brothers and Barnum and Bailey Circus, *Disney on Ice,* and headliners such as New Edition, Alan Jackson, Reba McEntire, Brooks & Dunn, Paul Simon, Liza Minnelli, Luther Vandross, and Vince Gill.

To get here by car, take I-95 north to I-395 (stay in the left lane) to the Inner Harbor exit and follow Howard Street to the Arena. You can also take a MARC train from Union Station.

MCI Center

601 F St. NW, where it meets 7th St. ☎ **301/499-6300.** Metro: Gallery Place.

Set on 5 acres in a prime downtown location, the MCI Center is the new home for basketball teams, the Washington Wizards (formerly the Bullets) and the Georgetown Hoyas, and hockey team, the Washington Capitals, with seats for 20,600 fans to watch the games. This is also the site for the world championship figure skating competition and the Franklin National Bank Classic competition for college basketball.

The center is open 365 days a year, not just as a sports facility but as a location for rock and country music concerts and business conferences. Within the three-story complex are a 25,000 square-foot Discovery Channel store, a Destination D.C. retail store, a National Sports Gallery (an interactive sports museum), and three restaurants.

The Patriot Center

George Mason University, 4400 University Dr., Fairfax, VA. ☎ **703/993-3000.** ☎ 800/551-SEAT or 202/432-SEAT to charge tickets. The facility has 4,000 free parking spaces.

This 10,000-seat facility hosts major headliners. Performers here have included Randy Travis, David Copperfield, Gloria Estefan, Tom Petty, Natalie Cole, Sting, Counting Crows, and Kenny Rogers. There are family events such as *Sesame Street Live* here, too. To get here by car, take the I-495 to Braddock Road West, and continue about 6 miles to University Drive.

US Airways Arena

One Harry S. Truman Dr., Exit 15A or 17A off the Capital Beltway in Landover, MD. ☎ **800/551-SEAT** or 301/350-3400.

This 19,000-seat arena hosts a variety of concerts and headliner entertainment, including Pavarotti, AC/DC, Rod Stewart, Neil Diamond, and Garth Brooks, the Washington Warthogs indoor soccer games, Washington International Horse Show, and monster trucks events.

OUTDOOR PAVILIONS & STADIUMS

When summer comes to Washington, much of the entertainment moves outdoors. As city theaters go dark or cut back on performance schedules in July and August to catch their breath and gear up for a new season, a handful of Washington area amphitheaters pick up the slack. Performers who might have appeared indoors from fall through spring now show up on the stages listed below. It's a happy arrangement for everyone.

Carter Barron Amphitheater

16th St. and Colorado Ave. NW. ☎ **202/260-6836.** Take Metro to Silver Spring, transfer to S2 or S4 bus, with "Federal Triangle" destination sign, and let the driver know you wish to hop off at the 16th St. bus stop nearest the Carter Barron; the amphitheater is a 5-minute walk from that stop.

Way out on 16th Street (close to the Maryland border) is this 4,250-seat amphitheater in Rock Creek Park. Summer performances include a range of gospel, blues, and classical entertainment, though each year is different; my husband still talks about the Bruce Springsteen concert he saw here years ago. You can always count on Shakespeare: The Shakespeare Theatre Free For All takes place at the Carter Barron usually for 2 to 3 weeks in June, Tuesday through Sunday evenings; the free tickets are available the day of performance only, on a first-come, first-served basis (call ☎ 202/628-5770 for details). The 1997 Free For All featured Harry Hamlin in the title role of *Henry V;* the 1998 Free For All will star Kelly McGillis as Helena in *All's Well That Ends Well.*

Merriweather Post Pavilion

10475 Little Patuxent Pkwy. (just off Rte. 29 in Columbia, MD). ☎ **410/730-2424** for information; 800/955-5566, 410/481-6500, or 703/218-6500 to charge tickets. Tickets $17–$50 pavilion, $15–$23 lawn.

During the summer there's celebrity entertainment almost nightly at the Merriweather Post Pavilion, about 40 minutes by car from downtown D.C. There's reserved seating in the open-air pavilion (overhead protection provided in case of rain) and general-admission seating on the lawn (no refunds for rain) to see such performers as James Taylor, Tina Turner, Van Halen, the Beach Boys, Liza Minnelli, Sting, Julio Iglesias, Joan Rivers, Hootie and the Blowfish, Jimmy Buffett, Elton John, Al Jarreau, and Barry Manilow. If you choose the lawn seating, bring blankets and picnic fare (beverages must be bought on the premises).

Nissan Pavilion at Stone Ridge

7800 Cellar Door Dr. (off Wellington Rd. in Bristow, VA). ☎ **800/455-8999** or 703/754-6400 for concert information; 800/551-SEAT or 202/432-SEAT to charge tickets.

With a capacity of 25,000 seats (10,000 under the roof, the remainder on the lawn), this immense state-of-the-art entertainment facility just 25 minutes from the Beltway features major acts varying from classical to country. Since its opening in the summer of 1995, featured performers have included Yanni, Dave Matthews Band, Rush, Melissa Etheridge, Phish, Reba McEntire, The Cranberries, James Taylor, Van Halen, Jimmy Buffett, David Bowie, Nine Inch Nails, R.E.M., and Elton John. The action is enhanced by giant video screens inside the pavilion and on the lawn. To get here by car, take I-66 west to Exit 43B, turn left on Route 29, continue half a mile, and turn left onto Wellington Road; the Nissan Pavilion is about a mile down on your right.

Robert F. Kennedy Memorial Stadium/D.C. Armory

2400 E. Capitol St. SE. ☎ **202/547-9077;** 800/551-SEAT or 202/432-SEAT to charge tickets. Metro: Stadium-Armory.

RFK, until this year, has been the home stadium for the Washington Redskins football team, who now play at the new Jack Kent Cooke facility in Raljohn, MD. The stadium continues as an excellent summer event facility, packing crowds of 55,000-plus into its seats to hear concerts by the Rolling Stones, the Eagles, and other big name groups, and to watch D.C. United Major League soccer and college football.

The D.C. Armory, right next door, is a year-round venue for the Ringling Brothers Barnum & Bailey Circus, antique shows, and other events that require space for as many as 10,000 people.

Wolf Trap Farm Park for the Performing Arts

1551 Trap Rd., Vienna, VA. ☎ **703/255-1868**, or Protix (703/218-6500) to charge tickets. Filene Center seats $7–$45, lawn $7–$16; Barns tickets average $14–$20.

The country's only national park devoted to the performing arts, Wolf Trap, just 30 minutes by car from downtown D.C., offers a star-studded **Summer Festival Season** from late May to mid-September. The 1997 season featured performances by the National Symphony Orchestra (it's their summer home), adopted daughter Mary Chapin Carpenter, Patti LaBelle, Willie Nelson, The Neville Brothers, Ray Charles, and the dances of Pilobolus, Riverdance, and Twyla Tharp.

Performances take place in the 7,000-seat **Filene Center,** about half of which is under the open sky. You can also buy cheaper lawn seats on the hill, which is sometimes the nicest way to go. If you do, arrive early (the lawn opens 90 minutes before the performance), and bring a blanket and a picnic dinner; it's a tradition.

Wolf Trap also hosts a number of very popular festivals. The park features a day-long Irish music festival in May; two major festivals in June, the Louisiana Swamp Romp Cajun Festival and a weekend of jazz and blues; and the International Children's Festival each September.

From late fall until May, the 350-seat Barns of Wolf Trap, just up the road at 1635 Trap Rd., features jazz, pop, country, folk, bluegrass, and chamber musicians. The Barns are the summer home of the Wolf Trap Opera Company, which is the only entertainment booked here May through September. Call ☎ **703/938-2404** for information.

Take the Metro to West Falls Church; in summer only, the Wolf Trap Express Shuttle ($3.50 round-trip) runs from the Metro every 20 minutes starting 2 hours before performance time and (return trip) 20 minutes after the performance ends or 11pm (whichever comes first). By car, take I-495 (the Beltway) to Exit 12W (Dulles Toll Road); stay on the local exit road (you'll see a sign) until you come to Wolf Trap. The park is also accessible from Exit 67 off I-66 West. There's plenty of parking.

3 The Club & Music Scene

You don't have to go to an enormous auditorium or a fancy concert hall to enjoy live entertainment in the capital. If you're looking for a tuneful night on the town, Washington offers smoky jazz clubs, lively bars, warehouse ballrooms, places where you sit back and listen, places where you can get up and dance, even a roadhouse or two. If you're looking for comic relief, Washington can take care of you there, too (the pickings are few but good).

A lot of nightlife sites fall into more than one category: for example, the Black Cat is a bar and a dance club, offering food and sometimes poetry readings; Coco Loco is a hot Brazilian restaurant and an even hotter nightclub on weekend nights. So I've listed each nightspot according to the type of music it features, and included the details in its description.

The best nightlife districts are **Adams-Morgan;** the area around **U and 14th streets NW,** a newly developing district yet still a relatively dangerous part of town; and the **7th Street NW corridor** near Chinatown and the MCI Center. In fact, each of these neighborhoods can be slightly dubious. As a rule, while clubbing, stick to the major thoroughfares and steer clear of deserted side streets.

COMEDY

In addition to the below-listed, be sure to catch Gross National Product (see box below). Big-name comedians also perform around town at such places as **Constitution Hall.**

The Improv

1140 Connecticut Ave. NW (between L and M sts.). ☎ **202/296-7008.** Cover $10 Sun–Thurs, $12 Fri–Sat, plus a 2-drink minimum (waived if you dine). Metro: Farragut North. Parking garage next door $4.

The Improv features top performers on the national comedy club circuit as well as comic plays and one-person shows. *Saturday Night Live* performers Ellen Cleghorne, David Spade, Chris Rock, and Adam Sandler have all played here, as have comedy bigs Ellen DeGeneres, Jerry Seinfeld, David Alan Grier, Robin Williams, Rosie O'Donnell, and Brian Regan. Shows are about 1 1/2 hours long and include three comics (an emcee, feature act, and headliner). Show times are 8:30pm from Sunday to Thursday, 8:30 and 10:30pm on Friday and Saturday. The best way to snag a good seat is to have dinner here (make reservations), which allows you to enter the club

Today's Headlines, Tomorrow's Punchlines

Washington's hilarious political-comedy troupe, **Gross National Product,** does first-rate impersonations of all the capital's major players, from a Clinton look-alike who is a virtual clone to a definitively Doleful Bob. With clever acts and brilliant improvisation, they've been spoofing government since 1980 in shows like *BushCapades, Clintoons, A Newt World Order, GNP on the Dole,* and, most recently *Hell to the Chief.* "The great thing is the constant source of material," says GNP creator/Dole impersonator John Simmons. "You have power, money, and sex all along the Potomac—GNP is a growth industry." Some snippets from past shows include:

Clinton on welfare reform: "My plan will also apply to Congress. For the first term, you'll receive all the support and job training you need at the government's expense, but if you're re-elected to a second term, you must work."

Newt Gingrich on the death penalty: "Let's privatize the death penalty, the government can't do the job. Let's give it to General Motors. You can cram eight to ten criminals in the back of one of those Chevy pickups with exploding gas tanks . . . now that's efficiency for you!"

Clinton on Hillary: "Hillary will play any role in my administration she wants. After all, she's a hell of a lot smarter than me. And if you vote for me, I promise Hillary will handle all your future investments."

On Colin Powell: "I understand they're going to make a movie out of Colin Powell's book, and the studio is tossing out names of stars who share his black experience. Their first choice is Robert Redford."

And an oldie from the George Bush years: "We're offering a thousand points of light in a kinder, Gentile nation."

Be sure to catch a GNP show while you're in town. It's an archetypal Washington experience. They play at the Bayou in Georgetown. Best bet: Call GNP directly at ☎ **202/783-7212** for show information and reservations.

---

as early as 7pm. Dinner entrées ($7.95 to $13.95) include prime rib, sandwiches, and pasta and seafood selections. Drinks average $3.25. You must be 18 to get in.

Chelsea's
1055 Thomas Jefferson St. NW. ☎ **202/298-8222.** $50 for dinner and show, $33.50 for show alone. Fri and Sat nights. Metro: Foggy Bottom, with a 10-minute walk.

This nightclub in the Foundry Building on the C&O Canal is home base for the Capitol Steps comedy satire troupe, whose claim to fame is poking fun at Washington institutions through song. You may have heard of them via their many albums and appearances on national TV shows. And, they certainly know their material: The Steps are ex-Congressional staffers, well acquainted with the crazy workings of government.

POP/ROCK

The Bayou
3135 K St. NW (under the Whitehurst Fwy, near Wisconsin Ave.). ☎ **202/333-2897.** Cover $5–$25.

This lively nightclub, located on the Georgetown waterfront, features a mixed bag of live musical entertainment, mostly progressive, reggae, and alternative sounds. Performers are up-and-coming national groups, with occasional big names (Hootie and the Blowfish, Red Hot Chili Peppers, Phish, Melissa Etheridge, the Kinks, Todd Rundgren) playing the club for old time's sake. In addition, there are occasional comedy group shows such as political satirists Gross National Product (see box above). Show times vary.

The Bayou is a funky, cavelike club, with exposed brick-and-stone walls and seating on two levels. Sandwiches and pizza are available during the show. Except for shows appealing to all age groups, no one under 18 is admitted. There's convenient parking at the corner of Wisconsin and K streets.

Black Cat

1831 14th St. NW (between S and T sts.). ☎ **202/667-7960.** Cover $5–$10 for concerts; no cover in the Red Room. Metro: U Street–Cardozo.

This comfortable, low-key Gen-X grunge bar has a large, funky, red-walled living-roomy lounge with booths and tables, a red-leather sofa, pinball machines, a pool table, and a jukebox stocked with alternative and classic rock. There's live music in the adjoining room, essentially a large dance floor (it accommodates about 400 people) with stages at both ends. Entertainment includes alternative rock and jazz performers (mostly locals, but some bigger names such as John Zorn, Blur, Morphine, Foo Fighters, The Offspring, and The Cramps) and occasional poetry readings. The Red Room Bar is open until 2am from Sunday to Thursday, and until 3am Friday and Saturday. Concerts take place 4 or 5 nights a week, beginning at about 8:30pm (call for details). Light fare, such as kebob dinners, is available, and the bar has European and microbrew beers on tap.

Capitol Ballroom

Half and K sts. SE. ☎ **202/554-1500.** Cover Fri–Sat $7 before 11pm, $9 after 11pm; other nights $5–$25, depending on the performer. Metro: Navy Yard.

Occupying a vast converted boiler-company warehouse consisting of a cavernous space, a bigger cavernous space, and a half dozen bars, the Capitol Ballroom is generally a Gen-X mecca (though some performers attract an older crowd). It's also D.C.'s largest club, accommodating upward of 1,500 people a night. Friday night Buzz Parties here feature six DJs playing techno, house, and jungle music from 10pm to 6am (except for once-a-month raves, when the action continues until about 9am). Saturday nights are similar, though the music mix is alternative/ industrial, progressive, and techno. The rest of the week is given over to live concerts, mostly featuring nationally known acts (such as Bruce Hornsby, Iggy Pop, Tears for Fears, Lenny Kravitz, Rage Against the Machine, and Ozzy Osbourne), and, occasionally, local groups. You can buy tickets in advance via Ticketmaster (☎ **202/432-SEAT**). You must be 18 to get in, 21 to have your wrist stamped for drinks. The game room and state-of-the-art lighting/laser/sound systems are a plus.

Chief Ike's Mambo Room

1725 Columbia Rd. NW. ☎ **202/332-2211.** $3 cover on weekends. Metro: Woodley Park– Zoo, with a 20-minute walk.

No live music but a wide selection of contemporary music played by New York DJ Eddie Rivera. People come to this Adams-Morgan club on Thursday, Friday, and Saturday nights to dance, drink, flirt, and yes, to eat. Chief Ike's, unlike other clubs, sets great store by its grub: Cajun/Southern food. Doors open at 4pm daily; happy hour lasts nightly from 4 to 8pm. The crowd is (for the most part) young, with lots of politicos and local artists stopping in. Downstairs is where you'll find the dancing, upstairs is good for kibitzing and pool-playing.

Club Heaven and Hell

2327 18th St. NW. ☎ **202/667-HELL** (club phone), or 703/522-4227 (for bookings and information). Cover: $3 Tues, $2 Wed, $4 Thurs, $5 Fri and Sat; no cover in Hell Sun and Mon (Heaven is closed those days).

This schizophrenic club is in Adams-Morgan. Heaven (upstairs, of course) is a psychedelic version of paradise with black walls and strobe lights, Buddhas, Egyptian art, and paintings based on Michelangelo's *David* and *God Creating Adam*. The balcony allows an escape from the dense mob of dancers and very loud music. The crowd is interracial, clean-cut, casual, 25 to 35 (picture the cast of *Friends*). The music (till 2am Tuesday to Thursday, 3am Friday and Saturday) is alternative, Gothic, and industrial on Tuesday; progressive, alternative, and techno on Wednesday; '80s retro (Prince, Madonna, Michael Jackson), DC's Original Dance Party, played by DJs Jim'n'Jon on Thursday; hip-hop, progressive, and alternative on Friday and Saturday. The ground floor is occupied by a dark, minimalist Italian restaurant called the Green Island Cafe; it serves pastas and veal dishes, and features live traditional/mellow jazz on Friday and Saturday nights. Go down a flight of stairs to the smoke-filled, low-ceilinged cellar that comprises Hell, with its mural of hellfire and backlit eerie masks. The crowd is not especially satanic; it's basically the same as upstairs.

9:30 Club

815 V St. NW. ☎ **202/393-0930.** Tickets $5–$40, depending on the performer. Metro: U Street–Cardozo.

Housed in yet another converted warehouse, this major live-music venue hosts frequent record company parties and features a wide range of top performers. You might catch Sheryl Crow, the Wallflowers, Smashing Pumpkins, Shawn Colvin, and even Tony Bennett. It's only open when there's a show on (call ahead), and, obviously, the crowd varies with the performer. The sound system is state of the art. There are four bars, two on the main dance-floor level, one in the upstairs VIP room (anyone is welcome here unless the room is being used for a private party), and another in the distressed-looking cellar. The 9:30 Club is a standup place, literally; there are no seats. Tickets to most shows are available through Protix (☎ **800/955-5566** or 703/218-6500).

Madam's Organ

2461 18th St. NW. ☎ **202/667-5370.** Cover is never more than $5–$8.

This beloved Adams-Morgan hangout fulfills owner Bill Duggan's definition of a good bar: where there's great sound and people sweating. Guitarist/singer/bluesman-in-residence Bobby Parker provides the great sounds; you provide the sweat. DJ and local "character" Stella Neptune spins funk and dance tunes on Thursday nights. Recently relocated from down the street, the club features a wide open bar decorated eclectically with a 150-year-old gilded bar mirror, stuffed fish and animal heads, and paintings of nudes. The second-floor bar is called Big Daddy's Love Lounge & Pick-Up Joint, which tells you everything you need to know. Other points to note: You can play darts, and redheads pay half-price for drinks.

State of the Union

1357 U St. NW. ☎ **202/588-8810.** Call for cover information. Metro: U Street–Cardozo.

DJ and live music highlight reggae, hip-hop, and acid jazz sounds in this nightclub that plays on a Soviet Union theme: hammer and sickle sconces, a bust of Lenin over the bar, and a big painting of Rasputin on a back wall. The hip crowd ranges from mid-20s to about 35, interracial, and international. The music, both live and DJ-provided, is very avant-garde. On Friday and Saturday nights, renowned D.C. DJs play rare grooves, funk, soul, hip-hop, and house; Sunday there's reggae; Monday nights from 9pm to midnight an acoustic jazz trio plays; and other nights there's live entertainment, generally, straight, funk, and acid jazz. You might also happen upon a poetry reading. The music is pretty loud. Weather permitting, the back room has an open-air screen (actually more like a cage wall). There's an interesting selection of beers and flavored vodkas. Open through 2am Sunday to Thursday, 3am Friday and Saturday.

JAZZ/BLUES

Blues Alley

1073 Wisconsin Ave. NW (in an alley below M St.). ☎ **202/337-4141.** Cover $13–$40, plus $7 food or drink minimum.

Blues Alley, in Georgetown, has been Washington's top jazz club since 1965, featuring such artists as Nancy Wilson, McCoy Tyner, Sonny Rollins, Flora Purim, Herbie Mann, Wynton Marsalis, Charlie Byrd, Ramsey Lewis, Rachelle Ferrell, and Maynard Ferguson. There are usually two shows nightly at 8 and 10pm; some performers also do midnight shows on weekends. Reservations are essential (call after noon); since seating is on a first-come, first-served basis, it's best to arrive no later than 7pm and have dinner. Entrées on the steak and creole-seafood menu (for example, jambalaya, chicken creole, and crabcakes) are in the $14 to $20 range; snacks and sandwiches are $5.25 to $9, and drinks are $5.35 to $9. The decor is of the classic jazz club genre: exposed-brick walls, beamed ceiling, and small candlelit tables. Sometimes well-known visiting musicians get up and jam with performers; one night when Jerry Lewis was in the audience, he got up on stage and told a few jokes.

City Blues

2651 Connecticut Ave. NW. ☎ **202/232-2300.** Cover: Thur–Sat $5. Metro: Woodley Park-Zoo.

This is a neighborhood club that offers live entertainment 7 nights a week, mostly blues and some jazz, performed mainly by locals but with big names sitting in from time to time. Look for groups like the Mary Ann Redmond Band, and names like Timothy Ford, who plays piano with the Marianna Previti Band. The 5-year-old club is a cozy den of three interconnected rooms on one floor of a converted town house. Seating is at tables and at the bar. The full menu features New Orleans cuisine. The crowd ranges in age from 21 to 65, and includes lots of repeat customers.

New Vegas Lounge

1415 P St. NW. ☎ **202/483-3971.** Cover only on weekends, usually about $10. Metro: Dupont Circle.

When the Vegas Lounge is good, it's very good. When it's bad, it's laughable. This dark, one-room joint is crowded with tables at which sit a mix of Washingtonians, black and white, college kids and their elders. If you're lucky, you might find a blues band out of Chicago playing Otis Redding's "Try a Little Tenderness," making the room swoon, and eventually putting everyone on their feet dancing. On the other hand, on an open-mike night, you're likely to hear a neighborhood group who has no business appearing in public. Thursdays are college nights. The lounge is open Tuesday through Sunday.

One Step Down

2517 Pennsylvania Ave. NW. ☎ **202/331-8863.** Cover: $10 with 2-drink minimum on weekends; no or low cover weeknights. Metro: Foggy Bottom.

This quintessential, hole-in-the-wall jazz club is the constant on this stretch of Pennsylvania Avenue just outside of Georgetown. After 35 years, One Step Down has seen its neighbors change names and owners too many times to count. The One Step showcases the talents of names you often recognize, and some you don't: sax player Paul Bollenbeck, the Steve Wilson Quartet, Ronnie Wells, and Ron Elliston. Saturday and Sunday from 3:30 to 7:30pm, the club stages a jam session; no cover. Live music plays here 7 nights a week; the club is open from 11:30am to 2am daily, until 3am on weekends. The people who come to the One Step tend to be heavy jazz enthusiasts who stay quiet during the sets.

Twins Lounge

5516 Colorado Ave. NW. ☎ **202/882-2523.** No cover, but a $7 minimum weeknights; variable cover weekends, plus a $10 minimum. Take a taxi or drive.

Four blocks from the Carter Barron Amphitheater (see listing above) on the outskirts of town is this intimate jazz club, which offers live music every night. On weeknights you'll hear local artists (open mike on Wednesday nights); weekends you'll hear out-of-town acts, such as Bobby Watson, Gil Scott Heron, and James William. Sunday night is a weekly jam session well attended by musicians from all over town. Menu features Italian, Ethiopian, and Caribbean dishes. Crowd is mixed, "75% white, ages 25 to 90," according to the staff.

Twist and Shout

4800 Auburn Ave., Bethesda, MD. ☎ **301/652-3383.** Cover averages $10. Metro: Bethesda, with a 10-minute walk—call for directions from the Metro station.

If you like your blues down and dirty, your ceilings low, your beer straightforward, and your crowd eclectic, this is your place. Eat before you come (there are plenty of restaurants in Bethesda). Open only on Friday and Saturday nights, the Twist and Shout is in a bare-bones room of an American Legion Hall, a bar along one side, wooden booths along the other, with a smattering of tall bar stools with tall round tables at the back. The band plays on a slightly raised platform stage, inviting the audience to dance or just stand and watch. You'll hear legendary musicians from around the country, not necessarily headliners, but people like Bob Margolin, who played guitar in Muddy Waters' last band; bluesman and harmonica-player Junior Welles, a longtime player with Buddy Guy; and local legends Bobby Radcliff, Bill Kirchen, and Tom Principato. The music is mostly rhythm and blues, with zydeco and rock and roll thrown in from time to time. This is the place made famous by Mary Chapin Carpenter in her hit single, "Twist and Shout." The cover charge is very reasonable, considering the excellence of the music.

Utopia

1418 U St. NW. ☎ **202/483-7669.** No cover. Metro: U Street–Cardozo.

Unlike many music bars that offer snack fare, the arty New York/Soho–style Utopia is serious about its restaurant operation. A moderately priced international menu features entrées ranging from lamb couscous to blackened shrimp with creole cream sauce, not to mention pastas and filet mignon béarnaise. There's also an interesting wine list and a large selection of beers and single-malt scotches. The setting is cozy and candlelit, with walls used for a changing art gallery show (the bold, colorful paintings in the front room are by Moroccan owner Jamal Sahri). The eclectic crowd here varies with the music, ranging from early 20s to about 35, for the most part, including South Americans and Europeans. On Wednesday nights live blues and jazz groups perform; Thursday there's live Brazilian jazz; Friday there's jukebox only (everything from Algerian Ray to the Gypsy Kings); and on Sunday, bluesy jazz singer Pam Bricker takes the stage. There's no real dance floor, but people find odd spaces to move to the tunes. Open Sunday through Thursday until 2am, Friday and Saturday until 3am.

INTERNATIONAL SOUNDS

Bukom Café

2442 18th St. NW. ☎ **202/265-4600.** No cover or minimum.

An African ambience prevails at the Bukom Café, an Adams-Morgan restaurant serving dishes from Sierra Leone, Nigeria, Ghana, Senegal, and the Ivory Coast. But, unless you come early, expect to drink and dance rather than eat on a weekend night, when very good African bands play until 3am, and this smoke-filled club is packed wall to wall with Africans and young locals. Somehow, people manage to find small spaces to dance here and there. No cover or minimum.

Coco Loco

810 7th St. NW (between H and I sts.). ☎ **202/289-2626.** Cover $5–$10. Valet parking $4. Metro: Gallery Place.

This is one of D.C.'s liveliest clubs, heralded by marquee lights. Thursday through Saturday nights, come for a late tapas or mixed-grill dinner (see chapter 6 for details) and stay for international music and dancing, with occasional live bands. On Saturday night, the entertainment includes a sexy 11pm floor show featuring Brazilian exhibition dancers who begin performing in feathered and sequined Rio Rita costumes and strip down to a bare minimum. Laser lights and other special effects enhance the show, which ends with a conga line and a limbo contest. There's dancing until 2am on Thursday, and until 3am on Friday and Saturday. Coco Loco draws an attractive upscale international crowd of all ages, including many impressively talented dancers. It's great fun.

Kala Kala

2439 18th St. NW. ☎ **202/232-5433.**

This is another Adams-Morgan African club whose owner originally hails from Madagascar. Just down from Bukom Café (see above), it's a claustrophobic narrow club with a variety of African sculptures displayed on the wall. The clientele is about half African/Caribbean, the rest comprised mostly of young neighborhood residents. You can order up an African beer or a spicy shish kebab. Open Wednesday through Sunday until 2am, Friday and Saturday until 3am, a DJ plays African reggae, zouk (French Caribbean), soca (from Trinidad), salsa, and the occasional Top 40 tune.

Latin Jazz Alley

1721 Columbia Rd. NW, on the 2nd floor of the El Migueleno Cafe. ☎ **202/328-6190.** $5 per hour of dance instruction; $3–$5 cover charge on Fri nights for live jazz.

Another place to get in on Washington's Latin scene, this one in Adams-Morgan. At the Alley, you can learn to dance: Argentine tango on Wednesday night from 7pm to 9pm, and salsa and merengue Thursday, Friday, and Saturday night from 7:30pm to 9:30pm. Latin jazz groups play Friday nights from 10pm to 2am.

GAY CLUBS

Dupont Circle is the gay hub of Washington, D.C., with at least 10 gay bars within easy walking distance of one another. At either of the two Dupont Circle locales listed below, you'll find natives happy to tell you about (or take you to) the others.

The Circle Bar & Tavern

1629 Connecticut Ave. NW (between Q and R sts.). ☎ **202/462-5575.** No cover. Metro: Dupont Circle.

This impressively slick-looking three-story club is the largest gay bar in the Dupont Circle area. It attracts a racially mixed gay and lesbian crowd (about 80% male), mostly in the 25 to 35 age range. The Underground level, which has a dance floor, is the setting for many weekend events: lesbian rugby team parties, Log Cabin Club parties (they're a gay Republican group), gay rodeos, and gay proms; Candice Gingrich (Newt's sister) has held receptions here. The main floor, with black-painted brick walls donning Matisse prints, has two bars, a great jukebox stocked with rock classics, and a pool table. But most simpatico is the upstairs Terrace, which centers on a big rectangular bar adorned with fabulous floral displays. Up here, there are monitors airing music videos, plus pinball and video games, and, when the weather is fine, the big open-air terrace is a delight. Wednesday there's karaoke on the Terrace, and it's Women's Night Underground. Tuesday, drinks are half price and there's a grab bag after 10pm (everyone wins something, perhaps a key chain or funny hat). Sunday there's a 9pm drag show Underground. Open until 2am Sunday through Thursday, 3am Friday and Saturday.

J.R.'s

1519 17th St. NW (between P and Q sts.). ☎ **202/328-0090.** No cover. Metro: Dupont Circle.

More intimate than the above, this casual all-male Dupont Circle club draws a crowd that is friendly, upscale, and very attractive. The interior—not that you'll be able to see much of it, because J.R.'s is always sardine-packed wall to wall—has a 20-foot-high, pressed-tin ceiling and exposed-brick walls hung with neon beer signs. The big screen over the bar area is used to air music videos and the weekly saga of *Melrose Place* (much fun). The balcony, with a pool table, is a little more laid-back. No food is served. Open until 2am Sunday through Thursday, 3am Friday and Saturday.

Tracks

1111 1st St. SE. ☎ **202/488-3320.** Cover $5–$10. Metro: Navy Yard.

This vast high-energy club (a converted auto dealership, with 21,000 square feet inside and a 10,000-square-foot patio) is a favorite place to dance in D.C. Its chic-rather-than-funky interior houses a main dance floor centered on a mirrored ball, another with a zigzag display of video monitors, both offering great sound and light systems. DJs provide the music, and the crowd is appealingly unhinged. Thursday nights there's progressive house and techno in the main room, progressive industrial video in another, and the crowd is predominantly straight (there's an open bar from 9 to 10pm, and pitchers of beer are $4 all night; some nights there are rave parties). Friday also draws a straight crowd for progressive and house music. Saturday is a gay night (mostly men but some women and a sprinkling of straights); the music is high-energy house in the main room, deep underground and club house in the video room. Gay country-and-western tea dances are featured Sunday afternoons through 9:30pm followed by house music, and the crowd is mostly gay and African-American. And the last Tuesday of every month is lesbian night. On warm nights, much of the action centers on the fountained outdoor deck which has a volleyball court! Other pluses: a pool table, video games, and a snack bar. Liquor service is available through 2am Thursday and Friday, till 3am Saturday and Sunday; the club often stays open until 6am. You must be 18 to get in, 21 to have your wrist stamped for drinks.

4 The Bar Scene

Washington has a thriving and varied bar scene. If you're in the mood for a sophisticated setting, seek out a bar in one of the nicer hotels, like The Jefferson, the Willard, the Ritz-Carlton, or the Carlton (see chapter 5 for more information and suggestions). If you want a convivial atmosphere and decent grub, try bars that double as restaurants. Refer to chapter 6 for details about these in particular: Capital City Brewing Company, Clyde's, Martin's, Music City Roadhouse, Old Ebbitt Grill, Old Glory, Paolo's, Sequoia, U Street Wine Bar and Tapas Bistro, and Xing Kuba.

But if you're looking for the more typical, drink and mingle, or drink and converse type of place, try these:

The Big Hunt

1345 Connecticut Ave. NW (between N St. and Dupont Circle). ☎ **202/785-2333.** Metro: Dupont Circle.

This casual and comfy Dupont Circle hangout for the twentysomething-to-thirtysomething crowd—billing itself as a "happy hunting ground for humans"—has a kind of *Raiders of the Lost Ark*/explorer/jungle theme. A downstairs room (the floor where music is the loudest) is adorned with exotic travel posters and animal skins; another area has leopard-skin–patterned booths under canvas tenting. Amusing murals grace the balcony level, which adjoins a room with pool tables. The candlelit basement is the spot for quiet conversation. The menu offers typical bar food; more to the point is a beer list with close to 30 varieties on tap, most of them microbrews. Open Sunday through Thursday until 2am, Friday and Saturday until 3am.

Brickskeller

1523 22nd St. NW. ☎ **202/293-1885.** Metro: Dupont Circle or Foggy Bottom.

If you like beer and you like a choice, head for Brickskeller, which has been around for nearly 40 years and offers about 1,000 beers from the world over. If you can't make up your mind, ask one of the waiters, who tend to be knowledgeable about the brews. The tavern draws students, college professors, embassy types, and people from the neighborhood. Brickskeller is a series of interconnecting rooms filled with gingham tablecloth–covered tables; upstairs rooms are only open weekend nights. The food is generally OK; more than OK are the burgers, which include the excellent Brickburger, topped with bacon, salami, onion, and cheese; and the Ale burger, made with beer.

Cafe Milano

3251 Prospect St. NW. ☎ **202/333-6183.**

Located just off Wisconsin Avenue in lower Georgetown, Cafe Milano has gained a reputation for attracting beautiful people, including the likes of Marlene Cooke, widow of Redskins owner Jack Kent Cooke. You might see a few glamorous faces—and then again, you might see a bunch of people on the prowl for glamorous faces. It's often crowded, especially Thursday through Saturday nights. The food is better than you might expect: Try the salads and pastas.

Champions

1206 Wisconsin Ave. NW (just north of M St.). ☎ **202/965-4005.**

Smells like beer. This is a sports bar, where both sports fans and athletes—Redskins players among them—like to hang out. Champions lies at the end of an alley off Wisconsin Avenue—be careful at night. The two-story bar is a clutter of sports paraphernalia, with TV monitors airing nonstop sporting events. Conversation has two themes: sports and pickup lines. Champions is often packed and doesn't take reservations; in the evening, you can expect to wait for a table, so arrive early. It's open nightly.

The Dubliner

In the Phoenix Park Hotel, at 520 N. Capitol St. NW, with its own entrance on Massachusetts Ave. NW. ☎ **202/737-3773.** Metro: Union Station.

This is your old Irish pub, the port you can blow into in any storm, personal or weather-related. It's got the dark wood paneling and tables, the etched-and-stained glass windows, Irish-accented staff from time to time, and, most importantly, the Auld Dubliner Amber Ale. You'll probably want to stick to drink here, but should

Nothing Beats a Good Cigar & a Dry Martini

Ozio is a trendy subterranean cigar-and-martini club at 1835 K St. NW (☎ 202/822-6000). Its motto is Winston Churchill's rule of life: "Smoking cigars and drinking of alcohol before, after, and if need be, during all meals, and intervals between them." It has a whimsical/upscale art-deco interior, with distressed-look walls and columns, Persian rugs strewn on concrete floors, and comfortable seating in plush armchairs, sofas, and banquettes. The lighting is nightclubby, and the music mellow (light jazz, blues, Sinatra, Tony Bennett). People dance wherever they can find a space. Ozio is the kind of place where limos are parked out front, and the suit-and-tie crowd is comprised of senators, hotshot professionals, and local sports figures. Exotic-looking cigar men (the stogie equivalents of sommeliers) come by during the evening with humidors; if you're a novice, they'll help you make a selection and guide you through the rituals. You can, however, avoid the markup by bringing your own; regular customers (Redskin football player Gus Frerotte and D.C. police chief Larry Soulsby to name two) maintain humidors in lockers on the premises. Perfect vodka and gin martinis and other sophisticated libations (including a choice of 20 single-malt scotches) enhance the experience. There's also a restaurant menu (Ozio hosts the occasional cigar dinner with noted chefs) ranging from tapas and pastas to filet mignon. Part of the fun is the atmosphere of open rebellion against earnest PC mores. Open Monday through Thursday until 2am, Friday and Saturday until 3am. Closed Sunday. Happy hour weekdays from 4 to 7pm. Closest Metro station is Farragut North or Farragut West.

you look at a menu, choose a burger, grilled chicken sandwich, or the roast duck salad. The Dubliner is frequented by Capitol Hill staffers and journalists who cover the Hill. Irish musical groups play nightly.

Fox and Hounds

1533 17th St. NW (between Q and Church sts.). ☎ 202/232-6307. Metro: Dupont Circle.

Though it's in the heart of the Dupont Circle gay district, Fox and Hounds is a basically straight and very friendly neighborhood bar that offers pretty good singles action. It's under the same ownership as the Trio restaurant and offers its identical extensive menu (see details in chapter 6). Genial owner George Mallios describes it as "*Cheers* for the twentysomething set." In the beery-smelling interior, the walls are hung with equestrian fox-hunting prints and posters from the Disney movie *The Fox and the Hound*. The jukebox blares the latest hits, and sporting events are aired, to enthusiastic commentary, on a TV over the bar. Spring through fall, the large patio fronting 17th Street is packed nightly. Customers like the wide variety of coffee-liqueur drinks, premium wines by the glass, imported beers, and microbrews.

Froggy Bottom Pub

2142 L St. NW. ☎ 202/338-3000. Metro: Foggy Bottom.

A hangout for students from George Washington University and Howard University, and for employees of the World Bank and other nearby offices, Froggy Bottom is a hospitable place, though pretty plain. The most attractive spot is its outdoor cafe, but if you sit out here, you may find yourselves shouting to be heard over the siren of an ambulance racing to GW Hospital, just down the block. Inside, a restaurant is upstairs, the bar downstairs. Daily specials start at 6pm, like the free appetizers available on Friday nights. On Saturday night, from 8pm until midnight, you pay $10 for all-you-can-drink house wine or beer.

Mr. Smith's of Georgetown
3104 M St. NW. ☎ **202/333-3104.**

Mr. Smith's bills itself as "The Friendliest Saloon in Town," but the truth is that it's so popular among regulars, you're in danger of being ignored if staff don't know you. The bar, which opened about 30 years ago, has a front room with original brick walls, wooden seats, and a long bar, at which you can count on finding pairs of newfound friends telling obscene jokes, loudly. At the end of this room is a large piano around which customers congregate each night to accompany the pianist. (Have a daiquiri— Mr. Smith's is known for them.) The garden room, an interior light-filled room that adjoins an outdoor garden area, lies beyond.

Nathan's
3150 M St. NW. ☎ **202/338-2600.**

Nathan's is on the corner of M Street and Wisconsin Avenue in the heart of George-town. If you pop in here in mid-afternoon, it's a quiet place to grab a beer or glass of wine and watch the action out on the street. (I know someone who uses Nathan's as an in-town office for his suburban Virginia–based business.) Visit at night, though, and it's the more typical bar scene, crowded with locals, out-of-towners, students, and a sprinkling of couples in from the suburbs. That's the front room. The back room at Nathan's is a civilized, candlelit restaurant serving decent Italian fare on linen-laid tables.

Planet Fred
1221 Connecticut Ave. NW. ☎ **202/466-2336.** Metro: Dupont Circle or Farragut North.

Latin dance is currently taking Washington by storm, and Planet Fred is yet another place you can learn the moves. Every Monday from 7pm to 9pm, a local instructor teaches salsa and merengue, for free, to a young and enthusiastic bunch of Washing-tonians. On other nights, the bar is a scene of wild revelry, including an intriguing bingo game.

Polly Esther's
605 12th St. NW. ☎ **202/737-1970.** Metro: Metro Center.

Seventies decor and music reign here, with artifacts from that decade hanging on the walls (anything to do with the Brady Bunch), and disco dance music (think YMCA, ABBA, the BeeGees) blaring from the sound system. Downstairs is more culture-clubish, where you dance to '80s tunes by artists like Madonna and Prince. Polly Esther's is open Thursday through Sunday, charging a $6 cover on Friday nights, $8 on Saturday nights.

Post Pub
1422 L St. NW. ☎ **202/628-2111.** Metro: McPherson Square.

This joint fits into the "comfortable shoe" category. Situated between Vermont and 15th streets, across from the offices of the *Washington Post,* the pub gets busy at lunch, grows quiet in the afternoon, and picks up again in the evening, but the place is never empty. Post Pub has two rooms, which are furnished with old-fashioned black ban-quettes, faux wood paneling, mirrored beer insignias, juke boxes, cigarette machines, and a long bar with tall stools. There are different happy hour specials every night, like the 5 to 9pm Thursday "Anything Absolute," which offers drinks made with Absolut vodka for $2.50 each. The food is homey and inexpensive (under $10)— onion rings, sandwiches, chicken parmigiana, and the like.

The Rock
717 6th St. NW. ☎ **202/842-7625.** Metro: Gallery Place.

The Rock is the District's latest sports bar, situating itself in probably the best location a sports establishment could have: across the street from the MCI Center. The three-floor bar fills a former warehouse, its decor a montage of pre-existing exposed pipes and concrete floors, and TV screens, pool tables, and sports memorabilia. The most popular spot is the third floor, where the pool tables and a cigar lounge are located. A rooftop tiki bar is planned.

The Tombs
1226 36th St. NW. ☎ **202/337-6668.**

Housed in a converted 19th-century Federal-style home, the Tombs, which opened in 1962, is a favorite hangout for students and faculty of nearby Georgetown University. (Bill Clinton came here during his college years.) GU types tend to congregate at the central bar and surrounding tables, while local residents tend to head for "the Sweeps," the room that lies down a few steps and has red leather banquettes.

Directly below the upscale 1789 Restaurant (see chapter 6 for details), the Tombs benefits from menu supervision from 1789 chef Riz Lacoste. The menu offers burgers, sandwiches, and salads, as well as more serious fare.

The Tune Inn
33¹/₂ Pennsylvania Ave. SE. ☎ **202/543-2725.** Metro: Capitol South.

Capitol Hill has a number of bars that qualify as "institutions," but the Tune Inn is probably the most popular. Capitol Hill staffers and their bosses, apparently at ease in dive surroundings, have been coming here since it opened in 1955. Or maybe it's the cheap beer and greasy burgers that draw them. Anyway, stop in.

Tunnicliff's Tavern
222 7th St. SE. ☎ **202/546-3663.** Metro: Eastern Market.

Directly across from Eastern Market, another Capitol Hill institution, named for the original, circa-1796 Tunnicliff's Tavern. (This Tunnicliff's opened in 1988.) An outdoor cafe fronts the tavern, which includes a great bar and a partly set-apart dining room. You're likely to see Hill people here; the last time I was there, Louisiana Senator John Breaux and his wife stopped by. Proprietress Lynne Breaux, though not related to the senator, hails from New Orleans and cultivates a Mardi Gras atmosphere that includes live music on Saturday nights. The menu features some standard New Orleans items, like po'boys, gumbo, and fried oysters, as well as nachos and other bar fare. Breaux likes to make everyone feel welcome, including families, and has toys and coloring books at the ready.

5 More Entertainment

CINEMA

With the advent of VCRs, classic film theaters have almost become extinct. Other than the Mary Pickford Theater in the John Adams Building of the Library of Congress (see chapter 7), there is only one choice in this category:

AFI (American Film Institute) Theater
At the Kennedy Center, New Hampshire Ave. NW and Rock Creek Pkwy. ☎ **202/828-4090** (information) or 202/785-4601 (box office). $6.50; $5.50 for members (AFI Theater memberships are $20 a year), senior citizens, and students under 18 with ID. Metro: Foggy Bottom.

This marvelous facility features classic films, works of independent filmmakers, foreign films, themed festivals, and the like in a 224-seat theater designed to offer the highest standard of projection, picture, and sound quality. There's something showing almost every Wednesday to Sunday evening and weekend afternoon. The AFI also sponsors audience-participation discussions with major directors, film stars, and screenwriters; for example, Linda Yellin, Sigourney Weaver, Milos Foreman, Gore Vidal, Nora Ephron, Faye Wray, and Jonathan Demme.

Underground parking at the Kennedy Center, subject to availability, is $8 for the entire evening after 5pm.

FREE SHOWS

In D.C., some of the best things at night are free—or very cheap. See chapter 7 for information about free entertainment offered year-round by individual museums and historic sites; see information earlier in this chapter about the free performances staged by the Kennedy Center, the Shakespeare Theatre, and the Carter Barron Amphitheater.

The city comes especially alive in summer with numerous outdoor concerts performed around town. Choose a night, any night, and you will find a **military band** playing at one of three locations in Washington, D.C.: the U.S. Capitol, the Sylvan Theater on the grounds of the Washington Monument, and the Navy Memorial Plaza. These bands perform jazz, show tunes, blues, music for strings—you name it. The concerts begin at 8pm and continue every night June through Labor Day. For details about military events, call the individual branches: the U.S. Army Band, "Pershing's Own" (☎ **703/696-3399**); the U.S. Navy Band (☎ **202/433-2525** for a 24-hour recording, or 202/433-6090); the U.S. Marine Band, "The President's Own" (☎ **202/433-4011** for a 24-hour recording, or 202/433-5809); and the U.S. Air Force Band, "America's International Musical Ambassadors" (☎ **202/767-5658** for a 24-hour recording, or 202/767-4310).

On the southeast side of town, you'll find renowned Washington blues and jazz artists doing their thing at the **Fort Dupont Summer Theatre,** Minnesota Avenue SE at Randle Circle, in Fort Dupont Park (☎ **202/426-7723** or 202/619-7222) every Friday and Saturday at 8:30pm from sometime in July to the end of August. Bring a blanket and a picnic dinner; arrive early to get a good spot on the lawn. Fort Dupont features both talented local performers and nationally known acts such as Marion Meadows, Miles Jaye, The Sensational Nightingales, Pieces of a Dream, and Roy Ayers. No tickets required; admission is free.

Concerts at the Capitol, an American Festival, is sponsored jointly by the National Park Service and Congress. It's a series of free summer concerts with the **National Symphony Orchestra** that takes place at 8pm on the west side of the Capitol on Memorial Day, July 4, and Labor Day. Seating is on the lawn, so bring a picnic. Major guest stars in past years have included Ossie Davis (a narrator and host), Leontyne Price, Johnny Cash, Rita Moreno, Mary Chapin Carpenter, and Mstislav Rostropovich. The music ranges from light classical to country to show tunes of the Gershwin/Rodgers and Hammerstein genre. For further information call ☎ **202/619-7222.**

Two only-in-Washington, not-to-be-missed outdoor events are the Smithsonian's annual **Festival of American Folklife,** which offers a potpourri of musical and cultural performances; and the **National Independence Day Celebration** on the Mall; for more information, see chapter 2's calendar for June and July.

Finally, the **Washington National Cathedral** and its grounds are a magnificent setting for the cathedral's annual Summer Festival series of musical events, which include a weekly carillon recital ("best heard from the Bishop's Garden," according to a staff member). Call ☎ **202/537-6200** for details.

Side Trips from Washington, D.C.

Within an easy drive, bike ride, or jaunt on the Metro from Washington are a number of historic and tourist attractions. If you'd like a break from Washington proper, head for one of these sites. But don't expect to find them less crowded; their suburban locations and proximity to the downtown make them popular spots for local tourists and out-of-towners alike.

1 Mount Vernon

No visit to Washington would be complete without a trip to Mount Vernon, the estate of George Washington. Only 16 miles south of the capital, this southern plantation dates back to a 1674 land grant to a certain Washington—the president's great-grandfather.

ESSENTIALS

GETTING THERE   If you're going **by car,** take any of the bridges over the Potomac into Virginia to the George Washington Memorial Parkway (Rte. 1) going south; the parkway ends at Mount Vernon. **Tourmobile** buses (☎ 202/554-5100) depart daily, April through October only, from Arlington National Cemetery and the Washington Monument. The round-trip fare is $20 for adults, $10 for children 3 to 11 (free for children under 3) and includes the admission fee to Mount Vernon (for details on the Tourmobile, see "Getting Around" in chapter 4).

The Gray Line bus tours go to Mount Vernon, as do some boat tours; see "Organized Tours" in chapter 7, for further information about Gray Line Tours; the **Spirit of Washington Cruises,** which leave from the Washington waterfront; and the **Potomac Riverboat Cruise's** *Cherry Blossom* three-decker paddlewheeler, which departs from the pier behind the Torpedo Factory, at the bottom of King Street in Old Town Alexandria.

If you're in the mood for exercise in a pleasant setting, rent a bike (see "Participatory Sports" in chapter 7 for rental locations) and hop on the pathway that runs along the Potomac. In Washington, this is the Rock Creek Park Trail; once you cross Memorial Bridge into Virginia, the name changes to the Mount Vernon Trail, which, as it sounds, is a straight shot to Mount Vernon. The section from Memorial Bridge to Mount Vernon is about 19 miles in all.

TOURING THE ESTATE

Mount Vernon (☎ 703/780-2000) was purchased for $200,000 in 1858 by the Mount Vernon Ladies' Association from John Augustine Washington, great-grandnephew of the first president. Without the group's purchase, the estate might have crumbled and disappeared, for neither the federal government nor the Commonwealth of Virginia had wanted to buy the property when it was earlier offered for sale. The restoration is an unmarred beauty; many of the furnishings are original pieces acquired by Washington, and the rooms have been repainted in the original colors favored by George and Martha.

Mount Vernon's mansion and grounds are stunning. Some 500 of the original 8,000 acres (divided into five farms) owned by Washington are still intact. Washington delighted in riding horseback around his property, directing planting and other activities; the Bowling Green entrance is still graced by some of the trees he planted. The American Revolution and his years as president took Washington away from his beloved estate most of the time. He finally retired to Mount Vernon in 1797, just 2 years before his death, to "view the solitary walk and tread the paths of private life with heartfelt satisfaction." He is buried on the estate. Martha was buried next to him in May 1802. Public memorial services are held at the estate every year on the third Monday in February, the date commemorating Washington's birthday; admission is free that day.

Mount Vernon has been one of the nation's most-visited shrines since the mid–19th century. Today more than a million people tour the property annually. There's no formal tour, but attendants stationed throughout the house and grounds provide brief orientations and answer questions. The best time to visit is off-season; during the heavy tourist months, avoid weekends and holidays if possible, and year-round, arrive early to beat the crowds.

The house itself is interesting as an outstanding prototype of colonial architecture, as an example of the aristocratic lifestyle in the 18th century, and of course, as the home of our first president. There are a number of family portraits, and the rooms are appointed as if actually in day-to-day use.

After leaving the house, you can tour the outbuildings: the kitchen, slave quarters, storeroom, smokehouse, overseer's quarters, coachhouse, and stables. A 4-acre exhibit area called "George Washington, Pioneer Farmer" includes a replica of Washington's 16-sided barn and fields of crops that he grew (corn, wheat, oats, and so forth). Docents in period costumes demonstrate 18th-century farming methods. A museum on the property exhibits Washington memorabilia, and details of the restoration are explained in the museum's annex; there's also a gift shop on the premises. You'll want to walk around the grounds (most pleasant in nice weather), and see the wharf, the slave burial ground, the greenhouse, the tomb containing George and Martha Washington's sarcophagi (24 other family members are also interred here), the lawns, and the gardens.

The house and grounds are open to the public daily 8am to 5pm April through August; 9am to 5pm in March, September, and October; and 9am to 4pm November

---

Special Activities at Mount Vernon

There's an ongoing schedule of events at Mount Vernon, especially in summer. For adults, these might include tours focusing on 18th-century gardens, slave life, colonial crafts, or archaeology; for children there are hands-on history programs and treasure hunts. Call to find out if anything is on during your visit.

Side Trips from Washington, D.C.

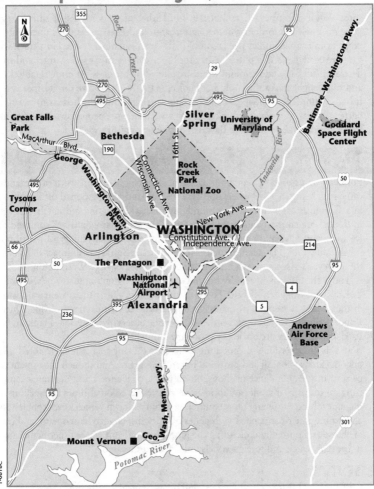

through February. Allow at least 2 hours to see everything. Admission is $8 for adults, $7.50 for senior citizens, $4 for children 6 through 11, under 6 free. A map is provided at the entrance.

WHERE TO DINE

At the entrance to Mount Vernon you'll find a **snack bar** serving light fare, and there are picnic tables outside. If a picnic is what you have in mind, drive a mile north on the parkway to **Riverside Park,** where you can lunch at tables overlooking the Potomac.

Mount Vernon Inn

Near the entrance to Mount Vernon. ☎ **703/780-0011.** Reservations recommended at dinner. Main courses $4.50–$8.50 at lunch, $12–$24 at dinner; prix-fixe dinner $14. AE, DISC, MC, V. Daily 11am–3:30pm and Mon–Sat 5–9pm. AMERICAN.

Lunch or dinner at the inn is an intrinsic part of the Mount Vernon experience. It's a quaintly charming colonial-style restaurant, complete with period furnishings and three working fireplaces. The waitstaff is in 18th-century costume. Be sure to begin your meal with an order of homemade peanut and chestnut soup. Lunch entrées range from colonial turkey pye (a sort of Early American quiche served in a crock with garden vegetables and a puffed pastry top) to a 20th-century–style burger and fries. There's a full bar, and premium wines are offered by the glass. At dinner, tablecloths and candlelight make this a plusher choice. Happily, a prix-fixe dinner means that it is also affordable. The meal includes soup (perhaps broccoli cheddar) or salad, an entrée such as Maryland crabcakes or roast venison with peppercorn sauce, home-made breads, and dessert (like Bavarian parfait or English trifle).

2 Alexandria

Founded by a group of Scottish tobacco merchants, the seaport town of Alexandria came into being in 1749 when a 60-acre tract of land was auctioned off in half-acre lots. Colonists came from miles around, in ramshackle wagons and stately carriages, in sloops, brigantines, and lesser craft, to bid on land that would be "commodious for trade and navigation and tend greatly to the ease and advantage of the frontier inhabitants. . . ." The auction took place in **Market Square** (still intact today), and the surveyor's assistant was a capable lad of 17 named George Washington.

Today the original 60 acres of lots in George Washington's hometown (also Robert E. Lee's) are the heart of **Old Town,** a multimillion-dollar urban-renewal historic district. Many Alexandria streets still bear their original colonial names (King, Queen, Prince, Princess, Royal—you get the drift), while others like Jefferson, Franklin, Lee, Patrick, and Henry are obviously post-Revolutionary.

In this "mother lode of Americana," the past is being increasingly restored in an ongoing archaeological and historical research program. And though the present can be seen in the abundance of shops, boutiques, art galleries, and restaurants capital-izing on tourism, it's still easy to imagine yourself in colonial times by smelling the fragrant tobacco; listening for the rumbling of horse-drawn vehicles over cobblestone; envisioning the oxcarts piled with crates of chickens, country-cured ham, and casks of cheese and butter; and picturing the bustling waterfront where fishermen brought in the daily catch and foreign vessels unloaded exotic cargo.

ESSENTIALS

GETTING THERE   If you're traveling **by car,** take the Arlington Memorial or the 14th Street Bridge to the George Washington Memorial Parkway south, which be-comes Washington Street in Old Town Alexandria. Washington Street intersects with King Street, Alexandria's main thoroughfare. Turn left from Washington Street onto one of the streets before or after King Street (southbound left turns are not permit-ted from Washington onto King Street), and you'll be heading toward the waterfront and the heart of Old Town. Turn right onto King Street and you'll find an avenue of shops and restaurants. You can obtain a free parking permit from the visitors as-sociation (see below), or park at meters or in garages.

The easiest way to make the trip may be the **Metro's** Yellow Line to the King Street station. From there, you can catch a blue-and-gold DASH bus (AT2 or AT5 east-bound) to the Visitors Association, or you can walk, although it's about a mile from the station into the center of Old Town. The town is compact, so you won't need a car once you arrive.

VISITOR INFORMATION   The **Alexandria Convention and Visitors Associa-tion,** located at Ramsay House, 221 King St., at Fairfax Street (☎ **703/838-4200;**

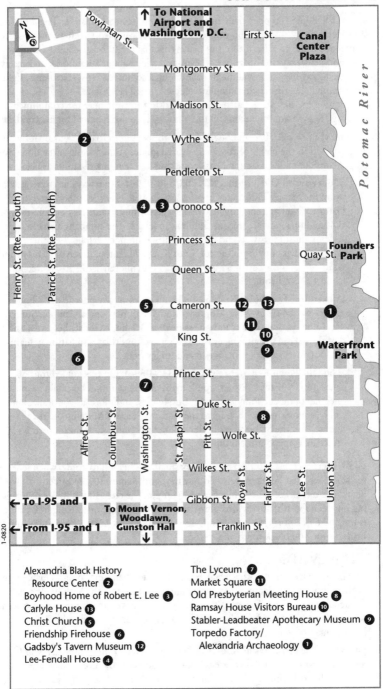

Old Town Alexandria

Alexandria Black History
  Resource Center ❷
Boyhood Home of Robert E. Lee ❸
Carlyle House ⓭
Christ Church ❺
Friendship Firehouse ❻
Gadsby's Tavern Museum ⓬
Lee-Fendall House ❹

The Lyceum ❼
Market Square ⑪
Old Presbyterian Meeting House ❽
Ramsay House Visitors Bureau ⑩
Stabler-Leadbeater Apothecary Museum ❾
Torpedo Factory/
  Alexandria Archaeology ❶

fax 703/838-4683) is open daily from 9am to 5pm (closed January 1, Thanksgiving, and December 25). Here you can obtain a map/self-guided walking tour and brochures about the area; learn about special events that might be scheduled during your visit and get tickets for them; see an 8-minute video about Alexandria; and receive answers to any questions you might have about accommodations, restaurants, sights, or shopping. The association supplies materials in 20 languages.

If you come by car, get a free **1-day parking permit** here for complimentary parking at any 2-hour meter for up to 24 hours. It can be renewed for a second day.

ORGANIZED TOURS Though it's easy to see Alexandria on your own by putting yourself in the hands of colonially attired guides at the various attractions, you might consider taking a comprehensive walking tour. Among the tours available are:

Doorways to Old Virginia (☎ 703/548-0100). **Doorways** has tours leaving from the Stabler-Leadbeater Apothecary Shop at 11am Monday through Saturday, and at 2pm Sunday (weather permitting); tours cost $4 for anyone 12 and older, and are free for children under 12. The company also offers 1-hour ghost tours weekend evenings spring through October (weather permitting), departing from the corner of King and Fairfax streets at 7:30pm and again at 9pm; the cost is $4 for adults, $3 for children ages 7 to 17, free for children 6 and younger.

Alexandria Tours (☎ 703/461-0955). This company offers daily 1-hour **Overview Tours** at 11am Monday through Saturday and at 2pm on Sunday, for $5 per person (ages 6 and under free); and 1-hour **Ghost, Legends, and Folklore Tours** beginning at Market Square, on Friday and Saturday nights at 7pm, for $5 per person (ages 6 and under free).

The Old Town Experience (☎ 703/836-0694). On this guided tour of Alexandria's historic district, you learn about Alexandria's hospitality symbols, merchant houses, flounder houses, busybodies, and more, as you walk along cobblestone streets with visits to the Gadsby's Tavern Museum, Carlyle House, and the Stabler-Leadbeater Apothecary Shop. Call ahead; their $5 tours are by appointment only.

CITY LAYOUT The Old Town is very small. It's helpful to know, when looking for addresses, that Alexandria is laid out in a grid. Union to Lee Street is the 100 block, Lee to Fairfax the 200 block, and so on up. The cross streets (more or less going north and south) are divided north and south by King Street. King to Cameron is the 100 block north, Cameron to Queen the 200 block north, and so on. King to Prince is the 100 block south and so forth.

SPECIAL EVENTS

The below-listed are only the *major* events. If you're planning to participate in any of them, book your accommodations far ahead and contact the Visitors Association for details and advance tickets. Whenever you come, you're sure to run into some activity or other—a jazz festival, tea garden or tavern gambol, quilt exhibit, wine tasting, or organ recital.

January The **birthdays of Robert E. Lee** and his father, Revolutionary War Colonel **"Light Horse Harry" Lee,** are celebrated together at the Lee-Fendall House and Lee's Boyhood Home the fourth Sunday of the month. The party features period music, refreshments, and house tours.

February Alexandria celebrates **George Washington's Birthday,** on the weekend preceding the federal legal holiday, usually the third Monday in February.

Festivities typically include a colonial-costume or black-tie banquet followed by a ball at Gadsby's Tavern, a 10-kilometer race, special tours, a Revolutionary War encampment at Fort Ward Park (complete with uniformed troops engaging in skirmishes), the nation's largest George Washington Birthday Parade (50,000 to 75,000 people attend each year), and 18th-century comic opera performances.

March On the second Saturday in March, King Street is the site of a popular **St. Patrick's Day Parade.**

April Alexandria celebrates **Historic Garden Week in Virginia** with tours of privately owned local (usually historic) homes and gardens the fourth Saturday of the month.

June The **Red Cross Waterfront Festival,** the second week in June, honors Alexandria's historic importance as a seaport and the vitality of its Potomac shoreline today with a display of historic tall ships, ship tours, boat rides and races, nautical art exhibits, waterfront walking tours, fireworks, children's games, an arts and crafts show, food booths, and entertainment. Admission is charged.

July Gather with the clans for **Virginia Scottish Games,** a 2-day Celtic festival the fourth weekend of the month that celebrates Alexandria's Highland heritage. Activities include athletic events (such as the caber toss, in which competitors heave a 140-pound pole in the air), musicians (playing reels, strathspeys, and laments), fiddling and harp competitions, a parade of clan societies in tartans, a Celtic crafts fair, storytelling, Highland dance performances and competitions, booths selling Scottish foods and wares, dog trials featuring Scottish breeds, and a Scottish Country Dance Party. Tickets at the gate are about $9 for 1 day, $15 for the entire weekend; children 15 and under are admitted free with a paying adult. You can get a small discount on tickets purchased in advance at the Ramsay House Visitors Center.

August A **Civil War Living History** program is featured the second Saturday of the month at Fort Ward, with authentically equipped and costumed military units demonstrating camp life with drills, music, a review of troops, and a torchlight tour. Admission is charged.

September Chili enthusiasts can sample "bowls of red" at the **Hard Times Chili Cookoff** in Waterfront Park. Contestants from almost every U.S. state and territory compete, and for an admission charge of a few dollars, you can taste all their creations. Proceeds go to charity. Fiddling contests, jalapeño-eating contests, and country music are part of the fun.

October Explore the ghosts and graveyards of Alexandria on a **Halloween Walking Tour** with a lantern-carrying guide in 18th-century costume. The tour focuses on eerie Alexandria legend, myth, and folklore. See "Organized Tours," above, for phone numbers and costs.

November The **Historic Alexandria Antiques Show,** on the third weekend of the month, features several dozen dealers from many states displaying an array of high-quality antiques in room settings, including jewelry, silver, rare books, rugs, paintings, folk art, furniture, pottery, and decorative objects. Admission charged; proceeds help restore historic sites. Pricier activities include a gala opening party (about $75 admission) and a champagne brunch with a featured speaker (about $40).

There's a **Christmas Tree Lighting** in Market Square the Friday after Thanksgiving; the ceremony, which includes choir singing, puppet shows, dance performances, and an appearance by Santa and his elves, begins at 7pm. The night the tree is lit, thousands of tiny lights adorning King Street trees also go on.

Planning Note

Many Alexandria attractions are closed on Monday.

December   Holiday festivities continue with the **Annual Scottish Christmas Walk** on the first Saturday in December. Activities include kilted bagpipers, Highland dancers, a parade of Scottish clans (with horses and dogs), caroling, fashion shows, storytelling, booths (selling crafts, antiques, food, hot mulled punch, heather, fresh wreaths, and holly), and children's games. Admission is charged for some events.

The **Old Town Christmas Candlelight Tour,** the second week in December, visits seasonally decorated historic Alexandria homes and an 18th-century tavern. There are colonial dancing, string quartets, madrigal and opera singers, and refreshments, too. Tickets, which are $12 for adults and $5 for students 6 to 17, are available at the Ramsay House Visitors Center.

There are so many holiday season activities, the Visitors Association issues a special brochure about them each year. Pick one up to learn about decorations, workshops, walking tours, tree lightings, concerts, bazaars, bake sales, crafts fairs, and much more.

WHAT TO SEE & DO

In addition to the annual events mentioned above, there's much to see and do.

About Admissions: Available at Ramsay House (see "Visitor Information," above) is a money-saving **block ticket** for admission to five historic Alexandria properties: Gadsby's Tavern, Lee's Boyhood Home, the Carlyle House, Stabler-Leadbeater Apothecary Shop, and the Lee-Fendall House. The ticket, which can also be purchased at any of the buildings, costs $12 for adults, $5 for children ages 11 to 17; children under 11 enter free. You can also purchase block tickets for three sights ($7 adults, $3 children) or two sights ($6 adults, $2 children), but I would recommend that you visit all five.

Alexandria Black History Resource Center

638 N. Alfred St. (at Wythe St.). ☎ **703/838-4356.** Free admission (donations accepted). Tues–Sat 10am–4pm.

In a 1940s building that originally housed the black community's first public library, the center exhibits historical objects, photographs, documents, and memorabilia relating to African-American Alexandrians from the 18th century forward. In addition to the permanent collection, the museum presents twice-yearly rotating exhibits and other activities. If you're interested in further studies, check out the center's Watson Reading Room.

✪ Boyhood Home of Robert E. Lee

607 Oronoco St. (between St. Asaph and Washington sts.). ☎ **703/548-8454.** Admission $3 adults, $1 children 11–17, free for children under 11; or buy the block ticket. Tours given Mon–Sat 10am–3:30pm, Sun 1–3:30pm. Closed Easter, Thanksgiving, and Dec 15–Jan 31 (except for the Sun closest to Jan 19, Robert E. Lee's birthday).

Revolutionary War cavalry hero Henry "Light Horse Harry" Lee brought his wife, Ann Hill Carter, and five children to this early Federal-style mansion in 1812, when Robert, destined to become a Confederate military leader, was just 5 years old. A tour of the house, built in 1795, provides a glimpse into the gracious lifestyle of Alexandria's gentry. George Washington was an occasional guest of two earlier occupants, John Potts (the builder of the house) and Col. William Fitzhugh. In 1804 the Fitzhughs' daughter, Mary Lee, married Martha Washington's grandson, George

Washington Parke Custis, in the drawing room. And the Custises' daughter, Mary Ann Randolph, married Robert E. Lee.

General Lafayette honored Ann Hill Carter Lee with a visit to the house in October 1824 in tribute to her husband, "Light Horse Harry" Lee, who had died in 1818. Lafayette had been a comrade-in-arms with Lee during the American Revolution. The drawing room today is called the Lafayette Room to commemorate that visit.

On a fascinating tour, you'll see the nursery with its little canopied bed and toy box; Mrs. Lee's room; the Lafayette Room, furnished in period antiques, with the tea table set up for use; the morning room, where *The Iliad* translated into Latin reposes on a gaming table (both "Light Horse Harry" and Robert were classical scholars); and the winter kitchen. The furnishings are of the Lee period but did not belong to the family. The house was occupied by 17 different owners after the Lees left. It was made into a museum in 1967.

✪ Carlyle House

121 N. Fairfax St. (at Cameron St.). ☎ **703/549-2997.** Admission $3 adults, $1 children 11–17, free for children under 11; or buy a block ticket. Tues–Sat 10am–4:30pm, Sun noon–4:30pm.

Not only is Carlyle House regarded as one of Virginia's most architecturally impressive 18th-century houses, it also figured prominently in American history. In 1753 Scottish merchant John Carlyle completed the mansion for his bride, Sara Fairfax of Belvoir, a daughter of one of Virginia's most prominent families. It was designed in the style of a Scottish/English manor house and lavishly furnished. Carlyle, a successful merchant, had the means to import the best furnishings and appointments available abroad for his new Alexandria home.

When it was built, Carlyle House was a waterfront property with its own wharf. A social and political center, the house was visited by numerous great men of the time, including George Washington. But its most important moment in history occurred in April 1755 when Maj. Gen. Edward Braddock, commander-in-chief of his majesty's forces in North America, met with five colonial governors here and asked them to tax colonists to finance a campaign against the French and Indians. Colonial legislatures refused to comply, one of the first instances of serious friction between America and Britain. Nevertheless, Braddock made Carlyle House his headquarters during the campaign, and Carlyle was less than impressed with him. He called the general "a man of weak understanding. . . very indolent. . . a slave to his passions, women and wine. . . as great an Epicure as could be in his eating, tho a brave man." Possibly these were the reasons his unfinanced campaign met with disaster. Braddock received, as Carlyle described it, "a most remarkable drubbing."

A **tour** of Carlyle House takes about 40 minutes. Two of the original rooms, the large parlor and the adjacent study, have survived intact; the former, where Braddock met the governors, still retains its original fine woodwork, paneling, and pediments. The house is furnished in period pieces; however, only a few of Carlyle's possessions remain. In an upstairs room an architecture exhibit depicts 18th-century construction methods with hand-hewn beams and hand-wrought nails. Tours are given every half hour on the hour and half hour.

Christ Church

118 N. Washington St. (at Cameron St.). ☎ **703/549-1450.** Free admission. Mon–Fri 9am–4pm, Sat 9am–noon, Sun 2–4:30pm. Closed all federal holidays.

This sturdy redbrick Georgian-style church would be an important national landmark even if its two most distinguished members had not been Washington and Lee. It has been in continuous use since 1773.

First in the Hearts of His Countrymen: George in Alexandria

Though Alexandria calls itself George Washington's hometown, it was never his primary residence. He did spend a great deal of time here, though. As a 17-year-old surveyor, he helped lay out the town. As an adult, he had a home on Cameron Street, worshipped at Christ Church, trained his troops in Market Square, and bid them farewell at Gadsby's Tavern.

Born into a Virginia planter family in 1732, George Washington pursued his lifelong interest in military arts from an early age. At 22, he was already a lieutenant colonel fighting for the British in the French and Indian War. An aide to General Braddock, he escaped injury, though four bullets rent his coat and two horses were shot from under him. Like many Virginia planters, however, he began to feel exploited by the British government. On July 3, 1775, he assumed command of the Continental Army, a position he would hold for 6 years.

After the British surrender at Yorktown, Washington, who was respected as a great military hero, retired to his Potomac estate, Mount Vernon. However, he was unable to ignore the needs of the fledgling nation for which he had fought so valiantly. He agreed to preside over the 1787 Constitutional Convention. Washington also reluctantly accepted the presidency, taking office on April 30, 1789. His presidency was unique in that every action established a tradition for the new republic. "As the first of everything . . . will serve to establish a Precedent," he wrote James Madison, "it is devoutly wished on my part that these precedents may be fixed on true principles."

Washington finally retired to Mount Vernon in 1797, 2 years before his death. He is buried there next to his wife Martha. Consider this tribute to Washington made by Abigail Adams: "He never grew giddy, but ever maintained a modest diffidence of his own talents. . . . Possessed of power, possessed of an extensive influence, he never used it but for the benefit of his country. . . . If we look through the whole tenor of his life, history will not produce to us a parallel."

There have, of course, been many changes since Washington's day. The bell tower, church bell, galleries, and organ were added by the early 1800s, the "wineglass" pulpit in 1891. But much of what was changed later has since been restored to its earlier state. The pristine white interior with wood moldings and gold trim is colonially correct, though modern heating has obviated the need for charcoal braziers and hot bricks. For the most part, the original structure remains, including the handblown glass in the windows that the first worshipers gazed through when their minds wandered from the service. The town has grown up around the building that was first called the "Church in the Woods" because of its rural setting.

Christ Church has had its historic moments. Washington and other early church members fomented revolution in the churchyard, and Robert E. Lee met here with Richmond representatives to discuss assuming a command of Virginia's military forces at the beginning of the Civil War. You can sit in the pew where George and Martha sat with her two Custis grandchildren, or in the Robert E. Lee family pew.

It's a tradition for U.S. presidents to attend a service here on a Sunday close to Washington's birthday and sit in his pew. One of the most memorable of these visits took place shortly after Pearl Harbor, when Franklin Delano Roosevelt attended services with Winston Churchill on the World Day of Prayer, January 1, 1942.

Of course, you're invited to attend a service. There's no admission, but donations are appreciated. A guide gives brief lectures to visitors. The old Parish Hall today houses a gift shop and an exhibit on the history of the church. Walk out to the weathered graveyard after you see the church. It was Alexandria's first and only burial ground until 1805; its oldest marked grave is that of Isaac Pearce, who died in 1771. The remains of 34 Confederate soldiers are also interred here.

Fort Ward Museum & Historic Site

4301 W. Braddock Rd. (between Rte. 7–Leesburg Turnpike–and Seminary Rd.). ☎ **703/838-4848.** Free admission. Park, daily 9am–sunset; museum, Tues–Sat 9am–5pm, Sun noon–5pm. Closed Jan 1, Thanksgiving, and Dec 25. From Old Town, follow King St. west, go right on Kenwood Ave., then left on West Braddock Rd.; continue for ³/₄ mile to the entrance on the right.

A short drive from Old Town is a 45-acre museum, historic site, and park that take you on a leap forward in Alexandria history to the Civil War. The action here centers, as it did in the early 1860s, on an actual Union fort that Lincoln ordered erected. It was part of a system of Civil War forts called the "Defenses of Washington." About 90% of the fort's earthwork walls are preserved, and the Northwest Bastion has been restored with six mounted guns (originally there were 36). A model of 19th-century military engineering, the fort was never attacked by Confederate forces. Self-guided tours begin at the Fort Ward ceremonial gate.

Visitors can explore the fort and replicas of the ceremonial entrance gate and an officer's hut. There's a museum of Civil War artifacts on the premises where changing exhibits focus on subjects such as Union arms and equipment, medical care of the wounded, and local war history.

There are picnic areas with barbecue grills in the park surrounding the fort. Concerts are presented on selected evenings June to mid-August in the outdoor amphitheater. A living-history program takes place in mid-August (call for details).

Friendship Firehouse

107 S. Alfred St. (between King and Prince sts.). ☎ **703/838-3891** or 703/838-4994. Free admission. Fri–Sat 10am–4pm, Sun 1–4pm.

Alexandria's first fire-fighting organization, the Friendship Fire Company, was established in 1774. In the early days, the company met in taverns and kept its fire-fighting equipment in a member's barn. Its present Italianate-style brick building dates from 1855; it was erected after an earlier building was, ironically, destroyed by fire. Local tradition holds that George Washington was involved with the firehouse as a founding member, active firefighter, and purchaser of its first fire engine, although extensive research does not confirm these stories. Fire engines and fire fighting paraphernalia are on display.

✪ Gadsby's Tavern Museum

134 N. Royal St. (at Cameron St.). ☎ **703/838-4242.** Admission $3 adults, $1 children 11–17, free for children under 11; or buy the block ticket. Tours given Apr–Sept, Tues–Sat 10am–5pm, Sun 1–5pm; Oct–Mar, Tues–Sat 11am–4pm, Sun 1–4pm. Closed all federal holidays except Veterans Day.

Alexandria was at the crossroads of 18th-century America, and its social center was Gadsby's Tavern, which consisted of two buildings (one Georgian, one Federal) dating from circa 1770 and 1792, respectively. Innkeeper John Gadsby combined them to create "a gentleman's tavern," which he operated from 1796 to 1808; it was considered one of the finest in the country. George Washington was a frequent dinner guest; he and Martha danced in the second-floor ballroom and it was here that Washington celebrated his last birthday. The tavern also saw Thomas Jefferson, James Madison, and the Marquis de Lafayette. It was the scene of lavish parties, theatrical performances, small circuses, government meetings, and concerts. Itinerant merchants used the tavern to display their wares, and traveling doctors and dentists treated a hapless clientele (these were rudimentary professions in the 18th century) on the premises.

The rooms have been restored to their 18th-century appearance with the help of modern excavations and colonial inventories. On the 30-minute tour, you'll get a good look at the Tap Room, a small dining room; the Assembly Room, the ballroom; typical bedrooms; and the underground icehouse, which was filled each winter from the icy river. Tours depart 15 minutes before and after the hour. Inquire about a special "living history" tour called Gadsby's Time Travels, which is given four or five times a year. Cap off the experience with a meal at the restored colonial-style restaurant that occupies three tavern rooms (see "Where to Dine," below).

✪ Lee-Fendall House

614 Oronoco St. (at Washington St.). ☎ 703/548-1789. Admission $3 adults, $1 children 11–17, free for children under 11; or buy the block ticket. Tues–Sat 10am–3:45pm, Sun noon–3:45pm. Tours depart frequently throughout the day. Closed Jan 1, Thanksgiving, and Dec 24–25.

This handsome Greek Revival–style house is a veritable Lee family museum of furniture, heirlooms, and documents. "Light Horse Harry" Lee never actually lived here, though he was a frequent visitor, as was his good friend, George Washington. He did own the original lot, but sold it to Philip Richard Fendall (himself a Lee on his mother's side), who built the house in 1785. Fendall married three Lee wives, including Harry's first mother-in-law and, later, Harry's sister.

Thirty-seven Lees occupied the house over a period of 118 years (1785 to 1903), and it was from this house that Harry wrote Alexandria's farewell address to Washington, delivered when he passed through town on his way to assume the presidency. (Harry also wrote and delivered, but not at this house, the famous funeral oration to Washington that contained the words: "First in war, first in peace, and first in the hearts of his countrymen.") During the Civil War, the house was seized and used as a Union hospital.

Thirty-minute guided tours interpret the 1850s era of the home and provide insight into Victorian family life. You'll also see the colonial garden with its magnolia and chestnut trees, roses, and boxwood-lined paths. Much of the interior woodwork and glass is original.

The Lyceum

201 S. Washington St. (off Prince St.). ☎ 703/838-4994. Free admission. Mon–Sat 10am–5pm, Sun 1–5pm. Closed Jan 1, Thanksgiving, and Dec 25.

This Greek Revival building houses a museum that depicts Alexandria's history from the 17th through the 20th century. It features changing exhibits and an ongoing series of lectures, concerts, and educational programs.

Information is also available here about Virginia state attractions, especially Alexandria attractions. You can obtain maps and brochures, and a knowledgeable staff will be happy to answer your questions.

But even without its many attractions, the brick and stucco Lyceum merits a visit. Built in 1839, it was designed in the Doric temple style to serve as a lecture, meeting, and concert hall. It was an important center of Alexandria's cultural life until the Civil War, when Union forces appropriated it for use as a hospital. After the war it became a private residence, and still later it was subdivided for office space. In 1969, however, the city council's use of eminent domain alone prevented The Lyceum from being demolished in favor of a parking lot.

Old Presbyterian Meeting House

321 S. Fairfax St. (between Duke and Wolfe sts.). ☎ 703/549-6670. Free admission. Mon–Fri 9am–3pm; Sun services at 10am.

Presbyterian congregations have worshipped in Virginia since the Rev. Alexander Whittaker converted Pocahontas in Jamestown in 1614. This brick church was built by Scottish pioneers in 1775. Although it wasn't George Washington's church, the Meeting House bell tolled continuously for 4 days after his death in December 1799, and memorial services were preached from the pulpit here by Presbyterian, Episcopal, and Methodist ministers. According to the Alexandria paper of the day, "The walking being bad to the Episcopal church the funeral sermon of George Washington will be preached at the Presbyterian Meeting House." Two months later, on Washington's birthday, Alexandria citizens marched from Market Square to the church to pay their respects.

Many famous Alexandrians are buried in the church graveyard, including John and Sara Carlyle, Dr. James Craik (the surgeon who treated—some say killed—Washington, dressed Lafayette's wounds at Brandywine, and ministered to the dying Braddock at Monongahela), and William Hunter, Jr., founder of the St. Andrew's Society of Scottish descendants, to whom bagpipers pay homage on the first Saturday of December. It is also the site of a Tomb of an Unknown Revolutionary War Soldier, and of the minister between 1789 and 1820, Dr. James Muir, who lies beneath the sanctuary in his gown and bands.

The original Meeting House was gutted by a lightning fire in 1835, but parishioners restored it in the style of the day a few years later. The present bell, said to be recast from the metal of the old one, was hung in a newly constructed belfry in 1843, and a new organ was installed in 1849. The Meeting House closed its doors in 1889, and for 60 years it was virtually abandoned. But in 1949 it was reborn as a living Presbyterian U.S.A. church, and today the Old Meeting House looks much as it did following its first restoration. The original parsonage, or manse, is still intact. There's no guided tour, but there is a recorded narrative in the graveyard.

Stabler-Leadbeater Apothecary Museum

105–107 S. Fairfax St. (near King St.). ☎ **703/836-3713.** Admission $2 adults, $1 children 11–17, free for children under 11; or buy a block ticket. Mon–Sat 10am–4pm, Sun 1–5pm. Closed Jan 1, Thanksgiving, and Dec 25.

When its doors closed in 1933, this landmark drugstore was the second oldest in continuous operation in America. Run for five generations by the same Quaker family (beginning in 1792), its famous early patrons included Robert E. Lee (he purchased the paint for Arlington House here), George Mason, Henry Clay, John C. Calhoun, and George Washington. Gothic Revival decorative elements and Victorian-style doors were added in the 1840s.

Today the apothecary looks much as it did in colonial times, its shelves lined with original handblown gold-leaf–labeled bottles (actually the most valuable collection of antique medicinal bottles in the country), old scales stamped with the royal crown, patent medicines, and equipment for bloodletting. The clock on the rear wall, the porcelain-handled mahogany drawers, and two mortars and pestles all date from about 1790. Among the shop's documentary records is this 1802 order from Mount Vernon: "Mrs. Washington desires Mr. Stabler to send by the bearer a quart bottle of his best Castor Oil and the bill for it."

There are **tours** Sundays from 1 to 5pm; other times a 10-minute recording will guide you around the displays. The adjoining gift shop uses its proceeds to maintain the apothecary.

✪ Torpedo Factory

105 N. Union St. (between King and Cameron sts. on the waterfront). ☎ **703/838-4565.** Free admission. Daily 10am–5pm; archaeology exhibit area, Tues–Fri 10am–3pm, Sat 10am–5pm, Sun 1–5pm. Closed Easter, July 4, Thanksgiving, Dec 25, and Jan 1.

This block-long, three-story building, once a torpedo shell-case factory, now accommodates some 160 professional artists and craftspeople who create and sell their own works on the premises. Here you can see artists at work in their studios: potters, painters, printmakers, photographers, sculptors, and jewelers, as well as those who make stained-glass windows and fiber art.

On permanent display here are exhibits on Alexandria history provided by **Alexandria Archaeology** (☎ **703/838-4399**), which is headquartered here and engages in extensive city research. The special exhibit area and lab are open to the public during the hours listed above with a volunteer or staff member on hand to answer questions. An ongoing exhibit, "Archaeologists at Work," highlights current excavation finds and methodology.

SHOPPING

Old Town has hundreds of charming boutiques, antique stores, and gift shops selling everything from souvenir T-shirts to 18th-century reproductions. Some of the most interesting are at the sights (for example, Museum Shop at The Lyceum), but most are clustered on King and Cameron streets and their connecting cross streets. Plan to spend a fair amount of time browsing in between visits to historic sites. A guide to antique stores is available at the Visitors Association. Also see chapter 9, which includes some Alexandria shops.

WHERE TO DINE

There are so many fine restaurants in Alexandria that Washingtonians often drive over just to dine here and stroll the cobblestone streets.

EXPENSIVE

Landini Brothers

115 King St. (between Lee and Union sts.). ☎ **703/836-8404.** Reservations recommended. Main courses $9–$12 at lunch. $12.50–$24.50 at dinner. AE, CB, DC, DISC, MC, V. Mon–Sat 11:30am–11pm, Sun 4–10pm. NORTHERN ITALIAN.

The classic, delicate cuisine of Tuscany is featured at this rustic, almost grottolike restaurant with stone walls, a flagstone floor, and rough-hewn beams overhead. It's especially charming by candlelight. There's additional seating in a lovely dining room upstairs. Everything is homemade: the pasta, the desserts, and the crusty Italian bread. At lunch you might choose a cold seafood salad or spinach and ricotta-stuffed agnolotti in buttery Parmesan cheese sauce. At dinner, try the prosciutto and melon or the shrimp sautéed in garlic with tangy lemon sauce. Many proceed to an order of prime aged beef tenderloin medallions sautéed with garlic, mushrooms, and rosemary in a Barolo wine sauce. Others opt for linguine with scallops, shrimp, clams, mussels, and squid in a garlic/parsley/red-pepper and white-wine sauce. Dessert choices include tiramisu and custard-filled fruit tarts.

Le Refuge

127 N. Washington St. (1 block from King St.). ☎ **703/548-4661.** Reservations recommended. Main courses $8–$13 at lunch, $14–$20 at dinner; pre-theater $16. AE, DC, DISC, MC, V. Mon–Sat 11:30am–2:30pm and 5:30–10pm. FRENCH.

This is a cramped, but still appealing, space. Le Refuge is dark and busy and inexorably French. The food is mostly old fashioned: onion soup, bouillabaisse, rack of lamb, and chicken in mustard cream sauce. Perfectly prepared vegetables surround all entrées: potatoes lyonnaise, coins of zucchini, and bright bunches of broccoli florets. Desserts, like everything here, are homemade and include fruit tarts, creme brulée, and profiteroles.

MODERATE

East Wind

809 King St. (between Columbus and Alfred sts.). ☎ **703/836-1515.** Reservations recommended. Main courses $6–$8 at lunch, $8–$14 at dinner; prix-fixe lunch $7. AE, CB, DC, DISC, MC, V. Mon–Fri 11:30am–2:30pm; Mon–Thurs 5:30–10pm, Fri–Sat 5:30–10:30pm, Sun 5:30–9:30pm. VIETNAMESE.

The decor of this Vietnamese restaurant is very appealing: The works of Vietnamese artist Minh Nguyen adorn the sienna stucco and knotty pine–paneled walls, accompanied by flowers on each pink-clothed table and a large floral display up front. The owner personally visits the market each morning to select the freshest fish.

An East Wind meal might begin with an appetizer of *cha gio* (delicate Vietnamese egg rolls) or a salad of shredded chicken and vegetables mixed with fish sauce. A favorite entrée is *bo dun:* beef tenderloin strips marinated in wine, honey, and spices, rolled in fresh onions, and broiled on bamboo skewers. Also excellent are the grilled lemon chicken or charcoal-broiled shrimp and scallops served on rice vermicelli. Vegetarians will find many appealing selections on East Wind's menu. There's refreshing ginger ice cream for dessert. A good bargain is the prix-fixe lunch, which includes soup, an entrée, and coffee or tea.

Gadsby's Tavern

138 N. Royal St. (at Cameron St.). ☎ **703/548-1288.** Reservations recommended. Main courses $6.50–$10 at lunch/brunch, $15–$23 at dinner. Half-price portions available on some items for children 12 and under. CB, DC, DISC, MC, V. Mon–Sat 11:30am–3pm, Sun 11am–3pm; nightly 5:30–10pm. COLONIAL AMERICAN.

In the spirit of history, pass through the portals where Washington reviewed his troops for the last time, and dine at the famous Gadsby's Tavern. The setting evokes the 18th century authentically, with period music, wood-plank floors, hurricane-lamp wall sconces, and a rendition of a Hogarth painting over the fireplace (one of several).

Servers are dressed in authentic colonial attire. George Washington dined and danced here often. A strolling violinist entertains Sunday and Monday nights and at Sunday brunch. Tuesday through Saturday night an "18th-century gentleman" regales guests with song and tells the news of the day (200 years ago). In clement weather, it is possible to dine in a flagstone courtyard edged with flower beds.

All the fare is homemade, including the sweet Sally Lunn bread baked on the premises daily. You might start off with soup from the stockpot served with homemade sourdough crackers, followed by an entrée of baked ham and cheese pye (a sort of Early American quiche), or hot roast turkey with giblet gravy and bread and sage stuffing on Sally Lunn bread, or George Washington's favorite: slow-roasted crisp duckling served with fruit dressing and Madeira sauce. For dessert, try the English trifle or creamy buttermilk-custard pye with a hint of lemon. Colonial "coolers" are also available: scuppernong, Wench's Punch, and such. The Sunday brunch menu adds such items as thick slices of toast dipped in a batter of rum and spices, with sausage, hash browns, and hot cinnamon syrup. And a "desserts and libations" menu highlights such favorites as Scottish apple gingerbread and bourbon apple pye, along with a wide selection of beverages.

Bilbo Baggins

208 Queen St. (at Lee St.). ☎ **703/683-0300.** Main courses $7.50–$12 at lunch/brunch, $15–$17 at dinner. AE, DC, DISC, MC, V. Mon–Fri 11:30am–2:30pm, Sat 11:30am–5:30pm, Sun 11am–2:30pm; Mon–Sat 5:30–10:30pm, Sun 4:30–9:30pm. AMERICAN/CONTINENTAL.

Named, in case you didn't know, for a character in *The Hobbit,* Bilbo Baggins is a charming two-story restaurant offering scrumptious fresh and homemade fare. Plants flourish in the sunlight throughout the rustic downstairs area and among the stained-glass windows and murals of scenes from *The Hobbit* upstairs. Candlelit at night, it becomes an even cozier setting. The restaurant adjoins a skylit wine bar with windows overlooking Queen Street.

The restaurant offers many pasta dishes, such as tortellini stuffed with crabmeat, fresh salmon, and dill, in an apple-ginger chardonnay cream sauce. Other entrées range from grilled salmon and scallops in lemon-dill vinaigrette to chicken breast stuffed with feta cheese, accompanied by potato croquettes or seasonal vegetables. An extensive wine list is available (32 boutique wines are offered by the glass), as are all bar drinks, 10 microbrewery draft beers, and out-of-this-world homemade desserts such as the Lord of the Rings—seven layers of raspberry-filled white and chocolate cake topped with chocolate ganache.

INEXPENSIVE

The Deli on the Strand

211 The Strand #5 (entrance on S. Union St. between Duke and Prince sts.). ☎ **703/548-7222.** Sandwiches $2.75–$5.25. AE, MC, V. Daily 8am–8pm. DELI.

Who could refuse a sunlit picnic in Fort Ward Park (described above), in the Old Town at Founders Park, bordering the Potomac at the foot of Queen Street, or in the Market Square? The park doesn't have picnic tables, but there are benches and plenty of grass to sit on. Buy the fixings at the Deli on the Strand. The divine aroma of baking bread wafts through the air, and you can get reasonably priced cold-cut sandwiches on it, as well as muffins, brownies, and (on the weekend) bagels. Also available are homemade seafood or pasta salads, cheeses, beer, wine, and champagne. There are a few picnic tables outside under an awning.

✪ Hard Times Cafe

1404 King St. (near S. West St.). ☎ **703/683-5340.** No reservations. Main courses $4–$7. AE, MC, V. Mon–Thurs 11am–10pm, Fri–Sat 11am–11pm. Sun noon–10pm (hours extended in summer). AMERICAN/SOUTHWESTERN.

Will Rogers once said he "always judged a town by the quality of its chili." He would have loved Alexandria, where the fabulous Hard Times Cafe serves up top-secret-recipe homemade chilis and fresh-from-the-oven cornbread. It's a laid-back hangout where waiters and waitresses wear jeans and T-shirts; country music is always playing on the 100-CD jukebox; and the Texas decor features Lone Star flags, a longhorn steer hide overhead, and historic photos of the Old West on the walls. The chili comes in three varieties: Texas, Cincinnati (cooked with sweeter spices, including cinnamon), and vegetarian. I favor the Texas style: coarse-ground chuck simmered for 6 hours with special spices in beef sauce. If chili isn't your thing, order grilled chicken breast, a burger, or salad. Side orders of steak fries cooked with the skins, cheddar-filled jalapeños, and deep-fried onion rings are ample for two. Wash it all down with one of the menu's 30 beers, including a Hard Times label and many selections from western microbreweries. The Hard Times has garnered many a chili cookoff award, and CHILI-U.S.A., a resolution before Congress "to make chili the official food of this great nation," was conceived by Oklahoma lobbyists over a "bowl of red" here. There's additional seating upstairs; the Colorado flag overhead was brought in by a senator from that state.

La Madeleine

500 King St. (at S. Pitt St.). ☎ **703/739-2854.** No reservations. Main courses $4–$10 at lunch and dinner. AE, DISC, MC, V. Sun–Thurs 7am–10pm, Fri–Sat 7am–11pm. FRENCH CAFE.

This is part of a self-service chain, charming nonetheless. Its French-country interior has a beamed ceiling, bare oak floors, a wood-burning stove, and maple hutches displaying crockery and pewter mugs. The walls are hung with copper pots and antique farm implements.

Come in the morning for fresh-baked croissants, Danish, scones, muffins, and brioches, or a heartier bacon-and-eggs breakfast. Throughout the day, there are delicious salads (such as roasted vegetables and rigatoni), sandwiches (including a traditional croque monsieur), and hot dishes ranging from quiche and pizza to rotisserie chicken with a Caesar salad. After 5pm, additional choices include pastas and specials such as beef bourguignon and salmon in dill cream sauce, both served with a crispy potato galette and sautéed broccoli. There are about two dozen fabulous fresh-baked French desserts, including yummy fruit tarts and a chocolate, vanilla, and praline triple-layer cheesecake with graham-cracker crust.

✪ South Austin Grill

801 King St. (at S. Columbus St.). ☎ **703/684-8969.** Reservations not accepted. Lunch, Sat–Sun brunch and dinner $6–$13. AE, DC, DISC, MC, V. Mon–Thurs 11:30am–11pm, Fri–Sat 11:30am–midnight, Sun 11am–11pm. TEX-MEX.

One of four Austin Grills in the area, this one is larger than the original outpost in Glover Park. The two dining floors are cheerfully decorated, with roomy booths painted in bright primary hues and walls hung with Austin music club posters and other Texiana. A corner location permits lots of sunlight to stream in.

Otherwise, menu, music, and ambience are the same as at the Glover Park location; see chapter 6 listing for that information.

The Tea Cosy

119 S. Royal St. (between King and Prince sts.). ☎ **703/836-8181.** No reservations. Tea cakes and sandwiches $2–$5; full afternoon tea $8.75; main courses $3.50–$8.25. DISC, MC, V. Sat–Thurs 10am–6pm, Fri 10am–7pm. BRITISH TEAROOM.

An authentic British tearoom, with posters advertising Bovril and Colman's Mustard on whitewashed walls, a beamed ceiling, and a magazine rack stocked with British periodicals and newspapers. Tables are set with pretty floral-patterned place mats. A shop in the back sells archetypal British foodstuffs: digestive biscuits, ginger wine, Irish oatmeal, chutney, and such.

Come in for a full afternoon tea, including assorted tea sandwiches and oven-fresh scones (date/pecan, lemon, raisin, apricot, or cheese) served with jams and Devonshire cream. Crumpets, shortbread, and trifle are also à la carte options. For heartier meals, your choices include steak-and-kidney pie, shepherd's pie, Cornish pasty, cheese-and-vegetable pasty, Scottish sausage rolls, and bangers and mash. Everything, including vegetables, is fresh and homemade. There are daily dessert specials such as apple-blackberry pie with custard. Possible libations: British ales and beers, hard cider, and a soft drink called orange quosh.

Appendix: Useful Toll-Free Numbers & Web Sites

LODGINGS

Best Western International, Inc.
800/528-1234 North America
800/528-2222 TDD

Budgetel Inns
800/4-BUDGET Continental USA and Canada

Budget Host
800/BUD-HOST Continental USA

Clarion Hotels
800/CLARION Continental USA and Canada
800/228-3323 TDD
http://www.hotelchoice.com/cgi-bin/res/webres?clarion.html

Comfort Inns
800/228-5150 Continental USA and Canada
800/228-3323 TDD
http://www.hotelchoice.com/cgi-bin/res/webres?comfort.html

Courtyard by Marriott
800/321-2211 Continental USA and Canada
800/228-7014 TDD
http://www.courtyard.com

Days Inn
800/325-2525 Continental USA and Canada
800/325-3297 TDD
http://www.daysinn.com/daysinn.html

Doubletree Hotels
800/222-TREE Continental USA and Canada
800/528-9898 TDD

Drury Inn
800/325-8300 Continental USA and Canada
800/325-0583 TDD

Econo Lodges
800/55-ECONO Continental USA and Canada
800/228-3323 TDD
http://www.hotelchoice.com/cgi-bin/res/webres?econo.html

Embassy Suites
800/362-2779 Continental USA and Canada
800/458-4708 TDD
http://www.embassy-suites.com/

Exel Inns of America
800/356-8013 Continental USA and Canada
Fairfield Inn by Marriott
800/228-2800 Continental USA and Canada
800/228-7014 TDD
http://www.marriott.com/fairfieldinn/
Fairmont Hotels
800/527-4727 Continental USA
Forte Hotels
800/225-5843 Continental USA and Canada
Four Seasons Hotels
800/332-3442 Continental USA
800/268-6282 Canada
Friendship Inns
800/453-4511 Continental USA
800/228-3323 TDD
http://www.hotelchoice.com/cgi-bin/
res/webres?friendship.html
Guest Quarters Suites
800/424-2900 Continental USA
Hampton Inn
800/HAMPTON Continental USA and Canada
800/451-HTDD TDD
http://www.hampton-inn.com/
Hilton Hotels Corporation
800/HILTONS Continental USA and Canada
800/368-1133 TDD
http://www.hilton.com
Holiday Inn
800/HOLIDAY Continental USA and Canada
800/238-5544 TDD
http://www.holiday-inn.com/
Howard Johnson
800/654-2000 Continental USA and Canada
800/654-8442 TDD
http://www.hojo.com/hojo.html
Hyatt Hotels and Resorts
800/228-9000 Continental USA and Canada
800/228-9548 TDD
http://www.hyatt.com
Inns of America
800/826-0778 Continental USA and Canada
Intercontinental Hotels
800/327-0200 Continental USA and Canada
ITT Sheraton
800/325-3535 Continental USA and Canada
800/325-1717 TDD
La Quinta Motor Inns, Inc.
800/531-5900 Continental USA and Canada
800/426-3101 TDD

Loews Hotels
800/223-0888 Continental USA and Canada
http://www.loewshotels.com
Luxury Collection Hotels
800/325-3589 Continental USA and Canada
Marriott Hotels
800/228-9290 Continental USA and Canada
800/228-7014 TDD
http://www.marriott.com/
Master Hosts Inns
800/251-1962 Continental USA and Canada
Meridien
800/543-4300 Continental USA and Canada
Omni Hotels
800/843-6664 Continental USA and Canada
Park Inns International
800/437-PARK Continental USA and Canada
http://www.p-inns.com/parkinn.html
Quality Inns
800/228-5151 Continental USA and Canada
800/228-3323 TDD
http://www.hotelchoice.com/cgi-bin/res/webres?quality.html
Radisson Hotels International
800/333-3333 Continental USA and Canada
Ramada
800/2-RAMADA Continental USA and Canada
http://www.ramada.com/ramada.html
Red Carpet Inns
800/251-1962 Continental USA and Canada
Red Lion Hotels and Inns
800/547-8010 Continental USA and Canada
Red Roof Inns
800/843-7663 Continental USA and Canada
800/843-9999 TDD
http://www.redroof.com
Renaissance Hotels International
800/HOTELS-1 Continental USA and Canada
800/833-4747 TDD
Residence Inn by Marriott
800/331-3131 Continental USA and Canada
800/228-7014 TDD
http://www.marriott.com/lodging/resinn.htm
Rodeway Inns
800/228-2000 Continental USA and Canada
800/228-3323 TDD
http://www.hotelchoice.com/cgi-bin/res/webres?rodeway.html
Scottish Inns
800/251-1962 Continental USA and Canada
Shilo Inns
800/222-2244 Continental USA and Canada

Signature Inns
800/822-5252 Continental USA and Canada
Super 8 Motels
800/800-8000 Continental USA and Canada
800/533-6634 TDD
http://www.super8motels.com/super8.html
Susse Chalet Motor Lodges & Inns
800/258-1980 Continental USA and Canada
Travelodge
800/255-3050 Continental USA and Canada
Vagabond Hotels Inc.
800/522-1555 Continental USA and Canada
Westin Hotels and Resorts
800/228-3000 Continental USA and Canada
800/254-5440 TDD
http://www.westin.com/
Wyndham Hotels and Resorts
800/822-4200 Continental USA and Canada

CAR RENTAL AGENCIES

Advantage Rent-A-Car
800/777-5500 Continental USA and Canada
Airways Rent A Car
800/952-9200 Continental USA
Alamo Rent A Car
800/327-9633 Continental USA and Canada
http://www.goalamo.com/
Avis
800/331-1212 Continental USA
800/TRY-AVIS Canada
800/331-2323 TDD
http://www.avis/com/
Budget Rent A Car
800/527-0700 Continental USA and Canada
800/826-5510 TDD
Dollar Rent A Car
800/800-4000 Continental USA and Canada
Enterprise Rent-A-Car
800/325-8007 Continental USA and Canada
Hertz
800/654-3131 Continental USA and Canada
800/654-2280 TDD
National Car Rental
800/CAR-RENT Continental USA and Canada
800/328-6323 TDD
http://www.nationalcar.com/index.html
Payless Car Rental
800/PAYLESS Continental USA and Canada
Rent-A-Wreck
800/535-1391 Continental USA

Sears Rent A Car
800/527-0770 Continental USA and Canada
Thrifty Rent-A-Car
800/367-2277 Continental USA and Canada
800/358-5856 TDD
U-Save Auto Rental of America
800/272-USAV Continental USA and Canada
Value Rent-A-Car
800/327-2501 Continental USA and Canada
http://www.go-value.com/

AIRLINES

American Airlines
800/433-7300 Continental USA and Western Canada
800/543-1586 TDD
http://www.americanair.com/aa_home/aa_home.htm
Canadian Airlines International
800/426-7000 Continental USA and Canada
http://www.cdair.ca/
Continental Airlines
800/525-0280 Continental USA
800/343-9195 TDD
http://www.flycontinental.com:80/index.html
Delta Air Lines
800/221-1212 Continental USA
800/831-4488 TDD
http://www.delta-air.com/index.html
Northwest Airlines
800/225-2525 Continental USA and Canada
http://www.nwa.com/
Southwest Airlines
800/435-9792 Continental USA and Canada
http://www.iflyswa.com
Trans World Airlines
800/221-2000 Continental USA
http://www2.twa.com/TWA/Airlines/home/home.htm
United Airlines
800/241-6522 Continental USA and Canada
http://www.ual.com/
US Airways
800/428-4322 Continental USA and Canada
http://www.usairways.com/

Index

See also separate Accommodations and Restaurant indexes, below.

GENERAL INDEX

WHEREVER YOU TRAVEL, *H*ELP IS NEVER FAR AWAY.

From planning your trip to providing travel assistance along the way, American Express® Travel Service Offices are always there to help you do more.

Washington, D.C.

American Express Travel Service
1150 Connecticut Avenue N.W.
202/457-1300

American Express Travel Service
Mazza Gallerie, 5300 Wisconsin N.W.
202/362-4000

do more AMERICAN EXPRESS

Travel

http://www.americanexpress.com/travel

**American Express Travel Service Offices
are located throughout the United States.
For the office nearest you, call 1-800-AXP-3429.**